Fig. 1 Class P1 No. 2394 leaving Potters Bar tunnel on a New England – Hornsey coal train, 1936.

LOCOMOTIVES OF THE L.N.E.R.

Part 6B

TENDER ENGINES – CLASSES O1 to P2

Published by
THE RAILWAY CORRESPONDENCE AND TRAVEL SOCIETY
1983

ISBN 0 901115 54 1

CONTENTS

ACKNOWLEDGEMENTS

This Part is mainly the work of Messrs. M. G. Boddy, W.A. Brown, E. Neve and W. B. Yeadon, with assistance from Messrs. E. V. Fry and W. Hennigan. Special thanks are due to Messrs. B. R. Andrews, P. Neve, J. W. P. Rowledge, R. Willson and the Australian Railway Historical Society for their helpful assistance in connection with the War Department engines. Thanks are also due to Messrs. B. W. Calvert, J. M. Edgson and L. V. Wood for preparing the line drawings and others who have so willingly helped with information and advice.

Acknowledgement of Illustrations:-

F. R. Hebron (Figs. 1, 9, 28, 70, 118/9/46), T. G. Hepburn (Figs. 2, 6, 8, 13, 32/3/5, 69, 73/7, 80/4, 107/10/2/31/6/9/45), W. L. Good (Figs. 3, 65, 130), L.N.E.R. (Figs. 4, 5, 12/4/5/7-22, 62, 78, 91/2/3/7, 109/11/3/4/21-4/6/7/8/33/4/5), H. G. Tidey (Fig. 11), B. Hilton (Fig.24), K. Pirt (Fig. 25), P. Proud (Figs. 29, 71), R. Gee (Fig. 30), L. R. Peters (Figs. 31, 64, 98), P. H. Groom (Figs. 34, 83/7), W. H. Whitworth (Figs. 36, 44/7-50/8, 129/37), L. Hanson (Figs. 37, 43, 131), W. Potter (Figs. 38, 41/5, 57, 148), N. Fields (Figs. 40, 75), D. A. Dant (Fig. 46), T. M. S. Findlater (Fig. 52), P. J. Hughes (Figs. 55, 61/3, 81), E. V. Fry (Fig. 60), H. C. Casserley (Figs. 66, 100), J. P. Wilson (Figs. 68, 74, 115), G. H. Soole (Fig. 72), C. Ord (Fig. 76), C. L. Kerr (Figs. 82, 103/41/50), E. Oldham (Fig. 85), D. M. C. Hepburne-Scott (Figs. 88, 90), G. M. Staddon (Fig. 89), J. D. Darby (Figs. 95, 106), C. C. B. Herbert (Fig. 96), J. L. Stevenson (Fig. 99), C. R. L. Coles (Fig. 104), J. F. Henton (Fig. 105), A. F. Cook (Figs. 116/7), The Topical Press (Fig. 125), C. R. Gordon Stuart (Fig. 132), E. R. Wethersett (Figs. 140/3/9), K. A. C. R. Nunn (Fig. 144).

Figs. 7, 10/6, 26, 36, 44/7-50/6/67/94, 101/2/4/8/37/40/3/7/9 are reproduced by courtesy of Ian Allan Ltd., Fig. 11 of Lens of Sutton, Fig. 25 of The Gresley Society, Figs. 27, 39, 42, 53/4/9, 79, 86 of Photomatic Ltd., Fig. 144 of The Locomotive Club of Great Britain. The photographs of F. R. Hebron, T. G. Hepburn and D. M. C. Hepburne-Scott are reproduced by courtesy of B. Stephenson, Esq.

INTRODUCTION

This Part is concerned primarily with the 2-8-0 heavy goods engine type, large numbers of which ran on the L.N.E.R. system. Also featured are Gresley's two classes of 2-8-2, numerically small but of considerable interest.

The L.N.E.R. inherited 2-8-0's from only two of its constituent companies: for the G.N.R. Gresley had built both two and three-cylinder versions of his design, whilst on the G.C.R. Robinson's engines had already become famous in railway, if not military, circles. The G.C.R. design had been selected to be built in large numbers by the Government for service on the Continent during the 1914-18 War. Many of these R.O.D. (Railway Operating Division of the Royal Engineers) engines were subsequently purchased by the L.N.E.R. so that, together with the G.C.R. engines, they formed the mainstay of the Company's heavy goods engine fleet, despite the fact that Gresley built more of his three-cylinder 2-8-0's.

History was repeated after the 1939-45 War, when the L.N.E.R. purchased 200 of the "Austerity" 2-8-0's built for military service in that war. During that time the demands made on the L.N.E.R. traffic department were exceptional and many of the "Austerity" 2-8-0's, also the 2-10-0 counterpart, were received on loan for varying periods. The U.S. Army, too, had a 2-8-0 design which saw wartime service on the L.N.E.R. Finally, some L.M.S. Stanier 2-8-0's were built by the L.N.E.R. and Southern Railway and taken into the Company's stock, whilst others ran on loan. In view of this complicated situation and in order to present a co-ordinated account of their activities on the L.N.E.R., the authors decided to include in this book all these engines, whether owned by the Company or not. In the peak month, February 1944, there were no fewer than 530 engines on loan to the L.N.E.R., made up of 350 "Austerity" 2-8-0's, 168 U.S. Army engines, ten "Austerity" 2-10-0's and two Stanier 8F's.

Of the 2-8-2's, the two engines of the P1 class were also designed for goods service and were the counterpart of the Gresley Pacifics. The famous *Cock o' the North*, and its five sister engines of class P2, were for passenger work on the arduous line from Edinburgh to Aberdeen and earned the L.N.E.R. much attention.

In all, 784 engines owned by the L.N.E.R. feature in this book, together with 953 on loan, although many of the latter were subsequently taken into L.N.E.R. stock and therefore also came within the first total.

In this work the complete history of each engine owned by the L.N.E.R., or built to its design, is given. Dimensions are quoted as well as full lists of detail alterations and dates of building, rebuilding, renumbering and withdrawal. Illustrations are generally confined to the post-Grouping period.

Most of the information has been obtained from official sources and it will be noted that in several instances it is at variance with previously published accounts, including such classical works as those by E. L. Ahrons. In every case the greatest possible care has been taken to have the details verified and the authors are confident that the version now presented is authentic. Records kept at the various L.N.E.R. locomotive works and elsewhere were not on a uniform basis, particularly of course in the pre-Grouping period, and this has prevented full documentation of some of the detail variations in certain classes.

Acknowledgements will be found in Part 1, The Preliminary Survey, to firms, organisations and, not least, British Railways, for their assistance in providing material for this Part. In addition, readers are referred to Part 1 for full details of the L.N.E.R.'s history and its policy regarding locomotive construction, classification of engines and boilers, diagrams, numberings, naming, liveries, brakes, tenders, route restrictions and load and power classifications. A full list of locomotive classes and their subdivision into class parts is also included therein.

The individual class articles in this series have been arranged on a uniform basis, each class being divided under sub-headings. This method was preferred by the authors to a chronological history as it facilitates reference, but some unavoidable repetition does occur. The following notes on these sub-headings are offered to assist the reader:—

ENGINES AT GROUPING (or at subsequent date of absorption).—For convenience the locomotive numbers quoted are wherever possible on an L.N.E.R. basis. In some instances, however, locomotives were withdrawn without actually receiving new L.N.E.R. numbers.

STANDARD L.N.E.R. DIMENSIONS. – These are on a uniform basis for each class and have generally been taken from the first engine diagram issued by the L.N.E.R. for the class concerned, unless otherwise stated. The pitch of the boiler is its centre line height above rail level. Boiler diagram numbers refer to those brought into use from 1928 onwards by the L.N.E.R. These numbers have also been used for locomotive classes which became extinct before that date where the particular boiler type survived in use on some other class at 1928 and thus received a diagram number.

REBUILDING. – Generally this section is confined to major rebuilding, or reboilering with a different type of boiler. All other variations appear under other headings. e.g. "Details" and "Brakes".

ENGINE DIAGRAMS. – The diagrams issued by the L.N.E.R. are listed under this heading. Generally the diagrams were prepared at the end of the year quoted and issued early in the following year. In certain classes an indication is given of major variations not recognised by the issue of a diagram.

SUMMARY. – (i) Engine Numbers: An L.N.E.R. number shown in brackets indicates that it was never actually borne. Dates of renumbering are given, except in the case of many of the 1924 L.N.E.R. numbers where the relevant information is not uniformly available. (ii) Rebuilding and other alterations: As this work is primarily a history from Grouping to the present day, the Summary normally lists only alterations that occurred after 1923. Alterations made in pre-Grouping days are therefore generally confined to the body of the article on each class, except that, where a particular alteration to a class was initiated before Grouping and continued by the L.N.E.R., complete details will be given in the Summary.

Dates of building, rebuilding and detail alterations are on the basis customarily employed by the various companies before Grouping. For the L.N.E.R. and B.R. periods they are "to traffic", i.e. when the locomotive took up revenue earning work. Differences may thus occur between these and previously published information where, for instance, "ex-works" or "official" rebuilding dates may have been quoted. "Ex-works" frequently meant the date an engine emerged from the erecting shop; a further period then elapsed during which time it ran one or more trial trips and was painted and varnished. Rebuilding dates were often recorded when a new boiler was allotted to or installed on an engine then under repair and could precede the date the engine returned to traffic by several months. From about 1929, ex-works dates ceased to be quoted in L.N.E.R. records, dates to traffic being solely used thereafter.

2-8-0 CLASSES

SUMMARY OF CLASS TOTALS

Class	*Rly.*	1-1-23	1923	1924	1925	1926	1927	1928	1929	1930	1931	1932
			31st December									
O1*	**G.N.**	20	20	20	20	20	20	20	20	20	20	20
O2	**G.N.**	11	19	26	26	26	26	26	26	26	26	34
O4	**G.C.**	131	131	256	293	305	356	400	405	405	405	406
O5	**G.C.**	17	17	17	17	16	16	16	16	16	16	15
O6	—											
Total		179	187	319	356	367	418	462	467	467	467	475

Class	1933	1934	1935	1936	1937	1938	1939	1940	1941	1942	1943	1944
	31st December											
O1												16
O2	38	42	42	42	42	42	42	42	42	~~65~~ 64	67	67
O1*	20	20	20	20	20	20	20	20	20	20	20	20
O4	408	408	411	415	416	416	416	417	420	420	329	313
O5	13	13	10	6	5	5	5	4	1	1		
O6												25
Total	479	483	483	483	483	483	483	483	483	~~506~~ 505	416	441

Class	1945	1946	1947	1948	1949	1950	1951	1952	1953	1954	1955	1956
	31st December											
O1	37	50	51	53	58	58	58	58	58	58	58	58
O2	67	67	67	66	66	66	66	66	66	66	66	66
O3	20	20	17	15	15	14	4					
O4	292	279	278	276	271	271	271	266	266	266	266	266
O6†	43	68	68	68	68	68	68	68	68	68	68	68
O7‡		190	200	200	200	200	200	200	200	200	200	200
Total	459	674	681	678	678	677	667	658	658	658	658	658

Class	1957	1958	1959	1960	1961	1962	1963	1964	1965	1966	1967	1968
	31st December											
O1	58	58	58	58	58	30	18	10				
O2	66	66	66	62	56	40						
O3												
O4	266	265	222	215	196	116	88	57	13			
O6†	68	68	68	68	68	68	68	66	57	46	15	
O7‡	200	200	199	198	198	179	141	123	74	34		
Total	658	657	613	601	576	433	315	256	144	80	15	Nil

* Reclassified O3 in 1944.
† In 1948 class O6 was incorporated in the L.M.S. 8F class (Nos. 48705-72).
‡ In 1949 class O7 was incorporated in the W.D. 8F class (Nos. 90000-90100, 90422-90520).

2-8-0 CLASSES O1 TO O7

Until the 1939-45 War, the L.N.E.R. 2-8-0 engines were of two main designs: classes O1 and O2 originated on the G.N.R., whilst classes O4 and O5 were from the G.C.R. The classification O3 was left blank for a long time and was originally intended to provide for possible development of the Doncaster design.

Class O1 consisted of twenty 4ft. 8in. engines, the first of which appeared in 1913. This was Gresley's second design and was developed from his 2-6-0 (class K1 on the L.N.E.R.). It was of course very much bigger and carried a 5ft. 6in. diameter boiler. The two outside cylinders were, like the 2-6-0, driven by Walschaerts valve gear. The class was not added to, and further construction of the 2-8-0 type was a three-cylinder version. In 1944 the O1's were reclassified O3 so that O1 could be used for Thompson's new design. The O3's were withdrawn during 1947-52.

The first O2 engine was built in 1918 and carried the same type of boiler as the O1 class. This was Gresley's first use of three cylinders. Movement of the valve for the centre cylinder was derived from the outside valve gear for the other two cylinders. Ten more engines were built in 1921 and differed in having the alternative version of derived valve gear as introduced on the class K3 2-6-0's. Class O2 was adopted as a Group Standard design and a further fifteen were built soon after Grouping, but the large-scale acquisition of surplus R.O.D. engines during 1923-29 meant that it was unnecessary to build further O2's until 1932-34 when sixteen were delivered for use on the G.E. Section. A final batch of twenty-five was built in 1942-43 to partly compensate for the requisition of other engines for wartime use. The class then totalled sixty-seven engines. Apart from fitting the rather similar Thompson standard B1-type boiler, no major alterations were made to the O2's. The pioneer engine was scrapped in 1948 and the remainder were withdrawn in 1960-63.

The G.C.R. 2-8-0, classified O4 on the L.N.E.R., was introduced in 1911 by Robinson. It was a robust and straightforward design, developed from his earlier 0-8-0 engines, and had 4ft. 8in. coupled wheels and outside cylinders operated by inside Stephenson motion. The boiler had a Belpaire firebox and was similar to that used by Robinson on his Atlantics. By the end of 1914 126 were in service. During 1919-21 a further nineteen engines were built with larger diameter boilers and this variant was classified O5 on the L.N.E.R. Two of these engines had already been converted to the smaller boiler type before Grouping and the remainder were similarly rebuilt to class O4 by the L.N.E.R., this being completed in 1943.

During the First World War the original Robinson 2-8-0 design was selected by the Government to be built for military service and 521 were constructed. After hostilities ceased in 1918 many of these engines were temporarily loaned to the railway companies in Britain, whilst others were purchased. Eventually most of the loaned engines were put up for sale and, being standard with an existing class on the L.N.E.R., the Company decided to purchase 273 of them. By 1929, when all these engines were in traffic, together with three bought by the G.C.R., plus the 145 class O4 and O5 engines, the L.N.E.R. had 421 heavy goods locomotives of uniform design.

Through the ensuing years many O4's were rebuilt with a variety of types of boiler with round-topped firebox. However, in 1944 Thompson initiated a more drastic conversion programme in which the O4's were given his B1-type boiler and cylinders with outside Walschaerts valve gear. These rebuilds were classified O1 and fifty-eight were dealt with up to 1949, when such rebuildings were discontinued.

Withdrawal from stock of class O4 had begun in 1943, when ninety-two engines which had been "called up" for wartime service in 1941 were deleted from the Company's books, whilst a further five were taken for overseas service in 1952. Normal withdrawal commenced in 1958 and the class became extinct in 1966. The O1 rebuilds disappeared during the previous year.

The story of the wartime use of the 2-8-0 type on the L.N.E.R. cannot be complete without some mention of the U.S. Army S160 class engines, designed for use by the occupying forces in Europe, and shipped across to Britain in large numbers in readiness for the invasion. During 1942-45 210 of them were loaned to the Company, with a peak of 168 when the full allocation to the British main line companies settled down, and they were widely distributed throughout the system.

The L.M.S. class 8F Stanier-designed 2-8-0 was selected by the Government at the beginning of the 1939-45 War to be constructed as a standard type both for military use and to augment the heavy goods engine fleet in this country. For its part, the L.N.E.R. built and ran sixty of these engines during the period 1943-47. These bore L.M.S. numbers and livery. Sixty-eight more, numbered in the L.N.E.R. series, were built by the L.N.E.R. and Southern Railway during 1944-46 for use on the L.N.E.R. The classification O6 was introduced to cover these engines, which were transferred to the L.M.S. system during 1947-48.

The wartime Government eventually decided to have built a further 2-8-0 type, to be constructed in large numbers for use on the Continent once our forces had commenced the invasion. R. A. Riddles was the designer of these well-known "Austerity" engines and 935 were turned out during 1943-45. Many of these engines saw initial service on the L.N.E.R. system until they were required on the Continent. At the end of hostilities the L.N.E.R. again had engines of this type on loan and then in 1946 decided to purchase 200 of them. The classification O7 was given to these engines. After nationalisation, B.R. purchased further examples. Withdrawal occurred during the years 1959-67.

CLASS O1 (LATER O3)

G.N.R. CLASS O1 – GRESLEY
4ft. 8in. ENGINES

ENGINES AT GROUPING (Built 1913-19): 3456-60/2-76. TOTAL 20.

When Gresley took over from Ivatt in 1911 the G.N.R. possessed fifty-five 0-8-0 goods engines (L.N.E.R. classes Q1 and Q2) which were being worked to capacity. The Company's main line was carrying very heavy coal traffic from Grantham (off the Nottingham branch) to London and a reduction in the number of trains by means of increasing the loadings was desirable, double-heading not being a favoured solution to the problem. Consequently Gresley had in mind a larger design than the Ivatt 0-8-0 and the result was the class O1 2-8-0 mineral engine, with two 21in. diameter by 28in. stroke cylinders supplied by a 5ft. 6in. diameter boiler having a 24-element superheater.

This was Gresley's second new design for the G.N.R. and as in his previous 2-6-0 he employed outside cylinders and Walschaerts valve gear driving 10in. diameter piston valves. The same double-bolster swing-link pony truck provided not only support for the front end, but also made the engine a better vehicle for traversing the frequent diversions on to and out of the slow lines on the journey to London. The boiler was a considerable increase in diameter over that used on the initial ten 2-6-0's and in fact set the standard for future construction of that type of engine. However, when the O1's first appeared there were doubts about the ability of ordinary injectors to maintain an adequate feed with such large cylinders. Consequently the first five engines had Weir feed pumps, though these were removed before Grouping. No. 476 was given a Worthington feed pump in 1922, but this too was later removed.

The initial order placed in May 1913 was for five engines Nos. 456-60. However, six boilers were ordered, allegedly to provide a spare for the class, but Gresley may have been thinking already of a more powerful 2-8-0, and certainly when the sixth boiler was eventually used it was fitted to the prototype three-cylinder engine, No. 461, which appeared in 1918 (see class O2).

In January 1916 quotations for fifteen more 2-8-0's were called for but no contracts were issued. The G.N.R. needed these engines and in

G.N.R. Nos.	*Maker*	*Order No.*	*Works Nos.*	*No. built*	*Date*
456-60	Doncaster	274	1411/2/3/5/8	5	1913-14
462-71	N.B. Loco. Co. (a)	L705 (b)	22060-9	10	1919
472-6	,, (c)	L709 (d)	22099-103	5	1919

(a) Hyde Park Works.
(b) Doncaster E.O. 286 issued February 1918.
(c) Atlas Works.
(d) Doncaster E.O. 286A also quoted.

the summer of 1917, boiler plates, frame plates, tyres and axles sufficient for ten engines were ordered from America. The boiler order was issued in December 1917 and the engine order itself in February 1918. However, by April 1918 the construction order, together with the material, had been transferred from Doncaster to the North British Locomotive Co. for completion at their Hyde Park Works. In August 1918 five more engines were ordered from this firm and were built at their Atlas Works. Doncaster provided the tenders for all these engines. No more engines were ordered and the construction of the class is summarised above.

The remaining 2-8-0's which were built for the G.N.R. had three cylinders (see class O2). Both classes took the same type of boiler and it is worth observing that the two classes of engine were constructed over a period of thirty years (1913-43) without any significant change in the boiler design.

The introduction of the O1's coincided with that of the tango dance into Britain and so they were nicknamed "Tangos", a name which was also used in some parts of the system for the 0-6-0 tank engines of that period (L.N.E.R. classes J50 and J51). The O1's were altered little over the years, the most noticeable change being the fitting from 1940 of shorter chimneys and dome covers, together with the repositioning of the whistle in front of the cab instead of above it, in order to bring the class within the 13ft. 0in. gauge. This was the maximum permissible height under the wires of the projected Manchester to Sheffield electrification scheme.

In February 1944 the engines were reclassified O3 to enable class O1 to be used for the Thompson rebuilds from class O4. Withdrawals commenced in 1947 and by the beginning of 1952 there were only four left in service, Nos. 63476/82/4/8 (ex-3457/64/6/70). The class became extinct in December 1952 when No. 63484 was withdrawn.

Standard L.N.E.R. Dimensions at Grouping

Cylinders (2 outside)	21″ × 28″
Motion	Walschaerts with 10″ piston valves
Boiler:	
Max. diam. outside	5′ 6″
Barrel length	16′ 1⅜″*
Firebox length outside	9′ 6″
Pitch	8′ 7¼″
Diagram No.	2
Heating surface:	
Firebox	163.5 sq. ft.
Tubes (160 × 2″)	1340.5 sq. ft.
Flues (24 × 5¼″)	528.0 sq. ft.
Total evaporative	2032.0 sq. ft.
Superheater (24 × 1¼″)	430.5 sq. ft.
Total	2462.5 sq. ft.
Grate area	27.5 sq. ft.
Boiler pressure	180 lb./sq. in.
Leading wheels	3′ 2″
Coupled wheels	4′ 8″
Tender wheels	4′ 2″
Tractive effort (85%)	33,736 lb.
Length over buffers	60′ 9¾″
Wheelbase:	
Engine	7′ 10″ + 6′ 0″ + 6′ 6″ + 6′ 0″ = 26′ 4″
Tender	7′ 0″ + 6′ 0″ = 13′ 0″
Total	51′ 4¼″
Weight (full):	
Engine	76T 4C
Tender	43T 2C
Total	119T 6C
Adhesive	67T 8C
Max. axle load	17T 12C
Water capacity	3,500 gallons
Coal capacity	6T 10C

* The engine diagram quoted 15′ 5½″, which was the length of the barrel less the amount by which the smokebox tubeplate was recessed into it.

L.N.E.R. Renumbering

The engines had 3000 added to the G.N.R. numbers shortly after Grouping, becoming Nos. 3456-60 and 3462-76. Some confusion can arise over the 1946 renumbering when they became 3475-94 in order as the two series overlapped; in the original L.N.E.R. numbering Nos. 3475/6 were the last two engines whereas in the new scheme these numbers were taken by the first two engines of the class.

Details

The coupled wheels had laminated bearing springs. Equalising beams connected those for the leading and intermediate coupled wheels and also for the driving and trailing coupled wheels. These beams were removed from about 1940 when they were taken off the O2's and P1's. The coupled wheel axle journals were $8\frac{1}{2}$in. diameter and 9in. long, lubricated from the Wakefield mechanical lubricator which was mounted midway along the right-hand running plate. No. 3476 is recorded as receiving the Silvertown type in September 1929, but it is not known if this was for the axleboxes or the cylinders.

The pony truck employed Gresley's double swing-link suspension and centring arrangement. The original bearing springs were 2ft. 6in. across their centres (one $\frac{9}{16}$in. and six $\frac{7}{16}$in. thick plates). Nos. 456/8/9 quickly received replacement springs (seven $\frac{9}{16}$in. plates) as provided for Nos. 1640-7 (see class K2). Finally all five engines acquired helical bearing springs, probably during their first general repairs in 1916. The later O1's Nos. 462-76, had helical springs when new and also had dust shields in front of their axleboxes, a feature which the first five engines never acquired (cf. figs. 6 and 7).

The cylinders were the largest employed in a Doncaster design and were inclined at 1 in 40 from the horizontal, driving the third pair of coupled wheels. The cylinders had piston tail rod extensions (fig. 2), but in September 1924 it was decided to dispense with them and they were removed from Nos. 3456 (December 1924), 3468 (March 1925) and 3459 (April 1925) by way of an experiment in conjunction with the trial fitting of cast steel piston heads. The experiment appears to have been unsatisfactory, possibly because the piston heads were heavier than in other classes and wear of the cylinder walls was excessive, and the tail rods were put back again later. However, they were finally removed from all engines at a later date (fig. 4), though No. 3462 still had them in September 1940. The valve gear was reversed by lever whereas on the later three-cylinder counterparts screw reverse was employed. The radius rods were plain on Nos. 456-60 only and fluted on the later engines (cf. figs. 4 and 6). No. 3458, at least, acquired fluted radius rods in L.N.E.R. days. One minor detail which always distinguished Nos. 456-60 from the later engines of the class was the length of the casings above the running plate on the right-hand side alongside the firebox, which covered the reversing rod. These casings were 6ft. 4in. long on the earlier engines and 8ft. 6in. on the later ones (cf. figs. 2 and 9). A Wakefield mechanical lubricator was provided for the cylinders and valves and was mounted on the right-hand running plate just behind the cylinders.

The piston valves were 10in. diameter and the maximum travel was $5\frac{3}{8}$in. at 75 per cent cut-off. Nos. 456-60 when new had Doncaster-type "double admission" valves. The valve head, which was a $2\frac{11}{16}$in. long split ring, controlled the valve events, whilst supplementary ports were provided in the circumference. The latter were connected to similar ports in the other valve head by a sleeve which enclosed the valve spindle between them. They were arranged to open at the same time as the normal steaming edge of the valve, thereby doubling the steam admission to the cylinder, which was of benefit when running. However, as this feature also doubled the effective opening to "lead" steam there was a disadvantage on starting, though this was allowed for by providing only $\frac{1}{16}$in. steam lead. The exhaust clearance was $\frac{3}{8}$in. and the steam lap of the valve was $1\frac{5}{16}$in.

One difficulty with double admission piston valves was keeping the supplementary portways free from carbon deposits. This resulted in loss of power when running and the amount of lead steam was then insufficient. After a few months in service, No. 457's valves were altered (probably at the shed during April 1914) to give $\frac{5}{16}$in. exhaust clearance, $\frac{1}{8}$in. steam lead and $1\frac{1}{4}$in. steam lap. The other four engines were brought into line shortly afterwards.

A disadvantage with split ring piston valves is that as they are sprung in the steam chest liner to make a steamtight fit, surface lubrication is difficult, wear is heavy and a good deal of energy is wasted during the actual travel. In November 1918 No. 460 was fitted with new piston valves, based on Canadian Pacific practice. The valve head had a $1\frac{7}{16}$in. centre ring with a $\frac{5}{8}$in. wide split ring on each side of it. Together they presented a steamtight fit, whilst energy lost through friction was reduced as only the outer rings were sprung in the liner. When Nos. 462-76 appeared during 1919, the first ten engines had Doncaster-type valves like Nos. 456-9 and the last five engines had C.P.R.-type valves like No. 460.

The C.P.R.-type piston valve was not entirely satisfactory, because steam managed to find its way through the fine gaps between the individual rings that made up each head. From 1922 they were replaced on Nos. 460/72-6 by a new type of valve having a single split ring with a number of tiny holes in the circumference to admit just enough lubricated steam to the surface of the ring to overcome starting friction. Nos. 456-9/62-71 were not brought into line.

After Grouping G.E. pattern (Knorr type) piston valves became standard on all the O1's from about 1924. These had a solid valve head, $\frac{1}{32}$in. smaller in diameter than the valve liner, with four narrow split rings to provide the necessary steamtight fit. From October 1932 replacement piston valves were the "ring control" type, in which admission was controlled by the edges of the outer split rings.

Gravity sanding was applied in front of the leading coupled and to the rear of the trailing coupled wheels. In addition steam-operated sanders were provided in front of the driving wheels.

The boiler was based on that fitted to the Ivatt large Atlantics (see Part 3A class C1), but with a long narrow firebox. The barrel was almost identical except for the dome being on the rear ring instead of the front one. The barrel was made of two telescopic rings, the front being the smaller with a diameter of 5ft. $4\frac{3}{4}$in. The firebox tubeplate was $\frac{7}{8}$in. thick on Nos. 456-60 only, when new, and the distance between the tubeplates was 16ft. 0in. Replacement inner fireboxes and those on Nos. 462-76 when new had 1in. thick tubeplates which reduced the distance between the tubeplates to 15ft. $11\frac{7}{8}$in.

The original boilers fitted to the O1's, as well as to class O2 No. 461, had Ramsbottom safety valves and none of these particular boilers had a subsequent valve change. The original boilers generally rotated only amongst the O1's and No. 461, though one or two did appear on other O2's. All other Diagram 2 boilers had Ross pop safety valves and these boilers gradually appeared on the O1's, commencing with Nos. 3462/6/7/70/1 in 1924, (cf. figs. 2 and 3).

There were originally 167 small tubes, providing 1,399 sq. ft. of heating surface. The top row of tubes was dispensed with from 1918 and the amended heating surface figures are as shown under "Standard L.N.E.R. Dimensions at Grouping". The boiler pressure was originally 170 lb. per sq. in., raised to 180 lb. from 1919.

Robinson superheaters with 24 long-loop type elements were provided. The heating surface was at first quoted as 570 sq. ft., but this was afterwards amended to 430.5 sq. ft. when the later method of calculation was applied, which took into account only the area of the elements actually inside the flue tubes and was based on the internal diameter of the elements and not the outside figure.

The inner firebox was supported by twenty-two rows of vertical roof stays with two girder bar stays at the front end. The area between the side and roof stays caused Gresley some concern. He believed that when the boiler was working, the expansion of the copper firebox would tend to pull down the top of the outer wrapper plate and consequently force out the sides. The North British Locomotive Co. tested No. 468's new boiler under a hydraulic pressure of 250 lb. per sq. in. and found that in fact the expansion of the sides of the outer firebox tended to pull down the top, which in turn forced down the crown of the copper firebox. The maximum deflection at mid-length of the firebox was $\frac{7}{16}$in. and when the pressure was released there was a maximum permanent deformation of $\frac{3}{16}$in. Doncaster also conducted similar tests with a K2 boiler, with the same result. Horizontal transverse stays, seven in number and located just above the crown of the copper firebox, were fitted to the new boiler for No. 472. In the hydraulic tests N.B. Locomotive Co. found that the maximum deflection was only $\frac{3}{32}$in. and the permanent deformation was reduced to the small margin of $\frac{1}{64}$in. Gresley decided to fit all large diameter boilers with transverse stays and from then onwards they became standard. The first G.N. engine to have them was one of the 2-6-0's, No. 1642, which returned to traffic a week before No. 472 entered service (see also under class K2). The girder bar stays at the front of the firebox were replaced by a single row of expansion sling stays on new boilers constructed after 1931. There was no external evidence of this last change.

The boilers which were built before Grouping had four wash-out plugs on each side of the firebox above the handrails. The arrangement was staggered to ensure the best coverage of the top of the inner firebox. On the boilers which were originally fitted to Nos. 456-60 and also class O2 No. 461, the plugs on the right-hand side were slightly to the rear of those on the left.

Curiously, the opposite applied in the case of the boilers fitted to Nos. 462-76 and also class O2 Nos. 477-86, which were in fact arranged correctly according to the firebox drawing of April 1913. Presumably the first six boilers had been incorrectly drilled. Boilers built between 1923 and 1933 had three wash-out plugs on each side of the firebox instead of four (cf. figs. 4 and 6), which ensured that they were spaced well clear of the transverse stays. Boilers constructed after 1933 had hand holes instead of wash-out plugs in the same position as before.

The Diagram 2 boiler, in addition to being standard for class O2, was also used for the two class O4/4 rebuilds. Although Diagram 100A boilers were afterwards fitted to classes O2 and O4, none was fitted to any of the two-cylinder Gresley engines.

When Nos. 456-60 were new they had one live steam injector only, on the driver's side, whilst on the fireman's side a steam valve controlled the action of a Weir pump and water heater, which was itself located between the frames. The pump drew water from the tender, passed it through the heater and fed it into the boiler half way up on the left-hand side. The exhaust steam from the pump, together with some of the exhaust steam from the blastpipe, passed through the heater to heat the feed water. In September 1916 No. 459 was modified: the heater was dispensed with and the flange on the blastpipe blanked off. Cold feed water was pumped into the top of the boiler on to collection trays inside an additional dome casing which was located behind the ordinary dome. A single elongated cover was fitted over both domes. The other four engines were not altered. The Weir feed pumps and equipment were eventually removed from Nos. 456-60 and ordinary exhaust steam injectors substituted, bringing them into line with Nos. 462-76, as follows:-

No.	*Pump Removed*	*No.*	*Pump Removed*
456	10/1918	459	2/1920
457	2/1919	460	11/1918
458	1/1920		

No. 459 (later 3459) retained its boiler with the redundant extra dome until May 1927 (fig. 6). This boiler was afterwards fitted to class O2 No. 3461 and later took part in further top feed experiments (see under class O2).

In November 1922 No. 476 (later 3476) was fitted with a Worthington feed water heater and boiler feed pump, working on a similar principle to the original Weir arrangement on Nos. 3456-60, but mounted in a more accessible position on the left-hand side running plate (fig. 5). On 11th December 1923 the engine worked a coal train of seventy-five wagons from New England to Ferme Park – a journey which took 4½ hours. The pump was easy to operate and the boiler feed was easily maintained. It was then intended to carry out comparative tests between this engine and another O1 to determine the economy effected. Arrangements were made for No. 476 to work a special coal train from New England to Ferme Park for two weeks commencing 14th January 1924. The trials were cancelled at the last minute as the amount of coal in stock at that time had not yet returned to its normal level after the Christmas break, and there is no record of them being held later. The original pump was presumably found to be inadequate in size, because it was replaced by a larger one in December 1924. The whole equipment was removed in May 1927.

In December 1928 No. 3474 was fitted with a Gresham & Craven No. 20 feed water heater. This comprised a special coned nozzle which was attached to the end of the delivery pipe from one of the injectors so that steam mixed with the feed water just before the actual point of delivery. There was no external evidence of this fitting. Nos. 3464/73/6 were similarly fitted in 1929. The experiment was concluded and the engines returned to their normal state in 1931-32 as follows:-

	Feed water heater	
No.	*Fitted*	*Removed*
3464	3/1929	4/1931
3473	10/1929	4/1932*
3474	12/1928	1/1931
3476	9/1929	6/1932

* This date is not officially confirmed.

The smokebox was 4ft. 10in. long and projected about 15in. forward of the supporting saddle. The diameter of the door was 4ft. 9in. with the centres of the hinge straps 1ft. 3in. apart. A horizontal handrail was provided above the upper strap and below the top lampiron. The boiler handrails, which were separate, curved round the front of the smokebox and upwards. Latterly on some engines these handrails stopped short on the smokebox side but not all the engines were brought into line with this latest practice. The vacuum ejector exhaust pipe ran along the right-hand side of the boiler between the handrail and the boiler clothing plate so that they shared common pillar stanchions, which was unusual. On Nos. 456-60 only, when new, the steam from the blower valve in the cab to the smokebox passed through a separate tube on the left-hand side between the handrail and the boiler clothing plate so that they too shared common pillar stanchions (fig. 6). On Nos. 462-76 the steam pipe from the blower valve passed through the boiler to the smokebox and the first five engines were afterwards brought into line.

The diameter of the blastpipe orifice was 5½in. on Nos. 456-60 and 5⅜in. on the later engines. Churchward-pattern blastpipe jumper tops were fitted to three O1's, Nos. 3457 (February 1934), 3466 (May 1935) and 3463 (October 1935). In December 1938 it was agreed that there had been no advantage in fitting jumper tops and they were afterwards removed.

The chimney, 1ft. 7½in. high, was the pattern to be found on classes C1, K2 and O2 at Grouping. This type was retained until October 1940 from which date a 1ft. 4in. high chimney was substituted as the engines passed through shops to bring the engines within the 13ft. 0in. gauge in connection with the electrification proposals (figs. 2 and 4). This latest pattern chimney had been introduced in August 1923 for the class O2 2-8-0's and had subsequently appeared on class C1 No. 3279 and classes K4 and O4/5. The chimney was also later fitted to four other classes, B1, K1, K1/1 and L1. The height above rail level to the top of the stud which secured the dome cover was 13ft. 1$\frac{1}{16}$in. before Grouping (though shown as 13ft. 1⅛in. on the engine diagram). The height was reduced afterwards by the L.N.E.R. to 13ft. 0½in., then finally to 12ft. 11$\frac{15}{16}$in. after October 1940 to bring it within the 13ft. 0in. gauge mentioned above. In connection with this successive lowering, it should be noted that the height of the dome itself on the boiler barrel remained unaltered and the lowering was effected by making adjustments to the securing stud and to the distance piece which bridged the gap between dome and cover, thereby permitting the cover to be flattened down.

The whistle was originally located above the cab roof following usual G.N.R. practice with the operating lever at the top (fig. 3), and the height above rail level to the top was 13ft. 3⅜in. Later, the whistle was generally located in front of the cab, lower down than before and usually off-centre to either left or right (fig. 4), but occasionally in line with the safety valves. The alteration began before the general reduction in height to clear the 13ft 0in. gauge referred to earlier, but there were still engines latterly with the whistle in the original position, e.g. Nos. 3487/94 after 1946. Furthermore the change was not noted on the engine diagram so that officially the engines remained outside the new gauge. The engines retained to the end the original G.N.R. style cab, so that whilst the height at the centre cleared the 13ft. 0in. gauge, provided the whistle had been moved, the profile at the "shoulders" did *not* clear the L.N.E.R. Composite Load Gauge.

The engines had G.N.R. round case buffers, 1ft. 6in. long, which they retained to the end. Originally ordinary three-link couplings were fitted but screw couplings were substituted later, a start having been made by Grouping (cf. figs. 6 and 7).

Brakes

The engines had vacuum brakes following usual G.N.R. practice, but to obtain the necessary brake power there were four 18in. diameter brake cylinders between the frames. The brake rodding followed an unusual arrangement: the pair of cylinders under the reversing shaft applied brakes on the first two pairs of coupled wheels whilst the cylinders under the cab applied brakes on the driving and trailing coupled wheels.

Tenders

When new the O1's were normally attached to 3,500-gallon tenders which held 6½ tons of coal, though at one time Nos. 468/75 at least were noted attached to older Stirling tenders. Later, Ivatt 3,670 and 3,720-gallon tenders were substituted which, although they carried more water, only held 5 tons of coal.

This was the position in January 1928 when the Running Department complained that coal trains between New England and Ferme Park were frequently being delayed at Hitchin, whilst the engine went to the shed for more coal. It was decided to fit a division plate at the back of the coal space on the tenders which were attached to the O1's. This would prevent coal from rolling to the far end near the tank lid and would assist the stacking of coal at the back of the bunker. Fifteen tenders were thus altered before it was reported that the problem had not been solved. In January 1929 an instruction was issued that the early class B tenders (i.e. with 5 tons coal capacity) were to be replaced by the modern B type (i.e. the 6½ tons coal and 3,500 gallons of water variety, as originally provided), to be taken from class C2 4-4-2's. This was done as the O1's passed through works, commencing with No. 3470 in February 1929. The remaining engines were dealt with as follows: Nos. 3464/7/8/73/6 (later in 1929); 3460/3/71/2 (1930); 3462 (1931); 3458/69 (1932); 3456/7/65/6/74 (1933); 3475 (1935); and finally No. 3459 in March 1936 (cf. figs. 2 and 3).

No. 3469 reverted to the older 3,670-gallon type once more in January 1935, when tender No. 1380 was attached, but regained the more modern 3,500-gallon type in November 1938. There was one further reversion, in June 1942 when tender No. 1380 was then attached to No. 3465 (latterly 63483) with which engine it remained until withdrawn in April 1951.

As the object of these tender changes was simply to increase coal capacity, it may seem curious that no attempt was made at that time to use the ten class B tenders which were provided with a third coal rail in 1923 (see Part 3A, class C1). The facility of their extra capacity was probably overlooked, as it was certainly never given any cognisance in the Diagram Book. However, such tenders were afterwards attached to Nos. 3457 (1933-46) and 3460 (1936).

Maintenance

The class was normally shopped at Doncaster but between April 1932 and May 1935 they all visited Gorton Works for overhaul.

Liveries

When new the engines appeared in the dark grey livery which was introduced on the G.N.R. in 1912 for goods engines. Engines 462-76 were lined out in white, but not their tenders, whilst Nos. 456-60 were unlined. There were two official photographs of No. 456, one in grey and one in lined green. However, the latter is actually No. 457 posing as No. 456 and taken one week after the genuine one, simply to illustrate a new 2-8-0 in green livery. In L.N.E.R. days black was of course the livery for goods engines. Until June 1928 red lining was applied.

British Railways

Seventeen engines were taken over at nationalisation. Nos. 3489/94 were withdrawn during 1948 whilst the remaining engines survived long enough to carry their 60000 series B.R. numbers.

Allocation and Work

These engines were introduced to work the constantly increasing coal traffic from the producing areas in Nottinghamshire, Derbyshire and South Yorkshire. They were designed to haul up to eighty loaded wagons, weighing around 1,300 tons, from Peterborough to Ferme Park. This was twenty wagons more than were then being handled by the Ivatt 0-8-0's (L.N.E.R. classes Q1 and Q2). The first run with seventy-eight wagons and two 20-ton brake vans took place on 2nd January 1914, afterwards becoming regular.

All twenty engines were originally allocated to Peterborough (New England), but by the end of 1920 three had moved to Colwick to work two daily eighty-wagon coal trains from Colwick to New England, returning with empties. Strict instructions were laid down that these trains were not to leave Grantham North until a clear road was available to Stoke summit and in the reverse direction they were held at Stoke until the road was clear through Grantham and on to the Nottingham branch. On arrival at New England these trains were not remarshalled, but proceeded to Ferme Park after examination and engine change. The fastest booking occupied ten hours nineteen minutes throughout from Colwick to London.

By Grouping, there were four O1's at Colwick to work these trains, Nos. 464/9/70/1. These engines returned to New England in March 1925, which once more housed the entire class, but after eight months Nos. 3459/68/9/75 were transferred in time for the peak winter months to Colwick. No. 3468 was back at New England by 1930, but the other three remained at Colwick until 1934-35. Colwick engines were rarely seen south of Peterborough on the G.N. main line, but after Grouping they occasionally worked to Woodford over the G.C. lines and to March via Sleaford and Spalding.

Until 1930 at least, there were fifteen booked coal trains from New England to Ferme Park on weekdays, including the two which had originated from Colwick, taking between 6½ and 7½ hours on the journey according to the amount of time spent waiting for passenger trains to pass through the double track sections of the line. Stops were made at Offord for water and at Hitchin for both water and crew changing, the general pattern of operating being for New England crews to work as far as Hitchin where they changed over with Hornsey men who had worked down with empties. In addition there were a number of brick trains from Fletton to London and slow unbraked goods trains from New England to Hornsey and King's Cross.

For many years two full train loads of Lincolnshire potatoes ran to London. The first started from Old Leake at 4-35 p.m. and was worked to Spalding by a Boston J6 or K2. From Spalding, where the load was made up to eighty wagons if available, this train was worked through to King's Cross by a New England O1 or O2 which had run tender-first from New England to Spalding in the evening. The second train started from Sibsey at 4-44 p.m. and was operated similarly to Spalding, whence it was hauled to Peterborough by a New England J6 which had run earlier to Spalding coupled to the engine of the 2-18 p.m. Peterborough to Grimsby passenger train. It spent several hours shunting at Spalding before taking the potato train to New England where it was exchanged for a 2-8-0 if the load warranted it. In the late thirties the Old Leake train was routed via Hertford North from Langley Junction. These two trains between them often carried nearly 2,000 tons of potatoes to London five nights a week. Gradually the traffic was lost to road transport and the trains ceased to run.

The majority of 2-8-0's working from New England to London were detached from their trains at Ferme Park and then went to Hornsey for servicing before returning northwards. A small number worked to King's Cross Goods daily and were serviced at the Top shed.

In addition to working southwards, the New England engines also had a few duties to Doncaster via Spalding, Sleaford and Lincoln. On these they took empty wagons northwards and returned with loaded coal. From 1925 onwards these duties were mostly undertaken by O4's but the Gresley engines still appeared occasionally. The distance from New England to Doncaster by this route was some 97 miles compared with 78 miles by the main line, but congestion was eased on the latter route. Not all the loaded trains ran via Sleaford and a few were routed from Lincoln via Boston and Spalding instead.

Coal traffic over the southern section of the G.N. main line between Peterborough and Ferme Park was heavy in the late twenties. In the winter months it was usual for congestion to occur in the Ferme Park yards because of problems arising from the disposal of traffic to the Southern Railway via King's Cross (York Road) and the Metropolitan Widened Lines. In addition to the strictly limited loads, there were severe restrictions on times when transfer trips could be run. Each eighty-wagon coal train which arrived at Ferme Park conveying coal for Southern Railway destinations required four transfer trips. Between thirty-five and forty such trips were booked regularly on weekdays. As a result of this congestion, it was common at certain times for three coal trains to be standing nose to tail on the goods line between New Southgate station and Cemetery Box, another between Oakleigh Park and New Barnet South and perhaps two occupying the up slow line from Potters Bar to Brookmans Park. When Ferme Park was able to accept another train, the one standing at New Southgate would be released and the following trains moved up one stage. Many hours were spent in this manner and relief crews were sent out from Hornsey from time to time who took over from Hornsey men who had only worked up from Hitchin. Sometimes one of these heavy trains would be shunted back from New Southgate station into the sidings north thereof and left until congestion eased at Ferme Park. This operation was often accompanied by much slipping and spectacular pyrotechnic effects at night. In times of heavy pressure there would also be special coal trains on Sundays.

In 1932 a move was made towards reducing the number of heavy slow moving coal trains over the whole G.N. main line. Trains loaded to a maximum of sixty wagons were gradually introduced, hauled by class K3 2-6-0's. This eventually made some of the O1's redundant at New England, where for a while between August 1935 and January 1936 the whole class had once more been stationed. Between 1936 and 1940 Nos. 3456-9/65/6/71/4/5/6 moved north to Doncaster, Nos. 3456/7 first spending six months at Mexborough.

In November 1942 the remaining engines at New England were transferred to Grantham, with No. 3471 from Doncaster, to work the steeply graded iron ore branches from Highdyke to Stainby and Sproxton and the block ore trains to Frodingham via Lincoln and Barnetby. This traffic had hitherto been worked by O4's, which were then transferred to Doncaster and Mexborough. Two more of the G.N. engines, Nos. 3457/74, were transferred from Doncaster to Grantham in May 1945.

The O1's occasionally strayed away from the Southern Area and on 20th May 1940 No. 3456 was observed on a coal train at Gascoigne Wood. On 13th September 1942 this same engine made the first recorded appearance of the class in Edinburgh, when noted on St. Margaret's shed.

Fig. 2 Class O1 No. 3457 at New England shed, about 1928.

Original 1ft. 7½in. chimney, Ramsbottom safety valves, tail rod extension to pistons, short casing over reversing rod, 3,670-gallon tender.

Fig. 3 Class O1 No. 3458 at Doncaster shed, May 1937.

Ross pop safety valves, whistle still located above cab roof, 3,500-gallon tender.

Fig. 4 Class O3 No. 3468 at Doncaster Works, September 1946.

Final 1ft. 4in. chimney, whistle in front of cab off-centre to right, three wash-out plugs on left-hand side of firebox, tail rod extensions removed, fluted radius rod, handrail cut short at side of smokebox (cf. fig. 2).

Fig. 5 Class O1 G.N.R. No. 476 at Doncaster Works, June 1921.

Close-up view of Worthington feed water heater and pump.

Fig. 6 Class O1 No. 3459 at Colwick shed, about 1926.

Four wash-out plugs on left-hand side of firebox, redundant extra dome, separate tube for steam to blower valve behind boiler handrail, plain radius rod, screw coupling, no axlebox dust shields, 3,670-gallon tender.

Fig. 7 Class O1 No. 3473 on down goods near Sandy, about 1928.

Three-link coupling, axlebox dust shields.

Fig. 8 Class O3 No. 3473 on up class C goods near Ruddington, August 1946.

Fig. 9 Class O1 No. 3474 on up class C goods leaving Wood Green tunnel, 1928.

Long casing over reversing rod.

Fig. 10 Class O2 No. 3461 at New England shed, about 1927.

Gresley's first three-cylinder engine with inclined cylinders and rocking shaft to actuate inside valve, original 1ft. 7½in. chimney and tall dome cover, Ramsbottom safety valves, four wash-out plugs on side of firebox, boiler handrails curved round front of smokebox and upwards, footsteps at front, parallel shank buffers, 3ft. 2in. pony truck wheels, 3,720-gallon tender.

Fig. 11 Class O2/1 No. 485N at Hornsey shed, about 1924.

Reduced inclination of outside cylinders with inside valve actuated by alternative form of conjugate valve gear, no footsteps at front, 2ft. 8in. pony truck wheels, Ross pop safety valves, whistle above cab roof, Wakefield mechanical lubricators for cylinders and axleboxes, Spencer double case buffers.

Fig. 12 Class O2/2 No. 487N at Doncaster Works, October 1923 prior to entering traffic.

Altered cab profile but still with 1ft. 7½in. chimney, whistle in front of cab, three wash-out plugs on side of firebox, G.N.-type 3,500-gallon tender built after Grouping.

Fig. 13 Class O2/2 No. 3500 at New England shed, July 1926.

With Dabeg feed water heater and pump, shorter 1ft. 4in. chimney, whistle in front of cab in line with safety valves.

Fig. 14 Class O2/2 No. 3487 at Doncaster Works, April 1931.

Close-up view of motion levers in front of steam chests.

During 1943-46 all twenty were seen working over the G.C. main line southwards from Nottingham. For a short time during the War, when the cross-London routes were blocked due to bombing, there were some coal train workings by O1 (O3) and O2 class engines via Sandy Junction, the L.M.S. route to Bedford, Bletchley and Claydon Junction, and thence on to the G.C. main line. They were also observed at Stratford, e.g. Nos. 3459/68 both on 30th October 1944, having probably worked in via the Bounds Green – Palace Gates connection. On 5th September 1945 No. 3459 was observed at Dunford West on a westbound goods train and ten days later No. 3473 was seen at Guide Bridge station on a mineral train.

From June 1945 the Grantham iron ore workings were taken over by O2's received from New England. The O3's were transferred to Doncaster where the entire class was once again concentrated. In April 1946 they all moved to Frodingham, where traffic to and from the steel works had greatly increased, in exchange for O4's. By the end of 1947 three O3's had been withdrawn leaving seventeen to enter British Railways service.

In 1948 the surviving engines were transferred once more to Doncaster, Nos. 3489/94 being withdrawn soon afterwards. Between 1948 and 1950 Nos. (6)3475/9/80/2 were housed at Immingham after which date the survivors were shared between Doncaster and Retford, whence they were employed on somewhat lighter duties. Nevertheless they managed to travel extensively. One was withdrawn in 1950, a further ten followed during 1951 and the remaining four in 1952. Prior to being withdrawn the last three survivors, Nos. 63476/84/8, were all seen in the Manchester area.

Engine Diagram

Section N, 1924. 3,500-gallon tender depicted. Superheater element diameter corrected from 1¼in. to 1.244in., 12/1938. Alternative lower heights to tops of chimney and dome and empty weight of engine added, 12/1940. Note added "for alternative 3,670-gallon tender see D2 class", 12/1941. Reclassified O3, 2/1944.

Classification: Southern Area load class 8; Route availability 6; B.R. power class 8F.

Summary of O1 Class

B.R.No.		1946 *No.*		1924 *No.*		*Maker*	*Works No.*	*Built*	*With-drawn*
63475	11/49	3475	12/46	3456	12/24	Doncaster	1411	12/1913	7/51
63476	3/48	3476	11/46	3457	4/26	,,	1412	12/1913	3/52
63477	7/48	3477	10/46	3458	2/24	,,	1413	12/1913	10/51
63478	6/48	3478	11/46	3459	4/25	,,	1415	1/1914	10/51
63479	10/48	3479	9/46	3460	3/26	,,	1418	3/1914	5/51
63480	4/49	3480	10/46	3462	6/24	N.B. Loco. Co.	22060	5/1919	3/51
63481	1/49	3481	10/46	3463	3/26	,,	22061	5/1919	4/51
63482	6/50	3482	5/46	3464	10/24	,,	22062	5/1919	1/52
63483	4/48	3483	10/46	3465	2/25	,,	22063	5/1919	4/51
63484	10/48	3484	10/46	3466	5/24	,,	22064	5/1919	12/52
63485	8/48	3485	11/46	3467	8/24	,,	22065	5/1919	9/51
63486	9/48	3486	11/46	3468	3/25	,,	22066	6/1919	2/51
—		3487	9/46	3469	5/25	,,	22067	6/1919	7/47
63488	7/48	3488	9/46	3470	10/24	,,	22068	7/1919	2/52
(63489)		3489	9/46	3471	8/24	,,	22069	7/1919	7/48
—		3490	11/46	3472	2/25	,,	22099	10/1919	6/47
63491	12/48	3491	11/46	3473	11/24	,,	22100	10/1919	12/50
—		3492	11/46	3474	12/24	,,	22101	11/1919	5/47
63493	7/48	3493	12/46	3475	4/25	,,	22102	11/1919	2/51
(63494)		3494	10/46	3476	12/24	,,	22103	11/1919	3/48

CLASS O2

G.N.R. CLASS O2 — GRESLEY
4ft. 8in. ENGINES

ENGINES AT GROUPING (Built 1918-21): 3461/77-86. TOTAL 11.

ENGINES BUILT AFTER GROUPING (1923-43): 2430-7, 2954-61, 3487-3501, 3833-57. TOTAL 56.

In November 1915 Gresley applied for the patent rights for a conjugate valve gear for three-cylinder engines, employing either rocking shafts or motion levers. In February 1916 the frames were ordered for a three-cylinder 2-8-0, No. 461, though no engine order had yet been issued. The drawing for the motion layout was completed in the following April and one month later Gresley deposited with the Patent Office the Complete Specification for his valve gear, with a statement to the effect that he was aware that it had been previously proposed to actuate the valve of the central cylinder of a three-cylinder engine "by means of a two-to-one lever and a floating sway beam". (This may have referred to Joy's patent taken out in 1884). In August 1916 Gresley learned through his patent agents that there had been a more recent patent, taken out by Holcroft (No. 7859 of 1909). Fortunately, he was assured that this had lapsed in 1913 (presumably meaning that certain prescribed fees had not been paid) and Gresley therefore decided it would be advisable to proceed with the application, as his three-cylinder engine was under construction. The Complete Specification was accepted in October 1916 (No. 15769) which made it possible to issue the engine order in the following December for No. 461. This sequence of events has been set out in full in view of Gresley's written communication in December 1918 to the Institution of Locomotive Engineers, stating that "it was not until some twelve months after, that I discovered through the Patent Office that Mr. Holcroft had a gear for the same purpose".

Whilst the engine was under construction outline drawings appeared in August 1917 for a 2-8-0 mineral engine having two 21in. by 30in. cylinders. This scheme was not pursued and No. 461 appeared in May 1918. The engine was a development of Gresley's earlier two-cylinder 2-8-0 (L.N.E.R. class O1, later O3) and carried the same design of boiler. No. 461 was Gresley's first three-cylinder engine and it embodied the alternative form of his conjugate valve gear, with rocking shafts to operate the middle valve. Introducing three cylinders brought with it some important advantages. Comparable power was obtained from smaller cylinders, whilst the lighter pistons caused less cylinder wear. After No. 461 appeared, Gresley announced his intention of concentrating on three-cylinder designs in future.

A further ten O2's were ordered from Doncaster Works in March 1919, though the order was afterwards transferred to the North British Locomotive Co. for completion, without tenders, at their Atlas Works. Nos. 477-86 appeared in 1921 and comprised class O2/1 on the L.N.E.R. In this series the cylinder and steam chest layout was redesigned and permitted the use of the simpler form of conjugate valve gear with 2 to 1 levers as introduced in 1920 by Gresley on his large boiler 2-6-0 (L.N.E.R. class K3). This arrangement became standard for future construction of class O2 and No. 461 remained the sole example of its type.

Immediately after the formation of the L.N.E.R. a further fifteen engines were ordered and were turned out in 1923-24 as Nos. 487-95N, 3496-3501. To enable these engines to clear the new Composite Load Gauge (13ft. 1in.), the profile of the cab roof was altered, the whistle was positioned in front of the cab instead of above and a shorter chimney was fitted. These engines comprised class O2/2.

Fifty 2-8-0's appeared on the 1924 building programme and these are believed to have been intended as O2's, though only the wheel arrangement was given. They were however deleted from the programme in November 1923 following enquiries into the purchase of ex-R.O.D. 2-8-0's instead (see under class O4). Large numbers of O4's were added to stock from 1924 and this obviated the need to build any more O2's for some time.

In December 1929 fifteen O2's were ordered against the 1930 building programme, though three months later the order was reduced to eight engines, Nos. 2954-61. The outstanding seven engines reappeared on the 1931 programme, but still no orders ensued. In January 1932 sixteen engines appeared on the 1932 programme, but only eight of these were afterwards ordered, Nos. 2430-7. There was a depression in industry throughout this time and consequently no urgent need for new engines. Nos. 2954-61 and 2430-7 were eventually built between April 1932 and March 1934. They were in fact the only engines built at Doncaster during this period. They had slightly lower dome covers to enable them to clear the G.E. 13ft. 0in. load gauge, side-window cabs, steam brakes (instead of vacuum) and 4,200-gallon Group Standard tenders. These engines were classified O2/3.

In October 1934 the construction of twenty O2's was announced on the 1935 building programme, but these were deleted shortly afterwards without any orders having been placed when the programme was entirely recast to take into account the new V2 class.

The outbreak of War in 1939 brought a Government order for 300 O4's to be sent overseas, to be replaced on the L.N.E.R. by new O2's and V2's. The requisition was cancelled in November 1939 so that there was no longer the same urgency to build O2's. In June 1940 Doncaster ordered ten O2's in advance of authority, presumably to enable them to place orders for raw material which was at that time scarce. In January 1941 the L.N.E.R. noted that the Railway Executive Committee had allocated them material resources for 100 O2's and thirty-five V2's, of which twenty-five O2's would be built in the company's workshops and the rest by contractors. In February 1941 an Emergency Board meeting of the L.N.E.R. noted that the Railway Executive had now directed the L.N.E.R. to build twenty-five each O2's and V2's. As far as the O2's were concerned, this resulted in an order being placed with Darlington for the required number, about April 1941. Apparently this either overlooked the ten ordered from Doncaster in June 1940 or assumed that authority would be forthcoming for the balance of the thirty-five referred to in January 1941. In June 1941 the Darlington order for twenty-five was cancelled and the material transferred to Doncaster for completion. Doncaster however only issued fresh orders for fifteen which, together with the June 1940 order for ten, added up to the authorised total of twenty-five. These engines, which appeared in 1942-43, had vacuum brakes on the engine and tender, but were also included in class O2/3.

No more O2's were authorised for construction and the final batch of ten engines which had been ordered from Darlington Works was eventually cancelled in October 1943. Altogether sixty-seven were built over a period of twenty-five years, of which the last twenty-five appeared within a space of nine months in wartime conditions.

Meanwhile in March 1939 orders were issued to alter Nos. 3461/77-3501 to clear the 13ft. 0in. load gauge and the opportunity was taken to fit Nos. 3461/77-86 with side-window cabs. (The original cabs of Nos. 3487-3501 were already well within this gauge so they were not replaced).

In October 1943 No. 3479 received a Diagram 100A boiler, as fitted to the new class B1 4-6-0's, but working at 180 lb. per sq. in. Four more engines were similarly fitted in 1944 and a separate class part 4 was introduced in September 1945 to cover this variety. Where not already fitted, a side-window cab was provided when one of these boilers was applied. The position at nationalisation, when the entire class was handed over to British Railways, is set out in the accompanying table.

Class	*Engine Nos.*	*Former Nos.*	*Remarks*
O2	3921	3461	Original engine, now with side-window cab.
O2/1	3922/3/5-31	3477/8/80-6	G.N.R. engines, now with side-window cabs.
O2/2	3933-46	3488-3501	L.N.E.R. engines with plain cabs.
O2/3	3948/9/51-61/3-87	2955/6/8-61, 2430-6, 3833-57	Group Standard engines, with side-window cabs.
O2/4	3924/32/47/50/62	3479/87, 2954/7, 2437	Rebuilds with Diagram 100A boilers, with side-window cabs.

Although the class was intact at nationalisation, the pioneer engine, No. 3921, was withdrawn in May 1948 after a life of exactly thirty years. In February 1949 Doncaster was authorised to proceed with the gradual conversion of the remaining engines to class O2/4. As this decision coincided with the release of some serviceable Diagram 2 boilers from withdrawn O3's, Nos. 63932/47/62 in fact lost their Diagram 100A boilers in 1949-50 and reverted to their former class parts. No. 63932 retained its side-window cab and was thus the only O2/2 engine with one. From 1955, Diagram 100A boilers were gradually fitted to twenty-six O2's, including No. 63932 for the second time. Nos. 63933/5/8/45 acquired side-window cabs when they were altered from Part 2 to Part 4. Nos. 63950/3/9/70 were withdrawn in 1960 followed by six more in 1961. Sixteen were withdrawn in 1962 and the last forty in 1963.

L.N.E.R. Renumbering

The engines which were taken over at Grouping had 3000 added to their original numbers, becoming 3461/77-86. The first nine engines built by the L.N.E.R. were numbered in the G.N.R. series, with the Sectional suffix, thus: 487-95N. These later became 3487-95. The last six engines built in 1924 appeared with their new L.N.E.R. numbers, 3496-3501. All the later batches acquired numbers which filled in blanks in the number series where convenient. Under the 1943 renumbering scheme, which was implemented in 1946, the engines became 3921-87 in order of construction.

Standard L.N.E.R. Dimensions

	No. 3461	*Remaining engines*
Cylinders (3)	18″ × 26″	$18\frac{1}{2}$″ × 26″
Motion	Walschaerts/Gresley with 8″ piston valves	
Leading wheels	3′ 2″	2′ 8″
Coupled wheels	4′ 8″	4′ 8″
Wheelbase (engine)	7′ 10″ + 6′ 6″ + 6′ 0″ + 6′ 0″ = 26′ 4″	8′ 8″ + 6′ 6″ + 6′ 0″ + 6′ 0″ = 27′ 2″
Tractive effort (85%)	34,523 lb.	36,470 lb.
	No. 3461, *Parts* 1, 2 *and* 3	*Part* 4
Boiler:		
Max. diam. outside	5′ 6″	5′ 6″
Barrel length	16′ $1\frac{3}{8}$″ (a)	14′ $1\frac{1}{2}$″ (b)
Firebox length outside	9′ 6″	10′ $1\frac{1}{2}$″
Pitch	8′ $7\frac{1}{4}$″	8′ $7\frac{1}{4}$″
Diagram No.	2	100A
Heating Surface:		
Firebox	163.5 sq. ft.	168 sq. ft.
Tubes	1340.5 sq. ft.	1048 sq. ft. (c)
Flues	528.0 sq. ft.	460 sq. ft
Total evaporative	2032.0 sq. ft.	1676 sq. ft. (c)
Superheater	430.5 sq. ft.	344 sq. ft.
Total	2462.5 sq. ft.	2020 sq. ft. (c)
Grate area	27.5 sq. ft.	27.9 sq. ft.
Tubes	160 × 2″	143 × 2″ (d)
Flues	24 × $5\frac{1}{4}$″	24 × $5\frac{1}{4}$″
Elements	24 × $1\frac{1}{4}$″ (e)	24 × 1.244″
Boiler pressure	180 lb./sq. in.	180 lb./sq. in.

	No. 3461	*Part* 1	*Part* 2	*Part* 3	*Part* 4 (f)
Weight (full):					
Engine	76T 8C	75T 16C	75T 16C	78T 13C	74T 2C
Adhesive	66T 12C	67T 7C	67T 7C	69T 7C	64T 12C
Max. axle load	17T 2C	17T 12C	17T 12C	18T 9C	17T 3C

Leading particulars applicable to tenders fitted:-

	G.N.R.-type	*L.N.E.R.*
Wheel diameter	4′ 2″	3′ 9″
Wheelbase	7′ 0″ + 6′ 0″ = 13′ 0″	7′ 3″ + 6′ 3″ = 13′ 6″
Total wheelbase (engine and tender)	52′ 2¼″ (g)	53′ 3″
Length over buffers (engine and tender)	61′ 4¾″ (g)	63′ 3″
Weight (full)	43T 2C	51T 10C (h)
Water capacity	3,500 gallons	4,200 gallons
Coal capacity	6T 10C	7T 10C

(a) The engine diagram quoted 15′ 5½″, which was the length of the barrel less the amount by which the smokebox tubeplate was recessed into it.
(b) The engine diagram quoted the distance between tubeplates, 13′ 11⅞″ (13′ 11½″ from December 1950).
(c) 1033, 1661 and 2005 sq. ft. respectively from November 1945.
(d) 141 tubes from November 1945.
(e) Later 1 7/32″ and finally 1.244″.
(f) Strictly correct for No. 3479 only, former O2/1.
(g) 51′ 4¼″ and 60′ 9¾″ respectively for No. 3461.
(h) 52T 0C from December 1938.

Development and Rebuilding

G.N.R. SERIES

L.N.E.R. Nos.	*Maker*	*Order No.*	*Date Ordered*	*Works Nos.*	*No. Built*	*Date*	*Class Part*
3461	Doncaster	283	December 1916	1481	1	1918	—
3477-86	N.B. Loco. Co.	L742*	April 1920	22691-700	10	1921	1
3487-96	Doncaster	298	January 1923	1574-82/4	10	1923-24	2
3497-3501	,,	299	February 1923	1587/9/92/4/5	5	1924	2
				Total	26		

* Originally ordered from Doncaster in March 1919 as E.O. 288.

NO. 3461.—In order to provide clearance for the middle connecting rod, the drive from all three cylinders was taken by the second coupled axle instead of by the third as in the earlier two-cylinder arrangement of class O1. This entailed a slight alteration to the coupled wheel spacings, with the second pair 6in. further back. The middle cylinder was inclined at 1 in 8 from the horizontal to allow the connecting rod to clear the leading coupled axle. The outside cylinders were inclined at the same angle (fig. 10) so that the three connecting rod cranks could be set at 120 degrees to each other. The simple form of Gresley's conjugate valve gear was not used, as it would have meant arranging the 2 to 1 motion levers in the same inclined plane. The alternative arrangement was used in which the valve gear on either side of the engine drove the outer arms of a rocking shaft which operated an outside valve. The inner arms of these two shafts operated the middle valve and the 2 to 1 ratio was achieved by making the inner arm on the right-hand shaft twice the length of the inner arm on the left-hand shaft. The middle steam chest was located low down, to the left of the middle cylinder. The rocking shaft arrangement had more pins and joints than a third independent gear would have had and was criticised on this account. The arrangement was stated to have been remarkably free from maintenance trouble, but it was a fact that the exhaust beat at the chimney was more syncopated than that of a run-down V2 class 2-6-2. The pins and joints were always in a bad state of wear when the engine was received in the works, as if shed maintenance was virtually impossible. In L.N.E.R. days at least, Doncaster Works admitted that they were never able to set the valve gear correctly because of the accumulative effect of slackness in these pins and joints.

When new No. 461 had Doncaster-type double admission piston valves as fitted to the two-cylinder 2-8-0's (see class O1, p.7). The diameter however was 8in. instead of 10in. and the maximum travel was 5¼in. at 75 per cent cut-off. Shortly after entering service, the middle valve was replaced by the C.P.R. type, a feature of which was the exhaust clearance of the middle valve was ⅛in. whilst that of the outside valves remained $\frac{5}{16}$in. The reason for the modification is not recorded, but as the drawing was dated 6th June 1918 there had been little time for any irregularities in the valve gear to have shown up. Whatever the reason, the experimental valve was removed shortly afterwards and the middle valve reverted to the double admission pattern. After Grouping No. 3461 was brought into line with later practice with the substitution of Knorr-type piston valves and finally ring control type valves (see later).

Inside the smokebox there were two steam pipes which led down from the header and into the smokebox saddle casting. Here they each divided into two separate steam passages with one passage from each steam pipe leading to the middle steam chest.

The boiler was identical to those which had been fitted to the previous two-cylinder engines and was in fact the spare boiler from the February 1913 order (see page 5). A point of difference was the absence of the Weir pump. The engine had a live steam injector on the right-hand side of the firebox back plate and an exhaust steam injector on the left-hand side under the cab.

No 461 was completed and weighed in steam on 4th March 1918. The weight was 76 tons 2 cwt., with 18 tons 18 cwt. axle load on the driving wheels. Further adjustments were made before the engine left the works on 15th May, by which time the maximum axle load had been reduced to 17 tons 2 cwt., and the full weight was shown as 76 tons 8 cwt.

After Grouping, it was never given a class part in the L.N.E.R. classification system and was shown on the engine diagram as "O2, engine 3461".

Nos. 3477-86.—This batch was ordered ten months after the appearance of the prototype. Meanwhile Holcroft pointed out that it was not essential for the cylinders to be in the same inclined plane. All that was necessary was to displace the middle crank from the desired 120° setting by the angular difference in the inclinations of the middle and outside cylinders. By arranging the outside cylinders nearer to the horizontal it was then possible to use the simple form of the conjugate valve gear, with 2 to 1 motion levers in front of the steam chests (fig. 14).

Doncaster embodied this new principle in the three-cylinder 2-6-0's which first appeared in 1920 (L.N.E.R. class K3). However, little progress was made with the new motion arrangement for the 2-8-0's before design work was handed over to the North British Locomotive Co. in April 1920. Gresley had thought of arranging the outside cylinders at 1 in 43.2 from the horizontal, the inside cylinder at 1 in 8 and all three steam chests at 1 in 30. The contractor quickly recommended arranging the outside cylinders and all three steam chests at 1 in 40, thus keeping them parallel with each other. Gresley gave his approval to this on 7th June 1920. The diameter of the cylinders was increased from 18in. to 18½in., taking advantage of the middle steam chest being no longer sandwiched between the middle cylinder and the frame.

The layout of the steam pipes was improved. The header had three outlets, instead of only two, so that separate pipes could be provided to each steam chest. The pipes for the outside steam chests left the smokebox sides instead of passing through the saddle casting and steam pipe covers were provided above the level of the running plate. The main part of the running plate was 3in. lower because of the lower position of the outside cylinders and motion.

The reduced inclination of the outside cylinders (fig. 11) also meant that the pony truck wheels had to be reduced from 3ft. 2in. to 2ft. 8in. diameter and moved 10in. further forward for clearance purposes. The length of the main frame was increased from 36ft. 4in. to 36ft. 11in. There were changes too in the style of buffers and in the sanding gear (see under Details).

A comparison of the weights in working order of these engines and No. 3461 shows a reduction of 12 cwt. (see under Standard L.N.E.R. Dimensions). The diagram weight of 75 tons 16 cwt. was taken from the actual weighing of No. 477 when it was new, but the individual weights for the other engines of this batch ranged from 74 tons 12 cwt. to 76 tons 17 cwt. However, engines rarely weigh the same in working order because of the different amounts of water in their boilers, therefore the apparent saving in weight over No. 3461 due to the modified front end layout has to be treated with caution.

When new these engines had C.P.R.-type piston valves, similar to the one tried out on No. 461 for a short time (see earlier), with $\frac{1}{8}$in. exhaust clearance and $1\frac{1}{4}$in. steam lap. As described on p. 8 under class O1, this type was unsatisfactory because steam leaked between the individual rings that made up the heads. From February 1922 they were replaced by a new type of piston valve with a single split-ring, with a number of tiny holes in the circumference to admit just sufficient lubricated steam to the surface to overcome friction when starting. In October 1923 No. 483 was fitted experimentally with Knorr-type piston valves. The valve heads were machined with a $\frac{1}{64}$in. clearance all round within the steam chest valve liner and rendered steamtight by providing each head with four narrow packing rings. Surface lubrication was no longer a problem because the area of the valve in direct contact with the liner was less, wear was reduced and only a small amount of energy was lost through friction. The remaining engines of this series were afterwards brought into line, whilst from October 1932 replacement piston valves were the "ring control" type (see later under Group Standard Engines).

Nos. 3487-3501.—These engines were built in 1923-24 to the new L.N.E.R. Composite Load Gauge, which involved fitting a $3\frac{1}{2}$in. shorter chimney, repositioning the whistle in front of the cab and reducing the radius of curvature of the cab roof. The highest point of the engine was then 13ft. $0\frac{1}{2}$in. above rail level to the top of the dome securing stud. However, for a while Nos. 3487/90/5 (at least) ran with taller chimneys (cf. figs. 12 and 13).

The driving wheel crank axle was built up from separate parts instead of being forged in one piece as in pre-Grouping engines of the class. This permitted an increase in the bearing surface of the connecting rod big-end ($8\frac{1}{4}$in. diameter by 6in. long instead of 9in. by $5\frac{1}{2}$in.), though the smaller dimensions appeared in error on the engine diagram for Nos. 3487-3501 until corrected in December 1940. No. 3461 was marked up on the drawings to receive a built-up crank axle to the new dimensions when a renewal was necessary, but no date of change has been traced. Nos. 3477-86 are shown as retaining to the end forged crank axles to the old dimensions.

When new these engines had single split-ring piston valves, which were replaced later by the Knorr-type following trials with No. 483, referred to earlier. From October 1932 the "ring control" type became standard (see later).

In December 1924 No. 3479 took part in dynamometer car tests on goods trains between Peterborough, Boston and Firsby, competing against class O1 No. 3466. Further tests were conducted in February 1925 between Peterborough and London with the same two engines. The average results are summarised in the table below, from which it will be seen that the O2 showed a significant economy over the O1, when measured in terms of consumption per draw-bar horsepower hour.

The dynamometer car was again used in March 1925 for maximum pull tests with Nos. 3479 and 3501, and finally for smokebox draught tests from Peterborough to Firsby and back with No. 3501.

In January 1925 No. 3500 was fitted with a Dabeg feed water heater and pump (fig. 13). This was a horizontal tandem type and was mounted on the left-hand side running plate. Before being pumped into the side of the boiler, feed water from the tender was heated by exhaust steam taken from the blastpipe. The exhaust steam injector under the cab on the left-hand side was replaced by a live steam faceplate injector. The Dabeg was probably the most successful

	12/1924		2/1925	
Engine No.	3466	3479	3466	3479
Average results:				
Load (tons)	1368	1368	1319.5	1315
Speed (m.p.h.)	18.5	18.43	13.24	13.67
D.b.h.p.	376	422	356	394
Steam temp. (deg. Fah.)	510	535	500	535
Coal consumption (lb./d.b.h.p. hr.)	5.18	4.43	5.25	4.79
Water consumption (lb./d.b.h.p. hr.)	29.9	26.2	31.95	28.15

application of a feed water heater and pump inasmuch as it was not removed from No. 3500 until December 1942, and its removal then was to conform to a general directive signed by Thompson on 20th June 1941, to "remove all gadgets such as A.C.F.I., Dabeg, etc." and substitute exhaust steam injectors.

In December 1928 No. 3480 acquired a Gresham & Craven No. 20 feed water heater, though there was no external evidence of the fitting. This comprised a special coned nozzle which was attached to the delivery pipe inside the boiler from one of the injectors. Steam was mixed with the feed water just before the actual point of delivery. No. 3498 was similarly fitted two months later. The experiment was short lived and the fittings were removed from these engines in November 1930 and May 1931 respectively.

Following on from the last experiment, in August 1931 No. 3499 acquired two such feed water heaters, which were however incorporated in an external top feed fitting in front of the dome. The delivery pipes from the two injectors passed along the outside of the boiler, high up on each side and were suitably lagged with asbestos (fig. 15). The apparatus was removed from this engine in October 1937.

In February 1929 No. 3461 had acquired the double dome boiler previously carried by class O1 No. 3459, though for the time being it retained its normal injector arrangement. Then in December 1933 it acquired a similar feed water arrangement to No. 3499, just described, except that the top feed was located inside the extra dome (fig. 27). This particular experiment ended in November 1935 when the double dome boiler was condemned: No 3461 was reboilered and reverted to its original injector arrangement.

In October 1932 No. 3492's superheater header was fitted with a set of sine wave elements. Tests were made between Peterborough and Hitchin, with this engine working the 12-35 p.m. mineral train from New England. For comparison purposes No. 3490, with standard long loop elements, was afterwards tested on the same train. The results are summarised in the accompanying table. The special sine wave elements were removed from No. 3492 shortly afterwards, but were also tried on certain engines of classes A3 and P2 and are described on p. 183.

Engine No.	3492	3492	3490
Elements	Sine wave	Sine wave	Standard
Date	11/11/32	25/11/32	7/12/32
Load (wagons)	60	71	73
Max. steam temperature	550°F	570°F	595°F
Location	m.p. 64	m.p. 65	m.p. 65
Gradient	200 up	200 up	200 up
Boiler pressure	170 lb./sq. in.	170 lb./sq. in.	175 lb./sq. in.
Cut-off position	40%	30%	50%
Estimated speed	8 m.p.h.	10 m.p.h.	8 m.p.h.

GROUP STANDARD ENGINES

L.N.E.R. Nos.	*Maker*	*Order No.*	*Date Ordered*	*Works Nos.*	*No. Built*	*Date*	*Class Part*
2954-61	Doncaster	326	December 1929	1773-80	8	1932	3
2430-7	,,	328	February 1932	1781-8	8	1933-34	3
3833-42	,,	359	June 1940	1931-40	10	1942	3
3843-52	,,	364*	June 1941	1941-50	10	1942	3
3853-7	,,	365*	June 1941	1951-5	5	1942-43	3

* Originally ordered from Darlington about April 1941.

In 1932 the first Group Standard O2's appeared, Nos. 2954-61, followed by Nos. 2430-7 in 1933-34 (figs. 16 and 17). Improvements were incorporated which brought them into line with current practice. In particular they were arranged for left-hand drive, steam brakes were fitted (with vacuum ejector for the train) and larger capacity tenders were attached. Long travel valve gear was introduced and at the same time the steam lap of the valves was increased (see later). These engines had the same type of built-up crank axle as Nos. 3487-3501, with the big-end bearing also 8¼in. diameter by 6in. long, erroneously shown on the engine diagram as 9in. by 6in. until it was corrected in December 1940.

As far back as July 1927 Gresley considered fitting the new valve gear to the O2's. Priority was given to preparing drawings for fitting such gear to the class K3 2-6-0's (see Part 6A) and it was not until December 1930 that an estimate was produced for the cost of altering the existing O2's. This worked out at £228 per engine, which was apparently not justified because the alterations were never authorised. The new valve gear was however fitted to the Group Standard O2's and the principal changes were as follows. The throw of the eccentric crank was increased from 1ft. 0¾in. to 1ft. 3in. to lengthen the valve travel in full gear from 5½in. to 6⅝in.; the connection between the foot of the radius link and the eccentric rod was lowered to increase the radius swing of the link foot from 1ft. 6in. to 1ft. 9in., requiring the die block in the radius link to be lowered proportionately for any given cut-off position, thus making possible finer settings of short cut-off; the proportions of the combination lever were altered to permit a longer steam lap; the Knorr-type piston valves had 1$\frac{9}{16}$in. steam lap with an extra $\frac{1}{16}$in. on the inside valve only, to allow for the effects in the middle cylinder of over-travel of the valve at speed. The height of the running plate over the coupled wheels was raised 3 inches to clear the motion because of the longer radius link.

The Knorr-type piston valves fitted to Nos. 2954-61 had one disadvantage. The valve events were controlled by the outer edges of the valve heads which had a $\frac{1}{64}$in. clearance inside the steam chest valve liner. Steam leakage past the valve heads was probably negligible, but from October 1932 admission was controlled by the edge of the outer valve ring, with the outer end of the head reduced in diameter to offer minimum resistance to steam. (Exhaust continued to be controlled as before by the inner edge of the head). "Ring control" valves, as they were known, were fitted to the engines built from 1933 onwards when new and gradually replaced the Knorr-type on Nos. 2954-61.

The lower corners of the front bufferbeam were cut away for clearance purposes when operating away from the G.N. Section. The cab was 6in. longer, with side windows and a separate roof top. A shallower dome cover was fitted which reduced the overall height to 12ft. 11$\frac{15}{16}$in., which was just within the G.E. load gauge. Hand holes in place of wash-out plugs on the firebox casing made their appearance on some engines of the 2430 batch, henceforth becoming standard on the class. There were also other minor changes, such as to the sanding and lubrication arrangements and to the run of the boiler handrails (see Details). Drop grates were fitted to all the Group Standard O2's when new.

The final batch of twenty-five O2's appeared in 1942-43 (fig. 18). They incorporated the latest improvements, including "V" bolt superheater header with ball-jointed (Melesco-type) element ends, equalising beams omitted from the coupled wheel spring gear, 8¾in. diameter coupled wheel axle journals instead of 8½in. and vacuum brakes for engine and tender.

The Group Standard O2's were fitted with carriage warming apparatus with the hose connection at the tender end only. The G.N. series engines of the class were never so equipped.

Reduction in Height of G.N.R. Series

In March 1939 Doncaster was instructed to alter Nos. 3461/77-3501 to clear the 13ft. 0in. height limit set for engines likely to pass beneath the wires of the projected overhead electrification schemes. In the case of Nos. 3487-3501 it was only necessary to lower the dome cover. Nos. 3461/77-86 however needed new cabs and the opportunity was taken to fit the side-window type (fig. 21). Shorter chimneys and lower dome covers were also required where these had not already been fitted; No 3482 for example had already acquired a shorter chimney. No alteration was made to the front bufferbeam, which retained its squared corners. The dates when side-window cabs were fitted to Nos. 3461/77-86 are set out in the Summary.

Diagram 100A Boilers

Thompson succeeded Gresley in April 1941 and it was not long before details of his standardisation proposals appeared. One heavy goods 2-8-0 engine was required, to replace classes J19, J20, J38, O1, O2, O4 and O5, and any other small-wheeled engines which were not covered by an 0-6-0 design which was to be based on class J39. Thompson planned to reboiler the 2-8-0's with Diagram 100A boilers and to fit standard cylinders if renewals became necessary. In the event, no action was taken in respect of the Gresley O1's and the O2's retained to the end their three-cylinder arrangement. Doncaster also continued to build O2's until early 1943, but this was only the fulfilment of orders placed before Gresley's death.

In October 1943 No. 3479 was fitted with a Diagram 100A boiler (fig. 22). Because of the shorter barrel it was not possible to anchor it in the usual manner to the combined middle cylinder and saddle casting. The front of the barrel was therefore fastened to a special support bracket which was attached to the frames just in front of the dip in the running plate. The smokebox was lengthened and the anti-vacuum valve located well behind the chimney. Other features which distinguished the Thompson boiler were the dome further forward, safety valves well forward with the whistle behind them on the firebox top and additional firebox hand holes above the boiler handrail.

No. 3479 was the first O2 to be altered and the dimensions on the engine diagram therefore applied in particular to this engine. The diagram showed a saving in weight of 1 ton 14 cwt., compared with the O2/1 engine diagram, because of the shorter boiler. Four more O2's were altered in 1944, Nos. 2437, 2954/7 and 3487. The firebox backplate sloped forward by almost 1ft. 0in. in the Diagram 100A boiler whereas it was vertical in the Diagram 2. It was therefore necessary to fit a standard side-window cab to No. 3487, which was 6in. longer than the plain type (fig. 24).

Class Part 4 was introduced in September 1945 to cover O2's which had been given these new boilers. At nationalisation there were still only the five mentioned above (now numbered 3924/32/47/50/62), but Nos. 63932/47/62 lost their Diagram 100A boilers when they were overhauled in 1949-50 due to the rapid withdrawal of O3's which brought about a temporary increase in the availability of Diagram 2 boilers. Nos. 63924/50 (formerly 3479 and 2957) then remained the only O2/4's until 1955, when conversions recommenced.

Subsequent conversions to O2/4 comprised six O2/1's, five O2/2's (including No. 63932 for its second time) and fifteen O2/3's. The former O2/2's which were altered for the first time, Nos. 63933/5/8/45, received side-window cabs. The dates when the engines were altered are set out in the Summary.

Details

Frames and Running Gear

Nos. 3461/77-3501 had rectangular steel front bufferbeams which were 8ft. 5in. wide. Engines built from 1932 onwards had the bottom corners cut away to clear platform edges when working away from the G.N. Section (cf. figs. 24 and 26). The supporting brackets in the angle between the bufferbeams and main frames were less substantial because of this alteration and it was not long before reports came in of bent bufferbeams, including No. 2954 before it was three months old and apparently the result of being buffered up on a curve in the shed yard. The bufferbeams were afterwards strengthened on these Group Standard engines by introducing additional securing bolts. No. 3461 had parallel shank buffers with a circular base. All the later O2's had Spencer double case buffers (cf. figs. 10 and 11). Group Standard buffers never appeared on any of the O2's.

The overall width across the running plate was 8ft. 6in. except alongside the cab where it was 8ft. 9in. On No. 3461 the height above rail level to the underside was 5ft. 8in. over the cylinders and coupled wheels. On Nos. 3477-3501 the running plate was at two levels, 4ft. 11¼in. over the cylinders and 5ft. 5in. over the coupled wheels. The Group Standard engines with their modified valve motion had their running plates raised over the coupled wheels to 5ft. 8in. above rail level to clear the longer radius link. On No. 3461 a step was provided in the curve of the running plate at the front end and footsteps were also fitted alongside the pony truck wheels. Steps were provided in the curve of the running plate just in front of the cab on Nos. 3461, 2960/1, 2430-7 and 3833-57.

The pony truck employed Gresley's double swing-link suspension and centring arrangement. In the case of No. 3461 only, the wheels were 3ft. 2in. diameter and the radius arm was 6ft. 0½in. long, features common to the contemporary two-cylinder 2-8-0's. The later O2's had 2ft. 8in. diameter wheels and the radius arm was 6ft. 6in. long. In all cases the bearing springs were of the helical type as afterwards fitted to the O1's. Guard irons were originally fitted to both the main frames and pony truck. In common with a number of other classes, those on the main frames were removed during the fifties as the pair on the pony truck were better placed and gave adequate protection (cf. figs. 23 and 24). The minimum radius of curved track capable of being negotiated was 4½ chains.

Nos. 3477 onwards had a hinged horizontal door in the platform just in front of the smokebox. This lifted to give access to the motion levers both for lubricating purposes and shed maintenance. The engines which were built from 1932 onwards also had a vertical plate in front of the motion levers. On Nos. 2954-9 this plate was secured by two bolts at each side and a 4in. diameter hole in the plate enabled the driver to get at the grease cup on the equal motion lever. On Nos. 2960/1 and 2430-7 the plate was hinged at the bottom so that the driver could get at the other joints of the motion levers, and the hole was still provided. A hinged flap was afterwards fitted over the hole to prevent ash finding its way through it and on to the pony truck axleboxes when the smokebox was being emptied. The later O2's, Nos. 3833-57, had only this hinged plate without the hole.

In May 1931 No. 3487 received a set of connecting rods made of Hiduminium light alloy. Stories are told of fitters in Doncaster Works carrying connecting rods around on their shoulders, to the astonishment of their colleagues! Nothing is recorded of the benefits or otherwise of this novel feature, which was last referred to in January 1952 when Doncaster Works reported that only the outside connecting rods were of Hiduminium, the inside one being of conventional steel.

The engines built up to 1934 had coupled wheel axlebox journals 8½in. diameter by 9in. long. From November 1940 the diameter was increased to 8¾in. when axles were renewed but the engines built in 1942-43 had these larger journals from new. The O2's had a tendency to settle down on their springs and were booked for raising rather more frequently than any other class. It was known that this was due to the spring equalising beams, and these had already been removed from those A1's which originally had them (see Part 2A, p.35). It was not until July 1939 that Gresley decided to dispense with them from the other classes which still had them and they were gradually removed in 1940-43 from the O2's, and incidentally from the O1's and P1's.

Nos. 3461/77-86 had two Wakefield No. 7 mechanical lubricators on the right-hand side running plate (fig. 11), one for the axleboxes and one for the cylinders and valves. Nos. 3487-3501 instead had a Gresham & Craven mechanical lubricator for the axleboxes and a Hulburd No. 4 mechanical lubricator for the cylinders and valves. In 1928-29 the Hulburd lubricators were replaced by the Wakefield type as follows:-

No.	*Date*	*No.*	*Date*
3487	5/1929	3495	12/1928
3488	3/1928	3496	2/1929*
3489	3/1928	3497	7/1929
3490	3/1928*	3498	3/1929
3491	3/1929	3499	3/1929
3492	4/1928	3500	6/1929
3493	5/1929	3501	2/1928
3494	6/1928		

* These dates are not officially confirmed.

Engines built from 1932 onwards had two Wakefield No. 7 mechancial lubricators on the left-hand side running plate, one for the axleboxes and one for the cylinders and valves.

Whilst the axleboxes had mechanical lubricators, the horn cheeks were lubricated in a simpler manner. Those for the trailing wheels, which were in close proximity to the firebox, had a small siphon oilbox located above the running plate. The other horn cheeks simply had worsted trimmings (strands of green wool), which were lubricated by oil can before each journey. Commencing with No. 2956 in July 1936 a central lubricator was provided on each side of the engine, mounted above the running plate about half way along its length, which lubricated all the horn cheeks. All the O2's were brought into line as they passed through shops (fig. 18).

When new, No. 3461 had forward running sanders in front of the driving coupled wheels (gravity fed at first, but soon altered to steam operation), and gravity fed reverse running sanders behind the trailing coupled wheels. By the mid-twenties this engine had acquired additional steam-operated sanders in front of the leading coupled wheels, but the reverse running sanders had been abandoned. The redundant sandboxes under the cab were however retained.

Nos. 3477-3501 had steam-operated sanders in front of the leading coupled wheels and gravity fed sanders in front of the driving coupled wheels. For reverse running there were gravity fed sanders behind the trailing coupled wheels. The sandboxes for the leading sanders were located low down between the frames just behind the pony truck wheels, so the delivery pipe had only a shallow drop. The filler pipes for these front sandboxes led down from holes in the running plate above the front vaive guides, then through holes in the frames and downwards.

The engines which were built in 1932-34, Nos. 2954-61 and 2430-7, differed from Nos. 3477-3501 by having gravity fed sanders for the leading coupled wheels and steam-operated sanders for the driving coupled wheels. The front sandboxes were moved further back to provide a more vertical flow for the sand and the filler holes were just behind the smokebox saddle. The filler holes were also larger in diameter to reduce spillage when filling (fig. 16). The filler pipes for the trailing sanders passed through the front of the cab, which was longer than the plain cabs on the earlier engines. The final batch of engines which appeared in 1942-43, Nos. 3833-57, had the same sand gear arrangement as the previous engines except that the filler holes for the forward running sanders were not quite as large (fig. 18).

Boilers

The Diagram 2 boiler was identical with the type introduced in 1913 for class O1. The barrel and firebox casing were made of $\frac{5}{8}$in. plate throughout. The barrel had two telescopic rings with the diameter over the front (smaller) one 5ft. 4$\frac{3}{4}$in. The front tubeplate was $\frac{3}{4}$in. thick and the distance between the tubeplates was originally 16ft. 0in. The inner firebox was made of $\frac{9}{16}$in. copper plate throughout, except for the tubeplate which was originally $\frac{7}{8}$in. thick on No. 461 only, when new. Replacement copper fireboxes, and the new ones for all the later engines of the class, had 1in. thick tubeplates instead which reduced the distance between the tubeplates to 15ft. 11$\frac{7}{8}$in.

The outer firebox was 9ft. 0in. long at the bottom. The throat plate sloped back so that the overall length to the commencement of the flange where it joined the barrel was 9ft. 6in. Both these dimensions appeared on the engine diagram. It is convenient at this point to mention that a number of other classes had boilers with throat plates having a similar 6in. slope: D, D49, J38, J39, K2, K3, K5, O1 (later O3) and O4/5. The Diagram 100A boiler which was fitted to the O2/4 engines had larger throat plates which sloped back 1ft. 1$\frac{1}{2}$in. from the commencement of the flange. The other classes which had boilers with similar throat plates were B1, B2, B3/3, B17, K1 (Peppercorn), K1/1, K4, O1 (Thompson) and O4/8. It is desirable in this Part to present the dimensions of these respective classes using a common basis for comparison purposes. The firebox lengths quoted under the various Standard L.N.E.R. Dimensions include the throat plate. The alternative dimensions which have been quoted elsewhere have resulted from taking a different basis, as in the case of for example class D49 (see Part 4 of this series).

The inner firebox was supported by twenty-two rows of vertical roof stays with two girder bars at the front end. No. 461's original firebox had no transverse stays, leaving a large unstayed area between the top row of side stays and the end stay of each row of vertical roof stays. This was unsatisfactory and all later O2 boilers had seven transverse stays in their fireboxes to reduce distortion of the plates when subjected to pressure of steam. The girder bars at the front of the firebox were replaced by one row of expansion and sling stays on new boilers constructed after 1931. There was no external evidence of this change.

The boilers which were built before Grouping had four wash-out plugs on each side of the firebox above the handrails. The arrangement was staggered to ensure the best coverage of the top of the inner firebox. On the boiler which was originally fitted to No. 461 (and those also used on class O1 Nos. 456-60), the plugs on the right-hand side were slightly to the rear of those on the left. The opposite applied in the case of the boilers which were fitted to Nos. 477-86 when new (and also class O1 Nos. 462-76). The boilers built between 1923 and 1933 had three wash-out plugs on each side of the firebox instead of four, apparently to ensure that they were spaced well away from the transverse stays (cf. figs. 10 and 12).

Whilst the boilers for Nos. 2430-7 were under construction at Gorton, it was decided to fit hand holes instead of wash-out plugs in the same position as before and the last three boilers of this order were so arranged. The boilers were sent to Doncaster for fitting as a result of which they were not fitted in sequence – No. 2430 even received a new boiler from a different batch. Two of the boilers with hand holes were fitted to Nos. 2431/3 (new), whilst the third one went to No. 3491 (November 1933). All later Diagram 2 boilers had hand holes (fig. 18). The front transverse stay had to be repositioned $\frac{1}{2}$in. further forward to provide room for the front hand hole on the right-hand side.

The boiler which was originally fitted to No. 461 (and also to class O1 Nos. 456-60/2-76) had Ramsbottom safety valves (cf. figs. 10 and 11). All subsequent Diagram 2 boilers had the Ross pop variety. As a result of boiler changes, several of the early boilers with Ramsbottom safety valves appeared on later O2's, including Nos. 3477/8/9/81/2/3/5/7/93/4/7. The last of the boilers with Ramsbottom safety valves was condemned from No. 3493 in March 1941.

Originally the boilers had Robinson superheaters with 24 long-loop elements. The superheating surface was shown as 570 sq. ft. but this was afterwards amended to 430.5 sq. ft. when the later method of calculation was used. The same arrangement of elements was used in the Ivatt Atlantics (class C1 in Part 3A of this series) when Robinson 24-element superheaters were applied to them. The elements were 1½in. outside diameter and 9 S.W.G. thick (inside diameter approximately $1\frac{7}{32}$in.). From December 1932 the thickness was reduced to 10 S.W.G. (inside diameter 1.244in.), but reverted to 9 S.W.G. from (officially) November 1944, though this final alteration was not recognised on the engine diagram. Replacement superheater headers from October 1940, and those fitted to Nos. 3833-57 which appeared new in 1942-43, were the "V" bolt type with ball-jointed (Melesco) element ends. The heating surface figure remained the same.

The Diagram 2 boilers as fitted to the O2's had 160 small tubes whereas the original O1 boilers had 167. The boiler pressure was originally 170 lb. per sq. in. but this was raised to 180 lb. from 1919. The diameter of the blastpipe orifice was 5in., except that No. 461 may have been 5⅜in. when new for a short time. No change was necessary when Diagram 100A boilers were afterwards fitted to certain engines of the class.

In March 1932 No. 3478 acquired a drop grate which afterwards became a standard fitting for all the later engines of the class. The rodding was on the right-hand side of the engine and passed through the running plate at an angle (fig. 20). The fitting was latterly noted as being absent from No. 63962 (ex-2437), and there may have been other cases.

On the engines built up to 1924 the diameter of the smokebox door was 4ft. 9in. and it fitted flat against a steel sealing ring, 4ft. 11½in. outer diameter, which was the only means of preserving an air-tight fit. On the Group Standard engines a new style of joint ring was introduced, 5ft. 0¾in. outer diameter, with a ¾in. wide recess all the way round packed with asbestos. The edge of the door was rounded to provide a more satisfactory fit when pressed against this packing. As a wartime expedient rivets were dispensed with on replacement smokeboxes after October 1940 and on Nos. 3833-57 when new. The outer diameter of the joint ring was reduced to 4ft. 10¼in. and it was welded to the smokebox front. The door hinge straps, which were 1ft. 3in. apart, continued to be secured by rivets.

In the interests of standardisation, Diagram 100A boilers were gradually fitted to a number of engines of the class from 1943 onwards (fig. 22). Although designed to work at 225 lb. per sq. in., the pressure was reduced to 180 lb. when fitted to the O2 class. The overall length of the boiler was 1ft. 4⅜in. shorter than the Diagram 2 type so that it was necessary to fit an extension ring at the front. The firebox therefore remained in the same relative position over the trailing coupled axle. The dome cover was shallower and 1ft. 8in. further forward on the top of the boiler. Another feature which distinguished these boilers was the positioning of the five hand holes on each side of the firebox above the boiler handrails.

These new boilers had vertical slide regulator valves in common with the Diagram 2 boilers. The regulator handle in the cab however was the latest B1 quadrant type, replacing the traditional G.N.-style horizontal handle which was provided on all engines with Diagram 2 boilers, including the Group Standard members of the class. The superheater header was the "Through" bolt type and the elements were 1½in. outside diameter and 10 S.W.G. thick (inside diameter 1.244in.). From (officially) November 1944 the thickness was increased to 9 S.W.G. (inside diameter 1.212in.), though the engine diagram was not corrected. The elements had ball-jointed ends.

From November 1945 the number of small tubes in the Diagram 100A boiler was reduced from 143 to 141 and the heating surface from 1,048 to 1,033 sq. ft. This allowed space for wash-out plugs to be provided on either side of the blastpipe in place of the single one in an awkward position behind it. From December 1950 replacement smokebox tubeplates were ⅞in. thick instead of ¾in., with 1in. radius flange instead of ¾in., to reduce the incidence of fractures. This slightly reduced the distance between the tubeplates from 13ft. 11⅞in. to 13ft. 11½in. The Diagram 100A boiler is described more fully under class B1 (see Part 2B, p.130).

General

The engines which appeared before Grouping were built to the generous G.N. load gauge and the tops of their 1ft. 7½in. high chimneys were 13ft. 2¼in. above rail level (fig. 10). The post-Grouping engines had 1ft. 4in. high chimneys which brought the overall height well inside the L.N.E.R. Composite Load Gauge (fig. 13), though for a while Nos. 3487/90/5 had taller chimneys. The shorter pattern of chimney was afterwards fitted to all the earlier O2's. For a time in the thirties No. 2961 had an even shorter chimney of unknown origin (fig. 29).

The height above rail level to the top of the dome cover on Nos. 3461/77-3501 was originally 13ft. $0\frac{1}{2}$in. The later engines had shallower dome covers, 12ft. $11\frac{15}{16}$in. above rail level, which was just inside the G.E. Section load gauge. The height to the top of the dome cover on the O2/4's, which had Thompson Diagram 100A boilers, was 12ft. $8\frac{1}{8}$in. (cf. figs. 10, 16 and 22).

The whistle on Nos. 3461/77-86 was located above the cab roof following usual G.N.R. practice, with the operating lever at the top (fig. 11). The overall height above rail level was 13ft. $3\frac{3}{8}$in. On Nos. 3487-3501 the G.N.-type whistle was located in front of the cab, lower down than before and in line with the safety valves (fig.13). The engines built from 1932 onwards had the Group Standard whistle, with its valve in the base, located in front of the cab to the left of centre (fig. 23). Nos. 3461/77-86 were brought into line when they acquired side-window cabs in 1939-40. The engines which received Diagram 100A boilers had their whistles mounted directly on top of the firebox in line with the safety valves (which were located well forward), instead of being attached to the steam manifold fitting inside the cab (fig. 22).

On the engines which were built between 1918 and 1924 the boiler handrails passed alongside the smokebox, curved round to the front and upwards and stopped in line with the handrail on the smokebox door (fig. 10). On the engines which were built from 1932 onwards the handrails stopped short on the smokebox sides (fig. 16) and the earlier engines were afterwards brought into line. The vacuum ejector exhaust pipe ran alongside the boiler on the driver's side, between the handrail and the boiler clothing plate so that they shared common pillar stanchions. However, on the engines which had Diagram 100A boilers the pipe was located about $4\frac{1}{2}$in. higher up than before (cf. figs. 32 and 33).

The engines built up to the end of 1934 had ordinary three-link couplings when they were new, but screw couplings were substituted later.

Several engines, including Nos. 63929-32/40, were latterly provided with Whitaker's tablet exchange apparatus on both sides of the tender, for working on the Highdyke branch (figs. 24 and 33).

Brakes

With the exception of the engines which were built in 1932-34, vacuum brakes were provided for engine, tender and train brakes. There were four 18in. diameter brake cylinders between the frames arranged in pairs in similar fashion to the earlier O1's. Nos. 2430-7 and 2954-61 had steam brakes on the engine and tender with a vacuum ejector for train braking. One steam brake cylinder under the cab replaced the four brake cylinders needed on the vacuum-braked O2's.

A number of O2's were latterly equipped with the B.R. standard A.W.S. (fig. 25). Features of the system were the air reservoirs under the running plate in front of the cab – a small one on the driver's side and a large one on the fireman's side – and a battery box alongside the cab steps on one or other side of the engine.

Tenders

Nos. 3461/77-3501 (later 3921-46). – These engines were normally attached to G.N.-type 3,500-gallon tenders, which held $6\frac{1}{2}$ tons of coal, though from time to time odd engines were noted attached to 3,670 and 3,720-gallon tenders which, although they held more water, only carried 5 tons of coal (fig. 10). The position in early 1928, for example, was as follows:-

3,500 gallons: Nos. 3477/8/9/82/5-3501
3,670 gallons: Nos. 3480/1/4
3,720 gallons: Nos. 3461/83

The tenders which were attached to Nos. 3487-3501 were built after Grouping, to G.N.R. standard 3,500-gallon design (fig. 12).

About 1929 the 3,670 and 3,720-gallon tenders were mostly replaced by the 3,500-gallon type as the smaller coal capacity of the former was causing problems on the Peterborough-London coal trains (see also p.10). However, they were not replaced on Nos. 3480/1/3 until 1942, 1934 and 1936 respectively. Four others re-acquired 3,670-gallon tenders in the thirties: Nos. 3479 (1935-43), 3482 (1934-42), 3484 (1932-34) and 3491 (1938-42).

Ten of the 3,500-gallon tenders had had an extra coping rail added in 1923 during the time they were attached to Ivatt Atlantics. Three were attached to Nos. 3477/86/97 in the thirties and they were also noted attached to Nos. 3933/6/46 at nationalisation.

Group Standard 4,200-gallon tenders from withdrawn K3's were transferred to seven O2's in 1961-62. Nos. 63923/7/39/43/6 acquired the stepped-out type (fig. 25) whilst Nos. 63928/37 received the welded flush-sided type. The dates these particular engines acquired larger tenders were as follows:-

No.	Date	No.	Date
63923	8/1960	63939	1/1961
63927	11/1961	63943	5/1962
63928	7/1961	63946	10/1960
63937	10/1960		

NOS. 2954-61, 2430-7 (LATER 3947-62). – Nos. 2954-61, 2430-3 were given second-hand Group Standard 4,200-gallon tenders with stepped-out sides from J38's (fig. 16). Nos. 2434-7 acquired new Group Standard 4,200-gallon tenders with straight sides of riveted construction (fig. 17).

NOS. 3833-57 (LATER 3963-87). – Shortage of steel during wartime led to Nos. 3833-57 being paired with second-hand Group Standard 4,200-gallon tenders, with both straight sides or stepped-out coping plates (fig. 18), taken from D49's which in turn received spare G.C.-type 4,000-gallon tenders (see Part 4 of this series, p.103). At a meeting of the Emergency Board on 26th March 1942, reference was made to the intended rebuilding of twenty-five class Q4 0-8-0 mineral engines into class Q1 0-8-0 tank engines, and the fact that their tenders could be used for the new O2's, with the added comment that as each O2 neared completion, a Q4 would be brought in to the works and converted, and its tender would then be used for the O2. Therefore indirectly these conversions obviated having to build new tenders for the O2's. This was later stressed by photographing No. 3834 in company with a G.C. tender (fig. 19), though it never ran in this condition. The tenders which were provided for Nos. 3834/5 had previously been temporarily attached to class V2 Nos. 3657 and 3656 respectively, otherwise all twenty-five came directly from D49's.

From December 1945 to March 1947 No. 3839 (later 3969) was paired with a tender which had been previously attached to class V2 No. 4777. This was the only high-fronted tender to appear behind a class O2. The only other change of note was in December 1949 when No. 63967 acquired a tender of all-welded construction from class K3 No. 61943.

It remains to be mentioned that almost immediately after Nos. 3833-42 had been ordered from Doncaster Works, the corresponding order for ten new tenders was held in abeyance on 6th June 1940. This was at a time when schemes were being prepared to make use of spare tenders, though it was not until 15th May 1942 that the formal instruction was issued to Doncaster to attach second-hand tenders to Nos. 3833-57. This left Doncaster with material on hand for ten new tenders for which they had no order. The parts were eventually sent to Darlington with the intention of completion there for attaching to Sandringhams as they were rebuilt to class B2, but this scheme fell through. In November 1948 the parts were allocated to class B1 Nos. 61350-9 on order (see Part 2B, p.136), though two tank bodies were later used to rebuild two class K3 tenders (see Part 6A, p. 121).

Liveries

The first paintings of G.N.R. Nos. 461 and 477-86 were grey with white lining on the engine. No. 461's tender was unique in having a single white lining in a panel with scalloped corners, which however failed to survive the general repair in July 1920. At Grouping therefore all eleven engines were alike in their grey livery.

No. 484 was ex-works on 29th January 1923 in black livery, with single red lining, painted specially to take part in a display of various liveries from which the Directors were invited to choose the standard livery. The number was retained on the cab side in G.N.R. size but it also appeared in 12in. gold blocked transfers on the tender below the letters "L & N E R". Apart from a small cast plate replacing the cab side numbers, this became the standard goods engine livery although the ampersand was quickly discarded from the tender inscription and only No. 484 carried it in class O2.

From 1929 the number appeared on the cab side in 7½in. shaded numerals due to lack of space (fig. 15) though 12in. numerals appeared on the Group Standard engines built from 1932 (fig. 16). The single red lining was also dispensed with from June 1928, though it was evident on Nos. 2430 and 2954 when they were officially photographed new. Nos. 3461/77-86 changed from 7½in. to 12in. cab numerals in 1939-40 when side-window cabs were fitted (fig. 21), and No. 3487 was likewise changed in October 1944 when a side-window cab was fitted along with a Diagram 100A boiler.

No. 3833 was the last engine to have "L N E R" on its tender when new (fig. 18). An official photograph of No. 3834 new, shows it paired with a G.C. tender, lettered "L N E R", to make the point that steel was being saved by using second-hand tenders for these wartime built engines (fig. 19). However, this engine entered traffic with a Group Standard tender lettered "N E" only. The next engine, No. 3835, ran trials with painted unshaded numerals and a painted version of the L.N.E.R. totem (as carried by the class Q1 0-8-0 tank engine rebuilds, see p. 9 of Part 9B) on its tender (fig. 20). It has not been established if it entered traffic so adorned but this is thought to be unlikely. Nos. 3836-57 all had "N E" on their tenders when they first appeared.

From January 1946 "L N E R" in full was gradually restored to the tenders, in shaded transfers at first then in yellow paint without shading as the stocks of transfers ran out. As before, the size of cab numerals used depended on whether or not a side-window cab was fitted.

Apart from No. 3921 withdrawn in March 1948, all O2's received B.R. unlined black livery and smokebox door numberplates were fitted. Despite all being dealt with at Doncaster, their treatment varied appreciably, as instanced by the accompanying examples.

No. E3946 ex-works February 1948. 10in. painted plain numerals and "BRITISH RAILWAYS" on the tender. Number on front buffer-beam and no numberplate.
No. 63954 ex-works May 1948. 12in. plain numerals, numberplate.
No. 63960 ex-works March 1949. 10in. Gill Sans numerals (fig. 26).
No. 63953 ex-works June 1949. As No. 63960, except nothing on tender (fig. 31).
No. 63946 ex-works May 1949. Small B.R. emblem on tender.
No. 63962 ex-works April 1955. Larger version of original B.R. emblem.
No. 63943 ex-works June 1957. Later style B.R. emblem, larger version (fig. 25). The one on right-hand side of tender facing to the right (forwards), which is wrong in heraldry.
No. 63932 ex-works May 1958. Small version of later style emblem (fig. 24).
No. 63945 ex-works August 1959. Also small version, but with lion on right-hand side of tender correctly facing to the left (fig. 34).

Maintenance

The engines were normally shopped at Doncaster including those which worked on the G.E. Section, the only exceptions being Nos. 2954/6/7 which each had one heavy repair at Stratford, in July, March and July 1933, respectively. The official minimum mileage between general repairs was laid down as 50,000. Life mileage figures are not available for any members of the class.

British Railways

All sixty-seven engines were taken into British Railways stock on 1st January 1948 and duly acquired their 60000 series numbers and smokebox door numberplates, with the exception of the pioneer engine No. 3921 (originally 461) which was withdrawn in May 1948.

Allocation and Work

When built as G.N.R. No. 461 the original O2 was allocated to New England in company with the twenty two-cylinder O1's, and remained there for twenty-five years. The engines turned out in 1921-24 also went to New England except for No. 3496 which spent its first ten months at Doncaster and No. 3501 which went on trial to the North Eastern Area at, it is believed, Newport for some eight months. Both then joined the remainder at New England where they remained for a quarter of a century apart from No. 3490 which spent six weeks at Mexborough in 1929. During this long time the O2's worked the same duties as the two-cylinder O1's as described on pages 11-13. The advent of W.D. "Austerity" 2-8-0's in 1942 caused changes to take place in the allocation of all the New England-based O2's as will be described later.

The eight engines built in 1932 were delivered new to March and immediately took up workings on the G.E. Section coal trains from Whitemoor Yard to Temple Mills (Stratford). The further eight engines built in 1933-34 joined them on these duties. On up coal trains their permitted load was 65 wagons, less than that on the G.N. Section between New England and Ferme Park, but there were some steeper grades on the climb to Elsenham summit than on the G.N. main line and, except for the last few miles into London, the line was double track only. This meant that coal and goods trains had to run on the same lines as express and other passenger trains. Permitted loads for other classes on the coal trains were: J15 (35 wagons), J16-J19, J27, J39 (50 wagons), J20 (55 wagons) and O4 (60 wagons). There had been a limit of 50 wagons in G.E.R. and early L.N.E.R. days on account of the length of the refuge sidings. Conversion of many of these to loops allowed longer trains by 1932. After January 1937 the length limit of up trains hauled by O2's was increased to 80 wagons, when conveying ordinary goods traffic, as by then the only intermediate refuge siding restriction was at Elsenham which held only 70 wagons.

Fig. 15 Class O2/2 No. 3499 at Doncaster Works, August 1931.

Top feed water delivery to boiler with feed pipes running along outside of boiler from cab, 7½in. shaded numerals on cab side.

Fig. 16 Class O2/3 No. 2959 at March shed, about 1934.

Group Standard series. Arranged for left-hand drive, side-window cab, lower dome cover, boiler handrails stopped short on smokebox sides, front sandbox filler just behind smokebox saddle, rear sandbox filler in front of cab, 12in. shaded numerals on cab side, second-hand Group Standard 4,200-gallon tender from class J38.

Fig. 17 Class O2/3 No. 2434 at Doncaster Works, January 1934.

New straight-sided Group Standard 4,200-gallon tender.

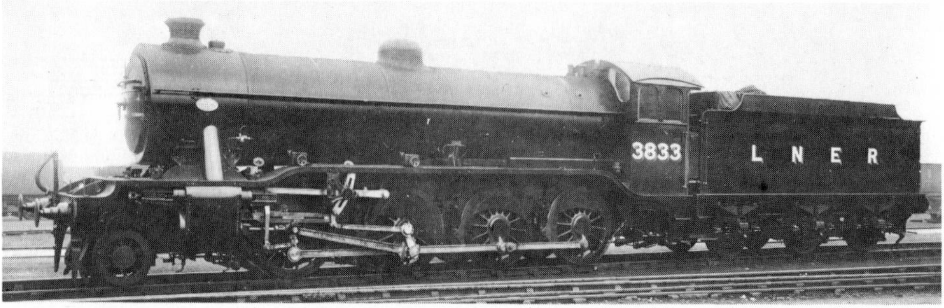

Fig. 18 Class O2/3 No. 3833 at Doncaster Works, May 1942.

Final Group Standard series. Central lubricator for horn cheeks located mid-way along running plate, hand holes in place of wash-out plugs on firebox side, small front sandbox fillers, second-hand Group Standard 4,200-gallon tender (lettered "L N E R") from class D49.

Fig. 19 Class O2/3 No. 3834 at Doncaster Works, June 1942.

Paired with second-hand ex-G.C. 4,000-gallon tender from class Q4 for photographic purposes only.

Fig. 20 Class O2/3 No. 3835 at Doncaster Works, June 1942.

Drop grate rod sloping down in front of cab, second-hand Group Standard 4,200-gallon tender from class V2 with L.N.E.R. totem displayed on side. (Note figs. 18, 19, 20 show steel shutters instead of glass windows in cab, for blackout conditions).

Fig. 21 Class O2/1 No. 3485 at Doncaster Works, June 1939.

Altered to clear 13ft. 0in. load gauge, G.N. cab replaced by side-window type.

Fig. 22 Class O2 (O2/4) No. 3479 at Doncaster Works, September 1943 before entering traffic rebuilt.

Diagram 100A boiler, anti-vacuum valve located well behind chimney on extension ring to boiler barrel, shallower dome cover further forward, safety valves further forward with whistle in line behind, five hand holes on side of firebox, side-window cab with 12in. shaded numerals.

Fig. 23 Class O2/3 No. 3965 at Colwick shed, August 1947.

Whistle in front of cab off-centre to left, guard irons on both main frames and pony truck, Gill Sans lettering and numerals.

Fig. 24 Class O2/4 No. 63932 at March shed, May 1958.

Diagram 100A boiler, side-window cab, front bufferbeam with square corners, guard irons removed from main frames, tablet exchange apparatus on side of tender, small version of later style emblem.

Fig. 25 Class O2/2 No. 63943 at Grantham shed, August 1962.

A.W.S. apparatus with air reservoir under running plate in front of cab, battery box alongside footsteps and shield behind coupling, stepped-out Group Standard 4,200-gallon tender from class K3, large version of later style emblem.

Fig. 26 Class O2/3 No. 63960 at Whitemoor Yard, March 1949.

Lower corners of front bufferbeam cut away, 10in. Gill Sans unshaded numerals on cab side.

Fig. 27 Class O2 No. 3461 on up coal train at Hadley Wood, about 1934.

Top feed delivery to boiler inside extra dome.

Fig. 28 Class O2/2 No. 3501 on a down class B goods at Greenwood, May 1926.

Fig. 29 Class O2/3 No. 2961 on Target No. 6 up goods near Broxbourne, April 1938.
Shorter chimney fitted.

Fig. 30 Class O2/4 No. 3924 on up class B goods near Wilbraham Road, Manchester, September 1947.

Fig. 31 Class O2/3 No. 63953 on up class C goods leaving Cambridge, about July 1949.

No ownership on tender.

Fig. 32 Class O2/3 No. 63958 approaching March on a Temple Mills – Whitemoor class B goods, July 1949.

Vacuum ejector exhaust pipe in original position behind boiler handrail.

Fig. 33 Class O2/4 No. 63930 with a train of iron ore empties on the Highdyke branch, July 1960.

Vacuum ejector exhaust pipe above boiler handrail, tablet exchange apparatus on side of tender.

Fig. 34 Class O2/4 No. 63945 leaving Great Ponton on up pick-up goods, August 1959.

Small version of later style of emblem with lion correctly facing left.

With empty wagon trains in the down direction overall limits also applied on account of length but from early L.N.E.R. days conditional schedules existed for empty trains of 100 wagons on Sundays from Temple Mills via Ely to March or Peterborough East (to be worked by engines from J16 upwards). At night Cambridge was allowed to make down empties up to 100 wagons when running via St. Ives to March or Whittlesea.

From 12th October 1936 the coal train workings between Whitemoor and Temple Mills were completely revised. There were thirteen O2 diagrams, each with a minimum turn-round of five hours at each end of the workings – ½ hour to and from shed, 3 hours shed duties and 1 hour to allow for late running. A "target", bearing a diagram number between 1 and 13, was carried on the front of each engine for identification purposes, in addition to the usual headlamps or discs (fig. 29). Instructions were issued for the engines to be released promptly from up trains at Temple Mills instead of being held up for grouping with other engines as was the usual practice.

Every endeavour was made to run each up train which was diagrammed to an O2, but if one had to be cancelled then the engine was to be retained at March to await the next up train in its own diagram. When a down train was cancelled, Stratford returned the O2 light at about the booked time of the train. Shortly afterwards, two O4 diagrams were added to the scheme, target Nos. 14 and 15.

The new diagrams proved satisfactory during the winter months and were revised from 3rd May 1937 in the light of experience. The turn-round time was cut, particularly at the Whitemoor end, and the number of O2 diagrams was reduced to twelve to provide four spare engines instead of only three. The two O4 diagrams were allocated target Nos. 1 and 2 and the O2's became 3 to 14 instead.

The O2's at March were kept in immaculate condition. This, combined with a modern cab and an L.N.E.R. Group Standard tender, made them look very different engines from the earlier members of the class at New England which, however good their mechanical condition, often looked neglected externally.

The workings of the O2 class on the G.E. Section were almost entirely confined to the lines between March and Temple Mills via Ely or St. Ives and, until 1939, they rarely appeared on any cross-country workings. On 3rd July 1935 a collision at Clapton Junction between up Cambridge and Chingford line trains in the later part of the evening rush hour blocked the lines there for a period. As a result of this the 7-38 p.m. Liverpool Street-Bishops Stortford was cancelled and its stock was worked empty from Tottenham to Bishops Stortford, following the 8-22 p.m. down Cambridge express. The stock was of standard Gresley L.N.E.R. non-corrider coaches, headed by one of the March O2's in well kept condition. If, as is believed, this train took up the normal forward working from Bishops Stortford at 9-17 p.m. (all stations to Cambridge), then it would probably have been the first occasion that an O2 appeared on a passenger train on the G.E. Section.

The first appearance of the class at Ipswich was in September 1935 when No. 2958 was seen there. Authority was given as late as 1937 for class O2 to work between March and Ipswich via Bury St. Edmunds and on 10th May 1938 No. 2437 was tested through the crossovers in Ipswich station and Top Yard. Most unusually No. 2954 worked a slow passenger train into Ipswich on 4th February 1946 from the west. In March 1943 No. 2431 was noted at Colchester, believed to have reached there via Long Melford and Marks Tey. The building of many airfields in the war years throughout East Anglia led to more varied workings in the region.

The twenty-five O2's built in 1942-43 were all first allocated to Doncaster whence there was ample heavy work available on wartime traffic in many directions. Late in 1942 two of this batch moved to New England to join the older members of the class in workings on the G.N. main line. During the course of 1943 twenty-one of the New England engines moved north to Doncaster following the introduction of W.D. "Austerity" 2-8-0's. During 1943 in particular, O2's had regular workings into the Manchester area and were frequently observed at Hull and Darlington, whilst Nos. 3842/56 were seen in Edinburgh.

A major redistribution of power in January 1944 saw all of Doncaster's O2's move to Colwick, no doubt to assist in the handling of the immense traffic generated by the movement of war materials to the South Coast ports in preparation for D-day in June 1944. Colwick retained this large stud of forty-four O2's for some eight months, after which the numbers were reduced by stages until in early 1945 all the O2/1 and O2/2 series had returned to New England together with four O2/3's. In June 1945 thirteen O2/2's replaced a like number of O3's at Grantham, the latter moving on to Doncaster.

By the end of 1945 New England had lost all its Gresley 2-8-0's and the southern end of the G.N. main line saw them only occasionally thereafter. The class was then divided between Colwick, Grantham, Doncaster and March.

The O2's at Grantham are best remembered on the iron ore workings centred on Highdyke, three miles south of Grantham. Block train loads were worked to Aldwarke near Rotherham and to Frodingham, with traffic that had originated at Sproxton and Stainby mines, respectively. (Calcinated iron ore also passed between Stainby and Stanton, but this was worked forward from Highdyke by Colwick engines and men). The single line branch from Highdyke to the mines was steeply graded and separately worked by other Grantham O2's, which were permitted to take sixteen empties outward to the mines and return with eighteen loaded wagons (fig. 33). Between Highdyke and Colsterworth Mines signal box, where single line tokens were exchanged, there were two rising gradients of 1 in 40 and a stretch of 1 in 60 falling. Between Colsterworth and Skillington Road Junction, where the Sproxton and Stainby branches separated, there was a 1 in 60 falling gradient followed immediately by a section of 1 in 40 rising. Later, some of the O2's had tablet catchers provided for exchanging tokens at Colsterworth Mines, but after one or two injuries caused by sleeves of clothing being caught in the apparatus, most firemen preferred to exchange by hand.

The next major move was in October 1946 when Langwith acquired thirty O2's, fourteen from Colwick, and sixteen from Doncaster. Langwith had hitherto been a preserve of G.C. O4's for the heaviest duties from that shed. Nevertheless, the enginemen there came to like the Gresley engines, mainly on account of the increased power they provided. At this time there was heavy traffic in coal from the concentration sidings at Mansfield and the O2's became common on many former G.C. routes, including the Woodhead line to Manchester. A year later Colwick lost its last four to Langwith and Doncaster sent one to Frodingham. Reduced traffic in iron ore from Highdyke enabled Grantham to release three engines to Frodingham in 1947.

The first withdrawal occurred in May 1948 when the pioneer No. 3921 was taken out of stock. The Langwith allocation was increased by one in March 1950 but three months later this shed lost its whole stud to Doncaster and Mexborough, mainly on account of the difficulty in finding sufficient staff to maintain three-cylinder engines.

In mid-1949 the sixteen engines at March had their first change since the initial allocation there, No. 63960 being moved to Grantham. Then in June 1950 the remaining fifteen were all sent to G.N. Section sheds, one to Grantham, two to New England and the rest to Doncaster. On the G.E. Section they will be remembered for the ease with which they lifted their heavy trains up the sharply curved 1 in 101 grade to Elsenham summit.

At the close of 1950 there were two O2's at New England, but Mexborough had acquired a substantial stud of eighteen engines and Frodingham retained six, leaving the remainder shared between Grantham and Doncaster. Gradually over the next two years the Mexborough and Frodingham allocations were reduced until at the end of 1955 only three sheds housed O2's, Grantham, Retford and Doncaster. It was during this latter period of their life that they began to travel more widely than hitherto. For instance, at the end of December 1954 No. 63954 was seen at Ripon on an up goods. In the autumn of 1955 Nos. 63926/33 were extensively employed on coal trains between Peterborough and Ferme Park, despite their allocation at Doncaster and Retford respectively. In June 1957 No. 63935 was observed on the Northallerton to Hawes pick-up goods, which on this occasion may only have worked as far as Redmire. In April 1960 No. 63981 was observed on Tyneside, whilst on 3rd February 1962 a most unusual task for this engine was the pick-up goods from Hull to Bridlington.

Withdrawal began in earnest in 1960 when four were taken out of stock. In the following year six more went and sixteen in 1962. The greatest single month's withdrawals came in September 1963 when no fewer than thirty went. The last five were taken out of stock in November 1963. In the closing months of their life Nos. 63969/81/4 were active in the Retford area working coal trains from Worksop to Wath Yard for Elland power station in the Calder Valley. Although all were withdrawn by November 1963, many were still stored for at least a year afterwards: No. 63966 was at Mexborough in October 1964, whilst no fewer than sixteen were still at Retford on 16th November, and Nos. 63932/40/2/3/6/62/74 at Doncaster on 8th December.

Engine Diagrams

Section N, 1924.	O2	No. 3461 only. Superheater element diameter corrected from $1\frac{1}{4}$in. to 1.244in., 12/1938. Empty weights of engine and tender added, 12/1939. Replaced by new diagram 12/1940.
Section N, 1924.	O2/1	Nos. 3477-86. Superheater element diameter corrected from $1\frac{1}{4}$in. to 1.244in., 12/1938. Note added; covers Nos. 3477/8/80/1/3/4/6 only, see new diagram for engines with altered cab, 12/1939. Remaining engines altered and diagram deleted 12/1940.
Section N, 1924.	O2/2	Nos. 3487-3501. Diagram replaced 12/1938.
Section L.N.E., 1932.	O2/3	Steam brake and vacuum ejector. Diagram replaced 12/1938.
Section N, 1938.	O2/2	Replacement diagram for Nos. 3487-3501 with lowered chimney and dome heights. Inside crank pin dimensions corrected from 9in. by $5\frac{1}{2}$in. to $8\frac{1}{4}$in. by 6in., 12/1940.
Section L.N.E., 1938.	O2/3	Replacement diagram, steam brake and vacuum ejector. Weight of tender altered from 51 tons to 52 tons; inside crank pin dimensions corrected from 9in. by 6in. to $8\frac{1}{4}$in. by 6in., 12/1940. Vacuum brakes for Nos. 3833-57 added, 12/1942. Diameter of coupled wheel journals corrected from $8\frac{1}{2}$in. to $8\frac{3}{4}$in., 12/1953.
Section N, 1939.	O2/1	New diagram for engines with altered (side-window) cabs.
Section N, 1940.	O2	Replacement diagram for No. 3461 only, with side-window cab.
1943.	O2	No. 3479 with Diagram 100A boiler. Class Part 4 added and reference to No. 3479 deleted, 12/1946. Diagram replaced 12/1947.
1947.	O2/4	Revised diagram for engines with Diagram 100A boiler; 141 small tubes instead of 143; G.N. tender depicted and diagram strictly correct for former Part 1 engines with new boiler. Diameter of coupled wheel journals altered from $8\frac{1}{2}$in. to $8\frac{3}{4}$in., 12/1953.

Classification: Southern Area load class 8; Route availability 6; B.R. power class 8F.

Summary of O2 Class

B.R. No.		*1946 No.*		*1924 No.*		*Maker*	*Works No.*	*Built*	*Class Part*	*Side Window Cab*	*Rebuilt to O2/4*	*Withdrawn*
(63921)		3921	7/46	3461	3/25	Doncaster	1481	5/1918	—	3/40	—	5/48
63922	12/49	3922	10/46	3477	7/25	N.B. Loco. Co.	22691	5/1921	1	6/40	—	11/62
63923	9/48	3923	8/46	3478	11/25	,,	22692	5/1921	1	7/40	—	12/62
63924	11/48	3924	6/46	3479	4/24	,,	22693	5/1921	1	7/39	10/43	11/63
63925	5/49	3925	10/46	3480	by 7/26	,,	22694	5/1921	1	10/40	7/58	9/63
63926	10/48	3926	10/46	3481	3/25	,,	22695	5/1921	1	10/40	3/61	9/63
63927	7/49	3927	5/46	3482	12/25	,,	22696	5/1921	1	10/39	—	9/63
63928	8/48	3928	8/46	3483	by 6/25	,,	22697	5/1921	1	5/40	7/61	9/63
63929	11/48	3929	8/46	3484	by 1/26	,,	22698	5/1921	1	8/40	7/59	7/62
63930	4/48	3930	9/46	3485	by 6/25	,,	22699	5/1921	1	6/39	8/59	12/62
63931	11/49	3931	9/46	3486	by 2/26	,,	22700	5/1921	1	5/40	1/62	9/63
63932	6/49	3932	9/46	3487	3/25	Doncaster	1574	10/1923	2	10/44	10/44-6/49; 5/58	9/63
63933	8/48	3933	6/46	3488	by 3/26	,,	1575	10/1923	2	1/58	1/58	12/62
63934	7/48	3934	3/46	3489	3/25	,,	1576	11/1923	2	—	—	7/62
63935	8/50	3935	9/46	3490	by 3/26	,,	1577	11/1923	2	4/58	4/58	9/63
63936	5/49	3936	10/46	3491	by 1/26	,,	1578	12/1923	2	—	—	9/63
63937	12/49	3937	9/46	3492	by 7/25	,,	1579	12/1923	2	—	—	9/63
63938	5/49	3938	11/46	3493	by 1/26	,,	1580	12/1923	2	7/58	7/58	9/63
63939	8/49	3939	10/46	3494	3/25	,,	1581	12/1923	2	—	—	9/63
63940	5/48	3940	12/46	3495	by 7/25	,,	1582	2/1924	2	—	—	9/63
63941	12/48	3941	10/46	3496	*new*	,,	1584	2/1924	2	—	—	9/63
63942	5/48	3942	7/46	3497	,,	,,	1587	3/1924	2	—	—	9/63
63943	6/48	3943	8/46	3498	,,	,,	1589	3/1924	2	—	—	9/63
63944	4/48	3944	6/46	3499	,,	,,	1592	4/1924	2	—	—	4/61
63945	10/48	3945	9/46	3500	,,	,,	1594	5/1924	2	11/56	11/56	9/63
63946	5/49	3946	3/46	3501	,,	,,	1595	6/1924	2	—	—	4/63

Summary of O2 Class (continued)

B.R. No.		*1946 No.*		*Original No.*	*Maker*	*Works No.*	*Built*	*Class Part*	*Rebuilt to O2/4*	*Withdrawn*
63947	5/48	3947	12/46	2954	Doncaster	1773	4/1932	3	8/44-6/50	4/61
63948	1/49	3948	12/46	2955	,,	1774	5/1932	3	8/59	10/62
63949	5/49	3949	3/46	2956	,,	1775	5/1932	3	8/55	9/63
63950	7/49	3950	12/46	2957	,,	1776	6/1932	3	7/44	11/60
63951	8/49	3951	3/46	2958	,,	1777	7/1932	3	—	6/62
63952	2/49	3952	1/47	2959	,,	1778	7/1932	3	—	4/61
63953	6/49	3953	3/46	2960	,,	1779	7/1932	3	—	11/60
63954	5/48	3954	12/46	2961	,,	1780	8/1932	3	—	3/61
63955	6/48	3955	5/46	2430	,,	1781	11/1933	3	4/59	5/62
63956	12/49	3956	9/46	2431	,,	1782	12/1933	3	12/61	9/63
63957	6/48	3957	3/46	2432	,,	1783	12/1933	3	—	7/61
63958	4/48	3958	9/46	2433	,,	1784	12/1933	3	—	5/61
63959	2/49	3959	9/46	2434	,,	1785	1/1934	3	—	10/60
63960	3/49	3960	10/46	2435	,,	1786	2/1934	3	8/59	9/63
63961	6/48	3961	10/46	2436	,,	1787	2/1934	3	3/59	12/62
63962	3/48	3962	10/46	2437	,,	1788	3/1934	3	5/44-1/50	9/63
63963	4/50	3963	11/46	3833	,,	1931	5/1942	3	—	9/63
63964	5/48	3964	8/46	3834	,,	1932	6/1942	3	3/61	9/63
63965	11/49	3965	6/46	3835	,,	1933	7/1942	3	9/59	10/62
63966	4/49	3966	11/46	3836	,,	1934	8/1942	3	1/58	12/62
63967	11/48	3967	9/46	3837	,,	1935	8/1942	3	—	11/62
63968	7/48	3968	9/46	3838	,,	1936	9/1942	3	3/61	9/63
63969	3/49	3969	9/46	3839	,,	1937	9/1942	3	—	11/63
63970	4/50	3970	9/46	3840	,,	1938	9/1942	3	—	5/60
63971	4/48	3971	11/46	3841	,,	1939	10/1942	3	—	12/62
63972	12/48	3972	11/46	3842	,,	1940	10/1942	3	—	5/63
63973	11/48	3973	9/46	3843	,,	1941	10/1942	3	—	9/63
63974	7/48	3974	8/46	3844	,,	1942	11/1942	3	—	9/63
63975	2/49	3975	11/46	3845	,,	1943	11/1942	3	7/62	11/63
63976	5/48	3976	9/46	3846	,,	1944	11/1942	3	12/60	9/63
63977	2/49	3977	11/46	3847	,,	1945	11/1942	3	—	9/63
63978	5/49	3978	12/46	3848	,,	1946	11/1942	3	—	5/63
63979	1/49	3979	11/46	3849	,,	1947	12/1942	3	6/59	9/62
63980	4/48	3980	12/46	3850	,,	1948	12/1942	3	—	9/63
63981	5/48	3981	10/46	3851	,,	1949	12/1942	3	—	11/63
63982	6/48	3982	10/46	3852	,,	1950	12/1942	3	8/57	12/62
63983	11/48	3983	5/46	3853	,,	1951	12/1942	3	7/56	7/63
63984	9/48	3984	12/46	3854	,,	1952	12/1942	3	—	11/63
63985	5/48	3985	10/46	3855	,,	1953	1/1943	3	—	9/63
63986	7/49	3986	11/46	3856	,,	1954	1/1943	3	—	6/63
63987	6/49	3987	4/46	3857	,,	1955	1/1943	3	—	9/63

CLASSES O4 AND O5

G.C.R. CLASSES 8K AND 8M
ROBINSON 4ft. 8in. ENGINES

ENGINES AT GROUPING:
CLASS O4 (Built 1911-19): 5001/5/8/26/69/93, 5102/33/55, 5271, 5331-5/46-55/75-99, 5400/2-8/12/3, 5966, 6183-6252. TOTAL 131.
CLASS O5 (Built 1918-21): 5010-5/7/9/22, 5414/5/7-22. TOTAL 17.

ENGINES PURCHASED AFTER GROUPING (Added to Stock 1923-29): 6253-6377, 6495-6642. TOTAL 273.

When Robinson introduced his 2-8-0 design on the G.C.R. in 1911 he can hardly have visualised the extensive role it was to play in the history of the railways of Britain over the ensuing fifty-five years. Not only was the design taken up by the Government for construction for military purposes in the First World War, but many of these engines saw similar service overseas during and after the 1939-45 War. In addition a number found their way to far distant countries such as China and Australia. The class also became the mainstay of L.N.E.R. heavy goods power during the whole of the company's existence. In all, 647 engines were built to the original design, together with nineteen more with a bigger boiler by the G.C.R. Although numerous reboilerings and rebuildings took place over the years many engines survived almost in their original form until withdrawn by B.R. in the sixties.

In 1902 Robinson had introduced his class 8A outside-cylinder 4ft. 8in. 0-8-0 design for mineral duties on the G.C.R. and eighty-nine were constructed up to 1910. The design was robust and straightforward and had a saturated Belpaire boiler and slide valves. It became class Q4 on the L.N.E.R. Additional mineral engines were required to handle the anticipated increase in coal traffic to the G.C.R.'s new port at Immingham, due to be opened in 1912. In August 1910 an order was issued for twenty enlarged engines of greater capacity to be built at Gorton for this traffic and the first engine, No. 966, appeared in September 1911. The new class 8K design had a superheated boiler, larger than on the 0-8-0 and similar in size to that used by Robinson on his Atlantics. To accommodate this heavier boiler, a leading pony truck was provided. The cylinder diameter was enlarged from 19 to 21in., and 10in. diameter piston valves were fitted between the frames.

The class was added to rapidly and by August 1914 there were 126 in service, built by Gorton and outside contractors. Three more were added to G.C.R. stock in 1919, purchased from the Ministry of Munitions. These were part of an intended order for twenty-five engines for the Government to be built at Gorton, cut to six, the remaining three passing to the Government as intended.

A development of the 8K design was worked out during the First World War, and although orders were placed for two batches each of ten engines in March 1916 and August 1917, the first of the new 8M engines did not enter traffic until January 1918. The new engines were essentially the standard 8K design but fitted with a 5ft. 6in. diameter boiler in place of the 5ft. 0in. pattern. Out of the order for the first ten 8M engines, only nine were built, the tenth being turned out as a 4-6-0 with the same size boiler, and as such forming the prototype of the 8N class (L.N.E.R. class B6). Due to difficulties caused by the hostilities the last of the nineteen 8M's did not appear until February 1921. An early decision appears to have been made not to perpetuate the design, as Nos. 412/3 were rebuilt to class 8K during 1922.

At Grouping, the L.N.E.R. took over from the G.C.R. 131 8K engines and seventeen of class 8M. These were classified O4 and O5 respectively by their new owners. The engines were very often referred to as "Tinies" on the G.C. Section of the L.N.E.R., although this nickname originated with the earlier class Q4 0-8-0's and is more correctly applied to that class.

The 1914-18 War saw the formation of the Railway Operating Division of the Royal Engineers, and this commenced operations in

France and Belgium in February 1916. The initial intention was to use rolling stock and locomotives from those countries, but the French deliberately kept their engines away from the fighting zone and the Belgians made similar difficulties, so British railways had to send engines to the Continent. Constituent companies of the L.N.E.R. which loaned engines to the R.O.D. during 1917-19 were the G.N.R., G.C.R., G.E.R., N.B.R. and N.E.R. (L.N.E.R. classes J4, J11 and Q4, J15, J36 and Q5). It was eventually decided that the best answer to the requirements of the R.O.D. was to build a single class of heavy goods engine and the G.C.R. class 8K was quickly chosen. The first orders were placed in February 1917 and 325 engines were built for service in France. In the autumn of 1918, when the War was drawing to a close, further orders were placed and 196 more were built, partly to keep British industry going during the run-down following the cessation of the construction of munitions and other articles of war. This total of 521 includes the six built at Gorton referred to earlier.

After the War was over, the now redundant R.O.D. 2-8-0's were loaned to many British railways (including the G.C.R., G.E.R. and N.E.R. which had ninety-three, forty-four and thirty-three respectively) until called in with the intention of finding buyers. The G.C.R. in fact showed interest in adding to their stock of 8K's, but the asking price proved to be too high and it was left to the newly-formed L.N.E.R. to purchase considerable numbers. The Company made its first selection late in 1923, followed by further batches in 1925 and 1927, totalling 273 engines. These were numbered and entered service as follows:-

Engine Nos.	*Date of order*	*Entered service*	*Total*
6253-6377	12/23	12/23-7/24	125
6495-6542	2/25	6/25-3/26	48
6543-6642	2/27	4/27-5/29	100

The price paid started at £2,000 each for the first batch, £1,500 for those ordered in 1925 and finally the real bargain price of £340 for the last hundred. It is incredible to realise that in 1927 for the sum of £34,000 the L.N.E.R. obtained one hundred heavy goods locomotives. The only undesirable feature of the ex-R.O.D. engines was that they had steel inner fireboxes which required early replacement.

By mid-1929 the L.N.E.R. owned 405 engines of class O4 made up of the 131 G.C.R. engines together with a further rebuild from class O5, plus the 273 engines purchased from the Government. At that time there were also sixteen O5's, making a grand total of 421 heavy goods engines of virtually uniform design.

Not surprisingly with the Doncaster influence on the L.N.E.R.'s locomotive department, several attempts were made over the years to rebuild the O4's with boilers incorporating round-topped fireboxes, but this did not really gather momentum until the Thompson era. However, the earliest such reboilering had taken place in G.C. days when in 1921 the prototype, No. 966, was given a 6ft. diameter boiler in connection with experiments then being conducted into the burning of pulverised fuel (see under Development and Rebuilding). A normal boiler was refitted in 1924.

The earliest rebuilding by the L.N.E.R. took place in 1929 when two engines were fitted with 5ft. 6in. diameter boilers as used in class O2, the alteration requiring an extension of the frames at the rear end. These rebuilds were classified O4/4. Three years later a shortened version of the O2 boiler was produced which could be fitted to class O4 without alteration to the frames. Four engines were rebuilt initially, followed by a further five in 1939, and were classified O4/5. Meanwhile conversion was continuing of the remaining O5 engines to O4, and these were accorded the separate classification O4/6 in 1938. The last O5 was rebuilt in 1943.

In 1939 the O2 boiler design was again taken for use in further rebuilding of class O4, but shortened even further. Such rebuilds were classified O4/7 and forty-seven were altered by 1947, when conversions ceased.

When Thompson became C.M.E. of the L.N.E.R. in 1941 he planned a small range of standard locomotives. Due to wartime stringencies several of the prototypes were produced by rebuilding existing engines, often drastically. For his heavy goods locomotive class, Thompson rebuilt No. 6595 in 1944 retaining the existing frames and wheels. To these he fitted his B1-type boiler and cylinders together with Walschaerts valve gear, new cab and raised running plate. The new class thus formed became class O1 and is dealt with in a separate chapter at page 88. Fifty-eight O4's were thus converted up to 1949. A less drastic rebuilding was carried out concurrently whereby the existing cylinders and Stephenson valve gear were retained but with the B1 boiler and new cab. These rebuilds became class O4/8 and ninety-nine were converted to this class during the years 1944-58.

Class	Date introduced	No. of engines	Description
O4/1	1923	126	Ex-G.C.R. engines, 4,000-gallon tender with scoop, vacuum brake for train. Eventually fitted with shorter chimneys and domes to suit L.N.E.R. Composite Load Gauge and scoops removed.
O4/2	1923	3	As O4/1, but with 3,250-gallon tender. Converted to O4/1 during 1923-25 by attaching larger tenders.
O4/2	1925	17	Engines cut down to suit N.B.R. load gauge. All transferred to O4/1 in December 1946.
O4/3	1927	273	Ex-R.O.D. engines purchased by L.N.E.R. Similar to O4/1, but without tender scoop and with steam brake only. Merged with O4/1 in December 1940.
O4/4	1929	2	Rebuilds with O2 type boilers (5ft. 6in. diameter and round-top firebox). Frames lengthened at rear end, new cab with single side window, G.N. type chimney.
O4/5	1932	9	Rebuilds with shortened barrel version of O2 boiler. Original cab retained, G.N. type chimney.
O4/6	1938	17	Conversions from class O5 with standard O4 boiler (from 1922 onwards). Wide cab (some with double side windows) retained.
O4/7	1939	41	O2 type boiler with shortened barrel and firebox. Original cab retained, G.C. type chimney.
O4/8	1944	99	B1 type boiler (5ft. 6in. diameter and round-top firebox). New cab with double side windows, G.N. type chimney.

It should be noted that some engines passed through more than one stage of rebuilding; one engine, No. 6320 (finally 63705), being rebuilt on three occasions to O4/5 (1939), O4/7 (1947) and O4/8 (1958).

The classifications O4/1, O4/2 and O4/3 were introduced during the early years after Grouping and related to comparatively minor differences connected with type of brake, pattern of tender and overall height. For ease of reference the principal distinguishing features of the variations of class O4 are given in the accompanying table.

When the Second World War broke out in September 1939 it was presumed that the military requirements for locomotives on the Continent would be repeated, and in October 1939 orders were issued to requisition 300 class O4 engines from the L.N.E.R. for this purpose. Work began on the preparation of these engines, but after fifty-seven had been dealt with the order was cancelled and they returned to service in this country.

In 1940 the L.N.E.R. loaned thirty O4's to the G.W.R. These were returned during 1941-43.

In 1941 the military supply route through Persia to Russia was opened up and fifty L.M.S. Stanier class 8F 2-8-0's and ninety-two O4's were immediately requisitioned for service in the Middle East. Of the O4's, sixty-one were ex-R.O.D. engines of which all but six had seen service in France during the First World War. The O4's never returned to Great Britain and were written off the L.N.E.R. books in December 1943. The actual sale price was not negotiated with the British government until February 1947, when a charge of £5,700 per engine was agreed. It should be noted that the total revenue from this sale, £524,400, was well in excess of the £356,000 which the L.N.E.R. paid to the Government some twenty years earlier, for the entire 273 ex-R.O.D. engines!

The British government retained a War Department base at Suez for some time after the end of the 1939-45 War and Stanier 2-8-0's were used to work the traffic there. Five of these were in need of heavy overhaul and it was decided to return them to Britain for this to be carried out. To replace them at Suez, the Government purchased five O4's from British Railways in February 1952. In the event, the Stanier engines never returned to Suez and the O4's remained out there. When the base was closed a few years later, the O4's passed into the hands of the Egyptian State Railways who had already obtained many of the earlier engines sent to the Middle East during the War.

Considering that more modern heavy goods locomotives were available to the Government in 1939, it is a considerable tribute to the O4 design that it had such a distinguished military career. There is no doubt that the O4 was one of the most successful classes for goods work ever built in this country. It is on record that Robinson himself regarded the class as his best design.

Quite a number of O4's were retained for colliery trip work in South Yorkshire until the end of steam in the Eastern Region. The last engine with original type of boiler of this remarkable class was not withdrawn until February 1966. This was No. 63764, an ex-R.O.D. engine built in 1918. The class finally disappeared from service in April 1966 when four class O4/8 engines were withdrawn.

Fortunately, G.C.R. No. 102 built at Gorton in 1912 has been preserved as part of the National Collection. The only others still in existence at the time of writing are three in Australia, originally purchased in 1925-26 for colliery work, and including two (former R.O.D. Nos. 2003/4) built at Gorton in 1918 but which never saw service on the L.N.E.R. (see p. 75).

L.N.E.R. Renumbering

The former R.O.D. engines purchased by the L.N.E.R. took numbers 6253-6377, 6495-6642 in the series allotted to G.C. Section engines under the 1924 general renumbering scheme. This is explained fully under Development and Rebuilding, on page 48 onwards, and the table showing R.O.D. and L.N.E.R. numbers will be found in the Appendix on page 194 onwards.

In the Thompson renumbering scheme, formulated in 1943, a valiant effort was made to sort out the entire O4 class into a logical sequence of numbers on the following basis:-

3500	Old No. 5966.
3501-8	Remaining Gorton-built G.C.R. engines, 1911.
3509-29	Gorton-built G.C.R. engines, 1912.
3530-99	Contractor-built G.C.R. engines, Nos. 6183-6252.
3600-25	Gorton-built G.C.R. engines, 1913-14.
3626/7/8	Gorton-built G.C.R. R.O.D. engines, Nos. 5001/5/8.
3629-42	Nasmyth Wilson-built R.O.D. engines.
3643-69	Kitson-built R.O.D. engines.
3670-3734	R. Stephenson-built R.O.D. engines.
3735-3901	N. B. Loco.-built R.O.D. engines.
3902-20	G.C.R. engines, rebuilds from class O5.

The order of renumbering within each of the above batches was not consistent. For example the engines which followed No. 966 from Gorton in 1911 were allotted 3501-8 in order of their old L.N.E.R. numbers, no regard being paid to construction order, and similar considerations applied to the O4's built at Gorton in 1912 and the former O5's built in 1919. The various R.O.D. batches generally followed the order of their works numbers, this being particularly noticeable in the case of the engines built by the North British Locomotive Co., whose three separate works were at one time building these engines simultaneously. However, there were one or two inconsistencies which cannot be explained, viz. Nos. 6340/9 were allotted new numbers 3693/4, instead of 3694/3 which would have been in accordance with their original R.O.D. numbers 1676/5, and No. 6298 was allotted 3883 instead of 3845, which would have been more logical when comparing its works number (22093) with those of the other engines built by N.B. Locomotive Co.

The ninety-two engines sent to the Middle East in the early war years were still in L.N.E.R. stock when the renumbering scheme was prepared in July 1943, and new numbers were allocated to them in the foregoing list. By the time the scheme was implemented in 1946 these engines had been deleted from stock (in December 1943) and the scheme went ahead leaving appropriate blanks in the numbering. Engines by then (and later) rebuilt to class O1 were not given fresh numbers and remained within the block allocated to class O4.

In December 1946, when the majority of L.N.E.R. locomotives had already been renumbered, the Company purchased 200 "Austerity" 2-8-0's (class O7). There was insufficient room for these engines at the end of the block of numbers (3100-3999) allotted to the eight-coupled goods classes and it was decided to number the O7's 3000-3199. This involved renumbering the Stanier design 2-8-0's of class O6 from 3100-67 to 3500-67. The latter numbers were of course already occupied by the O4 (and O1) class and the decision was taken to renumber the engines carrying numbers between 3500 and 3569 (so starting the O4 series at 3570) by using the blanks in the O4 list caused by the wartime deletions from stock. Therefore during February-April 1947 the fifty-nine engines concerned duly took the blanks in the range 3572-3809. Thus the carefully worked out scheme bringing logic to the O4 class numbering was largely destroyed after an interval of only a few months. Full details of the renumberings appear in the Summary. It will be noticed that Nos. 3512/20/3/30/2/43/4/9/51/9/64, 3810/1/4/5/20/5/6/30/1/4/44/66/71/5/92/6, 3903/9/10/6/8/9 were never used for the O4's (or O1's).

Standard L.N.E.R. Dimensions at Grouping

Cylinders (2 outside)	21″ × 26″				
Motion	Stephenson with 10″ piston valves				
	O4		No. 966	O5	
Boiler:					
Max. diam. outside	5′ 0″		6′ 0″	5′ 6″	
Barrel length	15′ 0″		15′ 0″	15′ 0″	
Firebox length outside	8′ 6″		8′ 6″	8′ 6″	
Pitch	8′ 6½″		8′ 8″	8′ 11″	
Diagram No.	15		—	15B	
	18-ele.	*22-ele.*	*28-ele.*	*28-ele.*	*42-ele.*
Heating surface (sq.ft.):					
Firebox	154	154	162	174	174.5
Tubes	1077	885	973	1050	437.0
Flues	380	464	487	591	1155.0
Total evap.	1611	1503	1622	1815	1766.5
Superheater	198	242	257	308	570.0
Total	1809	1745	1879	2123	2336.5
Tubes	134 × 2″	110 × 2″	147 × 2″	116 × 2¼″	67 × 2¼″
Flues	18 × 5¼″	22 × 5¼″	28 × 5¼″	28 × 5¼″	98 × 3″
Elements	18 × 1 1/16″	22 × 1 1/16″	28 × 1 1/16″	28 × 1 1/16″	42 × ¾″
Grate area (sq.ft.)	26.24	26.24	21.53	26.24	26.24
Boiler pressure	180 lb./sq.in.				
Leading wheels	3′ 6″				
Coupled wheels	4′ 8″				
Tractive effort (85%)	31,326 lb. *				
Wheelbase (engine)	8′ 4″ + 5′ 8½″ + 5′ 5½″ + 5′ 11″ = 25′ 5″				
Weight (full):					
Engine	73T 4C		76T 13C	75T 4C	
Adhesive	66T 4C		69T 13C	67T 18C	
Max. axle load	17T 1C		18T 13C	17T 5C	

Leading particulars applicable to tenders attached:

	O4/1, O5	O4/2	No. 966
Wheel diam.	4′ 4″	4′ 4″	2′ 9″
Wheelbase	6′ 6″ + 6′ 6″ = 13′ 0″	6′ 6″ + 6′ 6″ = 13′ 0″	5′ 6″ + 9′ 6″ + 5′ 6″ = 20′ 6″
Total wheelbase (engine and tender)	51′ 2½″	51′ 2½″	58′ 4½″
Length over buffers (engine and tender)	61′ 8½″	61′ 8½″	66′ 4½″
Weight (full)	48T 6C	44T 3C	52T 18C
Water capacity	4,000 gallons	3,250 gallons	4,150 gallons
Coal capacity	6T 0C	6T 0C	7T 0C

* Prior to 12/1927, engine diagrams quoted 30,827 lb., by the G.C. method of calculation, which allowed for the cross-sectional area of the piston rods.

G.C.R. CLASS 8K — L.N.E.R. CLASS O4

G.C.R. Nos.	*Maker*	*Order No.*	*Works Nos.*	*No. built*	*Date*
966, 331-5, 26, 69, 93, 102/33/55, 400/2-8	Gorton	340	—	20	1911-12
346-55	,,	404	—	10	1912
1183-1202	Kitson & Co.	415X	4891-4910	20	1912
1203-52	N.B. Loco. Co.	L496	19854-19908	50	1912-13
375-84	Gorton	413	—	10	1913
385-99, 271	,,	435	—	16	1913-14
1, 5, 8*	,,	653	—	3	1919

* G.C.R. Nos. 1, 5, 8 built as R.O.D. Nos. 2005/6/7.

O4/1 ENGINES.-Altogether 126 class 8K locomotives were built in the short period of three years between 1911 and 1914, to which were added three built at Gorton in 1919 for R.O.D. service (see p. 46) but purchased instead by the G.C. The pioneer engine No. 966 appeared in September 1911 and was equipped with Robinson's new 18-element superheater. This had been introduced three months earlier on class 9N 4-6-2T No. 24 (see Part 7, class A5) as a modified version of the Schmidt apparatus first used on class 9J 0-6-0 No. 16 in 1909 (see Part 5, class J11). Nine 2-8-0's had the Robinson pattern whilst a further nine had the Schmidt type. In addition four engines had an enlarged Robinson 24-element superheater of the type introduced shortly before this on class 8B 4-4-2 No. 361 (see Part 3A, class C4). Thus within a period of nine months twenty-two engines were built in which were represented three types of superheater, as follows:-

Robinson 18-ele.:	Nos. 133/55, 331/3/5, 400/3/4, 966.
Schmidt 18-ele.:	Nos. 26, 69, 93, 102, 332/4/46/7,402.
Robinson 24-ele.:	Nos. 405-8.

The remaining 104 engines built up to 1914 all had Robinson 24-element superheaters. The respective heating surface particulars of the 18-element and 24-element varieties are set out in the next column.

It will be noted that the dimensions for the 18-element boilers differ from those quoted under "Standard L.N.E.R. Dimensions at Grouping" which in particular show a reduction in the number of small tubes from 144 to 134, and this, together with the adoption of short loop elements, resulted in a smaller heating

	18-element (long loop)	*24-element* (long loop)
Heating surface (sq.ft.):		
Firebox	153	154
Tubes	1538	981
Flues		504
Total evap.	1691	1639
Superheater	318	490
Total	2009	2129
Tubes (2in.)	144	122
Flues ($5\frac{1}{4}$in.)	18	24
Elements ($1\frac{3}{8}$in. O.D.)	18	24

surface figure for the superheater. However it is quite likely that at Grouping the 18-element variety was extinct, or at the most fitted to one engine, No. 1211, which carried No. 404's original boiler from May 1917 to August 1924.

The particulars for the 24-element boiler have been taken from the general arrangement drawing for the engines built by North British Locomotive Co. in 1912 and here again the use of long loop elements resulted in a large heating surface figure.

By 1916 it had been decided to standardise on the 22-element superheater and reduce the number of small tubes from 122 in the 24-element boiler to 110 (see under "Standard L.N.E.R. Dimensions at Grouping" for the heating surface figures for this final boiler arrangement). In some cases the boilers simply had their elements blanked off, whilst in others the change had to await major boiler work or new boilers. At the same time a start was made altering the engines with Schmidt superheaters to the Robinson pattern. The dates of alteration where known are shown below, though it should be noted that there are some slight differences in the various official sources. In addition, whilst this process was taking place No. 350, built new with the Robinson superheater, received No. 347's boiler in 1916.

Engine No.	*18-element Schmidt*	*18-element Robinson*	*22-element Robinson*
26	*new*	1/16	6/18
69	,,	–	6/18
93	,,	7/16	11/19
102	,,	–	6/16
133	–	*new*	12/20
155	–	,,	6/20
331	–	,,	11/19
332	*new*	–	2/18
333	–	*new*	4/18
334	*new*	3/17	1/20
335	–	*new*	9/19
346	*new*	–	3/16
347	,,	–	2/16
350	3/16	–	1/19
400	–	*new*	5/18
402	*new*	–	11/18
403	–	*new*	8/17
404	–	,,	3/17
966	–	,,	5/16
1211	–	?5/17	?8/24

During the 1914-18 War few spare boilers were built for the class, which was then of course still quite new, but exceptional demands on Gorton during the War led to the temporary fitting of saturated boilers to three 2-8-0's, as follows:-

Engine No.	*Saturated*	*Superheated*
1208	4/17	11/21
1240	5/17	10/21
1252	4/17	9/19

In April 1918 the G.C.R. Locomotive Committee authorised the building of twenty-five engines for R.O.D. use, subject to the Ministry of Munitions being able to provide the necessary material promptly. Two months later the number was reduced to an order for six and R.O.D. Nos. 2002-7 were completed in 1918-19. However the last three were purchased by the G.C.R. shortly after completion, for £6,066 each, and they became their Nos. 1, 5 and 8. In April 1919 the Locomotive Committee authorised the purchase of ten R.O.D. engines standing at Immingham, provided the cost was no more than £8,000 each. The price was not acceptable to the Ministry and the sale fell through. (The L.N.W.R. purchased these engines instead, for £10,000 each). In May 1920 the Locomotive Committee authorised tenders to be asked for twenty new engines but this action was deferred a month later. In the following November the G.C.R. sought to purchase the ninety-three engines they had on loan, but again the asking price (of £12,000) proved to be too high and the engines concerned were returned in 1921.

O4/2 ENGINES.—This class part was issued to cover the three engines running at Grouping (Nos. 377/80/3) attached to smaller capacity tenders, holding 3,250 gallons of water and 6 tons of coal. The class part was discontinued in December 1924 and the two remaining engines still attached to such tenders, Nos. 380/3, were included in class part 1 (see also under Tenders). Class part 2 was later revived to cover the O4's cut down in height for use in Scotland (see p. 50).

L.N.E.R. ALTERATIONS.—The most obvious alterations made after Grouping, other than rebuilding with round-topped boilers which will be described later under their respective class parts, were the various styles of chimney fitted. The original pattern was of course Robinson's standard, 1ft. 10¼in. high (fig. 35). In June 1923 No. 1185 was modified for trials in Scotland, including the fitting of a B7-type Robinson style chimney, 1ft. 3in. high (fig. 36). Similar chimneys were afterwards fitted to the ten ex-R.O.D. engines prepared at Darlington Works in 1924 for service in Scotland (fig. 52). In addition No. 5408 was noted with one of these chimneys in the mid-thirties.

The original Robinson chimneys were unfortunately liable to crack and from October 1923 they were gradually replaced by Doncaster style flowerpot castings. No. 6496 received one of these in September 1925, which appears to have been a 1ft. 3in. high casting of the pattern fitted as replacements to the B7's for example. From April 1927 the remaining O4's in England gradually received taller chimneys, 1ft. 9in. high (fig. 37), though this process was not completed (see later). Meanwhile the five ex-R.O.D. engines prepared at Gorton Works in 1928 for service in Scotland, Nos. 6544/8/50/1/82, acquired flowerpot castings, 1ft. 5½in. high (fig. 53), as also fitted at about this time as replacements to the G.C.-built A5's (see Part 7 of this series). A sixth engine prepared at Gorton Works for service in Scotland, No. 6543 in March 1929, was photographed shortly afterwards at Cowlairs Works with a 1ft. 9in. chimney, which was presumably straightaway changed before it entered traffic. The two types of chimney fitted to the Scottish engines were occasionally interchanged during visits to Cowlairs Works for repair (see also under O4/2 on page 51). Gorton kept no records of chimneys changed, but a list supplied by them to Doncaster in 1933 showed 128 O4's altered, by which time the final L.N.E.R./Gorton pattern had evolved.

From March 1933 onwards the unrebuilt O4's gradually received the L.N.E.R./Gorton plain waisted chimney, 1ft. 5½in. high (fig. 39), which along with the reduced dome height enabled the engines to clear the L.N.E.R. Composite Load Gauge. At the same time the old G.C. arrangement of separate petticoat below the liner of the chimney was replaced by the Doncaster arrangement of liner only. The diameter of the blastpipe top was then increased from 5¼in. to 5½in. Unlike other former G.C. classes, no separate class part was issued to cover the altered engines, and they were not added to class part 2. The Scottish O4/2's visited Gorton Works for general repair from 1933, and they too gradually acquired the new pattern chimney.

As a wartime measure the number of small tubes in the Diagram 15 boiler was reduced from 110 to 108 from March 1941 and finally to 104 from March 1943, reducing the tube heating surface from 885 to 869 and 837 sq. ft. respectively. No. 3528 (later 3677) carried a Diagram 105 boiler from November 1946 to December 1948, as normally fitted to class S1 (see Part 9B of this series, p. 25). The crown of the inner firebox sloped downwards towards the rear instead of being horizontal and was 3⅜in. lower at the back than at the front, which was only of relevance to an engine engaged on hump duties. This reduced the firebox heating surface slightly from 154 to 151 sq. ft.

Other alterations carried out by the L.N.E.R. were of a minor nature, such as the different methods of lubrication, and are described under Details. The last Diagram 15 boiler was completed in December 1941, as the programme of replacement by round-topped boilers was gathering momentum. This process was never completed and was brought to a halt in December 1958, leaving fifty-seven ex-G.C.R. O4's in very much their original condition, with small boilers and Belpaire fireboxes. The last of these unrebuilt engines, Nos. 63586/93 (ex-5332, 6246), were withdrawn in October 1965.

G.C.R. Class 8M – L.N.E.R. Class O5 and Conversions to O4/6

G.C. Nos.	*Maker*	*Order No.*	*No. built*	*Date*
412-5/7-21	Gorton	555*	9	1918-19
422, 10-5/7/9, 22	,,	622	10	1919-21

* 10 engines ordered; No. 416 constructed instead as a 4-6-0 (L.N.E.R. class B6).

O5 Engines.—These engines were essentially the standard class O4 2-8-0 but fitted with a shortened "Sir Sam Fay" 4-6-0 boiler (L.N.E.R. class B2). This was 5ft. 6in. diameter compared with 5ft. 0in. of the O4's and had a deeper firebox, so that the pitch of the boiler was raised from 8ft. 6½in. to 8ft. 11in.

Although two orders each for ten engines were issued to Gorton Works in March 1916 and August 1917, it was not until January 1918 that delivery began. Eight of the first order were turned out by September of that year, but one of these was constructed as a 4-6-0 and is described in Part 2B of this series under class B6. The next O5 entered traffic in April 1919 and deliveries continued straight on into the second order, until October of that year when construction halted with five engines yet to be built. These last five engines (Nos. 14/5/7/9, 22), which were turned out between November 1920 and February 1921, were given double side windows to the cab and an extended roof (fig. 42), as introduced by Robinson on his "Improved Director" 4-4-0's of 1919 (L.N.E.R. class D11). The earlier O5's had cabs without side windows (fig. 41). To suit the larger diameter boilers, the O5 cabs were 7in. wider than on class O4 and were also taller. Even so, the front spectacles were much smaller and of different layout, being one-piece windows with parallel sides, square cut lower edge and the top curved to follow the radius of the cab roof and the shoulder of the firebox.

The standard arrangement of superheater on class O5 had 28 elements, six more than the normal O4 arrangement. However, five of the engines turned out during 1919 (Nos. 421, 10-13) had Robinson's small tube superheater which had 42 elements of only $\frac{3}{4}$in. inside diameter instead of the normal $1\frac{1}{16}$in. There were 98 flues of 3in. diameter and the elements were arranged so as to pass through two or more flues. The number of ordinary tubes was reduced from 116 to 67.

The small tube superheater had previously been tried by Robinson on a Pollitt 4-4-0 (class D6) and on an 0-8-0 (class Q4), but class O5 were the only new engines to be given this pattern of superheater. Subsequent boiler changes resulted in a small tube superheater appearing on No. 417, which received the boiler off No. 11 in July 1923. This pattern of superheater gradually disappeared from use and reference to it was finally deleted from the engine diagram in December 1936. However there was no reference to the small tube variety on the boiler diagram issued in December 1932 for the Diagram 15B boiler, though this may not have been significant if this pattern was by then obsolescent. From an inspection of the boiler allocations on the O5's, which show some significant periods when they were spare, up to nineteen months in one case, it is possible to deduce that small tube superheaters were possibly fitted to the following engines. It is however emphasised that official confirmation is lacking.

No.	*Fitted*
10	new-1/25
11	new-7/23
12	new-3/26
13	new-3/29
417	7/23-1/26
421	new-9/24

REBUILDS. – All the O5's were rebuilt to O4 by fitting the smaller boiler. The process began as early as July 1922 when the first two members of the class, Nos. 412/3, were rebuilt. This was probably done in order to create two spare boilers for class O5 and the three engines of class B6 which shared the same type of boiler. No further conversions took place until 1926 when No. 5012 was dealt with (fig. 44) and a further six years elapsed before the next one, No. 5017, was rebuilt. Henceforth until the outbreak of war in 1939 ten more O5's were converted, leaving five still to be dealt with. One was rebuilt in 1940 and three in 1941, two of which (Nos. 5420/1) were immediately despatched to the Middle East (see p. 63). The final rebuild was No. 5422 in January 1943.

O4/6 ENGINES. – At first the conversions from class O5 were included in the O4/1 classification, but from December 1938 were separately classified O4/6. This was due to the initial retention of the original large sized cab which was outside the L.N.E.R. Composite Load Gauge both as regards maximum height and at the eaves. When the O4 boiler was fitted to the O5's, the one-piece style of the front spectacles was retained though made wider and, because of the narrower firebox, no longer had to be shaped to follow the contour of the shoulders. In order to widen the sphere of operation of the class in view of the likelihood of the outbreak of war, it was decided to cut down the cabs to suit the L.N.E.R. gauge (chimney and dome height were already being dealt with in common with the rest of class O4). No. 5019 was the first to be altered, in May 1939, and all the engines rebuilt by that time were similarly changed during the following two years, whilst the five reboilered during the War were dealt with at the time of rebuilding. The alteration to the roof profile necessitated a further change to the shape of the front spectacles and these were now similar to the type on the class B7/2 4-6-0's, rectangular and with top and bottom of half-round shape (cf. figs. 44 and 46). The double side windows on Nos. 5014/5/7/9/22 were retained. The principal dimensions for class O4/6 were the same as shown for class O4 (with 22-element superheater) under "Standard L.N.E.R. Dimensions at Grouping".

The dates of rebuilding from O5 to O4 and subsequent alterations to the cabs are summarised as follows:-

Engine No.	*Rebuilt*	*Cab altered*
5010	7/41	7/41
5011	5/36	3/41
5012	8/26	9/40
5013	6/40	6/40
5014	1/33	10/41
5015	6/35	6/40
5017	10/32	10/41
5019	8/33	5/39
5022	10/35	5/40
5412	7/22	1/40
5413	7/22	10/41
5414	11/36	3/41

5415	10/36	1/41
5417	2/37	5/40
5418	2/36	4/40
5419	4/35	7/41
5420	9/41	9/41
5421	10/41	10/41
5422	1/43	1/43

Two of the O4/6 engines were further rebuilt to class O4/8, No. 63914 (ex-5012) in July 1955 and No. 63915 (ex-5013) in January 1956. On rebuilding they lost their distinctive cabs in favour of the standard double side-window type. Class O4/6 became extinct with the withdrawal of No. 63913 in June 1965.

Pulverised Fuel Experiments 1917-24

The use of coal dust as a fuel for steam raising has over the years attracted quite a lot of work and although success has been achieved in stationary steam plant, its use on locomotives has never been really successful. The First World War provided an opportunity for attempts to find an alternative to locomotive steam coal, the price of which had increased and at the same time the quality of coal available had deteriorated. J. G. Robinson became interested in the use of coal dust mainly for these reasons but also because in any case this material was much cheaper and offered the prospect of almost total combustion. Altogether four separate experiments were made, all on his 2-8-0 engines, and these are summarised as follows:-

Engine No.	*Date*	*Fuel*
353	1917-20	Coal dust
422	1919-23	Pulverised coal
420	1920-23	Mixture of coal dust and oil
966	1921-24	Pulverised coal

Engine No. 353.—In the U.S.A. attempts had been made to use powdered coal in steamship boilers and they may well have influenced Robinson in his thinking and hence his first attempt to find an alternative fuel was to use this method. The locomotive selected for this conversion was a standard 2-8-0 of G.C. class 8K and all Robinson's subsequent experimental work involved either this class or the larger boilered class 8M. No. 353 was rebuilt at Gorton in July 1917 and outwardly showed no physical difference except that the standard six-wheel tender carried an enclosed container in the coal space for the fuel, with a large periscope-like air-intake pipe at the front which curved to the rear. Internally a number of alterations were made in order to provide the right conditions for combining the coal dust with air before entering the firebox. The fuel was gravity-fed into rotating feed screws mounted at the bottom of the fuel container. On reaching the end of the feed screws the fuel was met by a blast of air from a fan mounted at the front of the tender on the left-hand side and driven by a De Laval steam turbine. The feed screws were driven initially by a four-cylinder petrol engine mounted on the opposite side of the tender-front to the fan and its turbine. (This arrangement was subsequently replaced by a horizontal two-cylinder steam engine driving this gearing). The gaseous mixture then passed through pipes to enter the firebox through two 7½in. diameter holes cut through the water space at the back of the firebox above the foundation ring. In the firebox the grate and ashpan were removed and the lower part was lined with firebrick, with a gap between the firebrick and the actual sides of the firebox. In place of the grate and ashpan, a damper box was provided behind the rear axle having front and back doors which allowed supplementary air to enter the firebox through a series of apertures cut into the firebrick lining. When starting from cold it was necessary to provide an external source of steam in order to work the machinery on the tender and a suitable connection point was provided. Due to wartime conditions, no provision could be made at that time for fuel preparation and the coal dust recovered from colliery screens had to be dried over the flues of a battery of Lancashire boilers. In these circumstances it was a brave attempt which did not achieve complete success. The initial problems involved obtaining a correct mixture of air and coal dust and several alterations to the firebox and its lining had to be tried.

The early trials involved nothing more strenuous than the engine hauling an inspection saloon. In some cases the trial run terminated in a failure to maintain steam and an ignominious return to Gorton behind conventially-fired motive power. Little further information has survived beyond a drawing office report of November 1917, except for a rather optimistic report in "The Engineer" dated 25th April 1919 in which brief details of trial runs between Ashburys and Woodhead hauling a train of 80 empty wagons are given; these trials also involved a standard coal-fired class 8K. Reference was made to another trial which involved a loaded coal train of 41 wagons and guard's van worked from Sheffield to Dunford Bridge. The average horsepower quoted for No. 353 was 1,000 h.p. with the empty wagon train, and for every pound of fuel consumed the engine evaporated 0.25 lb. more water than the coal-fired engine – a result which could hardly be said to be significant. The firebox drawing shown in "The Engineer" article differs from those shown in the drawing office report mentioned earlier and it is assumed that in the meantime a reasonable method of combustion had been achieved, although still not giving satisfaction; an assumption which is supported by the very low mileage of 2,747 run by No. 353 in the three years it ran in the converted condition. The main reason why the conversion of the small boilered No. 353 had not proved entirely successful was considered to be that its firebox was too small to achieve the correct conditions for the combustion of the coal dust and air mixture. The engine entered Gorton Works in January 1920 and emerged in the following month converted back to ordinary coal firing.

ENGINE NO. 422. – The second experiment involved using one of the larger boilered 2-8-0's, class 8M No. 422, built at Gorton in June 1919 and equipped to burn pulverised coal (fig. 47). By this time the War was over and conditions were slowly easing, so that although the basic principle of using coal dust as a fuel was tried again in much the same way as in 1917, several alterations were made in the light of experience. The most important change made was that it was now possible to provide facilities for fuel preparation and the necessary equipment was duly erected in the shed yard at Gorton consisting of a grinding mill for producing pulverised fuel (powdered coal) and also with facilities for drying. Facilities were also provided for refuelling with Colloidal fuel.

A special bogie tender was provided for No. 422, with a capacity for 7 tons of fuel and 4,150 gallons of water. The tender machinery comprised two vertically mounted twin-cylinder steam engines; the one on the left-hand side of the tender front drove the fan whilst the one on the right-hand side drove the feed screws. Each steam engine was operated by engaging a dog clutch. A third dog clutch was provided which engaged into a common drive shaft between the two engines, so that if for any reason either engine failed, then by engaging this clutch both sets of machinery could be operated by one steam engine. On No. 422 itself the greatest difference was in the layout of the fuel pipes which now entered the firebox below the foundation ring and a secondary air supply was admitted to the fuel by a pipe underneath the cab. The firebox was again lined with firebrick with ports let into it to provide a third air supply, admitted by dampers placed this time in front of the rear axle below the firebox. In this condition No. 422 entered traffic with a much better chance of achieving the right conditions for combustion due to the larger air supply available, and also utilising the much larger firebox volume which was partly due to the repositioned fuel entry pipes to the firebox.

Little information is available of the work done by No. 422 and it was eventually converted back to conventional coal firing in March 1923, having run 22,638 miles since June 1919.

ENGINE NO. 420. – In January 1920 another large-boilered 2-8-0 was converted, this time to burn Colloidal fuel which was a mixture of oil and coal dust, the only external evidence of the conversion being the tender fitted with an oil tank in the coal space. No. 420 was the engine in this trial (fig. 48) and few alterations were necessary to the firebox except for lining the rear portion of the ashpan with firebrick and a thin layer of broken firebrick strewn over the firebars. The burner used was of the triplex type with the nozzles so arranged that one, two or all three could be used at any one time depending upon the steam requirements of the locomotive. A steam warming coil was provided in the tender fuel tank to reduce the viscosity of the oil in cold weather and a compressed air pipe with a number of small holes was used to agitate the oil and its solids; this latter feature, or rather its failing, led to the eventual abandonment of using Colloidal fuel. The use of compressed air in the foregoing description is taken from a contemporary account in the "Locomotive Magazine" for July

1922. This account does not state how the supply of compressed air was obtained and all known photographs of No. 420 show no sign of an air compressor.

Several types of liquid fuel were successfully tried out, including creosote and pitch, as well as conventional fuel oil. The solid material used was mainly coal dust, though smokebox ashes and coke breeze were also used. The triplex burner could also be used with straight fuel oil and it is thought that No. 420 did run for a period as an oil-burner. In the issue of the "Railway Gazette" dated 9th July 1920, an account is given of trial runs made between Dewsnap Sidings and Dunford Bridge in which coal-fired 2-8-0 No. 419 was tried against No. 420 burning Colloidal fuel and No. 422 using pulverised fuel. The nominal load was 80 empty wagons and guard's van, with No. 422 hauling one wagon less to allow for the heavier weight of the bogie tender. As with the earlier trial run made by No. 353, little in the way of evidence to prove the advantage of one system of firing over the others was forthcoming, except that the average superheat temperature was higher in the case of the Colloidal fuel engine.

No. 420 was converted back to conventional coal firing in October 1923, having run 38,725 miles since January 1920.

ENGINE NO. 966. – The problem of firebox volume would seem to have still not been solved with the pulverised fuel engines, and a final attempt was made by providing a specially designed boiler and firebox. The engine chosen to be the subject of this next rebuilding was the pioneer small-boilered class 8K No. 966, built in 1911, which came out of Gorton in September 1921 rebuilt with a round-topped boiler six feet in diameter (fig. 49). The firebox was specially designed for burning pulverised fuel and in section was pear-shaped, with the widest part at the top. The firebox had no conventional grate or ashpan, but instead had a water jacket completely encircling it with the feed water delivered into the bottom of the water space below the firebox. The firebox had an extension in the form of a combustion chamber, whose cross-section was much narrower where it left the firebox but widened out at the tubeplate. The purpose of this chamber was to give a final mixing to any residual fuel and oxygen before entering the tubes. The special boiler was known as the "No. 1 design" but no evidence has been found to show an alternative design despite the inference in the title.

An official Gorton photograph shows the engine coupled to a standard six-wheel tender, but this may have been for photographic purposes only. No additional tender was modified in connection with this final experiment, so that there were then two special tenders shared between three modified engines. The inference here is that at any one time, one of these engines was either laid up without a tender or running as a coal-burner. According to the surviving records, No. 966 acquired the special bogie tender from No. 422 in May 1922, which suggests that it may have run during the eight preceding months coupled to the oil fuel tender from No. 420. (Its special boiler prohibited its use in a conventional manner). The records then show that at unrecorded dates No. 420's oil fuel tender finished up attached to No. 422 and No. 966's ordinary tender finished up attached to No. 420. This no doubt over-simplified matters and the tenders could have moved about more frequently. However the significance of the May 1922 date may be connected with an item in the "Locomotive Magazine" for July 1922 which recorded that Nos. 420 and 966 had been inspected at Marylebone Station by delegates to the congress of the Institute of Transport. It would appear likely that at this inspection No. 966 being the subject of the latest experiment would have had the bogie tender and that No. 420 would have had the six-wheeled oil fuel tender.

No account has been found of the work done by No. 966 and no recorded tests are known to have been published unlike the earlier conversions. The rebuilding of No. 966 in June 1924 with a conventional 5ft. 0in. diameter boiler brought to an end Robinson's attempts at finding an alternative fuel to coal and the engines concerned eventually reverted to normal methods of firing. No. 966 was possibly the least successful experiment as evidenced by its low mileage run, 9,648 between September 1921 and June 1924.

Following the final rebuilding of No. 966, the bogie tender was dismantled and the tender tank used for oil storage, whilst the bogies were used by Dukinfield Carriage Works in the construction of a 50-ton well trolley wagon built in 1926. One of the two steam reciprocating engines used for driving the tender machinery was installed in the Repair Shop at Gorton shed and used for driving the shop machinery. The engine boiler of course could not be used on a conventional steam locomotive and was scrapped in August 1927. No. 966's special double side

Fig. 35 Class O4/1 No. 5408 at Annesley shed, September 1926.

G.C. engine. Robinson 1ft. 10¼in. chimney, four uncased Ramsbottom safety valves, tail rod extension to pistons, footsteps and handgrip mid-way along running plate, vacuum ejector and hose connection.

Fig. 36 Class O4/1 No. 1185 at Guide Bridge, June 1923.

Altered for trial in Scotland, B7-type 1ft. 3in. chimney, flattened top to dome cover, Ross pop safety valves, no tail rod extensions, early lettering "L. & N. E. R." (with ampersand and full points). Note G.C.R. numberplate still carried on cab side.

Fig. 37 Class O4/1 No. 5383 at March shed, June 1935.

L.N.E.R. 1ft. 9in. flowerpot chimney, Ramsbottom safety valves separately cased, no footsteps or handgrips mid-way along running plate, substantial support plate with two steps on slide-bar bracket.

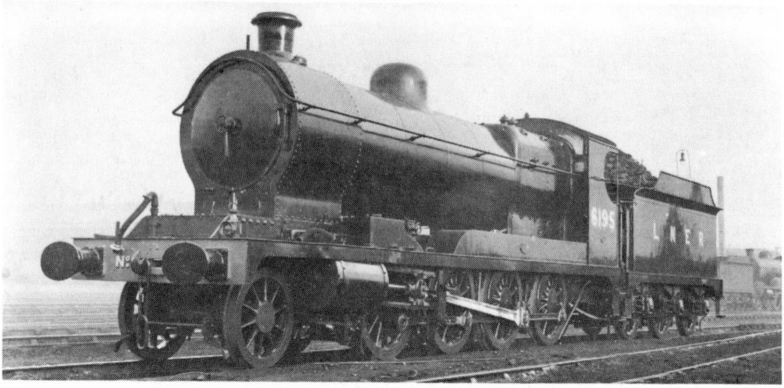

Fig. 38 Class O4/1 No. 6195 at Gorton shed, May 1935.

Fig. 39 Class O4/1 No. 6202 at Annesley shed, about 1936.

L.N.E.R./Gorton 1ft. 5½in. plain waisted chimney, Gresley anti-vacuum valve, wheel and handle fastening for smokebox door.

Fig. 40 Class O4/1 No, E3680 at Gorton Works, January 1948.

Twin-handle fastening for smokebox door, tender with coal rails plated on outside, still lettered "L N E R".

Fig. 41 Class O5 No. 5422 at Mexborough shed, April 1925.

Robinson 1ft. 3in. chimney, top feed to boiler, header discharge valve on smokebox side, plain cab with no side windows, wheel and handle fastening for smokebox door, Intensifore lubricator.

Fig. 42 Class O5 No. 5015 at Mexborough shed, July 1933.

L.N.E.R. 1ft. 3in. flowerpot chimney, side-window cab with tall casing in front covering part of screw reversing gear.

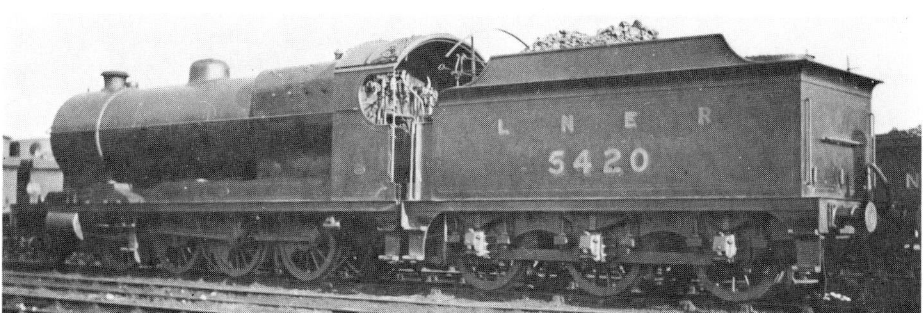

Fig. 43 Class O5 No. 5420 at March shed, June 1935.

Gresley anti-vacuum valve behind chimney, tender with frame to take tarpaulin sheet, still showing evidence of G.C. livery.

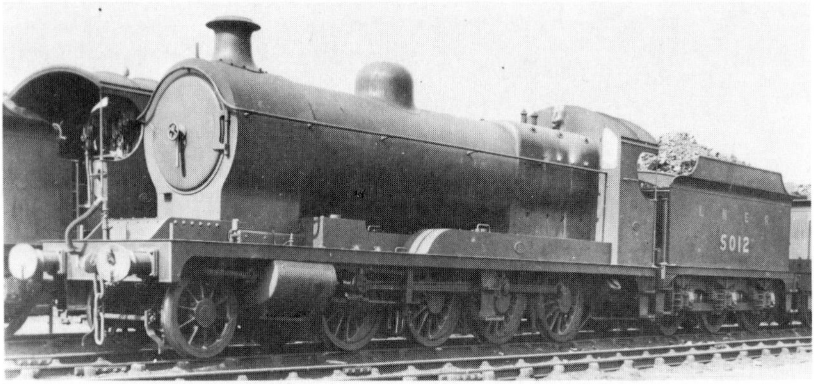

Fig. 44 Class O4/1 (O4/6) No. 5012 at Mexborough shed, about 1928.

Engine rebuilt from class O5 in 1926. Robinson chimney, retaining plain cab with no side windows and shaped spectacles in cab front plate.

Fig. 45 Class O4/1 (O4/6) No. 5014 at York shed, May 1938.

Engine rebuilt from class O5 in 1931. L.N.E.R. flowerpot chimney, retaining side-window cab.

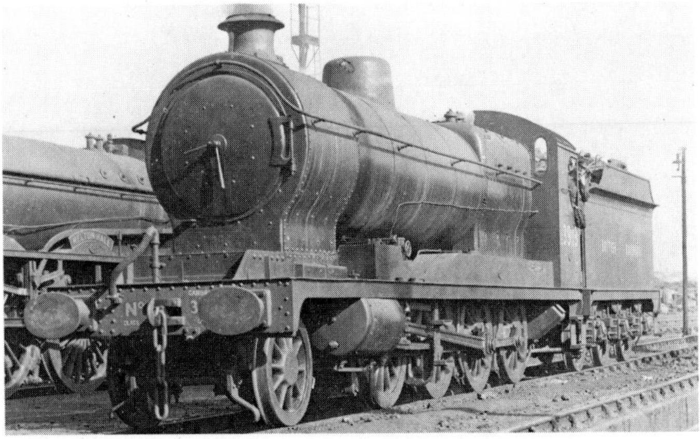

Fig. 46 Class O4/6 No. E3913 at Cambridge shed, 1948.

Reduced cab height with altered front spectacle windows, later L.N.E.R./Gorton chimney, retaining fixing bracket on bufferbeam for steam heat fitting.

window cab was removed and replaced by a standard O4 cab again. The rear sandboxes however were retained in their altered position under the running plate attached to the frames below the cab.

Sixty years after these experiments, it might be tempting to dismiss these manifestations of Robinson's ingenuity as a waste of time and money, but at that period the purchase of coal was a very large proportion of a railway company's budget, and anything which might have led to locomotive fuel economies was worth trying. The Colloidal fuel did show some evidence of being successful, but difficulty was experienced in maintaining the solids in suspension in the oil and probably showed no overall advantage over conventional oil firing methods; indeed the successful use of oil firing on the G.C. during two coal strikes in the 1920's could no doubt be credited to the work done on No. 420. In the case of the pulverised fuel, mention has been made earlier of the difficulties in obtaining ideal conditions for combustion, but some progress appears to have been made, as shown by the successful trial runs carried out. However, as the economic position eased, the expense of coal preparation and the provision and maintenance of ancillary machinery would have made this method of firing too expensive. In conclusion it may be of interest to quote from a Doncaster drawing office letter dated 13th May 1941 to Gorton headed "Dust Fired Locomotives", as it is obvious that with wartime conditions worsening, someone had revived Robinson's earlier work in this field. The letter is a reply to a suggestion and the final paragraph puts the case against pulverised fuel certainly from a practical point of view, with the comment that if the writer "has any new information so far unrevealed it would receive every consideration, but unless he can eliminate the auxiliary machinery in the form of blowers, conveyor screws and pulverising plant, with which the previous applications have been encumbered, there appears to be no justification for doing anything with the scheme at present".

L.N.E.R. Class O4 — Ex-R.O.D. Engines

R.O.D. Engines. — Because the L.N.E.R. was the major purchaser of the R.O.D type 2-8-0's built to Government order, it is appropriate to cover in detail their early history, and their construction is summarised on p. 47. It is convenient to divide the R.O.D. engines into three series, distinguished by the type of brake or method of lubricating the cylinders.

The initial orders were placed in February 1917 and by the following June there were 233 engines on order as follows:-

R.O.D. Nos	*Maker*	*Total*
1601-32	Kitson	32
1651-86	R. Stephenson	36
1701-24	Nasmyth, Wilson	24
1801-1941	N.B. Loco. Co.	141

The first engine to be completed, No. 1801, was handed over in September 1917 for immediate despatch to France, to be followed ultimately by the remaining engines from the above orders.

Several changes were made to the basic G.C.R. design, the better to suit the intended field of operation in France, no modifications being regarded as necessary to aid large-scale production. The most significant alteration was the use of $\frac{3}{8}$in. thick steel plate, instead of $\frac{9}{16}$in. and $\frac{7}{8}$in. copper, for the inner firebox together with steel stays. This was brought about by wartime shortage of copper rather than choice although steel fireboxes were used extensively on the Continent. Minor changes to the boiler were the use of a pair of Ross pop safety valves, instead of the four-column Ramsbottom type, and feed water introduced via clack valves on the faceplate in the cab instead of mounted on top of the boiler. The superheater had 22 elements, by this time standard on the G.C.R. engines, but the heating surface of the superheater was shown as increased from 242 to 255 sq. ft.

These engines were expected to handle coaching stock as well as goods traffic on the Continent and this required air brake equipment in place of the vacuum system. Steam brake was provided on engine and tender (as on the G.C. engines) together with a Westinghouse pump, for train braking, mounted on the right-hand side of the smokebox. Operation of the air brake valve applied the steam brake in proportion. The single steam brake cylinder was placed centrally beneath the cab floor between the frames. As troop trains were to be worked, steam heat connections were fitted at the front of the engine and back of the tender.

Apart from some engines which had ordinary buffers, the pattern mostly used had the Continental shape of ribbed casing. The heads were circular, not oval as with the G.C.R. type, and had a hole in the centre. To conform to Continental practice a pair of safety chains and hooks were fitted on either side of the drawhook. A further item, long obsolete on British locomotives, was the provision of a pair of screw jacks for dealing with derailments. These were carried on the running plate at the front end. To suit the marginally ($\frac{3}{16}$in.) wider track gauge on the Continent, the profile of the wheel tyres was changed. The centre pair of wheels on the tender were given slightly more side play than on the G.C. tenders and their tyres were thinner too. The tender was very similar to the G.C. pattern but was devoid of water pick-up gear, this being an unnecessary fitment for service on the Continent. In consequence the coal carrying capacity was shown as increased from 6 to 7 tons.

The engines were painted black all over, even the bufferbeams. Rectangular number plates were fitted to the cab sides and on the back of the tender, the latter carrying the same number as the engine. The maker's plates were attached to the long splashers. No lettering regarding ownership was at first displayed but as soon as the first engines began to arrive in France, large white-painted letters "R O D" together with the engine number were put on the tender sides (although the cast number plates were retained). Until this time these engines had been known solely as type MM (Ministry of Munitions), but thereafter they were popularly referred to as the R.O.D. type.

Between February and August 1918 orders were placed for the second series, of 100 engines. These differed in one major respect from the earlier R.O.D. engines, in having Westinghouse brake only, for engine, tender and train. This change could be detected by the presence of the brake cylinders, now two in number, located one on each side of the outside of the frames below the cab with a drum-shaped air reservoir immediately in front of each brake cylinder. The engines took up some of the vacant numbers in the R.O.D. list above 1601, as follows:-

R.O.D. Nos.	*Maker*	*Total*
1647-50/87-99, 1700	R. Stephenson	18*
1725-32	Nasmyth, Wilson	8*
1787-1800	N.B. Loco. Co.	14
1942-2001	,,	60*

* These engines were destined for France, of which Nos. 1647-50/87-95, 1942-69/72-99 were actually sent.

Between June and October 1918, orders were placed for the final series: 188 engines including Nos. 2002-7 from the G.C.R.'s Gorton Works following the decision earlier in the year to build up to twenty-five of these engines for the R.O.D. if conditions were favourable, as recorded earlier on page 39. In the event, the last three of these engines were purchased by the G.C.R., entering traffic in June 1919 as Nos. 1, 5 and 8 respectively. These three engines were therefore not counted as R.O.D. locomotives in the final analysis. The engines of this final series had air brake only, like the engines of the second series referred to earlier. However, in place of the Wakefield mechanical lubricator they were fitted instead with Robinson's Intensifore sight-feed lubricator for the cylinders and valves (fig. 50). In addition Nos. 2002-7 had copper instead of steel plate inner fireboxes. The engines took up most of the remaining vacant numbers in the R.O.D. list above 1601, care being taken not to duplicate engines which had been requisitioned from the L.N.W.R., some of which were numbered in the 16XX and 20XX series. As a result the R.O.D.'s with air brake only and Intensifore lubricators were allocated numbers as follows:-

R.O.D. Nos.	*Maker*	*Total*
1633/5/6/8/40-6, 1733-49	R. Stephenson	28
2002-7	Gorton	6*
2008-13/5-31/ 3-44/6/7/8/ 51-84/6-99, 2100-67	N.B. Loco. Co.	154

* These engines were destined for France: Nos. 2002/3/4 were actually sent whilst Nos. 2005/6/7 were purchased instead by the G.C.R. as Nos. 1, 5 and 8.

With the cessation of hostilities in November 1918 the need for the R.O.D. engines rapidly diminished. By mid-1919 most of those which had been sent to the Continent had returned to Great Britain and were stored. The remaining engines still in the course of delivery were also put into store on completion. The last two engines built, R.O.D. Nos. 1748/9, were not completed until April 1920. For completeness full details of orders and manufacturers are set out below:-

R.O.D. Nos.	*Maker*	*Order No.*	*Works Nos.*	*No. built*	*Date*
1601-12	Kitson & Co.	477Z	5183-94	12	1918
1613-32	,,	479C	5199-5218	20	1918
1633/42-6	R. Stephenson & Co.	E108	3749-54	6	1919
1635/6/8/40/1, 1733-49	,,	E109	3755-76	22	1919-20
1647-50/87/8	,,	E106	3731-6	6	1918
1651-70	,,	E104	3695-3714	20	1917-18
1671-86	,,	E105	3715-30	16	1918
1689-1700	,,	E107	3737-48	12	1918-19
1701-24	Nasmyth, Wilson & Co.	L926	1244-67	24	1917-18
1725-32	,,	L1550	1281-8	8	1919
1787-1800	N.B. Loco. Co. (a)	L707	22080-93	14	1919
1801-41	,, (c)	L689	21768-21808	41	1917
1842-91	,, (b)	L692	21819-68	50	1918
1892-1941	,, (c)	L693	21869-21918	50	1918
1942-71	,, (b)	L703	22000-29	30	1918-19
1972-2001	,, (c)	L704	22030-59	30	1918-19
2002-7 (d)	Gorton	653	—	6	1918-19
2008-13/5-20	N.B. Loco. Co. (b)	L710	22104-15	12	1919
2021-31/3	,, (c)	L711	22116-27	12	1919
2034-44/6/7/8/51-84/6/7	,, (b)	L712	22128-77	50	1919
2088-2137	,, (c)	L713	22178-22227	50	1919
2138-67	,, (a)	L714	22228-57	30	1919

(a) Atlas Works.
(b) Hyde Park Works.
(c) Queen's Park Works.
(d) Nos. 2005/6/7 were sold to the G.C.R. as soon as completed.

Several British companies showed interest in purchasing the now surplus engines and in May/June 1919 the G.C.R., G.W.R. and L.N.W.R. boards agreed to buy three, twenty and thirty respectively. (The purchase by the G.C.R. has already been mentioned). In August 1919 the Ministry of Transport assumed responsibility for the unsold engines and further sales were stopped, the Government having decided that all such engines would be placed in a pool of rolling stock held by them. Loans from this pool to a number of British railways were negotiated during 1919, mainly to allow the companies concerned to deal with the arrears of maintenance on their own engines. The companies hiring R.O.D. 2-8-0's at this time were as follows:-

Company	*Number*	*Period of hire*
Caledonian	50	1919-21
Great Central	93	1919-21
Great Eastern	44	1919-21
Great Western	76(a)	1919-22
Lancashire & Yorkshire	27	1919-20
London & North Western	152(b)	1919-21
London & South Western	17	1919-20
North Eastern	33	1919-21
South Eastern & Chatham	6	1919-20
	498	

(a) In addition, 6 were received from the L.Y.R. and 2 from the L.S.W.R.
(b) Also 21 from the L.Y.R., 6 from the S.E.C.R. and 2 from the L.S.W.R.

Only on the G.W.R. and L.N.W.R. were these engines allotted numbers in these companies' lists, the remainder retaining their R.O.D. numbers although company initials or insignia were added in some cases in place of the R.O.D. lettering. The Great Central Railway apparently carried out modifications to some of the engines they had on loan, in particular recording the alteration from air brake to steam brake in several instances (see under Brakes). Government control of the railways, imposed during the war, came to an end on 15th August 1921 and all the R.O.D. 2-8-0's were quickly returned to the Government, the only exceptions being sixty-four retained by the G.W.R. until 1922 and of course those which had been purchased outright by the G.C.R., G.W.R. and L.N.W.R.

During the period of the above-mentioned loans, efforts to sell the engines had continued, but with little success, only twenty being purchased (in 1920) by the L.N.W.R. and three (in 1923) by the Richmond Vale Railway in Australia. At the end of April 1923 the Ministry of Munitions War Surplus Disposals Board ceased activities and from 1st May the disposal of surplus war material, including the R.O.D. engines, was put into the hands of private enterprise in the form of George Cohen & Armstrong Disposals Corporation. The asking price of from £10,000 (in 1919) to £12,000 (in 1920) per engine and tender then fell to £2,000, but even so it took until 1928 (with the price then down to £340) to clear the stock.

O4/3 ENGINES.—When the Disposals Corporation took over there were 465 2-8-0's stored at Government sidings, as listed in the accompanying table.

Location	*Number*	*Remarks*
Aintree	29	5 ex-G.C.R., 15 ex-G.E.R., 9 ex-N.E.R.
Beachley, near Chepstow	64	All ex-G.W.R.
Gretna	50	All ex-C.R.
Morecambe	41	All ex-G.C.R.
Queensferry, near Chester	198	18 ex-G.C.R., 29 ex-G.E.R., 151 ex-L.N.W.R.
Royds Green, near Leeds	33	9 ex-G.C.R., 24 ex-N.E.R.
Stratton, near Swindon	50	20 ex-G.C.R., 20 ex-G.W.R., 10 ex-L.S.W.R.

The L.N.E.R. made their first selections from the dumps at Beachley and Queensferry in November 1923 and one month later placed an initial order for 125. Delivery commenced immediately although payment was not made for these until December of the following year. Along with these 1923 selections, thirteen spare boilers were also purchased (for £1,200 each) and some of these had been built as late as 1922 by Kerr Stuart & Co. of Stoke. In February 1925 forty-eight more engines were bought, followed two years later by a final 100. The remaining engines not purchased by the L.N.E.R. were disposed of to the G.W.R. (80), L.M.S. (75), and for use in Australia (10) and China (24), whilst one engine was broken up as a costing exercise and two more were sold to create spares for those sent to China. The L.M.S. resold thirty of their engines for use in China too, twenty-two of which were sent and the other eight were used as spares. The 273 engines purchased by the L.N.E.R. were numbered in groups according to manufacturer as follows:-

Engine Nos.	*Maker*	*Into service*
FIRST ORDER (125) 12/1923		
6253-6306	N.B. Loco. Co.	1923-24
6307-56	R. Stephenson	1923-24
6357-74	Kitson	1924
6375/6/7	Nasmyth Wilson	1924
SECOND ORDER (48) 2/1925		
6495-6503	R. Stephenson	1925-26
6504-35	N.B. Loco. Co.	1925-26
6536/7/8	Nasmyth Wilson	1925
6539-42	Kitson	1925
FINAL ORDER (100) 2/1927		
6543-7	Kitson	1927-29
6548-53	R. Stephenson	1927-29
6554-61	Nasmyth Wilson	1927-29
6562-6642	N.B. Loco. Co.	1927-29

Preparation for service on the L.N.E.R. included the replacement of the steel inner firebox by a new one made from copper, though in the case of the engines put into service in 1923-24 a considerable number ran in traffic for a few months with steel fireboxes, including the following at least: Nos. 6253/5/7-61/3/5-8/70/2-9/81/2/3, 6306/9/10/2-8/20-3/34/55/8/60-3/5/75/6/7. There seems little doubt that the Gorton boilershop was unable to cope with this sudden demand. The engines which had steam brake with Westinghouse for train braking had their Westinghouse equipment removed, though Nos. 6313 and 1334c at least were noted with Westinghouse pumps for a while (fig. 51). The later R.O.D. engines which had the full air brake were converted to steam brake. These ex-R.O.D. engines therefore always differed from the ex-G.C.R. O4's in having no provision for train braking. For a while a number of engines retained their Westinghouse pump mounting brackets on the side of the smokebox. The steam heating fitments were removed from the R.O.D. engines and also the side safety chains on the bufferbeams. In one or two cases the sockets for the chain anchorages cut into the bufferbeam were retained for a while and this necessitated the engine number being applied higher up. The Continental pattern buffers were replaced by the G.C.R. oval-headed type, though many of the earliest engines put into service on the L.N.E.R. kept their original buffers for a time, whilst No. 6288 is known to have received round headed buffers (fig. 52). By the time that the later purchases were being overhauled, Gresley flowerpot chimneys were being fitted to the class and this change was made when these later engines were first put into service on the L.N.E.R.

All the engines were overhauled and reconditioned at Gorton Works prior to entering service on the L.N.E.R. with the exception of ten engines dealt with at Darlington Works in 1924 for use in the Scottish Area. These engines were cut down in height to clear the N.B. load gauge and are referred to separately on page 50.

As time went by, such details as boiler mountings, superheaters, arrangement of boiler feed and buffers on the ex-G.C.R. and ex-R.O.D. engines were unified. Latterly, (see under Tenders) even the water pick-up gear was removed from the ex-G.C.R. engines, but the difference in braking always remained (except in the case of engines rebuilt to classes O4/4, O4/8 and O1).

The first batch of 125 O4's purchased by the L.N.E.R. from the Government were allocated numbers 1253-1377, which followed on after the then highest number in the G.C. Section Capital Stock list. The sectional suffix C was added to the numbers of the first engines to be put into service, but when the L.N.E.R. introduced its numbering scheme in February 1924 the suffix letters were dropped and G.C. Section numbers were increased by 5000, so that the class O4 engines which entered traffic from this date carried numbers in the 6000 series. All had been put into traffic by September 1924. The renumbering from R.O.D. to L.N.E.R. numbers was not particularly systematic other than that they were grouped according to manufacturers. The engines were taken from two dumps, sixty-four from Beachley (which was cleared) and the remainder from Queensferry. The Beachley engines took the lower numbers in each of the maker's groups, except that No. 6256 from Queensferry appeared within the Beachley series. It is apparent that the intention had been to number the engines within each maker's group in strict accordance with their sequence shown in the letter from the L.N.E.R., dated 18th November 1923, to the Disposals Corporation, which also listed them in random order within each maker's group. By some aberration which cannot be explained, two of the earliest engines put into traffic in December 1923, ex-R.O.D. Nos. 1841 and 2044 which should have become 1282c and 1300c respectively, were numbered 1255c and 1256c almost at the beginning of the series allocated. In consequence, the engines which should have been renumbered 1253-1377 in that order, eventually became 6253/4/7-83/55/4-99, 6300, 6256, 6301-77.

The second purchase of forty-eight engines in February 1925 were given numbers 6495-6542. The intervening numbers 6378-6494 had already been filled under the 1924 general renumbering scheme by new class D11/2 4-4-0's and the G.C.R. duplicate list engines (see Part 1 of this series, page 34). The allotment of numbers was again in groups according to manufacturer and was purely in the numerical order of the original R.O.D. numbers. Once more the engines taken from dumps (clearing the twenty-nine at Aintree and taking a further nineteen from Queensferry) were grouped, though the N.B. Locomotive Co. series had a batch from Queensferry interpolated between two batches from Aintree. These engines entered service between June 1925 and March 1926.

The final purchase of 100 engines in February 1927 cleared the dumps at both Gretna (21) and Morecambe (40), the balance of 39 coming from Queensferry. Nos. 6543-6642 were allotted to these engines, this time on a more orderly basis as, although the four manufacturers were again separated, the numerical order of the R.O.D. numbers was followed and the location of the dump whence the engines were obtained was ignored. There was one exception to this rule in that R.O.D. No. 1647 became L.N.E.R. No. 6550 between Nos. 1665 and 1672 (6549 and 6551). The L.N.E.R. was apparently in no hurry to overhaul and send into traffic its latest acquisitions. Beginning in April 1927 fifty-one entered service by the end of that year and forty-four more were dealt with during 1928. The final five (Nos. 6543/5/9/59, 6600) were put into traffic between March and May 1929.

In view of the somewhat haphazard relationship between the successive numbers carried, the engines purchased by the L.N.E.R. are listed in the Appendix in order of their first L.N.E.R. numbers, with their corresponding former R.O.D. numbers and post-1946 numbers. This list also gives their last use and subsequent location of storage prior to selection by the L.N.E.R.

Of the 273 engines purchased by the L.N.E.R., 149 were gradually fitted with round-topped boilers, sixty-one still with Belpaire fireboxes were sent to the Middle East in 1941-42 followed by one more in 1952, leaving sixty-two withdrawn by British Railways in 1959-66 in very much their original condition with small boilers and Belpaire fireboxes. The last unrebuilt engine, No. 63764 (ex-6581 former R.O.D. 1857), was withdrawn in April 1966. Meanwhile class part 3 had been dispensed with from December 1940 and the unrebuilt engines incorporated in class part 1 along with the former G.C. engines.

Scottish Area Engines—Class O4/2

No. 1185.—The N.B.R. had relied entirely on 0-6-0 tender engines to work its heavier goods and mineral traffic, but trials were held during 1921 of a G.W.R. 28XX class 2-8-0 and a N.E.R. three-cylinder 0-8-0 (L.N.E.R. class Q7). Just before Grouping an approach was made by the N.B.R. to the G.C.R. for the loan of a Robinson 2-8-0 for trial. It was realised that modification would be necessary to enable such an engine to clear the rather restricted N.B.R. load gauge and no action was taken until after the L.N.E.R. had been formed. In June 1923 No. 1185 was turned out from Gorton Works specially altered for trial in Scotland (fig. 36). The standard Robinson chimney was replaced by a shorter version 1ft. 3in. high as used on Robinson's large-boilered engines such as class B7 and a new dome cover with flattened top was fitted. Although the maximum height of the cab was 12ft. $8\frac{5}{16}$in., well within gauge, the angle irons used to reinforce the roof were replaced by flat strips and it is probable that the reason for this was that the existing eaves fouled the gauge. The whistle was removed from its position on top of the cab and put on the firebox, whilst short Ross pop safety valves completed the alterations. In this form No. 1185 was sent to Scotland for a trial period of five months. Whilst there it was allocated to Thornton shed and was used on the heavy coal traffic to Aberdeen. Today the existence of this traffic may seem strange but it should be remembered that at that time the considerable Aberdeen deep sea fishing fleet was coal fired. Although the trials with No. 1185 were successful, the engine was returned to Mexborough shed on the G.C. Section in November 1923. Despite the modifications made to it, this engine never returned to Scotland and remained allocated to Mexborough until taken by the War Department in 1941.

Later Engines.—During December 1923 the L.N.E.R. placed its first order for R.O.D. 2-8-0's with the Government and early in 1924 ten of these were earmarked for use in Scotland on the N.B. Section. The engines concerned had arrived at Gorton Works and were shown as taken into L.N.E.R. stock during February. At this time Gorton was under pressure from the work involved in reconditioning the R.O.D.'s in addition to the normal programme of overhauling existing stock. As a result the ten O4's for the N.B. Section were despatched to Darlington Works to be modified in the same way as No. 1185. As with the other ex-R.O.D. 2-8-0's, additional alterations were necessary, the major items being the replacement of the steel inner firebox by a new one made of copper and the replacement of the Westinghouse brake equipment by the steam pattern where applicable. The chimney was the same G.C. pattern, 1ft. 3in. high, fitted to No. 1185 (fig. 52). The side chains and rerailing jacks were removed but initially the R.O.D. pattern buffers with ribbed stocks were retained (fig. 69). A finishing touch by Darlington was the display of the engine classification on the bufferbeam, in this case "CLASS 2.8.0.". The ten reconditioned boilers fitted to these engines were given numbers S1467-76, the S indicating Scottish Area, in the Cowlairs boiler list. In October 1925 the classification O4/2 was allocated to these engines to differentiate them from the rest of class O4.

During the period from October 1928 to March 1929 six more ex-R.O.D. O4's were overhauled and sent to the Scottish Area. These were drawn from the final batch purchased from the Government in February 1927. Like the previous ten engines, they were cut down in height and classified O4/2. This time the work was done at Gorton and was of a similar nature to that carried out on the earlier engines, except that the chimney was an A5-type flowerpot casting, 1ft. 5½in. high (fig. 53). Several of these engines were given the short pattern of safety valves.

Details of the sixteen O4's sent to the Scottish Area are given in the accompanying table. It had been intended to send No. 6582 to the N.E. Area but this engine was exchanged with No. 6549 and sent to Scotland. Cowlairs Works carried out general repairs on the O4's in Scotland until about 1932 when the work was transferred to Gorton. During this period an engine repaired and repainted at Cowlairs could be recognised by the smaller size "L N E R" used by that works on tenders. In later years all sixteen engines received the L.N.E.R./Gorton pattern chimney, 1ft. 5½in. in height, (fig. 72) and standard taller Ross pop safety valves, but the flat reinforcing strips on the cab roof and altered position of the whistle were retained. During the thirties No. 6346 presented a curious appearance by acquiring one tall and one short pop valve. Most of the tenders attached to the O4's in Scotland received extensions to their tender front plates (fig. 55), a feature which they retained after the engines returned to England (see under Tenders).

With the eventual alteration of the whole of the O4 class to clear the L.N.E.R. Composite Load Gauge the need for a separate classification for the Scottish engines disappeared. From December 1946 class part 2 was dispensed with and these engines were incorporated in part 1.

Class O4 Modified for Service in Scottish Area

L.N.E.R. No.		*Into*	*Into*
First	*Second*	*Stock*	*Service*
6286	3880	2/24	8/24
6288	3879	,,	7/24
6290	3847	,,	8/24
6291	3848	,,	8/24
6328	3725	,,	8/24
6346	(3680)*	,,	7/24
6351	3674	,,	8/24
6352	3673	,,	8/24
6370	3653	,,	8/24
6372	3648	,,	8/24
6543	3644	3/29	3/29
6544	3647	10/28	12/28
6548	3682	8/28	10/28
6550	3704	11/28	12/28
6551	(3690)*	12/28	1/29
6582	3766	12/28	1/29

* Nos. 6346 and 6551 were included in the ninety-two engines sent to the Middle East in 1941-42 and therefore did not receive their new numbers.

Gresley Rebuilds — Classes O4/4, O4/5 and O4/7

The earliest known scheme for rebuilding during Gresley's time, was a Gorton proposal in 1927 to apply a boiler having a wide firebox with a grate area of 33 sq. ft. It is not clear whether or not the boiler would have had a round top firebox but this is a fair assumption. This scheme was not pursued.

Between 1929 and 1947 a number of engines were rebuilt with 5ft. 6in. diameter boilers. The first two were fitted with Diagram 2 boilers, as used in class O2, but this necessitated a frame extension at the rear end and a saddle for the smokebox. The next series of rebuilds had a modified O2 boiler, Diagram 15A, which avoided having to alter the frames under the cab. The final series had a shorter derivative, Diagram 15D, which dispensed with the smokebox saddle. The engines which were rebuilt are summarised as follows:-

O4 PART 4
1929 (2): Nos. 6287, 6371
O4 PART 5
1932 (4): Nos. 5008, 6207/32/42
1939 (5): Nos. 6299, 6320, 6500/92, 6606
O4 PART 7
1939 (3): Nos. 5390, 6241,6353
1940 (18): Nos. 5350/78/91, 5405, 6209/23/48/58, 6300/19/52, 6540/73/84/6, 6612/21/33
1941 (3): Nos. 5093, 6337/64
1942 (6): Nos. 5335, 6211/49, 6318/58, 6572
1943 (6): Nos. 5353, 6277/91/5, 6516, 6618
1944 (4): Nos. 6276/86, 6305, 6528
1947 (1): No. 3705

The main dimensions where they differed from the original O4 design are shown in the table on p. 53.

O4/4 ENGINES. — In July 1929 Nos 6287 and 6371 were rebuilt at Gorton with Diagram 2 boilers (fig. 56), as fitted to the Gresley 2-8-0's (see classes O1 and O2), complete with G.N.-pattern pull-out regulator handles working in a horizontal plane. Compared with the normal O4 boilers, they were 2ft. 1⅛in. longer overall and the barrel had two telescopic rings with the diameter over the rear (larger) one 5ft. 6in. The distance between the tubeplates was 15ft. 11⅞in., whilst the outer firebox, which was the round-top type, was 9ft. 0in. long at the bottom. The throatplate sloped back so that the overall length to the commencement of the flange where it joined the barrel was 9ft. 6in. Both these dimensions appeared on the engine diagram. The Robinson superheater had 24 long-loop elements, which increased the superheating surface from 242 sq. ft. in the Diagram 15 type to 430.5 sq. ft. The elements were 1½in. outside diameter and 9 S.W.G. thick (inside diameter approximately 1$\frac{7}{32}$in.). From December 1932 the thickness was reduced to 10 S.W.G. (inside diameter 1.244in.), but reverted to 9 S.W.G. from (officially) November 1944.

What could be regarded as a retrograde step was the arrangement of the firegate, which was horizontal over the back half with a drop of only 8½in. over the front section. These became features too of the final Diagram 100A boiler design, fitted to the O4/8 engines.

The smokebox was very similar to that fitted to the Gresley O2's. The boiler handrails curved round the front of the smokebox and stopped short on the front plate. A G.C. style smokebox door was fitted, complete with wheel and handle fastening, though this was changed later to the twin-handle arrangement (cf. figs. 56 and 57). A short handrail was provided on the door, similar to that on the O5's. The chimney was similar to the type fitted to the O2's, 1ft. 4in. high, but with a slightly larger diameter orifice at the top, 1ft. 4½in. The blastpipe top had a 5⅛in. diameter orifice.

The boilers fitted to Nos. 6287 and 6371 when they were rebuilt were part of a batch of seven constructed at Gorton, the remainder being fitted to O1's and O2's in the normal manner. Diagram 2 boilers were completely interchangeable between these three classes and it is of particular interest to note that when No. 6287 was next reboilered (in April 1934) it received the boiler previously carried by class O1 No. 3470, but which had started work in 1921 on class O2 G.N.R. No. 482.

Due to the provision of these longer boilers, 6in. long extensions were added to the frames below the cab. (Similar considerations were avoided in all later rebuilds by fitting shorter boilers). A cab with a single side window was provided, 4in. wider (at 8ft. 0in.) than the original type, shorter in length and set further back on the frame extension. A further point of difference was the rearward extension of the cab roof, similar to that of the O5's which also had short length cabs. The overall height remained the same as in the unrebuilt O4's. A casing was located in front of the cab, covering the front of the screw reversing gear, but not full depth as in the O5's. The running plate was widened alongside the cab and the reverse running sandboxes were visible below. The coupled wheel splashers were altered in front of the cab, where they now curved down to meet the running plate.

No further engines were rebuilt to class O4/4. No. 6371 was rebuilt by Thompson to class O1 in December 1945, whilst No. 3882 (ex-6287) was rebuilt to class O4/8 in August 1947. In both cases the frame extensions below the cab were removed, but No. 3882 retained its modified splasher arrangement until withdrawn.

O4/5 ENGINES. — Gresley's next rebuild appeared in June 1932. The Diagram 15A boiler fitted was a shortened version of the Diagram 2 boiler used for the O4/4's. The barrel was 7½in. shorter and consequently the distance between the

COMPARATIVE DIMENSIONS OF GRESLEY REBUILDS

Class	O4/4	O4/5	O4/7
Boiler:			
Max. diam. outside	5′ 6″	5′ 6″	5′ 6″
Barrel length	16′ 1⅜″ (a)	15′ 5⅞″ (b)	14′ 6″
Firebox length outside	9′ 6″	9′ 0″	9′ 0″
Pitch	8′ 6½″	8′ 6½″	8′ 6½″
Diagram No.	2	15A	15D
Heating surface (sq. ft.):			
Firebox	163.5	163.2	163.20
Tubes	1340.5	1288.1	1259.20
Flues	528.0	507.3	495.67
Total evap.	2032.0	1958.6	1918.07
Superheater	430.5	406.0	400.80
Total	2462.5	2364.6	2318.67
Tubes	160×2″	160×2″	160×2″
Flues	24×5¼″	24×5¼″	24×5¼″
Elements	24×1¼″	24×1.212″(c)	24×1.244″
Grate area (sq. ft.)	27.5	26.1	26.1
Total wheelbase (engine and tender)	51′ 8½″	51′ 2½″	51′ 2½″
Length over buffers (engine and tender)	62′ 2½″	61′ 8½″	61′ 8½″
Weight (full):			
Engine	73T 6C	74T 13C	73T 17C
Tender	47T 6C	48T 6C	48T 6C
Total	120T 12C	122T 19C	122T 3C
Adhesive	66T 6C	67T 5C	66T 14C
Max. axle load	16T 17C	7T 3C	17T 2C

(a) The engine diagram quoted 15′ 5½″, which was the length of the barrel less the amount by which the smokebox tubeplate was recessed into it.

(b) The engine diagram quoted 14′ 10″, which was the length of the barrel less the amount by which the smokebox tubeplate was recessed into it.

(c) 1.244″ from 12/1932.

Other leading dimensions will be found under "Standard L.N.E.R. Dimensions at Grouping".

tubeplates was reduced to 15ft. 4⅜in. The superheater elements were shorter, reducing their heating surface to 406 sq. ft. The firebox was 6in. shorter in length, which obviated the need to lengthen the frames. A further point of difference was that the grate sloped throughout with a drop of 1ft. 2½in. over its full length, as a result of which the reduction in the firebox heating surface was only marginal (from 163.5 to 163.2 sq. ft.). The G.N.-pattern horizontal regulator handle was again provided. The first boiler was distinguishable by the Doncaster-style wash-out plugs on the firebox side (fig. 58). The next four boilers, including the spare one put into service in 1935, had a combination of wash-out plugs and firebox hand holes (fig. 59). The remaining five boilers had hand holes only.

The original cab was retained (with however the angle irons used to reinforce the roof replaced by flat strips), necessitating the fitting of a "blister" on the right-hand side (fig. 59) to allow operation of the screw reverser, due to the larger diameter boiler. The front spectacle plate was altered to suit the contour of the round top firebox. The reverse running sandboxes remained inside the cab in the 1932 rebuilds, Nos. 5008, 6207/32/42 (fig. 58), but were visible below the cab in the 1939 rebuilds, Nos. 6299, 6320, 6500/92, 6606 (fig. 59).

The smokebox and internal arrangement were similar to those of class O4/4 (cf. figs. 56 and 58). The chimney was also the same pattern but the diameter of the orifice at the top was reduced to 1ft. 3⅞in., the same as that in the Gresley

O2's. The blastpipe top had the same $5\frac{3}{8}$in. diameter orifice.

Altogether ten Diagram 15A boilers were constructed and when they wore out they were not renewed. Seven engines were rebuilt again: No. 3705 (ex-6320) to class O4/7 (further rebuilt after nationalisation to class O4/8), Nos. 63579/89 (ex-6232/42) to class O1 and Nos. 63628, 63726/88, 63816 (ex-5008, 6500/92, 6606) to class O4/8. The remaining two engines, Nos. 63745, 63851 (ex-6207/99), were both withdrawn in April 1959, rendering class O4/5 extinct.

O4/7 Engines. — In February 1938 Doncaster prepared the boiler drawings for the final Gresley rebuilding. The Diagram 15D boiler was a shortened version of the Diagram 15A type used in class O4/5 to facilitate the retention of a G.C. style smokebox and thus avoid the expense of fitting a separate saddle. Compared with class O4/5, the barrel was $11\frac{7}{8}$in. shorter with the front tubeplate no longer recessed into the front ring. As a result the distance between tubeplates was only 4in. less, at 15ft. $0\frac{3}{8}$in. The superheater elements were shorter, reducing the superheating surface to 400.8 sq. ft. The firebox was identical to that of the Diagram 15A boiler. The G.N.-pattern horizontal regulator handle was once more provided.

The smokebox followed G.C. style and was 6ft. $3\frac{1}{2}$in. outside diameter, identical to that of the O5 pattern, though noticeably $11\frac{3}{4}$in. shorter (cf. figs. 42 and 60). As with the class O4/4 and O4/5 rebuilds, the boiler handrails curved round the front of the smokebox and stopped short on the front plate. The door was similar to the by then obsolescent O5 type, with wheel and handle fastening (later changed to twin handles, fig. 60) and horizontal handrail.

The chimney was 1ft. 3in. high, i.e. 1in. shorter than that fitted to the class O4/4 and O4/5 rebuilds on account of the larger diameter smokebox, and was the then standard L.N.E.R./Gorton pattern. The proportions of blastpipe and liner inside the smokebox closely followed those of the unrebuilt O4's, and not those of the previous Gresley rebuilds, being modified only as necessary to take account of the larger smokebox diameter and shorter chimney.

The original cab was retained, with however the angle irons used to reinforce the roof replaced by flat strips. The cab width was unchanged so that, as with class O4/5, a blister had to be provided on the right-hand side to allow operation of the screw reverser. The reverse running sandboxes remained inside the cab, as in the 1932 rebuilds to class O4/5.

Altogether, forty-three engines were rebuilt to class O4/7 between 1939 and 1947, including several undertaken at Stratford Works. The last rebuild, No. 3705 (ex-6320), appeared some three years after general rebuilding to this class part had been superseded by a programme of rebuilding with the Diagram 100A boiler to classes O1 and O4/8. No. 3705 had previously been an O4/5, and afterwards retained its modified rear sandbox arrangement below the cab (fig. 61). Altogether forty-six Diagram 15D boilers were constructed between 1939 and 1943, the last one being put into service in September 1945 on No. 6277.

The O4/7 engines had a more successful career than the other Gresley rebuilds, and only seven were rebuilt again by Thompson: No. 63596 (ex-6249) to class O1, and six others to class O4/8. The other thirty-four engines remained as class O4/7 until withdrawn. The last survivor was No. 63770 (ex-6584), withdrawn in December 1965.

Thompson Rebuilds — Class O4/8

In Thompson's standardisation proposals, one heavy goods 2-8-0 design was envisaged to replace the four classes of 2-8-0, four classes of 0-8-0, the J19, J20 and J38 0-6-0's and other small wheeled engines not covered by the standard 0-6-0 design. The O4 was a natural choice as the basis for the standard 2-8-0 and it was planned to gradually rebuild the Gresley O1's, O2's and the O4's with the standard boiler (Diagram 100A) and also to fit standard cylinders when renewals were necessary. Doncaster continued to build three-cylinder

2-8-0's until early 1943 (class O2), these being the fulfilment of orders placed before the drawing up of the new proposals. Then from late 1943 until mid-1946 almost the entire output from Doncaster was devoted to building L.M.S.-type 2-8-0's (class O6). To these were added the numerous "Austerities" (class O7), both on loan and purchased. Classes O6 and O7 were regarded as stop-gap measures until they could be entirely replaced by the standard engines. This was a formidable proposition and as it turned out the L.N.E.R. standard 2-8-0's (class O1) were well and truly outlived by many of the engines they were intended to supersede.

As early as October 1941, not long after Gresley's death, the first outline drawing appeared for the two-cylinder standard 2-8-0 (see under Thompson class O1) and in July 1943 the outline drawing appeared for the O4 fitted with the standard boiler only (class O4/8). The first rebuild (No. 6281) appeared in April 1944, only two months after the first O1 rebuild. Altogether ninety-nine engines were rebuilt in this manner between 1944 and 1958 (fig. 62), summarised as follows:-

1944 (11):	Nos. 5388, 6205/28/62/81/92/3, 6306, 6522/90, 6609
1947 (5):	Nos. 3633/51/3, 3818/82
1952 (2):	Nos. 63750, 63807
1953 (5):	Nos. 63683, 63703/4/63, 63858
1954 (6):	Nos. 63604/39/44, 63721, 63805/37
1955 (14):	Nos. 63573, 63602/6/12/24/8, 63776, 63816/50/2/73/95/9, 63914
1956 (17):	Nos. 63645/88/91, 63706/18/28/31/2/4/42/91, 63801/41/85/97/8, 63915
1957 (23):	Nos. 63631/6/41/9/55/72/4/5/9, 63720/54/65/88/94, 63800/23/40/61/2/4/77/8/84
1958 (16):	Nos. 63647/97, 63705/9/15/7/26/30/9/41/81/93, 63822/9/32/81

Rebuilding entailed the fitting of a Diagram 100A boiler and double side-window cab. The original cylinders and motion were however retained. In fact it is understood that in the L.N.E.R. period the condition of the cylinders determined the extent of the rebuilding, i.e. to class O1 or O4/8. Minor alterations were however necessary to accommodate the firebox which had a sloping throatplate unlike the vertical type fitted to G.C. engines. A saddle was fitted to carry the drumhead type smokebox. The new cab was 4in. wider, which allowed the screw reverser to be operated without difficulty despite the larger diameter boiler. Rebuilding ceased in 1958, largely due to pressure from the L.M. Region which took over responsibility for Gorton Works from 29th December 1958. Eight of these engines had been previously rebuilt by Gresley: Nos. 3882 (ex-O4/4), 63628 (ex-O4/5), 63655/75, 63705/6/94, 63884 (ex-O4/7). No. 3882, rebuilt in 1947, retained its short splashers, so modified when first rebuilt in 1929, though its frame extension was removed (fig. 63).

The main dimensions where they differed from the original O4 design are summarised as follows:-

Boiler:	
Max. diam. outside	5′ 6″
Barrel length	14′ 1½″ (a)
Firebox length outside	10′ 1½″ (b)
Pitch	8′ 6″
Diagram No.	100A
Heating surface:	
Firebox	168 sq.ft.
Tubes (143 × 2″)	1048 sq.ft.
Flues (24 × 5¼″)	460 sq.ft.
Total evaporative	1676 sq.ft.
Superheater (24 × 1.244″)	344 sq.ft.
Total	2020 sq.ft.
Grate area	27.9 sq.ft.
Length over buffers (engine and tender)	61′ 7¾″
Weight (full):	
Engine	72T 10C
Tender	48T 6C
Total	120T 16C
Adhesive	65T 10C
Max. axle load	16T 18C

(a) The engine diagram quoted the distance between tubeplates, 13′ 11⅞″ (13′ 11½″ from December 1950).

(b) An alternative figure was quoted on the engine diagram, see below.

The boiler had been introduced in 1942 for class B1 and was therefore designed to operate at 225 lb. per sq. in. However when used in class O4/8 the working pressure was reduced to 180 lb. This boiler type was used by Thompson in a number of rebuilds, including classes O1 and O2/4 which are also described in this Part. Full details will be found under class O1 at page 91.

The firebox was basically similar to that of the Diagram 2 boiler, used in class O4/4, but with a sloping back plate and a longer throatplate that sloped back 1ft. 1½in. from the commencement of the flange where it joined the barrel. The length of the casing at the bottom was 9ft. 0in., but allowing for the sloping throatplate the overall length was 10ft. 1½in. The engine diagram showed the overall length as 9ft. 7¼in., taking this measurement from the front of the firebox tubeplate to the extreme back end of the outer casing.

From November 1945 the number of small tubes was reduced from 143 to 141, reducing slightly the heating surface from 1,048 to 1,033 sq. ft. This allowed space for wash-out plugs to be provided on either side of the blastpipe, in place of the single one which was in an awkward place behind it.

The smokebox was similar to that of the Thompson class B1, being 5ft. 9⅜in. outside diameter, i.e. marginally less than that of the original O4 pattern, and was supported on a saddle. The smokebox door was the smaller B1-type, 4ft. 5¼in. diameter, 11ft. 0in. radius curvature, with the centres of the hinge straps 2ft. 0in. apart. The door had the standard twin-handle fastening and there was a small knob on the left-hand side, facing. The boiler handrails curved round the front of the smokebox and circled the door. The chimney was 1ft. 7$\frac{5}{16}$in. high, as fitted also to the Thompson class O1 rebuilds, significantly taller than the chimneys fitted to the earlier Gresley rebuilds, because the Thompson smokebox was smaller in diameter. The blastpipe top had a 5⅛in. diameter orifice.

A double side-window cab was fitted, which was 8ft. 0in. wide outside and 12ft. 10$\frac{9}{16}$in. overall height above rail level. The cab sides were horizontal at the bottom, as the original low running plate was retained, unlike all other classes with Diagram 100A boilers. The reverse running sandboxes were in view below the cab, in common with, for example, classes O4/4 and O4/5 (1939 rebuilds only). The reversing rod was supported on a vertical bracket mounted above the splasher, instead of on the side of the firebox.

Very few alterations were subsequently made to the O4/8's and self-cleaning smokeboxes were never fitted (as they were on the O1's). In the late fifties a number of engines were fitted with chemical water treatment gear, consisting of a blowdown valve on the boiler and provision on the tender for introducing chemicals into the water space. Despite increasing dieselisation, a handful of O4/8's remained in the Doncaster area, and they had the distinction of being the last engines of G.C. design to be withdrawn. Final withdrawals took place in April 1966, these also being amongst the last steam locomotives in the Eastern Region.

Details

The frames were spaced 4ft. 1½in. apart, except ahead of the intermediate (second pair) coupled wheels where they were set 3in. closer to provide adequate clearance for the 21in. diameter cylinders, and were very strong, being 1¼in. thick and braced by the front bufferbeam, pony truck bearer and pivot bracket, cylinder castings, cross beams in front of the driving coupled axle and in front of the firebox, trailing dragbox and rear bufferbeam. The G.C. pattern buffers were 1ft. 8¾in. long overall, including the 1½in. thick packing piece behind the base, with oval shaped heads. Some ex-R.O.D. engines ran for a short time while on the L.N.E.R. with Continental-style ribbed buffers (fig. 69), and one engine at least (No. 6288) ran for a short period with buffers having round heads (fig. 52). By the early thirties the packing piece behind the buffer base was being replaced by a ¾in. thick plate, which reduced the overall length to 1ft. 8in. to conform to Group Standard practice. Another type of buffer with oval head and stepped shank appeared about 1944, which was gradually fitted to a number of O4's (fig. 62) and Thompson class O1 rebuilds.

Three-link couplings were standard, but some O4's and most of the second batch of O5's had screw couplings when new, mainly for running-in purposes on passenger trains in the Manchester area. For the same purpose steam heat fittings were provided on these particular engines, and also on the first batch of O5's which had three-link couplings at the front. No. 966, too, had screw couplings and steam heat fittings whilst modified for burning pulverised coal (fig. 49). The screw couplings were generally replaced by the three-link type, by Grouping in the case of the O4's and subsequently in the case of the O5's, though they were still fitted in B.R. days to former O5's Nos. 63905/8/13. The steam heat fittings were also removed from the O4's at an early date and from the O5's between 1935 and 1939, though in some cases the fixing bracket on the bufferbeam was still in evidence after nationalisation (fig. 46). Screw couplings reappeared on selected engines in L.N.E.R. days, presumably in connection with special passenger workings, for example No. 6188 noted on a race special at Doncaster in September 1929. They were more numerous after nationalisation on engines provided with the vacuum ejector for train braking, and were noted for example on Nos. 63570/4/85/6/7/93, 63603/11/3/4/22/35/93, 63840, 63905/6/8/12/3/7/20. No. 63574 had this fitting when it worked a Sheffield-Manchester express to Penistone on 28th August 1954, and No. 63585 when it appeared on a rail tour in the Retford-Doncaster area on 12th October 1963 (fig. 77).

In the mid-thirties when class O5 Nos. 5420/1 were employed at Whitemoor as hump shunters, their drawgear was modified to prevent the drawbar between engine and tender being damaged when passing over the crest of the hump. Their dragboxes were altered at Cambridge shed. In addition, several O4's at March were similarly altered so that they could deputise for the O5's and for the class S1 0-8-4T's. Nos. 5420/1 were afterwards replaced on this duty by Nos. 5011 and 5414 (both by then rebuilt to class O4). No. 5414 at least is known to have had its dragbox altered.

In February and March 1934 ten O4's, Nos. 5350/82/6, 5412, 6280/5 6316/66, 6561 and 6625, had the clearance of their spring gear altered to clear the Frölich rail-brakes in Whitemoor yard. None of these engines was allocated to March and one, No. 6625, was from as far away as Gorton.

The axleboxes and horn guides originally had simple siphon lubrication. In October 1932 the sub-committee investigating the incidence of hot axleboxes recommended the trial fitting of the "Twin Plunger" mechanical lubricator, manufactured by Empire Engineering Co., Manchester, and largely used for diesel, gas and oil engines with successful results. Gresley however stated that in view of the satisfactory results obtained from the Wakefield Fountain siphon-feed lubricator fitted to selected B17's and D49's, he wished this method to be tried out on the O4's and to defer for the time being trials with the Empire type. During 1933-34 several O4's were fitted with two four-feed Fountain lubricators in the cab, including Nos. 5400 and 6359 (fig. 54). A distinctive feature of this system was the feed pipes running horizontally alongside the firebox and boiler, with U-shaped bends above the coupling wheels incorporating air inlets which revealed any blockage in the pipe at the axlebox end by emitting oil. Then during 1934 ten engines, Nos. 6255/83, 6362/8, 6521/3/4/97, 6605/17, were fitted with the Empire lubricator, and six engines, Nos. 5390, 6213/8/26, 6343, 6596, were provided with the Wakefield No. 2C mechanical lubricator. An improved Fountain lubricator was introduced in December 1935 on No. 5133. Eventually more than a hundred O4's were fitted with the new Fountain type. From 1943, the air inlet was dispensed with, the feed pipes were located lower down alongside the firebox just above the splasher, and test valves were provided close to the axleboxes between the frames.

The cylinders were 21in. diameter by 26in. stroke, these being proportions which eventually became standard in several G.C. classes of 4-6-0's, 4-4-2's and 0-8-0's. An entry in the Gorton drawing office register, dated 9th February 1917, covers the fitting of $19\frac{3}{4}$in. diameter cylinders to No. 1203, for which no explanation was given, and nothing further is known about this.

Each cylinder and its steam chest were machined from a single casting. The steam chest was passed through a hole cut in the frame, and the flange on the casting was then bolted to the frame around this hole. The two separate castings were then bolted together to form a rigid brace for the frames at the front end. The cylinders were inclined at 1 in 24 from the horizontal, and the drive was on to the third coupled axle. The pistons had tail rod extensions, but these were eventually removed (cf. figs. 35 and 36). (It is probable that one or two had their extensions removed prior to Grouping). The steam chests were inclined at 1 in 15, and the 10in. diameter piston valves, which were operated by Stephenson link motion between the frames, had a maximum travel of $4\frac{19}{64}$in. at $74\frac{3}{4}$ per cent cut-off.

The original G.C. broad ring piston valves were replaced by the multi-ring (Knorr) type, which remedied the problem of steam leaking passed the valves after running a high mileage. No. 1210 was fitted first, in September 1914, though it appears that no others were altered until after Grouping. The Knorr type was then gradually fitted to the O4's and O5's, mainly between 1934 and 1948.

The engines built between 1911 and 1914 had a Wakefield mechanical lubricator for cylinder and valve lubrication, mounted on the left-hand side running plate. From about 1917 a number were fitted instead with Robinson's Intensifore sight-feed lubricator in the cab, with vertical retention valves in view on the running plate above the cylinders. The O5's were also provided with this type of lubricator when new (fig. 41), as were the later R.O.D. engines (see p. 46) including the three purchased by the G.C.R. in 1919, L.N.E.R. Nos. 5001/5/8. This lubricator comprised a large vertical intensifier, which incorporated an oil reservoir for topping-up purposes and an oil chamber with a piston that lifted to draw oil from the reservoir into the chamber and then lowered to force oil under pressure to the sight-feed distributor, from which feeds led to the cylinders and valves via the retention valves mentioned earlier. Steam from the boiler was the normal method of providing pressure, but many of the later R.O.D. engines had a horizontal intensifier, controlled by air from the Westinghouse pump. Evidence from the Gorton records respecting the later R.O.D. engines, many of which worked on the G.C.R. in 1919-21, suggests that R.O.D. No. 2068-2107 were possibly fitted with the air-operated type, confirmed in the case of Nos. 2068 and 2107, whilst other engines in this range, e.g. Nos. 2095/6/7, 2102/5/6, appear to have been altered by the G.C.R. from air-operated to conventional steam-operated. The L.N.E.R. gradually replaced the Intensifore lubricators, generally by either the Wakefield Eureka or the Vacuum Detroit hydrostatic sight-feed type. Externally, the altered engines were distinguishable by the four oil feed pipes, which ran alongside the boiler barrel from the cab to the smokebox (fig. 58). In addition, the Intensifore retention valves above each cylinder were replaced by a single choke-plug of a different shape. (The choke-plugs for the steam chests were out of sight between the frames). One or two engines were also altered from mechanical lubrication to sight-feed, including Nos. 6336/71 (fig. 56). At the end of 1932 there were still seventy-two engines with Intensifore lubricators, made up of fifty-seven O4's, including forty-nine ex-R.O.D., and fifteen unrebuilt O5's. All were then quickly altered to the Wakefield mechanical type, the final O5 being altered in May 1937 and the last O4 three months later.

Gravity sanders were provided for forward running, in front of the leading and driving coupled wheels, and for reverse running behind the trailing coupled wheels. The tenders also had sanders, which operated in front of the first pair of wheels, but these were gradually dispensed with by the L.N.E.R., the process being completed about 1944. In the early thirties concern was being expressed at the possibility of sand interfering with track circuiting, and selected O4's and O5's were involved in a number of experiments with rail washing gear. Class O4 No. 6304 was fitted first, in June 1932, followed by class O5 Nos. 5420/1 in March and May 1933 respectively, in connection with their use at Whitemoor Yard. A pipe, which led down to a point behind the trailing coupled wheels, emitted water to clean the rails after the sand had served its purpose, and a similar pipe was located in front of the leading coupled wheels for the same purpose when running tender first.

O4 Engines. – The Diagram 15 boiler fitted to the original engines was also used in a number of other ex-G.C. classes: B5 (No. 5184 only), C4, C5 and S1. The boiler was designed for a pressure of 200 lb. per sq. in., but worked at the lower 180 lb. The barrel was constructed with three telescopic rings. The diameter over the largest one was 5ft. 0in., whilst that over the front ring was 4ft. 9½in. The distance between the tubeplates was 15ft. 4⅜in., later reduced to 15ft. 4¼in. when a thicker firebox tubeplate (1in. instead of ⅞in.) was fitted. The inner firebox was made of $\frac{9}{16}$in. copper plate throughout, except for the tubeplate which was ⅞in. (later 1in.). The outer firebox, which was the Belpaire type, was 8ft. 6in. long, with vertical throat and back plates. The grate sloped steeply, dropping 1ft. 2½in. over its length. The standard superheater fitted in L.N.E.R. days was the Robinson pattern, with 22 short-loop elements arranged in three rows of six, eight and eight respectively. The elements were 1⅜in. outside diameter and 9 S.W.G. thick. From December 1932 the thickness was reduced to 10 S.W.G., but reverted to 9 S.W.G. from (officially) November 1944. The engine diagram always showed the inside diameter as 1$\frac{1}{16}$in.

The smokebox door was secured by wheel and handle though this was changed to the twin-handle arrangement in the late forties (cf. figs. 39 and 40). There was a small footstep on the front plate, left-hand side facing. The boiler handrail circled the smokebox door and the upper lampiron was on the smokebox top. From June 1948 onwards the upper lampiron was fitted lower down on the door itself (cf. figs. 54 and 55).

At first, superheater dampers were provided to protect the elements from overheating, operated by a steam cylinder on the left-hand side of the smokebox, and all twenty engines of the first batch were so fitted. Later engines built up to 1914 had Robinson's draught retarder instead, which was recognisable by the steam valve on the left-hand side of the smokebox. Both arrangements were superseded from about 1917 by Robinson's combined blower and circulating valve under the driver's control. This had two opening positions. Either the blower could be operated alone, supplying live steam to the top of the blastpipe to draw the fire when the regulator was closed, or the blower could be operated at the same time that live steam was admitted to the saturated side of the header to circulate through the elements to prevent them overheating and also to prevent a vacuum being created which could draw smokebox ashes down the blastpipe into the steam chest. In conjunction with the combined blower and circulating valve, which it will be noted applied live steam to the header, Robinson's header discharge valve was fitted on the left-hand side of the smokebox (fig. 41). This automatically opened when the regulator handle was closed, to which it was linked by rodding that passed through the handrail along the left-hand side of the boiler, and so connected the superheated side of the header to the base of the blastpipe, bypassing the steam chest and cylinders.

The L.N.E.R. very quickly removed the header discharge valves though it is not known if the steam circulating facility was dispensed with at the same time. Gresley anti-vacuum valves were then fitted to the header, which automatically opened to the atmosphere when the regulator was closed, admitting air to the elements to prevent them overheating and to prevent a vacuum being created (fig. 39). However there were one or two engines in 1946-47 which had still to acquire anti-vacuum valves, although the other forms of element protection had long since been removed.

Top feed was introduced on the last batch of engines built at Gorton in 1913-14, Nos. 385-99, 271. In later years it was applied also to the earlier engines of the class, to Nos. 1, 5 and 8 purchased by the G.C.R. in 1919, and to the O5's when new (fig. 41). The clack valves for the top feed were mounted in a casing located on top of the boiler between chimney and dome, the feed pipe itself being hidden underneath the boiler clothing plate. The L.N.E.R. did not favour this arrangement and the engines lost this apparatus shortly after Grouping. In mid-1926 it was recorded that there were only nine O4's and eleven O5's still fitted (fig. 67) and these had probably all been altered by 1930.

In June 1921 No. 1234 was fitted with the Caille-Potonie feed water heater. A large diameter exhaust steam pipe left the smokebox on the left-hand side low down just in front of the tubeplate, ran back parallel to the running plate, passed through the splasher just in front of the cab and entered a box-shaped heater under the cab. Pre-heated water then entered the boiler through the top-feed arrangement. The whole apparatus was removed in December 1923.

Ross pop safety valves began to appear about 1919, but it is thought that few engines had been altered by Grouping, though ultimately all the original O4's were fitted to bring them into line with the ex-R.O.D. engines and the O5's, all of which had them when built. The original arrangement on the G.C.-built O4's had been four Ramsbottom valves in a rectangular casing (cf. figs. 65 and 36).

The original cabs on the O4's were 7ft. 8in. wide, simply laid out for right-hand drive. The cab sides had a large semi-circular cut-out with a full length vertical handrail. The forward view was good, with a large contoured spectacle on each side of the shoulder of the Belpaire firebox and a small square-shaped glass below. The cab roof was strengthened with strips of curved angle-iron and the overall height above rail level to the top was 12ft. $8\frac{5}{16}$in. The cab roofs on the engines altered for service in Scotland (see class O4/2, p. 50) had their angle-iron reinforcing strips altered to plain flat strips, as their outer edges at the eaves just fouled the N.B. Section load gauge. This reduced the overall helght by $1\frac{1}{8}$in. (fig. 69).

The width over the running plate was 8ft. 3in., except over the cylinders where it was 8ft. $9\frac{1}{2}$in. (fig. 69). The angle-iron below the running plate followed the same contour, with a set in it to clear the cylinder casing. Additional footsteps were provided at first, mid-way along this angle-iron, with a hand grip above the splasher close to the sandbox filler hole; these footsteps were removed at a later date (cf. figs. 35 and 37). A single step was provided on the cross-head slide bar support bracket, with a hand grip above the running plate. From 1929 a substantial support plate with two steps was attached to this bracket instead (figs. 35 and 37).

The sandboxes for reverse running were located inside the cab. However in L.N.E.R. days No. 6188 was noted in September 1929 with the sandboxes in view below the cab, as arranged for example in the O5's.

ENGINE NO. 966.—At Grouping this engine carried a large diameter boiler in connection with the pulverised fuel experiments already described on page 44 (fig. 49). A special double side-window cab was provided, 8ft. 5in. wide, and a tall casing was located in front of it on the right-hand side, covering the screw reversing gear. The sandboxes for reverse running were in view below the cab, as on the O5's which also had large diameter boilers which restricted the room for them inside the cab. The running plate was widened alongside the cab. When No. 5966 reverted to a standard O4 in 1924, it lost its side-window cab and widened running plate, but retained its outside sandboxes.

O5 ENGINES. – The Diagram 15B boiler fitted to the O5's was also used in class B6. Like the O4, the barrel was made of three telescopic rings, the diameter of these being 6in. larger than the O4 boiler. Other dimensions, e.g. distance between tubeplates, length of firebox and slope of grate, were the same. The normal superheater provided was the Robinson pattern, with 28 short-loop elements arranged in four rows of seven each. The elements were $1\frac{3}{8}$in. outside diameter and 9 S.W.G. thick. From December 1932 the thickness was reduced to 10 S.W.G. As with class O4, all engine diagrams showed the inside diameter as $1\frac{1}{16}$in.

The smokebox door was secured by the usual wheel and handle arrangement (fig. 41). Above the door centre was a handrail, 3ft. 4in. between pillar centres, which was not provided on the O4's. The boiler handrail circled the smokebox door and the top stanchion served to secure the upper lampiron.

The original chimney was a handsome casting, 1ft. 3in. high, which was gradually replaced after Grouping by a Doncaster-style "plant pot" chimney having the same height as before (cf. figs. 41 and 42). Later, a Gresley anti-vacuum valve was fitted, located behind the chimney (fig. 43). The blastpipe top had a $5\frac{3}{8}$in. diameter orifice.

The roof stays in the Diagram 15B boiler were pitched $\frac{3}{8}$in. closer than in the original O4 boiler, and there was an extra row (twenty-one instead of twenty). This necessitated a re-arrangement of the firebox hand holes and wash-out plugs above the handrail. In particular the rear hand hole on the left-hand side was located further back, in consequence of which the cab was 5in. shorter than that of the O4's. The cab was 7in. wider, at 8ft. 3in., because of the larger diameter boiler, and the overall height was 13ft. $1\frac{1}{2}$in. above rail level. One large spectacle on each side of the Belpaire firebox replaced the two separate ones in the O4's. Due to the provision of a shorter cab, a tall casing was located in front of it on the right-hand side, to cover the screw reversing gear (fig. 42). The last five O5's had a double side-window cab with extended roof. The sandboxes for reverse running were in view below the cab, whereas on the O4's they had been located inside the cab. The overall width over the running plate was 8ft. 9in. from the cylinders back, and 8ft. 3in. for the short portion at the front end. All these features were retained when the engines were rebuilt with Diagram 15 boilers to class O4.

At first footsteps were provided mid-way along the running plate and these (together with the cab footsteps) gave the impression of being set further in, due to the angle-iron above being further from the frame to match the running plate. The additional footsteps were dispensed with at a later date, possibly for reasons of safety. A single step was provided on the cross-head support bracket, with a hand grip above the running plate. From 1929 a substantial support plate with two steps was attached to this bracket instead.

Brakes

The engines built for the G.C.R. (both class O4 and O5) were equipped with steam brake on engine and tender, and with vacuum ejector for train braking (fig. 35). The only exceptions were the three O4's which became L.N.E.R. Nos. 5001/5/8, built to Government order and purchased in 1919. These had been built to the final specification for the R.O.D. engines and had Westinghouse brake for engine and train. Early photographs show them with pumps removed, but retaining the air tanks and brake cylinders below the cab and also with the hose connections at the front end. It is presumed that steam brakes were fitted before these engines went into service on the G.C.R. and it is known that the standard arrangement of steam brake with vacuum ejector was carried at the time they entered L.N.E.R. stock. It therefore seems likely that the change was made when they received their first heavy overhauls during 1921.

As recorded on page 46, the engines built to Government order for the R.O.D. all had Westinghouse pumps (fig. 50). In the first arrangement steam brakes were fitted to engine and tender and the air brake was for train braking, 233 engines being in this form. The remaining 288 had Westinghouse brake for engine and train. All the engines purchased by the L.N.E.R. had the Westinghouse equipment removed and, where required, steam brake substituted. Vacuum ejectors were not fitted, so there was no provision for train braking (fig. 52). Of the first 125 engines ordered in December 1923, a number retained the Westinghouse equipment for a short time (fig 51), but those

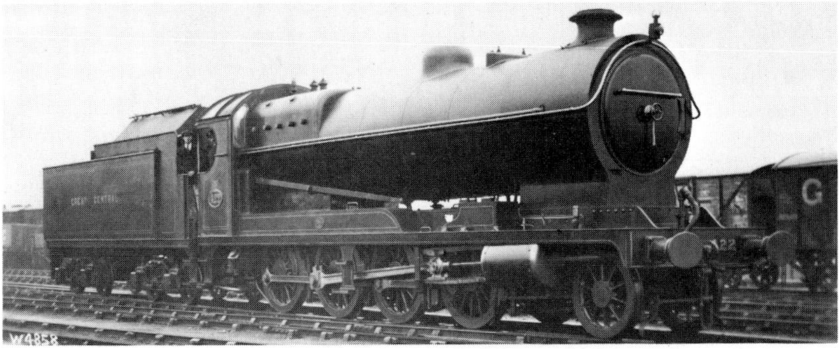

Fig. 47 Class O5 G.C.R. No. 422 at Guide Bridge, about 1921.

Fitted for burning pulverised coal, special bogie tender.

Fig. 48 Class O5 G.C.R. No. 420 on local passenger train at Guide Bridge, about 1920.

Fitted for burning Colloidal fuel.

Fig. 49 Class O4 G.C.R. No. 966 at Guide Bridge, about 1922.

Special 6ft. 0in. diameter boiler, fitted for burning pulverised fuel, double side-window cab with rear sandbox in view below, screw coupling and steam heating hose, special bogie tender from No. 422.

Fig. 50 Class O4 R.O.D. No. 2112, about 1920.

On loan to G.C.R., afterwards purchased from Government as L.N.E.R. No. 6286. Westinghouse pump, Intensifore sight-feed lubricator, Continental style buffers, rerailing jacks on running plate, "GREAT CENTRAL" displayed on tender.

Fig. 51 Class O4 No. 6313 at Colwick shed, about 1924.

Retaining Westinghouse pump on smokebox side and air brake reservoir below cab.

Fig. 52 Class O4/2 No. 6288 at Thornton, April 1927.

Steam brake and no vacuum ejector, B7-type 1ft. 3in. chimney, round headed buffers.

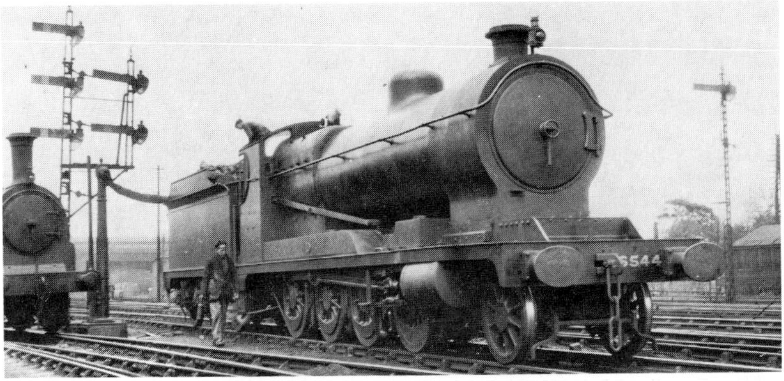

Fig. 53 Class O4/2 No. 6544 at Perth, about 1932.

A5-type 1ft. 5½in. flowerpot chimney, oval headed buffers.

Fig. 54 Class O4/3 No. 6359 at Lincoln shed, about 1937.

L.N.E.R./Gorton 1ft. 5½in. plain waisted chimney, Fountain lubricator for axleboxes, upper lampiron on top of smokebox.

Fig. 55 Class O4/1 No. 63847 at Staveley shed, June 1954.

Upper lampiron on smokebox door, tender with extended front plate.

Fig. 56 Class O4/4 No. 6371 at Doncaster shed, about 1936.

Rebuilt with Diagram 2 boiler. Frame extension at rear, modified splashers, single side-window cab, O2-type 1ft. 4in. chimney, wheel and handle fastening for smokebox door, sight-feed lubricator for cylinders.

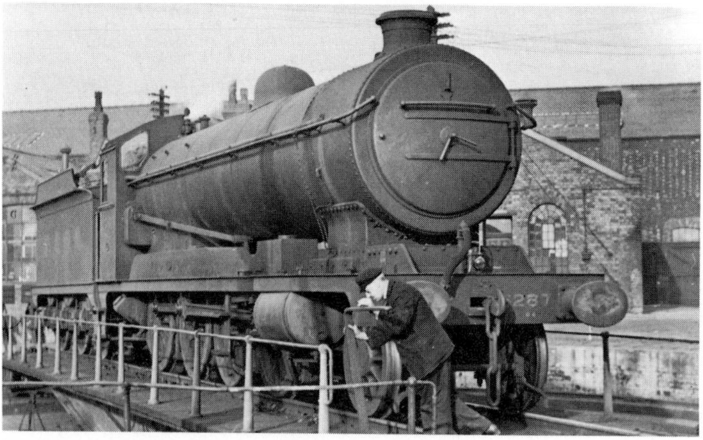

Fig. 57 Class O4/4 No. 6287 at Gorton shed, April 1939.

Vacuum ejector for train braking, twin-handle fastening for smokebox door.

Fig. 58 Class O4/5 No. 5008 at Doncaster shed, about 1932.

Rebuilt with Diagram 15A boiler. O2-type chimney, wash-out plugs on side of firebox, rear sandboxes remaining inside the cab, oil feed pipes for cylinders running alongside boiler from cab.

purchased subsequently were all altered prior to entering service on the L.N.E.R.

Subsequent rebuilding by the L.N.E.R. produced some variations in the above mentioned braking arrangements. The two class O4/4 engines (Nos. 6287 and 6371) rebuilt as such in 1929, were given vacuum ejectors (fig. 57) despite both being from the ex-R.O.D. series. However, when both were later rebuilt again, one to class O4/8 and the other to O1, the vacuum ejectors were removed. The other Gresley rebuilds, to O4/5 and O4/7, all retained their existing braking arrangements, i.e. steam and vacuum on the ex-G.C.R. engines and steam only for the ex-R.O.D. engines. Thompson's rebuilds to classes O4/8 and O1 had steam brake only, and this meant that the former G.C.R. engines lost their train brakes. Eventually, some O1's were given vacuum ejectors in B.R. days (see page 92).

Tenders

Robinson's standard 4,000-gallon tender was attached initially to all the class O4 and O5 engines. Those constructed for the G.C.R. had water pick-up gear whereas all the ex-R.O.D. tenders (including those attached to Nos. 5001/5/8) were without this fitment. Without pick-up the coal capacity was quoted as 7 tons against 6 tons for the G.C.-built tenders, and the laden weight of the R.O.D. tenders was about 49 tons, although only the weight of the G.C. version (48 tons 6 cwt.) was shown on the L.N.E.R. engine diagrams. In March 1946 authority was given to remove the pick-up gear from the tenders of the G.C.-built O4's. Whether or not all were dealt with is not known.

At Grouping three former G.C.R. engines were running with Robinson's smaller standard tender which held 3,250 gallons of water and 6 tons of coal. During 1923-25 4,000-gallon tenders were substituted. At first, the engines concerned were separately classified O4/2 whilst attached to the small tenders, but they were incorporated in O4/1 from December 1924. The classification O4/2 was later re-used to cover the engines cut down in height for use in Scotland (see page 50). Details of the engines with 3,250-gallon tenders were as follows:-

Engine No.	*3,250-gallon tender attached*
377	3/21 to 7/23
380	11/20 to 10/25
383	10/20 to 7/25

A number of O4's were at one time or another attached to an early variant of 4,000-gallon tender, which originally had four coal rails instead of sheet metal guards. From 1910 the rails were gradually plated over; tenders dealt with prior to 1923 appear to have been plated on the outside whilst the L.N.E.R. plated them on the inside, leaving the rails visible. From July 1929 to August 1942 No. 5385 had one of these tenders, previously attached to class J11 No. 5307 and which still had open rails when transferred to the O4. Several tenders with their rails plated on the outside (recognisable by the absence of beading around the edge), and mainly from classes C4, D9, J11 and Q4, were afterwards attached to O4's, e.g. Nos. 3628 and E3680 (fig. 40). Two tenders were latterly noted with their rails plated on the inside; one was from a C4 and attached successively to Nos. 63838, 63624, 63882 (and possibly finally to No. 63721), the other was from a D9 and was with No. 5001 (latterly 63626) from September 1940 to September 1952.

At Grouping No. 966 was attached to a bogie tender in connection with pulverised fuel experiments (fig. 49). This tender is described in the appropriate section on page 43.

The tenders with the O5's at March for hump shunting in the thirties, Nos. 5420/1, had a frame at the front (fig. 43), presumably to take a tarpaulin for added protection for the crew. Most of the tenders with the O4's working in Scotland had an extension added to the front plate (fig. 55), presumably to permit more coal to be carried, which was particularly desirable on the workings to Aberdeen. These extensions were retained after the engines returned south to England. As late as 1961 class O4/8 Nos. 63674/5, 63754, 63816 stationed at Colwick were given full-height tender weatherboards. The top edge of the weatherboard had the same contour as the cab roof and twin circular spectacle glasses were provided. It is understood that this addition to the tenders was made at the request of the enginemen to improve conditions when running light tender first to Highdyke to work iron ore trains to Stanton Ironworks.

Loans to G.W.R. 1940-43

During the War, in November 1940, thirty O4's were transferred on loan to the G.W.R. Most of the engines were in original Belpaire firebox condition but eight had been fitted with round topped boilers, seven being newly rebuilt Part 7 engines whilst the remaining engine (No.

6232) was a Part 5 having been rebuilt in 1932. The G.W.R. enginemen were of course no strangers to the O4's since they already had fifty 30XX class 2-8-0's of R.O.D. origin. The G.W.R. based the engines mainly in the Wolverhampton Division where Oxley shed had fourteen, with smaller numbers at Southall and Bristol. In April 1941 Nos. 6232/6 were returned to the L.N.E.R. at Sheffield but the reason for their early return is not known, although it should be noted that No. 6232 was the Part 5 engine. The remaining engines stayed on the G.W.R until 1942 when ten were returned, followed in 1943 by the other eighteen. The twenty-eight engines returned in 1942-43, with the exception of three sent to Gorton, were transferred to Woodford, but their stay at the latter shed was short following the arrival of the U.S. Army class S160 2-8-0's from April 1943. The dates the engines were on loan to the G.W.R. are summarised in the accompanying table.

L.N.E.R.	*On Loan to G.W.R.*	
No.	*From*	*To*
5391	11/40	7/42
5393	11/40	1/43
6205	11/40	7/42
6209	11/40	8/42
6220	11/40	2/43
6231	11/40	1/43
6232	11/40	4/41
6236	11/40	4/41
6245	11/40	2/43
6258	11/40	7/42
6265	11/40	1/43
6275	11/40	1/43
6277	11/40	2/43
6295	11/40	1/43
6321	11/40	1/43
6336	11/40	2/43
6350	11/40	2/43
6365	11/40	1/43
6524	11/40	1/43
6540	11/40	7/42
6562	11/40	1/43
6566	11/40	1/43
6573	11/40	7/42
6586	11/40	7/42
6594	11/40	2/43
6595	11/40	2/43
6621	11/40	7/42
6629	11/40	7/42
6633	11/40	1/43
6639	11/40	7/42

Government Requisitions 1939-45

The outbreak of War in September 1939 meant that for the second time a British Expeditionary Force would be sent across the Channel to France and, with memories of 1914-18 still in the minds of the Army Staff, plans were laid to cover engine requirements for the Royal Engineers. The L.N.E.R. was informed that 300 O4's would be required for overseas service and in return the L.N.E.R. agreed to replace them with 250 O2's and fifty further engines of a type not specified, all to be provided at Government expense. In November 1939 the proposal was cancelled and in the light of subsequent events in France, there is no doubt that had the engines been sent there, the subsequent history of class O4 would have been vastly different. By the time that Gorton Works was advised on 27th November that the arrangements had been cancelled, thirty-six engines had been repaired: Nos. 5347/9/75/86/92, 6186/7/9, 6211/4/35/72/3/5/88/91/7, 6327/38/44/6/58/69, 6507/12/27/41/53/60/3/72/89/99, 6607/27/34. Items of repair included new tyres, wheels or fireboxes, and depended on the condition of the engine concerned. A further engine, No. 6286, was to have received a new firebox under this scheme. In addition, twenty engines were ear-marked for which no repairs were needed: Nos. 5271, 5346/82, 6184/97, 6212/47/51/5/66/71, 6312/23/9/55, 6518/31/50/68, 6641. Preparation for overseas service was to have included the fitting of Westinghouse brake and steam heat connections with Continental type couplings. However when on 21st November 1939 the L.N.E.R. supplied a list of the first forty O4's which would be ready to go to France on 1st January 1940, it had to be pointed out the Westinghouse brake was not fitted as no materials had been received, and steam heating equipment was not fitted as no information had been received regarding the supply of Continental hose couplings.

In 1941, in order to supply our Russian allies, an overland supply route was opened up through Persia. To operate this route, 150 engines were to be released by Britain's railways, including ninety-two O4's. In the event, it was decided to send the newer L.M.S. class 8F 2-8-0's to Persia, and the O4's were redirected to Egypt and Palestine. Preliminary arrangements were made at a meeting held at the Ministry of War Transport on 5th September 1941 for the L.N.E.R. to supply these O4's as a matter of urgency. The main stipulations were that the mileages were not to exceed 20,000 since last general repair, the boilers were to be good with at least two years anticipated service before next overhaul, coupled wheel tyres to be not less than 2¼in. except that in a few cases 2in. would be accepted, engines to be given two coats of grey paint, L.N.E.R. number plates to be left on the cab sides, otherwise no numbering would be displayed. Later, Gorton was instructed to number the engines 700-91, in the order they were dealt with, with the numbers on front and rear bufferbeams only, in 1½ in. high matt golden yellow numerals. The target dates for despatch from Gorton Works were optimistic and not met. The first six had to be sent by 9th September, to be at Glasgow by the 16th. The next twelve had to be sent by the 13th, to be at Birkenhead by the 16th. Four more were to arrive at Birkenhead by the 28th, two at Glasgow by the 29th and the remainder to be available before the end of the first week in October for destinations to be advised later. There were a number of O4's already in Gorton Works when the instructions were received, but it was anticipated that a large number would be taken straight from traffic with just the paintwork to be dealt with speedily at Gorton. To facilitate necessary repairs, two O4's (Nos. 6234 and 6635) were immediately set aside at Gorton Works on 9th September to be stripped as necessary to provide spare parts. Engines were examined in traffic and where suitable they were directed to Gorton. Seven were rejected and returned to traffic on 12th September, these being Nos. 5353/77, 6246/71, 6523/5, 6641. A further six, Nos. 6224/91, 6372/6, 6538/67, were rejected the next day. Nos. 6276 and 6320 were also rejected at about this time. In addition, No. 6534 (of Frodingham) was to have been considered, but was laid up at the time on York shed with a hot axlebox.

After preparation at Gorton the engines were forwarded to the ports of embarkation, usually in pairs with one engine in steam and with additional wagons conveying spare parts. The first despatches were made on 11th September, No. 700 hauling No. 701 to Birkenhead Docks where they were loaded in the *Perthshire*. The first despatches to Glasgow were Nos. 711 (in steam) and 714/6 (both dead) on 15th September. The route taken to Glasgow was via York and Edinburgh, so that almost the entire journey was made over L.N.E.R. metals. Several engines were despatched to Greenock, following the same route as those for quays at Glasgow, but then handed over to the L.M.S. at St. Johns (Glasgow) for the final part of the journey. In addition to Birkenhead, a further Mersey port to receive these engines was Ellesmere Port. Others were sent to South Wales, to docks at Cardiff, Penarth and Swansea, travelling via the C.L.C. route to Chester, thence over the Great Western Railway via Shrewsbury. The only east coast port used was Hull, which handled four engines.

By the end of the first week in October 1941, when it had been intended that all the engines should have been despatched, only Nos. 700-21/3/4/5 had left Gorton, and in fact the last of these had been sent on 23rd September. Despatches were resumed on 8th October and by the end of the month Nos. 722/6-61/3/5/7 had been sent, which was quite an achievement. None was sent during November and only Nos. 766/8-74/81/2 in the first half of December. The last two to be sent in 1941 were Nos. 783/7 which left Gorton on Boxing Day, bound for Glasgow. Departure was at 10-35 a.m., with a recorded arrival at York at 5-0 p.m., by which time the dead engine, No. 783, was showing a marked tendency to run hot. By the time the engines reached Newcastle at 3-0 a.m. next morning, the trouble was causing more concern but they managed to reach Eastfield shed at 7-45 p.m. that evening. The trouble was caused by the cold weather and the Wakefield Fountain lubricator fitted to this engine not being operable when the engine was not in steam. Following this incident it was decided that as far as possible, engines fitted with Fountain lubricators should run in steam to avoid this difficulty. During January 1942, Nos. 762/4/75-9/84/5/6/8-91 were despatched from Gorton and finally No. 780 left on 3rd February for Swansea.

The ninety-two O4's were all engines with Belpaire fireboxes and Diagram 15 boilers, including no fewer than six original O5's, two of which were rebuilt at the time of preparation for war service and thus never ran on the L.N.E.R. as O4's. These were Nos. 733/81 (ex-5420/1). The engines were taken from sheds throughout the L.N.E.R. system, with the emphasis of course on the Southern Area (Western Section) which lost seventy-four. The Eastern Section provided nine, the North Eastern Area seven and two were from Scotland. They were a mixture of former R.O.D. engines from World War I (sixty-one) and G.C. built engines (thirty-one). The former had steam brake only and it was only in November 1941 that this fact came to light at the War Office. Instructions were then given that the ex-R.O.D. engines were to be fitted with vacuum brake equipment for train braking. This explains the lull in despatches at about this time, and the

W.D. No. (a)	*L.N.E.R. No.*	*Out of Traffic* (b)	*W.D. No.* (a)	*L.N.E.R. No.*	*Out of Traffic* (b)	*W.D. No.* (a)	*L.N.E.R. No.*	*Out of Traffic* (b)
700	6549	9/41	731	6345	9/41	762	6377	9/41
701	6196	9/41	732	6225	9/41	763	5376	9/41
702	6557	9/41	733	5420	9/41	764	6605	9/41
703	6279	9/41	734	6599	9/41	765	6580	9/41
704	6509	9/41	735	6504	9/41	766	5017	10/41
705	6239	9/41	736	6217	9/41	767	5346	10/41
706	6497	9/41	737	6204	9/41	768	5375	10/41
707	6597	9/41	738	6547	10/41	769	5402	10/41
708	6560	9/41	739	6202	9/41 (c)	770	5413	11/41
709	6565	9/41	740	6335	9/41 (c)	771	6197	10/41
710	6301	9/41	741	6551	9/41	772	6230	10/41
711	5383	9/41	742	6569	9/41	773	6235	10/41
712	6499	9/41	743	6369	9/41	774	6247	10/41
713	5382	9/41	744	6330	9/41	775	6260	10/41
714	6183	9/41	745	6593	9/41	776	6273	10/41
715	6368	9/41	746	5392	9/41	777	6266	10/41
716	6623	9/41	747	6233	9/41	778	6312	10/41
717	6339	9/41	748	6537	9/41	779	6362	10/41
718	6600	9/41	749	6613	9/41	780	6602	10/41
719	6212	9/41	750	6508	10/41	781	5421	10/41
720	6355	9/41	751	6541	9/41	782	6251	10/41
721	5019	9/41	752	6322	9/41	783	6563	10/41
722	6607	9/41	753	6348	10/41	784	6317	10/41
723	6520	9/41	754	6340	10/41	785	6297	10/41
724	5354	9/41	755	6332	9/41	786	6628	10/41
725	6514	9/41	756	5271	10/41	787	5014	10/41
726	6517	10/41	757	6346	9/41	788	6327	10/41
727	6530	9/41	758	6585	9/41	789	6603	10/41
728	6587	9/41	759	6315	9/41	790	6373	10/41
729	6610	9/41	760	6570	9/41	791	6527	10/41
730	6185	9/41	761	6238	9/41			

(a) After arrival in the Middle East, 9000 was added to these W.D. numbers. In September 1944 70000 was added to the *original* W.D. numbers.

(b) Withdrawn from L.N.E.R. stock, 12/1943.

(c) Lost at sea.

only O4's sent in the first half of December were ex-G.C. engines, already fitted for train braking. It is believed that the remaining ex-R.O.D. O4's despatched from the end of December 1941 onwards, were partially fitted with the necessary piping and other fittings before being sent overseas. The work was completed in the Middle East using material subsequently sent from Gorton as this became available; the last three vacuum ejectors were not despatched until September 1943.

Ninety O4's reached the Middle East, Nos. 739/40 being lost at sea en route. The engines subsequently saw service on the Egyptian State Railways, the Palestine Railway, the Haifa-Beirut-Tripoli Railway then under construction and the Damas, Hama & Prolongements Railway (Syria). After the War, six were purchased by the Iraqi Railways, lasting until 1955. The majority of the remaining engines were taken over by the Egyptian State Railways, and some of these survived until about 1961. Meanwhile the ninety-two engines were withdrawn from L.N.E.R. stock in December 1943, and are summarised in the above table.

Shortly after the last O4 required by the Government had left Gorton, the War Office decided to convert the engines to oil-firing, and drawings were supplied by Gorton and Doncaster for the necessary work to be carried out in the Middle East. The fittings were to be made as far as possible standard with those on the L.M.S. class 8F 2-8-0's, also in the Middle East. In this case the L.N.E.R. did not supply the equipment. The engines were gradually converted to oil-firing in the Middle East, but the work was never completed. No. 707 for example was withdrawn from W.D. service in Egypt in December 1943, still coal fired, and a list dated August 1944 quoted a further fourteen still to be altered.

Liveries

The 148 engines taken over from the G.C.R. at Grouping were in that Company's standard goods engine livery of black with red and white lining and with large oval brass number plates on their cab sides. At their next shopping, Gorton continued the black, but with the L.N.E.R. single red lining. The number plates were removed and replaced by 12in. transfer numerals, with shading, on the sides of the tender. Prior to June 1928, the engines taken over from the R.O.D. were generally treated similarly, except that several were first put into traffic with nothing more than a touching-up of their black paint. Sixteen ex-R.O.D. engines were dealt with at Gorton prior to the introduction of the full L.N.E.R. renumbering scheme and were therefore given the Sectional suffix C (e.g. 1255c) on the tender, but the majority went straight from R.O.D. number to 6XXX numbering.

From June 1928 their livery was unrelieved black, with the only variations being the move of the number from tender to cab side from March 1929, and the successive changes of indication of ownership on the tender, from "L N E R" to "NE" during the 1939-45 War and then briefly back again to "L N E R".

Before the class O4/2 engines in Scotland came south for repair from 1933 onwards, Cowlairs Works continued to use the 7½in. size lettering on their tenders, after the engine numbers had been moved to the cabside, whereas the English works invariably used the 12in. style. For some unaccountable reason, class O5 No. 5420 not only retained its number on the tender until October 1938, but also remained in G.C. style goods engine livery (fig. 43), with "GREAT CENTRAL" just visible below the "L N E R". This is all the more surprising when it had had general repairs at Gorton in June 1929, December 1931 and October 1935.

After nationalisation the tender inscription changed to "BRITISH RAILWAYS", followed later by the two versions of the emblem. During the currency of the first B.R. emblem (with lion above the wheel) from 1949 to 1957, it was customary for the larger size to appear on O4 tenders. However before this class changed over to the revised emblem (with lion holding the wheel), the opportunity was taken to use up the residual stock of the smaller size of the first emblem, and this style was mainly in evidence until about 1960. By this time the number of heavy repairs and repaintings had been curtailed, with the result that very few O4's received the final style of emblem.

British Railways

On Vesting Day, 1st January 1948, there were 278 class O4 engines in service, together with another fifty-one which had been rebuilt to class O1. The O4's were made up of the following varieties: O4 (213), O4/5 (8), O4/7 (41), O4/8 (16). All were ultimately renumbered into the 60000 series, though, as with certain other ex-L.N.E.R. classes, a number that were shopped in January to March of 1948 ran for a time with the "E" prefix to the L.N.E.R. numbers (fig. 46). The B.R. renumbering was completed in April 1951 when No. 3683, whose previous general repair had been in November 1947, at last became No. 63683.

Seven more engines (four O4, two O4/5 and one O4/7) were rebuilt to class O1 during 1948-49, when such rebuildings ceased. No engines were converted from one class part to another during the following two years, but in 1952 rebuilding to O4/8 recommenced. Eighty-three were dealt with up to 1958, four from O4/5, six from O4/7 and the remainder from O4.

Five O4's were withdrawn from stock in 1952 and sold to the Government. Normal withdrawal commenced in December 1958, with No. 63668, and proceeded steadily. The last two O4/5 engines (Nos. 63745 and 63851) were condemned in April 1959 and the final O4/7 (No. 63770) went in December 1965. At the beginning of 1966 there was one O4 in service (No. 63764) and twelve O4/8's, and these had all gone by April of that year.

It should be mentioned that the G.W.R. handed over forty-five R.O.D. class engines to B.R. and the last of these survived until 1958. Details of these engines may be found by reference to Part 10 of the Society's "The Locomotives of the Great Western Railway".

Government Purchase – 1952

In 1952 five O4's were sold to the Government for service in the Middle East, where they were intended to replace temporarily five L.M.S.-type class 8F 2-8-0's, sent back to England for overhaul. The Stanier engines never returned and the O4's continued to share the W.D. traffic with the few remaining 8F's until the base at Suez closed in 1954-55.

The O4's were repaired at Gorton and fitted for oil burning before shipment. They were painted unlined black and carried numbers 040 to 044 in plain yellow on the cab side surmounted by "W ↑ D", with the latter insignia also painted on the tender. All five engines ran the usual trial trips to New Mills before despatch to Southampton Docks. The final three sent, Nos. 042/3/4, were noted at Southampton on 19th March 1952 behind Lord Nelson class No. 30856. All five engines sailed on 7th April aboard M.V. *Belpareil* and were unloaded at Adabiya in May. Details of the engines concerned are as follows:-

W.D. No.	*B.R. No.*	*With-drawn*
040	63809 (ex-6222)	2/52
041	63849 (ex-6615)	,,
042	63778 (ex-6215)	,,
043	63580 (ex-5069)	,,
044	63627 (ex-5005)	,,

After arrival in Egypt the engines were named *Liss Forest, Weaversdown, Longmoor, Whitehall* and *Bordon*, possibly in the order of the W.D. numbers though this has not been confirmed. After the British base at Suez closed, the engines were taken over by the Egyptian State Railways and renumbered 9794-8 in order of their W.D. numbers, thus following on in the same series as the O4's sent to the Middle East in 1941-42, though the numbers 9792/3 were not used. It is believed that some of these engines lasted until 1961.

Allocation and Work

The building of the G.C. 8K class had been very much influenced by the construction of the new port at Immingham, with its excellent facilities for the export of coal from the colliery areas of South Yorkshire and North Midlands. The first 8K's came out in 1911, in advance of the opening of Immingham dock the following year. The initial allocation of the class was to Gorton, Mexborough, Annesley, Retford, Staveley, Sheffield and Immingham, although it is more than likely that some engines commenced their working life at the old shed at Grimsby which was partly replaced by the new shed at Immingham opened with the dock in 1912. By far the largest allocation was at Mexborough, a situation which continued until the outbreak of war in 1939.

The sheds on the London Extension south of Annesley did not house any of these engines at first, except for Nos. 394/5/6 which went new to Neasden in 1914 to work coal trains through from Annesley to London, though No. 395 was transferred to Gorton in 1917. The other two engines moved to Woodford in 1920, indicative of Woodford having by then become the marshalling point for goods and mineral traffic, which then continued to be the normal practice throughout the remaining life of the London Extension.

During that war the 8K's were built in large numbers for the Ministry of Munitions and many were loaned to the British main line railways in the period 1919-21. The constituent companies of the L.N.E.R. which had engines on loan were the G.C.R. itself (93), North Eastern (33) and Great Eastern (44). The N.E. engines were allocated to the York and Hull areas whilst the G.E. engines were at March and Doncaster. The latter engines were severely restricted in their sphere of operation because of their overall height and width, and when it was necessary to despatch engines to Stratford Works for attention their chimneys were removed. The March engines were thus generally restricted to the G.N. & G.E. Joint line northwards to Lincoln and Doncaster, although it is believed they also worked through to the L.D.E.C. line for coal traffic, a practice originally started in L.D.E.C. days and perpetuated after the G.C.R. took over that company in 1907.

Robinson's final goods engine design, the G.C. 8M class introduced in 1918, was not unnaturally allocated to the coal producing areas of South Yorkshire and the North Midlands with the largest number at Mexborough. The larger boiler compared with the 8K's does not seem to have made the engines superior in any way (no doubt the retention of the same 26 sq. ft. grate area was the main reason) and they were considered by engine crews to be more uncomfortable to work on because, like all the later Robinson engines, the back of the firebox was lagged (unlike the 8K's) and in consequence they were cold engines in winter. At Grouping the allocation was as follows: Mexborough 6, Retford 4, Sheffield 5, Gorton 2. (The engines at Gorton were Nos. 420/2 taking part in Robinson's experiments with alternative coal fuels). In the early part of 1924 Nos. 420/2, by then altered to conventional coal burning, went to Mexborough and were at the same time joined by the five Sheffield engines. Mexborough then had no fewer than thirteen members of the class allocated.

The formation of the L.N.E.R. and the decision to purchase ex-R.O.D. engines from the Government meant that the L.N.E.R. O4 class was to virtually fulfil the requirement for heavy goods engines throughout the life of the new company. Altogether 273 engines were added to stock and apart from the building of relatively small numbers of Gresley three-cylinder O2's, no further L.N.E.R. 2-8-0's were built or acquired until the Second World War.

In May 1929 when the last former R.O.D. engine was put into service, the distribution was as follows:-

Southern Area	381
North Eastern Area	24
Scottish Area	16

The first significant change was the loan of thirty engines to the G.W.R. in November 1940, all taken from the Southern Area and subsequently returned by early 1943. In 1941-42 ninety-two engines from all Areas were sent to the Middle East, on loan to the War Department but eventually deleted from stock at the end of 1943. Meanwhile the remaining O4's in Scotland were transferred to the Southern Area by the end of 1943. After nationalisation, the closure of Cudworth shed in 1951 resulted in six O4's operating for a short time from the former L.M.S. shed at nearby Royston, but by the end of that year the entire class of 271 O4's was allocated to Eastern Region sheds. Subsequent Regional changes were the result of boundary revisions. In June 1956 the sheds in the West Riding, together with eleven O4's, were transferred to the North Eastern Region. In February 1958 certain former G.C. sheds were transferred to the London Midland Region, including Gorton which at that time had twenty-seven O4's. Finally, Colwick shed was handed over to the L.M. Region in January 1966, along with five O4's which were immediately scrapped.

The accompanying table shows the number of O4's (with O5's added in brackets) at each shed at (i) 1st January 1923, (ii) 31st December 1939 before the wartime moves took place, (iii) 31st December 1947 on the eve of nationalisation and (iv) 31st December 1958 before mass withdrawal began. Details of the duties of classes O4 and O5 over the years follow, and are more conveniently dealt with under separate headings for the three Areas of the L.N.E.R. The reader is also referred to the separate chapter where the allocation and work of the Thompson rebuilds (class O1) is dealt with in detail.

Allocation at 31*st December*	1922	1939	1947	1958
Annesley	24	33	52	—
Barnsley	—	4	—	21
Frodingham	—	35	22	29
Gorton	24 (2)	27	—	27
Immingham	6	22	6	15
Keadby	2	—	—	—
Langwith	—	24	7	23
Mexborough	58 (6)	57 (3)	27	38
Retford	— (4)	14	15	10
Sheffield	8 (5)	19	23	38
Staveley	9	14	10	18
Tuxford	—	4	7	12
Woodford	—	14	—	—
Ardsley	—	—	1	11
Colwick	—	47	20	18
Doncaster	—	38	45	5
Grantham	—	7	—	—
Lincoln	—	2	—	—
Cambridge	—	3	14	—
March	—	12 (2)	3	—
Cudworth	—	9	—	—
Dairycoates	—	—	10	—
Springhead	—	15	3	—
Tyne Dock	—	—	13	—
Aberdeen	—	4	—	—
Dundee	—	3	—	—
Dunfermline	—	4	—	—
Thornton	—	5	—	—
Total O4	131	416	278	265
Total O5	(17)	(5)	—	—

Southern Area

Between the two wars the O4's virtually monopolised all normal goods and mineral traffic on the G.C. Section. Wath Yard was the focal point of much of the coal traffic from the South Yorkshire pits, which was worked eastward to Scunthorpe and Immingham, and westward via the Worsborough branch and

Woodhead to Lancashire and Cheshire. The nature of the Woodhead route was such that practically every train had to have assistance, the train loadings determining to what degree this was required. Trains originating at Wath received banking assistance from Wombwell Main Junction right through to the eastern end of the Woodhead tunnel, and again depending upon load additional assistance was given from Wentworth Junction. The Worsborough branch was short but steep, with a gradient of 1 in 40 for just over two miles from Wentworth Junction to West Silkstone Junction, where the branch joined the line from Barnsley to Penistone. Wentworth Junction maintained banking engines for providing assistance. The massive class U1 Garratt No. 2395 worked from here together with conventional engines. The Wentworth engines came on at the rear of the train and normally only banked as far as West Silkstone Junction, where they came off and ran back light to Wentworth to await the next train.

The traffic from Wath joined the G.C. main line at Barnsley Junction just to the east of Penistone, and was joined there by trains originating from the Langwith, Staveley and Worksop areas which had come via Sheffield Victoria. Westbound trains took a pilot engine from the start, if the loading warranted it, which then assisted at the head of the train as far as Sheffield Victoria, where it was usual practice to stop for water. The assisting engine then uncoupled and ran to the rear of the train to provide banking assistance to Dunford Bridge. In the up direction via Woodhead there was the inevitable procession of empty wagon trains running to the collieries, but no banking assistance was provided on the easterly climb to Woodhead. Not all the empty wagon trains went to the marshalling yards. Wagons were detached en route at the collieries involved, and on some of the Gorton workings to Langwith it was not unknown for the working to arrive at its destination consisting of engine and guard's van only.

The Robinson 2-8-0's predominated on all the workings via Woodhead up to the Second World War, with Mexborough shed having the largest number. In 1923 this shed had fifty-five O4's and six O5's, figures which were marginally reduced in total to fifty-seven O4's and three O5's by the end of 1939, notwithstanding the large numbers of ex-R.O.D. engines which had been added to stock. However it should be borne in mind that Doncaster had acquired some of Mexborough's work after 1923 (see later). Mexborough O4's were also to be found on banking duties to Dunford Bridge.

The year 1954 saw the inauguration of the Manchester-Sheffield-Wath electrification scheme, bringing to an end over one hundred years of steam working on the Woodhead line and the sight of an endless stream of coal trains with O4's at the head. For the next few years only dead O4's were seen on this line whenever they were hauled to Gorton Works for overhaul. In December 1958 the first O4 (No. 63668) was withdrawn for scrapping, and this was from Mexborough shed.

Doncaster shed acquired O4's in the early days after Grouping but it is not possible to give a definite date for the first acquisitions, because in the first few years of the L.N.E.R. transfers were shown to Districts and not to individual sheds. Mexborough shed was included in the Doncaster District and hence although the transfer lists showed engines to Doncaster it is certain that some of these moves were in actual fact to Mexborough. It is however known that in the Spring of 1924 some men and engines began to be transferred from Mexborough to Doncaster, it being considered that Doncaster was more conveniently situated for working G.C. traffic in that area. The acquisition of further O4's from the Government steadily built up Doncaster's allocation, which stood at fifty by December 1930, seven being former G.C. engines and the remainder newly acquired ex-R.O.D. engines. The O4's worked traffic from the former G.C. yards at Hexthorpe and also participated in the heavy flow of coal trains worked eastward to Scunthorpe and Immingham.

Doncaster O4's also undertook trip duties to and from the collieries from the former G.N. lines, including Rossington, and worked southwards through Lincoln to March on turns which were shared with March based O4's. The Doncaster allocation fell quite appreciably during the thirties, to thirty-eight at the end of 1939, increasing again to forty-five at nationalisation. The total then fell dramatically to only five at the end of 1958 but this handful of engines was to remain at Doncaster until almost the end of steam in the Eastern Region. The last O4 with a Belpaire firebox, No. 63764, was withdrawn from Doncaster shed in February 1966. Two months later the last four engines of the class, Nos. 63653, 63781, 63818/58, (all rebuilt engines of part 8), were withdrawn from Doncaster a few weeks before that shed was closed to steam in May 1966.

Coal was also carried over the G.C. main line from the North Derbyshire and Nottinghamshire collieries. The yard at Annesley provided marshalling facilities for onward despatch of the traffic south to Woodford, where it was further sorted, principally for transfer to the G.W.R. via the Banbury branch, or combined with goods traffic for the London area. On the London Extension the Annesley-Woodford trains were to a large extent in the hands of O4's until the mid-thirties, when a speeded up service was introduced worked by mixed-traffic engines of class K3 as the O4's were considered too slow. Woodford shed covered workings to London and trips to Banbury with their O4's, in addition to working northward. Neasden shed housed No. 6542 from December 1928 to January 1936, which worked to Woodford, but the latter shed normally worked most of the London traffic. In pre-war days the goods traffic on the London Extension was quite extensive and a considerable proportion passed on to the G.W.R. at Banbury.

The acquisition of the Lancashire, Derbyshire & East Coast Railway by the G.C.R. in 1907 added a further source of coal traffic from the newer collieries in the Dukeries. Mansfield Concentration Sidings were opened later in order to cater for the expansion of the Nottinghamshire coalfield in the Mansfield area, which took place in the period around the First World War. Coal trains originating in this area were worked eastward over the L.D.E.C. line to Immingham as well as to the north via Woodhead and to the south to Woodford. Langwith shed, where in pre-Grouping days the Q4's had been the mainstay, later housed a large number of O4's to cover this work, the total rising to a peak of forty-one briefly in August 1946. In October 1946 a major move resulted in Langwith acquiring thirty three-cylinder Gresley 2-8-0's (class O2) and most of its O4's went to Colwick and Doncaster. At nationalisation the number of O4's at Langwith was down to seven, but by the end of 1958 it had risen again, to twenty-three. Langwith was the last former G.C. shed to house O4's, retaining them mainly for colliery trip workings until the shed closed to steam in 1965.

The initial allocation of O4's at Colwick comprised engines transferred from Annesley, almost certainly as part of the rationalisation of traffic which took place in the Nottingham area early in 1924. Colwick was a former G.N. shed but thereafter some of its work was closely associated with the G.C. lines. The allocation built up steadily until at the end of 1930 twenty-seven O4's were on strength, twenty-three being recently acquired ex-R.O.D. engines. By the end of 1939 this number had been increased to no fewer than forty-seven, but by the end of the L.N.E.R.'s separate existence had dropped to twenty. However the O4's, albeit in rebuilt form as Part 8, almost saw the end of steam at Colwick, which they probably would have done but for the transfer of the shed to the London Midland Region in January 1966. This was followed by the immediate withdrawal by that Region of the five O4's taken over, Nos. 63644/74/5, 63816/73, and replacement by L.M.S. – type engines.

The Colwick engines were employed on the heavy mineral traffic originating in the Nottingham area, being principally coal, but there was also a considerable amount of iron ore from the mines in the area, mainly on the former L.N.W. & G.N. Joint line. The O4 part 8 engines managed to survive on iron ore trains to Stanton Ironworks until the end of 1965 when they were replaced by L.M.S. types as mentioned above. Coal traffic took Colwick O4's to Peterborough, though New England shed also participated in these workings. After nationalisation a Colwick O4 was sent out on one of that shed's former L.M.S. workings to Willesden, and it was reported that the cylinders fouled the platform edging on the L.N.W.R. main line, resulting in "Austerity" 2-8-0's being substituted on these workings.

There was heavy goods and mineral traffic in the North Lincolnshire area on which O4's were utilised to a great extent. Much of the traffic was connected with the vast steel works in the Scunthorpe area and the export of coal through the port of Immingham. Also, coal was worked to New Clee sidings for the trawlers based at Grimsby. In pre-war days Immingham engines worked to the South Yorkshire collieries as well as to Wath yard, though Doncaster also participated in these workings.

The Scunthorpe area prior to 1932 had been worked from the old South Yorkshire Railway shed at Keadby, on the west bank of the River Trent, and up to that date although they had six O4's the majority of that shed's work was in the hands of the older class Q4 0-8-0 engines. The reason for this was the inability of the Keadby turntable to accommodate O4's, although they could be turned on the North Lincolnshire Junction triangle at Frodingham. In 1932 the L.N.E.R. opened the new shed at Frodingham which was a great improvement, reducing light engine mileage to and from Keadby. With adequate turning facilities, O4's were drafted in until the allocation stood at thirty-four at the outbreak of war in 1939. An additional source of traffic in the area was iron ore and whilst considerable quantities were mined locally it was still necessary to import ore from other areas. Frodingham engines worked iron ore traffic from, and returned empties to, the Highdyke branch south of Grantham, in conjunction with O4's based at the latter shed (see later). There was also a daily working to the iron ore mine at Holton-le-Moor on the Lincoln to Barnetby line. Steel traffic was worked to Sheffield, Rotherham and Deepcar the normal route being via Barnetby. Additional traffic also took this route destined for South Wales and the West Midlands, with the Frodingham engines not usually working further south than Annesley. A well-known Frodingham duty for an O4 which lasted until the sixties was Gunness banker, a duty which called for assistance to eastbound goods trains climbing the 1 in 100 gradient approaching Frodingham from the River Trent. Towards the end the O4's were used almost exclusively on heavy trip workings between the steel works and marshalling yards and on the Gunness banking duty. The last ex-G.C. O4 in original condition with Belpaire firebox, No. 63586, was withdrawn from Frodingham in October 1965, the shed itself officially closing to steam four months later.

A most interesting task was undertaken by two O4's when they assisted in the refloating of a ship which had capsized in the dock at Immingham. During the night of 31st January 1953, a night of gales and floods on the East Coast, the S.S. *Hebble* and a lightship were under repair in the dry dock of the Humber Graving Dock & Engineering Co. Ltd. During the storm the bank of the River Humber was breached and the force of the water entering the dry dock knocked away the timbers supporting the ships and both fell over on to their sides. The larger ship, the *Hebble,* presented a difficult job to raise on to an even keel and planning the operation occupied several weeks until the task was undertaken in March. The rescue operation was carried out on 7th March 1953 and the Motive Power Department was asked to supply two engines to assist. Four steel pillars had been welded to the hull of the *Hebble*, to which were attached steel cables on a series of pulleys, and from these another cable passed alongside the dock to the railway sidings and was secured to the two O4's. The pulley system increased the pull of the O4's by fourteen times. The operation was a complete success and by admitting water slowly into the dry dock, with a steady pull exerted by the O4's, the ship was slowly raised on to an even keel within thirty minutes.

Gorton shed had a sizable allocation of O4's, whose principal duties lay in handling the coal traffic over Woodhead. Gorton engines however also worked west of Manchester on to the Cheshire Lines to Liverpool, Bidston, Chester and also on occasions reached Wrexham. For a time in the thirties the C.L.C. shed at Brunswick (Liverpool) housed an O4 (No. 6637) for working goods traffic to Sheffield. This duty had originally been worked by a class J10 to Dewsnap sidings (Guide Bridge) where the engine was replaced by an O4. The introduction of wartime constructed 2-8-0's, both British and American, inevitably meant that to some extent the O4's were replaced on main line work. Several O4's were placed in store about this time, including for example seven at Walton shed (Liverpool) in the spring of 1944, these being Nos. 6192, 6344, 6512/28/68/82/91, whilst others were stored at Trafford Park. The departure of the W.D. and U.S. Army 2-8-0's to the mainland of Europe in 1944 resulted in the O4's being returned to traffic.

Gorton was an Eastern Region shed after nationalisation until it was transferred to the London Midland Region in February 1958. A fairly large allocation of O4's was retained until 1962 for continuing their working on Cheshire Lines goods traffic. In September 1954 Nos. 63575 and 63681 were noted on one of the trains of bogie iron ore hopper wagons from Birkenhead Docks to the Shotton Steelworks of John Summers Ltd., a service then recently introduced. This working may have been in the nature of a trial, as L.M.S.-type class 8F 2-8-0's were the regular engines until succeeded by the B.R. Standard class 9F 2-10-0's. After the L.M. Region took over, Gorton O4's ventured away from their usual haunts and made appearances on former L.M.S. lines in the area. In 1958 No. 63598 was working on the old L.Y.R. main line, being noted at Todmorden with a goods train proceeding in the Manchester direction. (O4's were not new to this line as Barnsley shed had a daily working with a Wath to Rose Grove (Burnley) coal train which appears to have started in the autumn of 1956. It is believed that clearance problems with the O4's caused them to be replaced on this working after a short time by "Austerities"). Gorton also acquired the allocation and duties of the former L.M.S. shed at nearby Belle Vue and it was not unknown for O4's to work over the Midland lines as far south as Chinley on engineer's trains and on trips to Gowhole sidings. Ex-L.M.S. motive power gradually moved into Gorton and the O4's finally disappeared from the Manchester area with the withdrawal of Nos. 63598, 63600 and 63862 in October and November 1962.

The first recorded sighting of a G.C. 2-8-0 on the G.N. main line was on 27th July 1923 when an O5, still in G.C. livery as No. 17, worked an up coal train to Hornsey, and this working was repeated twice in September of the same year. The shed at New England received its first O4 in January 1925 and the allocation increased until at the beginning of 1926 there were thirteen, a figure which increased to twenty by 1930. The O4's worked both north and south of Peterborough although the long established service of coal trains for Hornsey was mainly in the hands of Gresley 2-8-0's (classes O1 and O2) and the two P1's, with the O4's tending to work the lighter trains. Northwards the class went to Colwick via Grantham, whilst Doncaster and Wath were reached via the loop line through Spalding and Lincoln. From May 1935 the O4's were moved away from New England when new K3's arrived.

Grantham first acquired O4's in 1928, the initial engine to arrive being No. 6628 in November of that year, and by September 1939 seven were allocated. The O4's were principally used on iron ore traffic originating at the mines on the Highdyke branch just to the south of Grantham on the main line. The ore trains were worked northward to York destined for Tees-side and Scotland, and to Scunthorpe for the local steel works. The Scunthorpe trains were originally sent via the main line and Doncaster, but were rerouted via Lincoln and Barnetby (reversing at both places) in 1932, following the speed up of East Coast main line express traffic. The Scunthorpe turns were also shared with Frodingham engines. One or two additional O4's went to Grantham in the early war years but two were withdrawn from traffic in 1941 and sent to the Middle East. In November 1942 all the Grantham O4's were transferred away to Doncaster and Mexborough and replaced by Gresley class O1 2-8-0's from New England.

In the West Riding the principal shed was at Ardsley which dealt with a not inconsiderable coal traffic originating from the collieries in the Wakefield area and on the West Riding & Grimsby line. The first O4 went to Ardsley in 1924 and was followed later by a further six, all being ex-R.O.D. engines. Two of these left in the early months of 1925 and the remaining five were exchanged in August 1926 for a like number of ex-G.C. engines, possibly in connection with the vacuum brake fittings on the latter. Then in 1928 all five Ardsley engines were transferred away and their work was taken over by class Q4 0-8-0's. The reason for this move was the inability of the turntable at Ardsley to accommodate O4's, which had to be turned on the triangle at Lofthouse. The Q4's henceforth were the mainstay of West Riding heavy goods traffic until the remaining engines were withdrawn after the War was over. They were gradually replaced from 1947 onwards by O4's, facilitated by the provision of a larger turntable at Ardsley shed. In June 1956 the West Riding sheds were taken over by the North Eastern Region and the following O4's were included in the allocations: Nos. 63570/84/8, 63605/33, 63724, 63823/57/64/85 (Ardsley), 63920 (Bradford). The Bradford engine had been transferred there from Ardsley in December 1953 and was a former O5. When Bradford shed closed, this engine went back to Ardsley in January 1958. Subsequent transfers were Nos. 63588, 63857/64, 63920 to the former L.M.S. shed at Wakefield in February 1959 and the return to Ardsley of Nos. 63857/64 in June 1961. No. 63570 was withdrawn first, in December 1961. The remaining ten engines were condemned together on 8th August 1962.

The Great Eastern Railway had gained experience with the class prior to Grouping when a number of R.O.D. engines had been loaned to that Company between 1919 and 1921. As mentioned earlier, the sphere of activity was limited to the Joint line north of March and they worked from Lincoln, Doncaster and March sheds. After 1923, O4's commenced working to March from the north via the Joint line and one or two were allocated to that shed during 1924-25, but only remained for brief periods as at that time they had not been cut down to clear the G.E. Section load gauge. In March 1929 the route from March to Stratford was passed for class O4 to work to Temple Mills and a permanent allocation of O4's was established at March. There were fourteen engines initially, one of which was No. 6498 which had in G.E. days been on loan as R.O.D. No. 1684, although this particular engine had been allocated to the G.E. shed at Doncaster. A further engine was transferred to March in April 1930 and it was only then that the O4's were first seen on goods trains through to Temple Mills. They remained on this work for some two years before they were ousted to a large extent by new class O2 2-8-0's from June 1932, with further O2's arriving in 1934. When the specially rostered Temple Mills workings were instituted in October 1936 (see class O2 p. 29), target Nos. 1 to 13 were diagrammed for the O2's and target Nos. 14 and 15 for the two regular workings still booked to O4's. The special instructions stipulated that if an O2 missed its rostered turn, owing to fog or mishap, a lower class of engine was to be substituted and the booked engine held back to take up its own diagram again at the next opportunity. Occasionally therefore O4's would appear on O2 duties. When the workings were revised in May 1937, the two O4 diagrams became target Nos. 1 and 2 instead. No. 1 covered the 9-20 a.m. daily Whitemoor – Temple Mills, returning with the 12-10 a.m. MX and 11-35 p.m. SO from Temple Mills. No. 2 covered the 11-15 a.m. daily Whitemoor – Temple Mills (terminating at Broxbourne on Saturdays), returning with the 11-35 p.m. SX and 11-55 p.m. SO from Temple Mills.

In 1931-32 three O4's were transferred from March to Cambridge shed (see later). At this time class O5 Nos. 5420/1 were transferred from Mexborough to March, in March and April 1932 respectively. Their normal employment was hump shunting at Whitemoor yard, on which duty they remained until withdrawn in 1941 for war service overseas. They were replaced at March in November 1941 by Nos. 5011 and 5414, former O5's but rebuilt to class O4 before the War. Both these engines moved on to Cambridge in December 1947 and finally back to the G.C. Section in May 1959.

The O4's at Cambridge worked coal empties to Whitemoor returning with loco coal for Cambridge shed at 8-25 p.m. and 1-35 a.m., with a further return working at 10-25 a.m. with coal for Cambridge Gas Works. The route both ways was via St. Ives (known locally as "the loop"). Cambridge O4's were additionally used on workings to Temple Mills and also on occasion deputised for March engines on the through workings from Whitemoor to London.

The O4's were normally only to be found on the route between Whitemoor and London via either Ely or the St. Ives loop. Due to clearance difficulties they were normally prohibited between Ely and Norwich, and likewise between Goodmayes and Norwich via Ipswich and on the East Suffolk line. In 1938 however an O4 was noted running into Ipswich via Bury St. Edmunds and there may have been other similar isolated workings. The total number of O4's allocated to the G.E. Section remained constant until 1941 at fifteen (plus two O5's after 1932), although there were several transfers of individual engines to and from the G.E. Section over the intervening years. Nine of the G.E. Section O4's were transferred to the War Department in 1941-42 (including Nos. 5420/1 after they had been rebuilt from class O5). Eight O4's remained and were concentrated at March shed from May 1942, where they continued working on goods and mineral trains. The balance was restored in September 1944 when an additional nine O4's were transferred to March shed. Extensive alterations were made to the goods workings at the end of the L.N.E.R.'s separate existence, when only three O4's were left at March, with no fewer than fourteen at Cambridge. Those at March were probably used on hump shunting at Whitemoor, a duty which they had also carried out on occasions in pre-war days when deputising for either the two O5's, Nos. 5420/1, or the class S1 0-8-4T's. The class was transferred away from the G.E. Section in the 1949-51 period, although the Thompson rebuilds (class O1) continued to see service at March after this date.

North Eastern Area

The year 1927 saw the first ex-Government O4's allocated to the North Eastern Area and by the autumn of 1928 Nos. 6576-81/3/4, 6607-18/30/1/2 were at work. No. 6582 had also been allocated but for some reason went to Scotland instead, and was not replaced until March 1929 (by No. 6549), at which time the planned allocation of twenty-four was shared between York (6) and Dairycoates (18). Incidentally, both these sheds had had experience with the class in North Eastern days when on loan from the Government. In September 1929 Nos. 6581 and 6613 were transferred from Dairycoates to the former Hull & Barnsley shed at Springhead for trial running in an attempt to overcome the use of the H. & B. 0-6-0's in pairs on coal trains. The trials were successful and one month later they were followed by Nos. 6612/4, also from Dairycoates, in their case shown to replace H. & B. 0-8-0's in addition to the avoidance of double-heading, whilst at the same time Nos. 6576 and 6611 went from York to Cudworth and Bullcroft, respectively. The latter was a tiny one-road shed which served Bullcroft Colliery on the Hull & Barnsley and Great Central Joint line from Aire Junction on the H. & B. main line. No. 6611 was sent there also to eliminate double-heading. By the summer of

1930 all the O4's allocated to the N.E. Area had been concentrated on the H. & B. Section. Springhead had no fewer than nineteen on its permanent allocation, with four at Cudworth (Nos. 6549/76/7/8) and No. 6611 at Bullcroft. The North Eastern Area allocation had meanwhile been temporarily increased by two in May 1930, by the loan of Nos. 6261/2 from the Southern Area to Springhead, where they remained until June 1933 when transferred to Doncaster. No. 6611 was transferred to Springhead on 5th December 1931 when Bullcroft shed closed.

During the years 1930-39 the only transfers away from the H. & B. were Nos. 6580, 6614/5 to Dairycoates in the period 1933-37. All twenty-four were back on the H. & B. by the latter date, with fifteen at Springhead and the remaining nine at Cudworth. In the thirties after the onset of the depression in industry, several O4's had been taken out of traffic and stored in the old Hull & Barnsley works at Springhead. In 1940 due to the heavy increase in goods traffic working south from the N.E. Area, twenty-one O4's left the H. & B. Section and were transferred to Heaton and West Hartlepool (for extra coal traffic) and York (for iron ore traffic), leaving only three engines at Cudworth, Nos. 6576/9 and 6614. A further six were transferred at the same time from G.C. Section sheds to Heaton (Nos. 6301/67) and York (Nos. 5378/95, 6514/74). In the following year seven O4's from the N.E. Area were included in the ninety-two engines sent to the Middle East, but were not replaced until 1942 when four more O4's (Nos. 5008, 5404, 6211, 6501) went to West Hartlepool from the Southern Area, followed by five more to this shed in 1943 (Nos. 6265, 6350, 6566/94/5). Meanwhile March 1943 saw the three Cudworth engines sent north to Heaton and in that year thirty-two O4's were allocated to the North Eastern Area.

During the war years O4's were a common sight on the N.E. main line on both coal and iron ore trains. An official letter of July 1941 refers to the iron ore traffic from Stainby mines to Rutherglen being worked from York to Newcastle by an O4 assisted by a class J26, J27 or J39 0-6-0 or another O4. The maximum load for a pair of O4's was 1,620 tons, requiring "a clear run Bensham to Gateshead". The building of the "Austerity" 2-8-0's in 1943 considerably eased the motive power situation and for a time one or two O4's were stored, including West Hartlepool's No. 6594 which was tallowed down at Trafford Park shed following a general repair at Gorton Works. In 1944 the Thompson O1 class began to appear and the first one to be rebuilt, No. 6595, was another West Hartlepool engine, although it was almost immediately exchanged for No. 6352 at Gorton. Meanwhile No. 6594 ex-store was exchanged for No. 6606 at Colwick, whilst later in 1944 No. 6631 was sent to Immingham in return for class O1 No. 6334.

After the War was over the class once again returned to the Hull sheds at Springhead and Dairycoates, and Cudworth also received an allocation of eight once more, whilst further north Tyne Dock acquired several O4's. The Dairycoates engines had regular workings to Bridlington, Scarborough, Stainforth, Thorne and Maltby. In 1951 the class was removed from the North Eastern scene (leaving the five class O1 rebuilds at Tyne Dock for the Consett iron ore trains). The first move took place with the closure of Cudworth shed on 30th July 1951 and its six O4's, Nos. 63751/4/72, 63845/9/57, were transferred to the nearby L.M.S. shed at Royston. The O4's did not remain there long and were exchanged with six "Austerities" from Colwick, which actually moved to Warrington ex-L.N.W.R. shed whilst Royston received Stanier class 8F 2-8-0's instead. A few weeks later the remaining O4's in the N.E. Region moved away, ten going to Eastern Region sheds and nine, surprisingly, to the Western Region. The latter engines were allocated to Oxley and Southall and in September 1951 sightings included No. 63881 on a down goods at Exeter on the 8th, whilst No. 63812 was noted at Taunton on the 10th and six days later at Oxford. Their stay on the Western Region was brief and by the end of September all nine had been exchanged with "Austerities" and transferred to the Eastern Region. Thus in September 1951 the whole of class O4 was for the first time entirely allocated to former L.N.E.R. Southern Area sheds.

Scottish Area

Reference has been made in Part 5 of this series (p. 224) to the trials of North Eastern and Great Western eight-coupled goods engines on the N.B.R., and soon after Grouping a further series of tests was carried out. However, whereas the earlier test runs were conducted between Perth and Glenfarg, the L.N.E.R. trials were between Thornton and Aberdeen. These involved classes O4 and Q6, the representative of the former class being No. 1185 (lettered

"L.& N.E.R."), which arrived in Scotland on 6th June 1923 and returned south on 2nd November. The Scottish Area authorities were favourably impressed by the performance of the O4, and so the following summer ten reconditioned ex-R.O.D. engines of this class were drafted north. The engines concerned were Nos. 6286/91, 6328 (to Dunfermline), 6288/90, 6346/52 (to Thornton), 6351/70 (to Aberdeen) and 6372 (to Dundee), and they arrived at these sheds during July and August 1924. They were put to work on the Fife to Aberdeen coal trains, but No. 6288 actually made its first trip from Thornton in the opposite direction – to Portobello. The O4's took over duties formerly worked by J37's, the Dunfermline, Thornton and Aberdeen engines being allotted to regular men who worked through and lodged. Typical duties of the period were the 2-15 a.m. and 4-20 p.m. Thornton – Aberdeen, and the 8-25 p.m. Townhill – Aberdeen, the corresponding departures from Aberdeen being at 12-5 a.m. and 6-25 p.m. to Thornton and 8-50 p.m. to Kelty. These trains ran as Class B goods but conveyed coal northwards, and the empties on the return journey. The O4's were booked to take forty wagons of coal as against thirty allowed to a J37.

In 1928-29 a further six reconditioned O4's were sent to Scotland, these being Nos. 6543/50 (Thornton), 6544/8 (Dunfermline), 6551 (Dundee) and 6582 (Aberdeen). There were only a few subsequent transfers of the sixteen engines, viz. 1930: No. 6582 to Dundee; 1931: Nos. 6286/91 to Dundee, the former soon passing on to Aberdeen; 1937: No. 6291 to Aberdeen; 1943 (for only two or three months): Nos. 6288, 6372, 6582 to Dunfermline. Initially, the instructions were that the O4's were not to be used on any route other than Edinburgh – Berwick, Edinburgh – Aberdeen, Edinburgh – Glasgow via Polmont, the Winchburgh – Dalmeny connection, Dunfermline – Thornton, the Methil branch and the line from Cowlairs to Yoker. They were not to be double-headed, speed was restricted to 30 m.p.h. and they were not allowed into colliery sidings. However, there was a heavy coal traffic from Fife to Perth worked by Dunfermline engines, and the O4's were subsequently allowed on this route. Like other large L.N.E.R. engines, they had to go to Perth South L.M.S. shed to turn, for which facility the L.M.S. charged one shilling per engine.

The class was little seen in Edinburgh, although not unknown on goods trains from Fife, until the outbreak of war in 1939 and for a time afterwards when English O4's appeared on the East Coast goods workings. This was when the "common user" policy was in vogue and crews changed over at Tweedmouth or Marshall Meadows. A St. Margaret's set of men had a thrilling trip on No. 6617 working home on a Heaton train from Tweedmouth. As used to be abundantly clear from the train graphs plotted by the Control to mark the progress of goods trains, these moved considerably faster on Saturdays than on other days of the week, with the men in a hurry to get home. This particular run was on a Saturday and the O4 was being pushed to make good speed down Cockburnspath bank. The fore-end was apparently well carbonised at the time and one of the cylinders actually burst into flames! In Fife the O4's were known descriptively as "Big Aggies", but at Aberdeen the topical nickname used was "Tin Lizzies" (the name applied to the D1's at Carlisle and the K2's at St. Margaret's!).

Two of the Scottish engines, Nos. 6346 and 6551, were among the ninety-two O4's taken out of traffic in 1941 for War Department use and they were not replaced in Scottish Area stock at that time. In the early months of 1943 however five O4's went to Scotland from English sheds, Nos. 5393, 6524, 6633 (to Thornton) and 6220, 6365 (to Dunfermline). They only worked in Scotland for a few months before returning to England, together with the remaining fourteen Scottish engines of the class. Henceforth, from October 1943 no O4's were ever again allocated to the Scottish Area, although two Thompson O1's spent some time in Fife (see class O1).

No. 63601

There can be few who would dispute that the O4's were a suitable subject for preservation and, gratifyingly, L.N.E.R. No. 5102 has been retained as part of the National Collection. No. 5102 (as B.R. No. 63601) was withdrawn in June 1963 from Frodingham shed and on the 23rd of that month was selected for preservation. At that time a fairly large number of Belpaire O4's of G.C. origin had already gone and No. 63601 was one of the three oldest survivors, having been built at Gorton in January 1912, and this was probably the reason for the choice. The engine was accepted by Doncaster Works later in 1963, no doubt with a view to restoration but this was not to be and, along with other preserved engines, No. 63601 was to lead a nomadic life during the next ten years.

The engine was moved from Doncaster in the first week of October 1964 (fig. 64) and by 15th November had arrived at Stratford Works (having run hot en route at Cambridge), where it was housed in No. 2 Paint Shop. In November 1967 it moved to Leicester (running hot en route at Luton), following a decision to make a permanent home for it in the Municipal Museum which was being established in that city. Some minor alteration work was then carried out at the former L.M.S. shed at Leicester. Almost three years later there was no sign of permanent housing for the engine in a museum and now British Railways was about to demolish the old engine shed which was its temporary home. In September 1970 the engine was therefore sent to the Pullman Car Shops at Preston Park, Brighton, to be under cover. In August 1972 No. 63601 returned by rail to Leicester, where it was initially housed in the Carriage and Wagon shops at Wigston before being transported by road to the proposed Leicester Railway Museum at Abbey Mills.

This was not the end of the story for in February 1976 No. 63601 was sent by road from Leicester Museum to Longsight Traction Depot, Manchester, en route to the Dinting Railway Centre. An enforced stay of four months was made at Longsight in order to deal with a hot box sustained during its last rail journey, from Brighton to Leicester. Repairs having been made, it was hauled by class 40 No. 40010 to its present home at Dinting on 20th June 1976. It is undergoing restoration and in the not too distant future it may be possible to see it working again, appropriately within sight of the sad remains of the Woodhead main line which the O4's graced for so many years.

R.O.D. Nos. 2002/3/4

Mention must be made of the fate of these three engines built at Gorton in 1918 but which were not acquired by the L.N.E.R. They were purchased in November 1926 by the New South Wales mining company, J. & A. Brown, for employment on their Richmond Vale Railway, which connected collieries in the Maitland coal-field with the New South Wales Government Railways at Hexham. This company also purchased a further ten R.O.D. engines. They were dismantled and shipped to Australia in parts, and reassembled in due course by the Hexham Engineering Works, No. 2003 as late as 1933.

No. 22 (ex-2002) was withdrawn in May 1966 but not disposed of as scrap until 1973. Steam working on the line ceased on 28th June 1973 and Nos. 23 (ex-2004) and 24 (ex-2003) were the last to work. No. 23 was preserved (as No. 21) by Coal & Allied Industries Ltd., successors to J. & A. Brown, and is at present displayed at the Freeman's Waterholes Mining Museum; whilst the genuine No. 21 (ex-R.O.D. 1615) was scrapped instead as (officially) No. 23. (It had been understood that No. 1615 hauled the train conveying Marshal Foch to the signing of the Armistice in November 1918, and was therefore thought to have had some historical significance. However No. 21 was in too poor condition to preserve and so No. 23 was substituted instead). No. 24 was purchased (together with another former R.O.D. engine) by the Hunter Valley Steam Railway & Museum Society and is preserved at Northern Colliery, Rhondda, N.S.W.

Engine Diagrams

Section C, 1924.	O4	"Eng. No. 966 only". 6ft. 0in diam. round top boiler, double side-window cab, tender carrying 7 tons pulverised coal and 4,150 gallons water on double bogies. Diagram deleted 12/1924 as boiler, tender and pulverised fuel apparatus removed.
Section C, 1924.	O4/1	Height over 13ft. 0in., details for 18 and 22 element superheaters included, tender with water scoop, no brake details, engines built between 1911 and 1919. Height to top of chimney altered to 12ft. $8\frac{5}{8}$in., 12/1927. Diagram deleted 12/1932.
Not issued, 1924.	O4	Ex-R.O.D. engines. The Diagram Book Index issued in 1924 simply referred to Nos. 6253 to 6377 inclusive added to stock as O4. Omissions rectified 12/1925 for the engines altered to suit N.B. load gauge (O4/2) and 12/1927 for the remainder (O4/3).
Section C, 1927.	O4/3	Ex-R.O.D. engines. Chimney and dome heights over 13ft. 0in., only 22-element superheater details, tender without scoop. Diagram deleted 12/1932.
Section C, 1932	O4	Composite diagram for Parts 1 and 3. Original chimney still fitted, Maximum height 13ft. $3\frac{1}{2}$in., only 22-element superheater details. Diagram deleted 12/1936.
Section C, 1932.	O4	Composite diagram for Parts 1 and 3. 1ft. 9in. chimney fitted, chimney height 13ft. $2\frac{1}{4}$in., dome height 13ft. $1\frac{1}{2}$in., only 22-element superheater details, no brake details, Part 1 tenders with water scoop, Part 3 tenders without scoop. Chimney altered to 1ft. $5\frac{1}{2}$in. and height to 12ft. $10\frac{3}{4}$in. for both Parts, 12/1936. Grate area altered from 26.24 to 26.34 sq. ft., 12/1937. Diagram deleted 12/1938.
Section C, 1938.	O4	Composite diagram for Parts 1 and 3. Chimney height 12ft. $10\frac{3}{4}$in., alternative dome heights of 12ft. $10\frac{7}{8}$in. and 13ft. $1\frac{1}{2}$in., brake type now included for Part 1 steam with vacuum ejector and Part 3 steam only. Diagram deleted 12/1940.
Section C, 1940.	O4	Composite diagram for Parts 1, 2 and 6. Drawing revised to show double side-window cab, three dimensions given for height to top of cab and radius of cab roof curve, alternative tender weights for with and without scoop, vacuum ejector specified for Nos. 5001-6252. Platform width altered from 8ft. 9in. to 8ft. $9\frac{1}{2}$in., width across cab 7ft. 8in. added for Parts 1 and 2 (diagram hitherto showed 8ft. 3in. which was applicable to Part 6), 12/1941. Note added that only Nos. 5010-22 have side-window cabs, 12/1942.
1946.	O4	Replacement diagram in Thompson style, applicable to Part 1 only.
Section C, 1924.	O4/2	"Eng. Nos. 377, 380 and 383". 22-element superheater details otherwise engine details as on Part 1 diagram, but tender of 3,250 gallon type with scoop. Diagram deleted 12/1924 and two remaining engines reclassified O4 Part 1.
Section C, 1925.	O4/2	Engines altered to suit N.B. load gauge. Both 18 and 22 element superheater details shown, tender shown as with scoop which was only applicable to No. 6185, no brake details shown. Diagram deleted 12/1926.
Section C, 1926.	O4/2	Replacement diagram to correct tender weights without scoop. Diagram deleted 12/1932.
Section C, 1932.	O4/2	Replacement diagram showing 22-element superheater. Minor alterations to thickness of flues and tubeplate, also length between tubeplates, 12/1938. Diagram deleted 12/1940, engines now included with Parts 1 and 6 on new composite diagram.
Section C, 1929.	O4/4	Engines rebuilt to take class O2 boiler. Steam brake with vacuum ejector added to diagram, 12/1938. Diagram deleted 12/1947, engines rebuilt to other Parts.

Fig. 59 Class O4/5 No. 3816 at Dairycoates shed, July 1948.

Both wash-out plugs and hand holes on side of firebox, "blister" on cab side to clear screw reverser, rear sandboxes in view below cab.

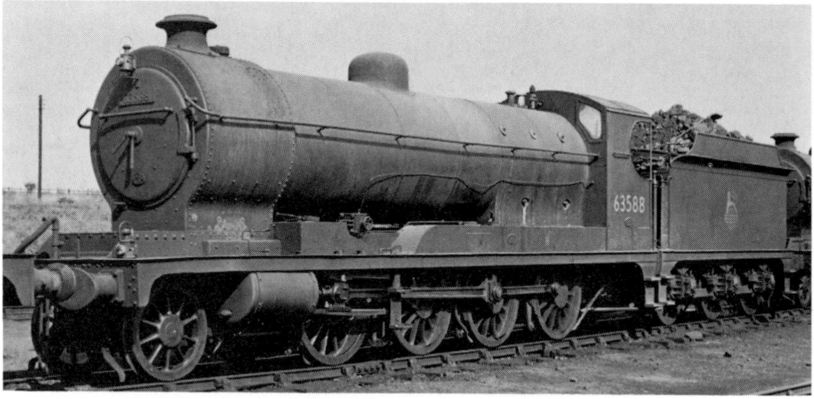

Fig. 60 Class O4/7 No. 63588 at Tuxford shed, September 1953.

Rebuilt with Diagram 15D boiler. Smokebox similar in style to class O5 but shorter (cf. fig. 42), twin-handle fastening for smokebox door, L.N.E.R./Gorton 1ft. 3in. chimney, handrail arrangement as classes O4/4 and O4/5.

Fig. 61 Class O4/7 No. 63705 at Staveley shed, July 1955.

Further rebuilt from class O4/5, retaining outside sandboxes below cab.

Fig. 62 Class O4/8 No. 6292 at Gorton Works, May 1944.

Rebuilt with Diagram 100A boiler. O1-type 1 ft. $7\frac{5}{16}$ in. chimney, new cab, new style buffers with stepped shanks, continuous handrail on smokebox front.

Fig. 63 Class O4/8 No. 3882 at Darnall shed, April 1949.

Further rebuilt from class O4/4. Frame extension removed but retaining shortened splashers.

Fig. 64 Class O4/1 No. 63601 at Oakington near Cambridge, October 1964.

After being withdrawn for preservation. Stopped with a hot axlebox en route from Doncaster to Stratford.

Fig. 65 Class O4/1 No. 6245 on a No. 1 vacuum braked goods near Rugby, August 1925.

Ramsbottom safety valves with single casing round valves (cf. figs. 35 and 37).

Fig. 66 Class O4/1 No. 6227 on down coal empties at Dukeries Junction, May 1946.

Still retaining smokebox door wheel and handle fastening and top lampiron in front of chimney.

Fig. 67 Class O5 No. 5010 on down goods near Peterborough, about 1926.
Still fitted with top feed to boiler and footsteps mid-way along running plate.

Fig. 68 Class O4/1 (O4/6) No. 5015 on down class B goods at Nottingham Trent Bridge, January 1936.

Fig. 69 Class O4/2 No. 6286 on class B goods from Perth between Glenfarg and Mawcarse, about 1929.

Still fitted with Continental style buffers with ribbed stocks, flat strips on cab roof, numbers high up on bufferbeam due to retention of side chain sockets, showing the wider running plate over the cylinders.

Fig. 70 Class O4/3 No. 6284 on down empty wagon train at Greenwood, 1925.

Fig. 71 Class O4/3 No. 6522 on Target No. 14 Whitemoor – Temple Mills goods near Broxbourne, June 1939.

Fig. 72 Class O4/2 No. 6544 on a class A goods from Perth near Glenfarg, about April 1934.

L.N.E.R./Gorton 1ft. 5½in. chimney.

Fig. 73 Class O4/7 No. 3794 on up class A goods at Nottingham Arkwright Street station, July 1947.

Gorton's angular style of dome cover.

Fig. 74 Class O4/8 No. 3633 on down class C goods at Nottingham Victoria station, May 1947.

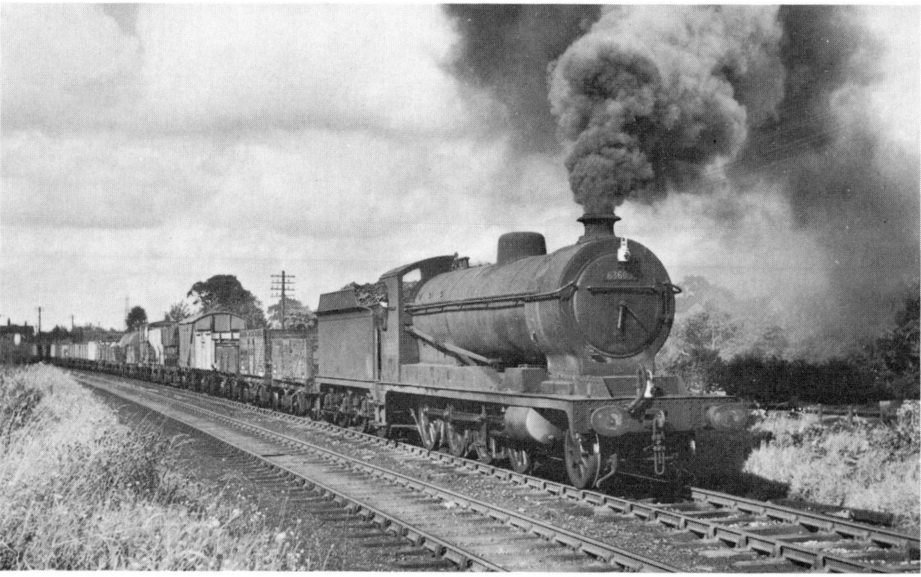

Fig. 75 Class O4/7 No. 63603 on down class H goods at Mobberley (ex-C.L.C.), August 1957.

Section C, 1932.	O4/5	Engines rebuilt to take modified O2 boiler. Steam brake with vacuum ejector added to diagram, 12/1938. Rebuilt date amended from 1932 to 1932-38, 12/1941. Diagram deleted 12/1959, last two engines withdrawn.
Section C, 1938.	O4/6	Engines rebuilt from class O5. Double side-window cab depicted, tender weights relevant for water scoop fitted but no scoop shown on diagram. Diagram deleted 12/1940, engines included with Parts 1 and 2 on new composite diagram.
Section C, 1939.	O4/7	Engines rebuilt with diagram 15D boiler, having round-top firebox. Diagram deleted 12/1965, last engines withdrawn.
1944.	O4	"With Diagram No. 100A boiler". Thompson rebuilds with standard round-top firebox boiler (but working at 180 lb. pressure), L.N.E.R.-type double side-window cab, diagram drawn in Thompson style. Engines reclassified O4 Part 8, 12/1946.
1947.	O4/8	Replacement diagram with reduction in tubes from 143 to 141 and revised heating surface. Diagram deleted 12/1966, last engines withdrawn.
Section C, 1924.	O5	Double side-window cab depicted, heights all over 13ft. 0in., centres of coupled wheel laminated springs incorrectly shown as 8ft. 6in., details shown for 28-element and 42-element superheaters. Laminated spring length corrected to 3ft. 6in., 12/1924. Details of 42-element superheater deleted, 12/1936. Empty weights added of engine and tender, 12/1937. Steam brake with vacuum ejector added to diagram, minor alterations to tubeplate thickness and length between tubeplates, 12/1938. Diagram deleted 12/1939.
Section C, 1939.	O5	Drawing revised to show cut-down variety, but heights given for both over and under 13ft. 0in., tender scoop not shown. Platform width altered from 8ft. 9in. to 8ft. 9½in., 12/1941. Note added that No. 5422 has no cab side windows, 12/1942. Diagram deleted 12/1943, last engine rebuilt to class O4 Part 6.

Classification: Southern Area load class 7; Route availability 6; B.R. power class 7.

Summary of O4 and O5 Classes

B.R. No.	*1947 No.*	*1946 No.*	*1924 No.*	*Maker*	*Built*	*Rebuilt G.C.*	*1923 Class*	*Rebuilt*	*With-drawn*
63572 6/49	3572 2/47	3500 12/46	5966 6/24	Gorton	9/1911	9/21	O4	O4/1 (6/24)	11/59
63577 7/49	3577 2/47	3501 4/46	5026 3/25	,,	12/1911	—	O4/1	—	12/63
63580 5/48	3580 2/47	3502 4/46	5069 11/25	,,	12/1911	—	,,	—	2/52 (p)
63582 1/49	3582 2/47	3503 4/46	5093 10/24	,,	12/1911	—	,,	O4/7 (2/41)	8/59
63585 10/50	3585 3/47	3504 1/46	5331 6/25	,,	10/1911	—	,,	—	12/63
63586 11/50	3586 2/47	3505 1/46	5332 3/25	,,	10/1911	—	,,	—	10/65
—	3594 2/47	3506 1/46	5333 11/25	,,	11/1911	—	,,	O1 (11/47)	—
63598 9/49	3598 2/47	3507 1/46	5334 12/24	,,	11/1911	—	,,	—	10/62
63600 10/49	3600 2/47	3508 1/46	5335 2/26	,,	11/1911	—	,,	O4/7 (9/42)	10/62
63601 9/49	3601 2/47	3509 4/46	5102 6/25	,,	1/1912	—	,,	—	6/63
63607 9/48	3607 2/47	3510 4/46	5133 5/25	,,	1/1912	—	,,	—	9/65
63608 12/48	3608 2/47	3511 1/46	5155 2/25	,,	1/1912	—	,,	—	5/61
—	—	(3512)	5346 7/25	,,	6/1912	—	,,	—	10/41 (k)
63617 5/50	3617 2/47	3513 8/46	5347 6/26	,,	6/1912	—	,,	—	12/62
63625 8/48	3625 2/47	3514 8/46	5348 2/25	,,	6/1912	—	,,	—	4/59
63632 11/50	3632 2/47	3515 9/46	5349 12/25	,,	7/1912	—	,,	—	1/64
63634 6/48	3634 2/47	3516 4/46	5350 4/25	,,	7/1912	—	,,	O4/7 (1/40)	9/62
63635 3/49	3635 3/47	3517 4/46	5351 5/26	,,	8/1912	—	,,	—	5/62
63640 11/49	3640 2/47	3518 11/46	5352 8/25	,,	8/1912	—	,,	—	5/59
63643 10/49	3643 2/47	3519 6/46	5353 7/24	,,	8/1912	—	,,	O4/7 (10/43)	11/60
—	—	(3520)	5354 2/25	,,	9/1912	—	,,	—	9/41 (k)
63654 4/49	3654 2/47	3521 8/46	5355 8/26	,,	9/1912	—	,,	—	6/59
63658 9/48	3658 2/47	3522 11/46	5400 7/26	,,	2/1912	—	,,	—	12/62
—	—	(3523)	5402 3/25	,,	2/1912	—	,,	—	10/41 (k)
63660 8/49	3660 2/47	3524 10/46	5403 11/24	,,	3/1912	—	,,	—	9/59
63664 5/48	3664 2/47	3525 11/46	5404 6/24	,,	3/1912	—	,,	—	9/62
63669 6/49	3669 2/47	3526 10/46	5405 4/27	,,	4/1912	—	,,	O4/7 (4/40)	11/60
63671 11/49	3671 2/47	3527 10/46	5406 4/26	,,	5/1912	—	,,	—	6/65
63677 1/49	3677 2/47	3528 9/46	5407 2/26	,,	5/1912	—	,,	—	3/62
—	—	3529	5408 7/26	,,	5/1912	—	,,	O1 (12/44)	—
—	—	(3530)	6183 3/25	Kitson & Co.	4891	7/1912	O4/1	—	9/41 (k)
63680 7/50	3680 2/47	3531 12/46	6184 8/25	,,	4892	7/1912	,,	—	9/59
—	—	(3532)	6185 8/25	,,	4893	7/1912	O4/1(s)	—	9/41 (k)
63683 4/51	3683 2/47	3533 9/46	6186 4/24	,,	4894	7/1912	O4/1	O4/8 (8/53)	3/65
63684 3/50	3684 2/47	3534 9/46	6187 6/24	,,	4895	7/1912	,,	—	12/63
63690 9/49	3690 2/47	3535 11/46	6188 6/24	,,	4896	7/1912	,,	—	12/62
63692 9/48	3692 2/47	3536 11/46	6189 8/24	,,	4897	7/1912	,,	—	2/65
63693 2/51	3693 2/47	3537 6/46	6190 12/24	,,	4898	8/1912	,,	—	11/62
63698 4/48	3698 2/47	3538 9/46	6191 11/24	,,	4899	8/1912	,,	—	12/62
63700 1/49	3700 2/47	3539 8/46	6192 4/27	,,	4900	8/1912	,,	—	12/60
63707 12/50	3707 2/47	3540 11/46	6193 10/24	,,	4901	9/1912	,,	—	7/65
63710 9/50	3710 2/47	3541 9/46	6194 12/26	,,	4902	9/1912	,,	—	7/59
—	—	(3542)	6195 5/25	,,	4903	9/1912	,,	O1 (10/44)	—
—	—	(3543)	6196 4/26	,,	4904	9/1912	,,	—	9/41 (k)
—	—	(3544)	6197 8/24	,,	4905	9/1912	,,	—	10/41 (k)
63719 11/50	3719 3/47	3545 9/46	6198 5/24	,,	4906	9/1912	,,	—	8/61
63722 3/49	3722 2/47	3546 9/46	6199 4/25	,,	4907	9/1912	,,	—	9/63

63723	1/49	3723	2/47	3547	9/46	6200	3/25	Kitson & Co.	4908	10/1912	O4/1	—	11/59
63727	12/49	3727	4/47	3548	9/46	6201	8/24	,,	4909	10/1912	,,	—	2/64
—		—		(3549)		6202	2/27	,,	4910	10/1912	,,	—	9/41 (k)
63736	10/49	3736	2/47	3550	10/46	6203	1/25	N.B. Loco. Co. (b)	19859	8/1912	,,	—	8/63
—		—		(3551)		6204	7/24	,,	19860	8/1912	,,	—	9/41 (k)
63738	5/48	3738	2/47	3552	11/46	6205	5/24	,,	19861	8/1912	,,	O4/8 (6/44)	8/65
63743	6/49	3743	3/47	3553	1/47	6206	2/25	,,	19862	8/1912	,,	—	6/62
63745	1/50	3745	2/47	3554	11/46	6207	4/25	,,	19863	8/1912	,,	O4/5 (6/32)	4/59
63757	6/48	3757	2/47	3555	12/46	6208	3/25	,,	19864	8/1912	,,	—	11/61
63761	2/49	3761	3/47	3556	11/46	6209	2/25	,,	19865	8/1912	,,	O4/7 (6/40)	6/59
63762	9/48	3762	2/47	3557	1/47	6210	8/25	,,	19866	8/1912	,,	—	3/62
63772	11/49	3772	2/47	3558	12/46	6211	11/24	,,	19867	8/1912	,,	O4/7 (6/42)	3/63
—		—		(3559)		6212	8/25	,,	19868	8/1912	,,	—	.9/41 (k)
—		—		(3560)		6213	4/25	,,	19869	8/1912	,,	O1 (4/46)	—
—		—		(3561)		6214	9/26	,,	19870	9/1912	,,	O1 (11/46)	—
63778	8/49	3778	2/47	3562	12/46	6215	2/24	,,	19871	9/1912	,,	—	2/52 (p)
—		—		(3563)		6216	8/25	,,	19872	9/1912	,,	O1 (1/46)	—
—		—		(3564)		6217	3/26	,,	19873	9/1912	,,	—	9/41 (k)
63797	1/50	3797	3/47	3565	11/46	6218	9/26	,,	19874	9/1912	,,	—	2/59
63799	5/48	3799	2/47	3566	11/46	6219	7/25	,,	19875	10/1912	,,	—	11/61
—		—		(3567)		6220	5/25	,,	19876	10/1912	,,	O1 6/45)	—
63805	11/49	3805	2/47	3568	12/46	6221	2/26	,,	19877	10/1912	,,	O4/8 (6/54)	11/62
63809	7/49	3809	2/47	3569	11/46	6222	7/25	,,	19878	10/1912	,,	—	2/52 (p)
63570	1/49	—		3570	11/46	6223	3/24	,,	19879	10/1912	,,	O4/7 (11/40)	12/61
(63571)		—		3571	12/46	6224	9/25	,,	19880	10/1912	,,	O1 (8/49)	—
—		—		(3572)		6225	8/25	,,	19881	11/1912	,,	—	9/41 (k)
63573	2/50	—		3573	12/46	6226	9/25	,,	19882	11/1912	,,	O4/8 (4/55)	4/61
63574	8/48	—		3574	12/46	6227	5/25	,,	19883	11/1912	,,	—	9/62
63575	10/48	—		3575	12/46	6228	10/26	,,	19884	11/1912	,,	O4/8 (9/44)	11/62
63576	4/50	—		3576	12/46	6229	4/26	,,	19885	11/1912	,,	—	11/63
—		—		(3577)		6230	3/26	,,	19886	11/1912	,,	—	10/41 (k)
—		—		(3578)		6231	2/24	,,	19887	11/1912	,,	O1 (10/45)	—
(63579)		—		3579	12/46	6232	9/25	,,	19888	11/1912	,,	O4/5 (10/32), O1 (3/48)	—
—		—		(3580)		6233	12/25	,,	19889	11/1912	,,	—	9/41 (k)
63581	12/49	—		3581	12/46	6234	10/27	,,	19890	11/1912	,,	—	2/59
—		—		(3582)		6235	1/25	,,	19891	11/1912	,,	—	10/41 (k)
63583	9/50	—		3583	11/46	6236	3/26	,,	19892	11/1912	,,	—	6/59
63584	1/50	—		3584	12/46	6237	2/25	,,	19893	11/1912	,,	—	8/62
—		—		(3585)		6238	7/26	,,	19894	11/1912	,,	—	9/41 (k)
—		—		(3586)		6239	2/24	,,	19895	12/1912	,,	—	9/41 (k)
63587	7/48	—		3587	12/46	6240	4/26	,,	19896	12/1912	,,	—	9/62
63588	7/48	—		3588	11/46	6241	11/24	,,	19897	12/1912	,,	O4/7 (11/39)	8/62
(63589)		—		3589	12/46	6242	2/24	,,	19898	12/1912	,,	O4/5 (10/32), O1 (4/49)	—
—		—		(3590)		6243	7/24	,,	19899	12/1912	,,	O1 (12/44)	—
—		—		(3591)		6244	11/24	,,	19900	12/1912	,,	O1 (4/44)	—
—		—		(3592)		6245	6/24	,,	19901	12/1912	,,	O1 (10/46)	—
63593	6/48	—		3593	11/46	6246	4/25	,,	19902	12/1912	,,	—	10/65

Summary of O4 and O5 Classes (continued)

B.R. No.	1946 No.	1924 No.	Maker	Works No.	Built	1923 Class	Rebuilt	With-drawn
—	(3594)	6247 3/25	N.B. Loco. Co. (b)	19903	12/1912	O4/1	—	10/41 (k)
63595 6/48	3595 12/46	6248 4/26	,,	19904	12/1912	,,	O4/7 (8/40)	4/61
(63596)	3596 1/47	6249 2/25	,,	19905	12/1912	,,	O4/7 (9/42), O1 (7/49)	—
63597 5/49	3597 12/46	6250 2/24	,,	19906	12/1912	,,	—	5/61
—	(3598)	6251 8/25	,,	19907	1/1913	,,	—	10/41 (k)
63599 2/49	3599 12/46	6252 3/24	,,	19908	1/1913	,,	—	2/62
—	(3600)	5375 1/26	Gorton	—	4/1913	,,	—	10/41 (k)
—	(3601)	5376 6/25	,,	—	4/1913	,,	—	9/41 (k)
63602 4/50	3602 10/46	5377 12/24	,,	—	5/1913	O4/2 (f)	O4/8 (3/55)	12/62
63603 11/48	3603 1/47	5378 7/26	,,	—	5/1913	O4/1	O4/7 (7/40)	7/62
63604 4/48	3604 11/46	5379 5/26	,,	—	6/1913	,,	O4/8 (1/54)	5/64
63605 4/48	3605 12/46	5380 12/25	,,	—	6/1913	O4/2 (g)	—	8/62
63606 7/48	3606 12/46	5381 8/25	,,	—	7/1913	O4/1	O4/8 (6/55)	6/65
—	(3607)	5382 11/25	,,	—	7/1913	,,	—	9/41 (k)
—	(3608)	5383 8/25	,,	—	8/1913	O4/2 (g)	—	9/41 (k)
63609 5/49	3609 8/46	5384 2/26	,,	—	9/1913	O4/1	—	9/62
—	(3610)	5385 5/26	,,	—	12/1913	,,	O1 (7/44)	—
63611 2/51	3611 10/46	5386 1/26	,,	—	1/1914	,,	—	3/64
63612 4/50	3612 10/46	5387 11/25	,,	—	1/1914	,,	O4/8 (7/55)	11/65
63613 10/48	3613 4/46	5388 2/24	,,	—	2/1914	,,	O4/8 (9/44)	7/65
63614 10/48	3614 3/46	5389 2/25	,,	—	2/1914	,,	—	4/59
63615 10/48	3615 10/46	5390 6/26	,,	—	2/1914	,,	O4/7 (12/39)	9/64
63616 12/50	3616 6/46	5391 2/24	,,	—	3/1914	,,	O4/7 (8/40)	9/62
—	(3617)	5392 5/24	,,	—	3/1914	,,	—	9/41 (k)
63618 3/49	3618 4/46	5393 3/26	,,	—	3/1914	,,	—	2/63
—	(3619)	5394 3/25	,,	—	4/1914	,,	O1 (3/45)	—
63620 3/50	3620 9/46	5395 7/25	,,	—	4/1914	,,	—	2/59
63621 5/50	3621 11/46	5396 5/24	,,	—	5/1914	,,	—	9/62
63622 10/48	3622 10/46	5397 2/24	,,	—	5/1914	,,	—	5/63
63623 7/48	3623 12/46	5398 5/25	,,	—	5/1914	,,	—	2/62
63624 8/50	3624 12/46	5399 11/25	,,	—	6/1914	,,	O4/8 (5/55)	12/62
—	(3625)	5271 3/24	,,	—	6/1914	,,	—	10/41 (k)

B.R. No.	1946 No.	1924 No.	Maker	Built	Former R.O.D. No.	To G.C. Stock	1923 Class	Rebuilt	With-drawn
63626 5/48	3626 12/46	5001 8/25	Gorton	1/1919	2005	6/1919	O4/1	—	6/61
63627 7/49	3627 12/46	5005 4/26	,,	3/1919	2006	6/1919	,,	—	2/52 (p)
63628 7/48	3628 11/46	5008 5/26	,,	3/1919	2007	6/1919	,,	O4/5 (6/32), O4/8 (2/55)	9/65

B.R. No		1946 No.		First L.N.E.R. No.	Date into Traffic	Maker	Works No.	Built	Former R.O.D. No.	Class (m)	Rebuilt	With-drawn
63629	11/49	3629	10/46	6554	6/27	Nasmyth, Wilson	1244	12/1917	1701	O4/3	—	2/59
—		(3630)		6555	5/27	,,	1255	2/1918	1712	,,	O1 (6/45)	—
63631	7/48	3631	11/46	6556	7/28	,,	1256	6/1918	1713	,,	O4/8 (1/57)	9/62
—		(3632)		6557	5/28	,,	1259	7/1918	1716	,,	—	9/41 (k)
63633	2/49	3633	11/46	6536	10/25	,,	1260	7/1918	1717	,,	O4/8 (4/47)	8/62
—		(3634)		6377	3/24	,,	1261	8/1918	1718	,,	—	9/41 (k)
—		(3635)		6537	10/25	,,	1262	8/1918	1719	,,	—	9/41 (k)
63636	7/48	3636	12/46	6376	2/24	,,	1264	10/1918	1721	,,	O4/8 (12/57)	12/64
63637	7/49	3637	11/46	6558	5/28	,,	1265	10/1918	1722	,,	—	12/62
63638	10/48	3638	12/46	6375	4/24	,,	1266	10/1918	1723	,,	—	3/59
63639	8/49	3639	1/47	6559	4/29	,,	1267	10/1918	1724	,,	O4/8 (12/54)	12/65
—		(3640)		6560	4/28	,,	1283	9/1919	1727	,,	—	9/41 (k)
63641	12/49	3641	1/47	6561	9/27	,,	1284	9/1919	1728	,,	O4/8 (6/57)	9/62
63642	2/50	3642	12/46	6538	10/25	,,	1285	—/1919	1729	,,	—	11/59
—		(3643)		6373	5/24	Kitson & Co.	5183	1/1918	1601	,,	—	10/41 (k)
63644	8/49	3644	11/46	6543	3/29	,,	5185	1/1918	1603	O4/2	O4/8 (8/54)	1/66
63645	8/48	3645	11/46	6366	2/24	,,	5186	2/1918	1604	O4/3	O4/8 (9/56)	4/64
—		(3646)		6374	5/24	,,	5187	2/1918	1605	,,	O1 (9/45)	—
63647	9/50	3647	12/46	6544	12/28	,,	5188	2/1918	1606	O4/2	O4/8 (3/58)	5/64
63648	2/51	3648	10/46	6372	8/24	,,	5189	2/1918	1607	,,	—	1/62
63649	1/50	3649	11/46	6365	3/24	,,	5190	3/1918	1608	O4/3	O4/8 (11/57)	3/61
—		(3650)		6545	5/29	,,	5191	3/1918	1609	,,	O1 (5/45)	—
63651	1/49	3651	9/46	6539	8/25	,,	5192	3/1918	1610	,,	O4/8 (1/47)	7/65
—		(3652)		6371	6/24	,,	5193	3/1918	1611	,,	O4/4 (7/29), O1 (12/45)	—
63653	6/49	3653	10/46	6370	8/24	,,	5194	4/1918	1612	O4/2	O4/8 (2/47)	4/66
—		(3654)		6369	5/24	,,	5200	5/1918	1614	O4/3	—	9/41 (k)
63655	10/48	3655	12/46	6364	2/24	,,	5202	6/1918	1616	,,	O4/7 (4/41), O4/8 (1/57)	12/62
63656	6/48	3656	12/46	6363	3/24	,,	5203	6/1918	1617	,,	—	11/62
63657	12/50	3657	1/47	6546	6/27	,,	5204	6/1918	1618	,,	—	9/62
—		(3658)		6368	4/24	,,	5205	7/1918	1619	,,	—	9/41 (k)
63659	5/50	3659	1/47	6360	2/24	,,	5206	7/1918	1620	,,	—	12/62
—		(3660)		6547	10/27	,,	5207	7/1918	1621	,,	—	10/41 (k)
63661	12/48	3661	1/47	6540	8/25	,,	5208	7/1918	1622	,,	O4/7 (8/40)	8/65
63662	5/48	3662	12/46	6358	2/24	,,	5210	8/1918	1624	,,	O4/7 (5/42)	5/61
—		(3663)		6359	2/24	,,	5211	8/1918	1625	,,	O1 (6/45)	—
—		(3664)		6541	8/25	,,	5212	8/1918	1626	,,	—	9/41 (k)
63665	1/50	3665	9/46	6357	3/24	,,	5213	9/1918	1627	,,	—	12/63
63666	5/48	3666	9/46	6542	10/25	,,	5214	9/1918	1628	,,	—	12/62
63667	6/50	3667	9/46	6367	2/24	,,	5215	9/1918	1629	,,	—	1/59
63668	7/49	3668	9/46	6361	2/24	,,	5217	10/1918	1631	,,	—	12/58
—		(3669)		6362	3/24	,,	5218	10/1918	1632	,,	—	10/41 (k)
—		(3670		6356	3/24	R. Stephenson & Co.	3695	9/1917	1651	,,	O1 (3/46)	—
—		(3671)		6355 (d)	1/24	,,	3696	9/1917	1652	,,	—	9/41 (k)
63672	8/50	3672	9/46	6354	6/24	,,	3697	10/1917	1653	,,	O4/8 (4/57)	12/63
63673	6/48	3673	12/46	6352	8/24	,,	3698	10/1917	1654	O4/2	O4/7 (3/40)	5/59

Summary of O4 and O5 Classes (continued)

B.R. No		*1946 No.*		*First L.N.E.R. No.*	*Date into Traffic*	*Maker*	*Works No.*	*Built*	*Former R.O.D. No.*	*Class* (m)	*Rebuilt*	*With-drawn*
63674	4/48	3674	9/46	6351	8/24	R. Stephenson & Co.	3699	10/1917	1655	O4/2	O4/8 (5/57)	1/66
63675	8/48	3675	11/46	6353	5/24	,,	3700	10/1917	1656	O4/3	O4/7 (12/39), O4/8 (2/57)	1/66
—		(3676)		6350	6/24	,,	3701	11/1917	1657	,,	O1 (1/45)	—
—		(3677)		6348	4/24	,,	3702	11/1917	1658	,,	—	10/41 (k)
—		(3678)		6332	5/24	,,	3703	11/1917	1659	,,	—	9/41 (k)
63679	6/50	3679	11/46	6325 (d)	1/24	,,	3705	12/1917	1661	,,	O4/8 (11/57)	5/65
—		(3680)		6346	7/24	,,	3706	12/1917	1662	O4/2	—	9/41 (k)
63681	5/48	3681	8/46	6347	4/24	,,	3707	12/1917	1663	O4/3	—	2/62
63682	6/49	3682	12/46	6548	10/28	,,	3708	12/1917	1664	O4/2	—	3/59
—		(3683)		6549	3/29	,,	3709	1/1918	1665	O4/3	—	9/41 (k)
—		(3684)		6345	2/24	,,	3710	1/1918	1666	,,	—	9/41 (k)
63685	2/49	3685	11/46	6344	5/24	,,	3711	1/1918	1667	,,	—	3/64
63686	4/48	3686	5/46	6495	7/25	,,	3712	2/1918	1668	,,	—	9/62
—		(3687)		6324	3/24	,,	3713	2/1918	1669	,,	O1 (12/45)	—
63688	1/49	3688	12/46	6343	3/24	,,	3714	2/1918	1670	,,	O4/8 (11/56)	9/65
—		(3689)		6341	5/24	,,	3715	3/1918	1671	,,	O1 (8/45)	—
—		(3690)		6551	1/29 (h)	,,	3716	3/1918	1672	O4/2	—	9/41 (k)
63691	10/48	3691	12/46	6342	3/24	,,	3717	4/1918	1673	O4/3	O4/8 (3/56)	6/65
—		(3692)		6339	4/24	,,	3718	4/1918	1674	,,	—	9/41 (k)
—		(3693)		6340	3/24	,,	3720	5/1918	1676	,,	—	10/41 (k)
63694	1/49	3694	1/47	6349	6/24	,,	3719	4/1918	1675	,,	—	10/59
63695	5/48	3695	6/46	6496	9/25	,,	3721	5/1918	1677	,,	—	12/62
63696	3/49	3696	12/46	6323	3/24	,,	3722	5/1918	1678	,,	—	4/59
63697	1/49	3697	9/46	6338	6/24	,,	3723	6/1918	1679	,,	O4/8 (5/58)	8/65
—		(3698)		6322	4/24	,,	3724	6/1918	1680	,,	—	9/41 (k)
63699	5/49	3699	9/46	6337	7/24	,,	3726	6/1918	1682	,,	O4/7 (4/41)	6/59
—		(3700)		6497	11/25	,,	3727	7/1918	1683	,,	—	9/41 (k)
63701	9/50	3701	5/46	6498	7/25	,,	3728	7/1918	1684	,,	—	8/65
63702	5/48	3702	4/46	6321	3/24	,,	3729	7/1918	1685	,,	—	9/64
63703	10/50	3703	9/46	6336	3/24	,,	3730	8/1918	1686	,,	O4/8 (1/53)	1/65
63704	11/50	3704	9/46	6550	12/28	,,	3731	10/1918	1647	O4/2	O4/8 (12/53)	3/63
63705	7/49	3705	9/46	6320	2/24	,,	3733	10/1918	1649	O4/3	O4/5 (8/39), O4/7 (12/47), O4/8 (8/58)	4/63
63706	12/48	3706	6/46	6319	2/24	,,	3734	10/1918	1650	,,	O4/7 (5/40), O4/8 (11/56)	9/65
—		(3707)		6499	10/25	,,	3735	11/1918	1687	,,	—	9/41 (k)
63708	5/48	3708	8/46	6318	4/24	,,	3736	11/1918	1688	,,	O4/7 (9/42)	9/62
63709	8/50	3709	8/46	6552	8/27	,,	3737	12/1918	1689	,,	O4/8 (2/58)	2/61
—		(3710)		6335	6/24	,,	3738	12/1918	1690	,,	—	9/41 (k)
—		(3711)		6317	3/24	,,	3739	1/1919	1691	,,	—	10/41 (k)
—		(3712)		6334 (d)	1/24	,,	3740	1/1919	1692	,,	O1 (5/44)	—
63713	10/49	3713	3/46	6553	11/27	,,	3741	1/1919	1693	,,	—	8/62
63714	2/50	3714	3/46	6316	4/24	,,	3742	1/1919	1694	,,	—	3/59
63715	6/48	3715	7/46	6333	6/24	,,	3743	2/1919	1695	,,	O4/8 (1/58)	1/64
63716	4/49	3716	6/46	6310	4/24	,,	3744	2/1919	1696	,,	—	7/60
63717	10/48	3717	7/46	6314	3/24	,,	3745	3/1919	1697	,,	O4/8 (3/58)	4/65

63718	6/48	3718	8/46	6313	3/24	R. Stephenson & Co.	3747	3/1919	1699	O4/3	O4/8 (6/56)	12/62
—		(3719)		6315	4/24	,,	3748	4/1919	1700	,,	—	9/41 (k)
63720	10/48	3720	5/46	6311	4/24	,,	3751	5/1919	1643	,,	O4/8 (2/57)	3/64
63721	8/49	3721	9/46	6331	6/24	,,	3753	6/1919	1645	,,	O4/8 (4/54)	11/62
—		(3722)		6312	2/24	,,	3756	7/1919	1636	,,	—	10/41 (k)
—		(3723)		6330	7/24	,,	3757	7/1919	1638	,,	—	9/41 (k)
63724	6/49	3724	9/46	6329	3/24	,,	3758	8/1919	1640	,,	—	8/62
—		(3725)		6328	8/24	,,	3759	8/1919	1641	O4/2	O1 (3/45)	—
63726	6/48	3726	10/46	6500	10/25	,,	3764	10/1919	1737	O4/3	O4/5 (9/39), O4/8 (1/58)	4/64
—		(3727)		6327	6/24	,,	3765	10/1919	1738	,,	—	10/41 (k)
63728	6/48	3728	7/46	6308	3/24	,,	3766	10/1919	1739	,,	O4/8 (2/56)	12/64
63729	6/48	3729	8/46	6309 (d)	12/23 (e)	,,	3768	11/1919	1741	,,	—	3/59
63730	2/49	3730	9/46	6326	4/24	,,	3770	11/1919	1743	,,	O4/8 (3/58)	1/66
63731	1/49	3731	9/46	6307	2/24	,,	3773	12/1919	1746	,,	O4/8 (9/56)	10/63
63732	6/48	3732	5/46	6501	6/25	,,	3774	12/1919	1747	,,	O4/8 (7/56)	9/65
63733	9/50	3733	3/46	6502	6/25	,,	3775	4/1920	1748	,,	—	1/60
63734	8/48	3734	6/46	6503	3/26	,,	3776	4/1920	1749	,,	O4/8 (6/56)	8/65
63735	12/48	3735	9/46	6562	10/27	N.B. Loco. Co. (c)	21772	9/1917	1805	,,	—	12/62
—		(3736)		6563	2/28	,,	21773	9/1917	1806	,,	—	10/41 (k)
63737	4/50	3737	8/46	6564	9/27	,,	21774	9/1917	1807	,,	—	12/62
—		(3738)		6565	12/27	,,	21776	9/1917	1809	,,	—	9/41 (k)
63739	3/48	3739	5/46	6285	2/24	,,	21778	10/1917	1811	,,	O4/8 (5/58)	10/65
—		(3740)		6566	5/27	,,	21779	10/1917	1812	,,	O1 (8/45)	—
63741	11/49	3741	8/46	6567	10/28	,,	21782	10/1917	1815	,,	O4/8 (7/58)	4/65
63742	10/48	3742	9/46	6568	6/27	,,	21783	10/1917	1816	,,	O4/8 (9/56)	2/63
—		(3743)		6569	6/27	,,	21784	10/1917	1817	,,	—	9/41 (k)
63744	5/48	3744	10/46	6284	3/24	,,	21786	10/1917	1819	,,	—	7/63
—		(3745)		6570	8/27	,,	21787	10/1917	1820	,,	—	9/41 (k)
(63746)		3746	9/46	6571	7/27	,,	21788	10/1917	1821	,,	O1 (11/48)	—
63747	4/48	3747	7/46	6572	5/27	,,	21791	11/1917	1824	,,	O4/7 (7/42)	5/61
63748	8/48	3748	8/46	6258 (d)	1/24	,,	21794	11/1917	1827	,,	O4/7 (5/40)	11/62
63749	8/48	3749	5/46	6573	4/28	,,	21796	11/1917	1829	,,	O4/7 (5/40)	10/59
63750	1/50	3750	8/46	6278 (d)	1/24	,,	21798	11/1917	1831	,,	O4/8 (10/52)	3/64
63751	2/49	3751	10/46	6574	9/27	,,	21800	12/1917	1833	,,	—	3/59
—		(3752)		6575	4/27	,,	21801	12/1917	1834	,,	O1 (11/45)	—
63753	3/50	3753	9/46	6576	4/28	,,	21803	12/1917	1836	,,	—	12/59
63754	9/49	3754	10/46	6577	3/28	,,	21806	12/1917	1839	,,	O4/8 (8/57)	2/64
—		(3755)		6578	1/28	,,	21807	12/1917	1840	,,	O1 (10/44)	—
63756	12/48	3756	6/46	6255 (d)	12/23 (e)	,,	21808	12/1917	1841	,,	—	6/59
—		(3757)		6279	3/24	N.B. Loco. Co. (b)	21822	1/1918	1845	,,	—	9/41 (k)
63758	8/48	3758	5/46	6276	2/24	,,	21824	1/1918	1847	,,	O4/7 (4/44)	5/62
63759	8/48	3759	5/46	6282 (d)	2/24	,,	21825	1/1918	1848	,,	—	9/62
—		(3760)		6579	5/28	,,	21826	2/1918	1849	,,	O1 (8/46)	—
—		(3761)		6580	5/28	,,	21831	3/1918	1854	,,	—	9/41 (k)
—		(3762)		6273	4/24	,,	21832	3/1918	1855	,,	—	10/41 (k)
63763	8/48	3763	4/46	6272 (d)	1/24	,,	21833	3/1918	1856	,,	O4/8 (10/53)	2/64

Summary of O4 and O5 Classes (continued)

B.R. No		1946 No.		First L.N.E.R. No.	Date into Traffic	Maker	Works No.	Built	Former R.O.D. No.	Class (m)	Rebuilt	With-drawn
63764	6/48	3764	6/46	6581	5/28	N.B. Loco. Co. (c)	21834	3/1918	1857	O4/3	—	2/66
63765	3/48	3765	8/46	6271	3/24	,,	21835	3/1918	1858	,,	O4/8 (12/57)	10/64
63766	5/48	3766	5/46	6582	1/29 (h)	,,	21836	3/1918	1859	O4/2	—	8/62
63767	5/49	3767	8/46	6274	2/24	,,	21837	3/1918	1860	O4/3	—	11/62
—		(3768)		6513	11/25	,,	21838	3/1918	1861	,,	O1 (12/45)	—
63769	7/49	3769	9/46	6583	1/28	,,	21839	4/1918	1862	,,	—	3/59
63770	10/49	3770	6/46	6584	3/28	,,	21840	4/1918	1863	,,	O4/7 (6/40)	12/65
63771	12/48	3771	3/46	6270	3/24	,,	21841	4/1918	1864	,,	—	11/62
—		(3772)		6585	10/27	,,	21843	4/1918	1866	,,	—	9/41 (k)
—		(3773)		6514	3/26	,,	21844	4/1918	1867	,,	—	9/41 (k)
63774	1/49	3774	4/46	6268	4/24	,,	21845	4/1918	1868	,,	—	3/63
63775	5/49	3775	11/46	6586	12/27	,,	21846	4/1918	1869	,,	O4/7 (8/40)	3/62
63776	9/50	3776	11/46	6267	2/24	N.B. Loco. Co. (b)	21847	4/1918	1870	,,	O4/8 (4/55)	12/62
—		(3777)		6504	8/25	,,	21850	5/1918	1873	,,	—	9/41 (k)
—		(3778)		6587	11/27	,,	21851	5/1918	1874	,,	—	9/41 (k)
63779	12/49	3779	9/46	6588	7/27	,,	21852	5/1918	1875	,,	—	4/62
—		(3780)		6505	7/25	,,	21853	5/1918	1876	,,	O1 (4/45)	—
63781	10/48	3781	6/46	6269 (d)	1/24	,,	21855	5/1918	1878	,,	O4/8 (4/58)	4/66
63782	5/49	3782	10/46	6506	7/25	,,	21856	5/1918	1879	,,	—	5/61
63783	12/48	3783	5/46	6589	2/28	,,	21857	5/1918	1880	,,	—	12/62
—		(3784)		6507	9/25	,,	21858	5/1918	1881	,,	O1 (6/44)	—
63785	2/49	3785	8/46	6590	1/28	,,	21859	5/1918	1882	,,	O4/8 (11/44)	3/66
—		(3786)		6515	10/25	,,	21861	6/1918	1884	,,	O1 (11/44)	—
63787	2/49	3787	9/46	6591	8/28	,,	21862	6/1918	1885	,,	—	6/62
63788	4/49	3788	10/46	6592	9/27	,,	21863	6/1918	1886	,,	O4/5 (9/39), O4/8 (3/57)	1/66
—		(3789)		6593	7/28	,,	21864	7/1918	1887	,,	—	9/41 (k)
63790	8/49	3790	5/46	6594	6/28	N.B. Loco. Co. (c)	21869	2/1918	1892	,,	—	3/59
63791	7/48	3791	7/46	6510	7/25	,,	21871	2/1918	1894	,,	O4/8 (10/56)	9/65
—		(3792)		6283 (d)	1/24	,,	21872	2/1918	1895	,,	O1 (9/44)	—
63793	9/50	3793	9/46	6280	3/24	,,	21873	2/1918	1896	,,	O4/8 (4/58)	5/65
63794	10/48	3794	7/46	6277	4/24	,,	21875	2/1918	1898	,,	O4/7 (4/43), O4/8 (5/57)	11/62
—		(3795)		6595	9/27	,,	21876	2/1918	1899	,,	O1 (2/44)	—
—		(3796)		6596	2/28	,,	21879	3/1918	1902	,,	O1 (4/46)	—
—		(3797)		6597	7/27	,,	21880	3/1918	1903	,,	—	9/41 (k)
63798	8/49	3798	7/46	6275	3/24	,,	21881	3/1918	1904	,,	—	5/62
—		(3799)		6517	10/25	,,	21882	3/1918	1905	,,	—	10/41 (k)
63800	6/48	3800	6/46	6511	6/25	,,	21884	3/1918	1907	,,	O4/8 (6/57)	5/64
63801	10/48	3801	9/46	6598	9/27	,,	21885	3/1918	1908	,,	O4/8 (8/56)	7/63
63802	5/49	3802	10/46	6281	2/24	,,	21887	4/1918	1910	,,	O4/8 (4/44)	6/64
—		(3803)		6599	7/27	,,	21888	4/1918	1911	,,	—	9/41 (k)
63804	3/49	3804	10/46	6512	10/25	,,	21890	4/1918	1913	,,	—	12/59
—		(3805)		6600	4/29	,,	21891	5/1918	1914	,,	—	9/41 (k)
—		(3806)		6601	3/28	,,	21892	5/1918	1915	,,	O1 (8/44)	—
63807	8/50	3807	7/46	6518	10/25	,,	21893	5/1918	1916	,,	O4/8 (11/52)	9/64
—		(3808)		6519	2/26	,,	21894	5/1918	1917	,,	O1 (2/45)	—
—		(3809)		6602	8/27	,,	21897	5/1918	1920	,,	—	10/41 (k)

—		(3810)		6603	1/28	N.B. Loco. Co. (c)	21898	5/1918	1921	O4/3	—	10/41 (k)
—		(3811)		6520	3/26	,,	21899	5/1918	1922	,,	—	9/41 (k)
63812	1/49	3812	6/46	6265	3/24	,,	21900	6/1918	1923	,,	—	5/59
63813	9/50	3813	11/46	6604	8/28	,,	21902	6/1918	1925	,,	—	3/65
—		(3814)		6605	1/28	,,	21904	6/1918	1927	,,	—	9/41 (k)
—		(3815)		6266	2/24	,,	21905	6/1918	1928	,,	—	10/41 (k)
63816	11/48	3816	11/46	6606	8/27	,,	21906	6/1918	1929	,,	O4/5 (10/39), O4/8 (12/55)	1/66
—		(3817)		6263	2/24	,,	21910	7/1918	1933	,,	O1 (4/45)	—
63818	9/49	3818	10/46	6264	2/24	,,	21913	7/1918	1936	,,	O4/8 (6/47)	4/66
63819	2/49	3819	11/46	6262	2/24	,,	21914	7/1918	1937	,,	O4/8 (11/44)	11/65
—		(3820)		6607	10/27	,,	21916	8/1918	1939	,,	—	9/41 (k)
63821	1/50	3821	11/46	6521	10/25	N.B. Loco. Co. (b)	22001	10/1918	1943	,,	—	12/62
63822	4/48	3822	12/46	6259 (d)	2/24	,,	22006	10/1918	1948	,,	O4/8 (12/58)	3/64
63823	9/48	3823	12/46	6608	6/28	,,	22007	10/1918	1949	,,	O4/8 (10/57)	8/62
63824	8/50	3824	12/46	6516	3/26	,,	22010	11/1918	1952	,,	O4/7 (6/43)	6/63
—		(3825)		6508	8/25	,,	22011	11/1918	1953	,,	—	10/41 (k)
—		(3826)		6509	8/25	,,	22012	11/1918	1954	,,	—	9/41 (k)
63827	10/49	3827	11/46	6306 (d)	12/23 (e)	,,	22014	11/1918	1956	,,	O4/8 (7/44)	1/64
63828	9/48	3828	11/46	6609	9/28	,,	22015	12/1918	1957	,,	O4/8 (9/44)	8/65
63829	9/48	3829	11/46	6304	2/24	,,	22017	12/1918	1959	,,	O4/8 (5/58)	3/64
—		(3830)		6610	12/27	,,	22020	1/1919	1962	,,	—	9/41 (K)
—		(3831)		6301	5/24	,,	22021	1/1919	1963	,,	—	9/41 (k)
63832	10/49	3832	9/46	6303	5/24	,,	22027	2/1919	1969	,,	O4/8 (2/58)	12/62
63833	3/48	3833	12/46	6531	6/25	,,	22029	2/1919	1971	,,	—	1/62
—		(3834)		6260	3/24	N.B. Loco. Co. (c)	22033	10/1918	1975	,,	—	10/41 (k)
63835	9/48	3835	10/46	6611	10/27	,,	22034	10/1918	1976	,,	—	2/59
63836	11/49	3836	11/46	6522	2/26	,,	22036	10/1918	1978	,,	O4/8 (10/44)	4/64
63837	12/48	3837	9/46	6523	1/26	,,	22037	11/1918	1979	,,	O4/8 (2/54)	12/62
(63838)		3838	9/46	6261	3/24	,,	22039	11/1918	1981	,,	O1 (6/49)	—
63839	6/49	3839	10/46	6305	4/24	,,	22049	12/1918	1991	,,	O4/7 (3/44)	4/59
63840	11/50	3840	11/46	6524	12/25	,,	22051	1/1919	1993	,,	O4/8 (8/57)	9/63
63841	2/49	3841	11/46	6302	5/24	,,	22053	2/1919	1995	,,	O4/8 (5/56)	3/64
63842	3/51	3842	11/46	6257	2/24	,,	22056	2/1919	1998	,,	—	4/65
63843	11/49	3843	11/46	6612	8/28	,,	22058	2/1919	2000	,,	O4/7 (2/40)	11/65
—		(3844)		6613	6/28	,,	22059	2/1919	2001	,,	—	9/41 (k)
63845	8/49	3845	11/46	6614	3/28	N.B. Loco. Co. (b)	22137	5/1919	2043	,,	—	6/61
63846	6/48	3846	11/46	6256 (d)	12/23 (e)	,,	22138	5/1919	2044	,,	—	6/64
63847	9/49	3847	12/46	6290	8/24	,,	22139	5/1919	2046	,,	—	5/59
63848	12/48	3848	12/46	6291	8/24	,,	22140	5/1919	2047	O4/2	O4/7 (7/43)	11/62
63849	11/48	3849	12/46	6615	2/28	,,	22141	6/1919	2048	,,	—	2/52 (p)
63850	6/50	3850	12/46	6294	3/24	,,	22143	6/1919	2052	O4/3	O4/8 (10/55)	6/65
63851	12/48	3851	11/46	6299	3/24	,,	22144	6/1919	2053	,,	O4/5 (11/39)	4/59
63852	6/50	3852	11/46	6289	4/24	,,	22145	6/1919	2054	,,	O4/8 (11/55)	1/64
63853	1/49	3853	8/46	6292 (d)	1/24	,,	22146	6/1919	2055	,,	O4/8 (5/44)	11/63
—		(3854)		6526	1/26	,,	22147	6/1919	2056	,,	O1 (6/46)	—
63855	9/48	3855	12/46	6616	10/27	,,	22150	6/1919	2059	,,	—	3/59

Summary of O4 and O5 Classes (continued)

B.R. No		1946 No.		First L.N.E.R. No.	Date into Traffic	Maker	Works No.	Built	Former R.O.D. No.	Class (m)	Rebuilt	With-drawn
(63856)		3856	12/46	6617	5/28	N.B. Loco. Co. (b)	22153	6/1919	2062	O4/3	O1 (10/49)	—
63857	6/49	3857	8/46	6618	3/28	,,	22154	7/1919	2063	,,	O4/7 (5/43)	8/62
63858	11/48	3858	9/46	6619	6/27	,,	22155	7/1919	2064	,,	O4/8 (5/53)	4/66
63859	5/49	3859	9/46	6620	11/27	,,	22156	7/1919	2065	,,	—	10/63
63860	4/50	3860	5/46	6621	9/27	,,	22157	7/1919	2066	,,	O4/7 (3/40)	10/61
63861	5/48	3861	9/46	6622	10/27	,,	22159	7/1919	2068	,,	O4/8 (11/57)	2/65
63862	3/49	3862	9/46	6532	6/25	,,	22164	8/1919	2073	,,	O4/8 (7/57)	11/62
—		(3863)		6533	7/25	,,	22165	8/1919	2074	,,	O1 (9/45)	—
63864	4/49	3864	7/46	6534	8/25	,,	22166	8/1919	2075	,,	O4/8 (9/57)	8/62
—		(3865)		6535	8/25	,,	22167	8/1919	2076	,,	O1 (2/46)	—
—		(3866)		6623	4/27	,,	22169	8/1919	2078	,,	—	9/41 (k)
—		(3867)		6624	8/28	,,	22170	8/1919	2079	,,	O1 (9/44)	—
—		(3868)		6625	4/27	,,	22172	8/1919	2081	,,	O1 (2/45)	—
—		(3869)		6626	6/27	,,	22173	8/1919	2082	,,	O1 (12/44)	—
63870	3/51	3870	7/46	6627	5/27	,,	22175	9/1919	2084	,,	—	1/62
—		(3871)		6628	4/27	,,	22177	10/1919	2087	,,	—	10/41 (k)
—		(3872)		6525	11/25	N.B. Loco. Co. (c)	22184	5/1919	2094	,,	O1 (5/46)	—
63873	12/48	3873	6/46	6629	11/27	,,	22185	5/1919	2095	,,	O4/8 (8/55)	1/66
—		(3874)		6630	3/28	,,	22186	6/1919	2096	,,	O1 (6/44)	—
—		(3875)		6527	12/25	,,	22188	6/1919	2098	,,	—	10/41 (k)
63876	11/48	3876	8/46	6528	12/25	,,	22189	6/1919	2099	,,	O4/7 (1/44)	3/59
63877	11/49	3877	6/46	6529	3/26	,,	22191	6/1919	2101	,,	O4/8 (4/57)	3/65
63878	5/50	3878	6/46	6631	5/28	,,	22194	6/1919	2104	,,	O4/8 (9/57)	3/65
—		(3879)		6288	8/24	,,	22200	7/1919	2110	O4/2	O1 (11/44)	—
63880	10/49	3880	8/46	6286	8/24	,,	22202	7/1919	2112	,,	O4/7 (3/44)	3/63
63881	4/48	3881	9/46	6632	3/28	,,	22206	7/1919	2116	O4/3	O4/8 (8/58)	12/62
63882	1/50	3882	4/46	6287	5/24	,,	22211	8/1919	2121	,,	O4/4 (7/29), O4/8 (8/47)	5/65
63883	3/49	3883	7/46	6298	4/24	N.B. Loco. Co. (a)	22093	4/1919	1800	,,	—	12/62
63884	2/50	3884	11/46	6633	5/27	N.B. Loco. Co. (c)	22216	8/1919	2126	,,	O4/7 (4/40), O4/8 (2/57)	6/64
63885	6/48	3885	5/46	6634	7/28	,,	22222	9/1919	2132	,,	O4/8 (10/56)	8/62
—		(3886)		6635	9/28	,,	22223	9/1919	2133	,,	O1 (8/46)	—
—		(3887)		6636	8/27	,,	22224	9/1919	2134	,,	O1 (3/46)	—
63888	7/50	3888	11/46	6637	4/27	,,	22225	9/1919	2135	,,	—	4/60
63889	9/50	3889	7/46	6638	5/27	,,	22226	9/1919	2136	,,	—	12/59
—		(3890)		6639	11/27	N.B. Loco. Co. (a)	22234	5/1919	2144	,,	O1 (7/46)	—
63891	8/48	3891	8/46	6295	6/24	,,	22235	5/1919	2145	,,	O4/7 (3/43)	9/61
—		(3892)		6297	4/24	,,	22237	6/1919	2147	,,	—	10/41 (k)
63893	5/49	3893	7/46	6293	5/24	,,	22238	6/1919	2148	,,	O4/8 (12/44)	6/65
63894	11/48	3894	6/46	6300 (d)	1/24	,,	22239	6/1919	2149	,,	O4/7 (2/40)	7/60
63895	8/48	3895	8/46	6296	7/24	,,	22240	6/1919	2150	,,	O4/8 (2/55)	7/62
—		(3896)		6530	2/26	,,	22242	6/1919	2152	,,	—	9/41 (k)
63897	8/49	3897	8/46	6254	3/24	,,	22243	6/1919	2153	,,	O4/8 (2/56)	5/63
63898	12/49	3898	8/46	6253	4/24	,,	22247	7/1919	2157	,,	O4/8 (4/56)	5/63
63899	12/48	3899	7/46	6640	6/27	,,	22250	10/1919	2160	,,	O4/8 (9/55)	5/63
63900	2/50	3900	8/46	6641	8/27	,,	22252	11/1919	2162	,,	—	9/62
—		(3901)		6642	6/27	,,	22255	12/1919	2165	,,	O1 (10/45)	—

B.R. No		1946 No.		1924 No.		Maker	Built	Rebuilt by G.C.R.	1923 Class	Rebuilt by L.N.E.R.	With-drawn
63902	5/48	3902	10/46	5412	10/25	Gorton	1/1918	7/22	O4/1 (i)	—	4/65
—		(3903)		5413	1/25	,,	3/1918	7/22	,,	—	11/41 (k)
63904	11/49	3904	8/46	5414	5/26	,,	4/1918	—	O5	O4/1 (11/36) (i)	11/61
63905	9/49	3905	4/46	5415	12/25	,,	5/1918	—	,,	O4/1 (10/36) (i)	4/59
63906	7/50	3906	10/46	5417	1/26	,,	6/1918	—	,,	O4/1 (2/37) (i)	1/65
63907	6/48	3907	3/46	5418	2/24	,,	8/1918	—	,,	O4/1 (2/36) (i)	5/64
63908	12/49	3908	11/46	5419	10/26	,,	9/1918	—	,,	O4/1 (4/35) (i)	10/63
—		(3909)		5420	8/26	,,	4/1919	—	,,	O4/6 (9/41)	9/41 (k)
—		(3910)		5421	11/24	,,	7/1919	—	,,	O4/6 (10/41)	10/41 (k)
63911	12/49	3911	9/46	5422	2/25	,,	6/1919	—	,,	O4/6 (1/43)	12/62
63912	3/49	3912	5/46	5010	2/25	,,	8/1919	—	,,	O4/6 (7/41)	12/62
63913	10/50	3913	8/46	5011	11/24	,,	8/1919	—	,,	O4/1 (5/36) (i)	6/65
63914	4/49	3914	10/46	5012	8/26	,,	9/1919	—	,,	O4/1 (8/26) (i), O4/8 (7/55)	5/64
63915	5/48	3915	8/46	5013	11/25	,,	10/1919	—	,,	O4/6 (6/40), O4/8 (1/56)	6/61
—		(3916)		5014	7/25	,,	11/1920	—	,,	O4/1 (1/33) (i)	10/41 (k)
63917	5/48	3917	8/46	5015	8/25	,,	12/1920	—	,,	O4/1 (6/35) (i)	6/62
—		(3918)		5017	12/25	,,	12/1920	—	,,	O4/1 (10/32) (i)	10/41 (k)
—		(3919)		5019	7/25	,,	1/1921	—	,,	O4/1 (8/33) (i)	9/41 (k)
63920	4/49	3920	9/46	5022	12/25	,,	2/1921	—	,,	O4/1 (10/35) (i)	8/62

(a) Atlas Works.
(b) Hyde Park Works.
(c) Queen's Park Works.
(d) These engines entered traffic numbered in the G.C. series with the sectional suffix C. They were subsequently renumbered into the 6000 series as follows:-

6255	7/24	6269	7/24	6282	2/25	6300	5/24	6325	8/24
6256	5/24	6272	6/24	6283	5/24	6306	7/24	6334	4/24
6258	5/24	6278	5/24	6292	8/24	6309	5/24	6355	8/24
6259	7/24								

(e) Did not figure in L.N.E.R. returns until 1924.
(f) Reclassified O4/1 when tender changed to 4,000-gallon type, 7/1923.
(g) Reclassified O4/1, 12/1924. Tenders subsequently changed to 4,000-gallon type:-

5380	12/25	5383	8/25

(h) Nos. 6551/82 were included in the stock figures for 1928 although not sent to traffic until January 1929.
(i) Reclassified O4/6, 12/1938.
(k) Sold to War Department and written off L.N.E.R. stock, 12/1943, having previously been on loan from 1941-42.
(m) O4/3 reclassified O4/1, 12/1940. O4/2 reclassified O4/1, 12/1946.
(p) Sold to War Department, 2/1952.
(s) No. 6185 reclassified O4/2 12/1925, although actually altered 6/1923.

CLASS O1

THOMPSON REBUILDS FROM ROBINSON 4ft. 8in. CLASS O4

ENGINES REBUILT AFTER GROUPING (1944-47): 3561/94, 3760/96, 3872/86/90, 5385/94, 5408, 6195, 6213/6/20/31/43/4/5/63/83/8, 6324/8/34/41/50/6/9/71/4, 6505/7/13/5/9/26/33/5/45/55/66/75/8/95, 6601/24/5/6/30/6/42. TOTAL 51.

ENGINES REBUILT AFTER NATIONALISATION (1948-49): 63571/9/89/96, 63746, 63838/56. TOTAL 7.

The requirements of the L.N.E.R. so far as heavy goods engines were concerned had been largely covered by the purchase of 273 ex-Government G.C.-pattern 2-8-0's in the twenties to swell the numbers of class O4. When further engines were required in the thirties, sixteen more class O2 three-cylinder 2-8-0's, with modern long travel valve gear, were built to Gresley design, and these were added to during the War when another twenty-five were constructed. Both these classes evolved in the era of relatively slow-moving coal trains which they handled with ease, thus assuring for themselves continued employment on this type of work for the foreseeable future. When Gresley died in 1941 his successor introduced new ideas, with simplicity in design as the keynote.

Thompson's first proposals included a heavy goods 2-8-0 which was intended to replace not only the existing 2-8-0's and 0-8-0's, but also the J19, J20 and J39 class 0-6-0's, together with any small-wheeled engines (e.g. class J38) not otherwise covered by the standard 0-6-0 proposal. The numerically large class O4 was a natural choice for development as the standard 2-8-0 and the first outline diagram appeared in October 1941 (see drawing). This depicted an O4 with the No. 2 standard boiler (Diagram 100A, introduced in 1942 on the class B1 4-6-0's), standard B1-type cylinders (based on class K2), Walschaerts valve gear, class L1-type pony truck with 3ft. 2in. diameter wheels, frames shortened by 9in. at the back, side-window cab, driving position altered from right to left hand, and Group Standard 4,200-gallon tender. The engine diagram, at first designated Type O, which appeared later differed chiefly in the following respects: boiler pressure increased from 220 lb. to 225 lb. per sq. in., straight running plate from ahead of the cylinders back to the cab and maximum axle load increased to 17 tons. Three features of the 1941 proposal were abandoned in the interests of economy: the original Robinson

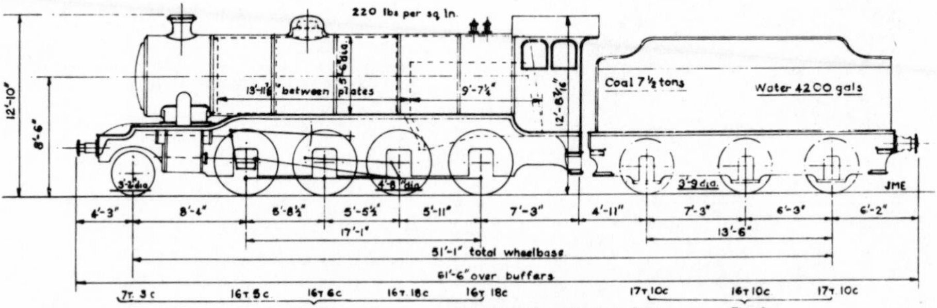

PROPOSED 2-8-0 FREIGHT ENGINE – OCTOBER 1941

pony truck was retained (as were the wheels and spring gear), the frames were not shortened and the G.C.-pattern 4,000-gallon tender was not changed.

Rebuilding commenced with No. 6595 in February 1944 (fig. 78) and ran concurrently with the less drastic rebuilding of class O4 to Part 8, with the condition of the cylinders and motion determining the extent of rebuilding, initially at least.

Class O1 figured in the L.N.E.R.'s post-war modernisation programme, announced at a meeting of the Emergency Board on 26th April 1945. The 1,000 engines in the five-year programme to the end of 1950 covered ten standard classes and included 160 class O1 rebuilds. However, from late 1943 to mid-1946, almost the entire output from the Company's own shops consisted of L.M.S.-type Stanier 2-8-0's (designated class O6 on the L.N.E.R.). Then in 1946-47 200 ex-W.D. "Austerity" 2-8-0's (class O7) were purchased to satisfy the L.N.E.R.'s immediate requirements for additional heavy goods engines. Both these additions to stock were regarded as stop-gap measures pending replacement by the standard 2-8-0's. However, these factors helped to slow down the O1 rebuilding programme, which was brought to an end in 1949 following a searching review by B.R. of schemes outstanding from before nationalisation. Altogether fifty-eight engines were rebuilt as follows, all being dealt with at Gorton Works:-

1944 (16): Nos. 5385, 5408, 6195, 6243/4/83/8, 6334, 6507/15/78/95, 6601/24/6/30.
1945 (21): Nos. 5394, 6220/31/63, 6324/8/41/50/9/71/4, 6505/13/9/33/45/55/66/75, 6625/42.
1946 (13): Nos. 3561, 3760/96, 3872/86/90, 6213/6/45, 6356, 6526/35, 6636.
1947 (1): No. 3594.
1948 (2): Nos. 63579, 63746.
1949 (5): Nos. 63571/89/96, 63838/56.

No major alterations were ever made to the class, although minor ones were carried out and are dealt with later. The class was chosen to represent the L.N.E.R. in the 1948 locomotive interchange trials and the results showed that the design was good, but in practice the engines, like other L.N.E.R. designs, soon became run-down without good maintenance, due to excessive wear in the motion. They also shared the firebox problems described under class B1 (see Part 2B, page 126). It has been said that the retention of the G.C.-pattern side rods was not successful when married to the new Walschaerts valve gear and it is perhaps a pity that completely new engines were never built to the O1 design. Withdrawals commenced in 1962 and were completed three years later. In the event, class O1 was itself outlived by three of the classes which it had been originally intended to replace—J38, O4 and Q6.

Standard L.N.E.R. Dimensions

Cylinders (2 outside)	20″ × 26″	
Motion	Walschaerts with 10″ piston valves	
Boiler:		
Max. diam. outside	5′ 6″	
Barrel length	14′ 1½″ (a)	
Firebox length outside	10′ 1½″ (b)	
Pitch	8′ 6″	
Diagram No.	100A	
	Original	*From* 11/1945
Tubes	143 × 2″	141 × 2″
Heating surface:		
Firebox	168 sq.ft.	168 sq.ft.
Tubes	1048 sq.ft.	1033 sq.ft.
Flues (24 × 5¼″)	460 sq.ft.	460 sq.ft.
Total evaporative	1676 sq.ft.	1661 sq.ft.
Superheater (24 × 1.244″)	344 sq.ft.	344 sq.ft.
Total	2020 sq.ft.	2005 sq.ft.

Grate area	27.9 sq.ft.
Boiler pressure	225 lb./sq.in.
Leading wheels	3′ 6″
Coupled wheels	4′ 8″
Tender wheels	4′ 4″
Tractive effort (85%)	35,518 lb.
Length over buffers	61′ 7¾″
Wheelbase:	
Engine	8′ 4″ + 5′ 8½″ + 5′ 5½″ + 5′ 11″ = 25′ 5″
Tender	6′ 6″ + 6′ 6″ = 13′ 0″
Total	51′ 2½″
Weight (full):	
Engine	73T 6C
Tender	48T 6C
Total	121T 12C
Adhesive	65T 17C
Max. axle load	17T 0C
Water capacity	4,000 gallons
Coal capacity	6T 0C

(a) The engine diagram quoted the distance between tubeplates, 13′ 11⅞″ (13′ 11½″ from December 1950). See under Details.

(b) Alternative figures were quoted on the engine diagram, see under Details.

L.N.E.R. Renumbering

Under the 1943 scheme class O4 had been allocated 3500-3920 and no amendment was made when rebuilding to class O1 began, these engines retaining their allotted numbers in the O4 series. Nos. 3529/42/60/1/3/7 were further renumbered 3678, 3711/73/7/89, 3803 in February-March 1947 to release their first numbers under the 1943 scheme for class O6 2-8-0's. See also under classes O4 and O5 (p. 36).

Details

The original frames, which were 1¼in. thick and quite substantial, were retained on rebuilding. These were spaced 4ft. 1½in. apart, except ahead of the second pair of coupled wheels where they were set 3in. closer to provide adequate clearance in the original O4 design for the 21in. diameter cylinders. As a result, on the class O1 rebuilds 1⅜in. thickness packing plates had to be fitted between the frames and the B1-type cylinders to maintain the correct distance between the centres of the cylinders, i.e. 6ft. 7½in. The G.C.-pattern buffers with oval heads were retained on rebuilding, though in later years several engines were fitted with buffers having stepped shanks similar to the Group Standard pattern, but retaining the oval heads (cf. figs. 78 and 79). Towards the end of the life of the O1's an additional frame stay was fitted ahead of the trailing axle in order to strengthen the frames. All engines except six (Nos. 63670, 63773/96, 63854/72/90) are recorded as altered between 1956 and 1960.

The cylinders were 20in. diameter by 26in. stroke of the type fitted to several other Thompson classes, with 10in. diameter piston valves. They were inclined at 1 in 50 and drove on to the third pair of coupled wheels, necessitating lengthy connecting rods. The reduction in the diameter of the cylinders as a result of rebuilding was amply compensated for by the increase in boiler pressure from 180 to 225 lb. per sq. in.

The reversing screw in the cab was set at an angle from the horizontal, in front of the driver's seat. The arrangement of the valve gear was modelled on that of class B1 to give similar valve events. The maximum cut-off position was 75 per cent in both fore and back gears and the maximum travel of the valves in full gear was 6$\frac{21}{32}$in. The eccentric (or return) crank was intended to be fitted with a ball race, but as a wartime expedient plain bearings were provided instead on fifteen rebuilt between June 1944 and February 1945, Nos. 5385, 5408, 6195, 6243/83/88, 6350, 6507/15/9/78, 6601/24/6/30. Ball bearings were generally substituted later, though it is not known if the process was completed.

In place of the class O4 arrangement of the leading footsteps attached to the motion bracket, simple steps consisting merely of an iron framework were provided just behind the front bufferbeam, together with a grab iron on the running plate. Similar steps were fitted to the prototype class L1 2-6-4T No. 9000.

A Wakefield No. 7 mechanical lubricator was located on the running plate on the left-hand side and supplied the steam chest and cylinders (fig. 78). The oil was led via the anti-carboniser fittings, the steam valve for which was on the right-hand side of the smokebox. Siphon feed was provided for the valve rods, piston rods and slide bars from small oilboxes on both sides of the running plate just behind the smokebox. The coupled wheel axleboxes and horn cheeks also had siphon feed. A central lubricator was fitted on each side of the engine, mounted on the running plate about half way along its length, serving the first three pairs of coupled axles (fig. 78). The siphon oilboxes for the trailing pair of wheels were located inside the cab.

Gravity-fed sanders were provided for forward running in front of the first and third pairs of coupled wheels. The sandboxes were out of sight between the frames and the filler pipes were brought up above running plate level with rectangular steel plates behind the filler caps to prevent sand spillage from entering the axleboxes. Gravity-fed sanders were also provided for reverse running behind the rear pair of coupled wheels, with the sandboxes in view below the cab bolted to the side of the frames. The sand spillage shields were found to be too short and in 1951 three engines were fitted experimentally with wider ones and the remaining engines were brought into line in 1956-58.

The Diagram 100A boiler had been introduced in 1942 for class B1. It was similar in construction to the Diagram 100 type which was used on class B17, but had thicker plates to withstand the higher working pressure. The barrel was made from two telescopic rings: the rear one was 5ft. 6in. outside diameter and the front one was 5ft. 4⅝in. The front tubeplate was ¾in. thick, recessed into the barrel, and the radius of the flange was ¾in. From December 1950, replacement smokebox tubeplates were ⅞in. thick with a 1in. radius flange, reducing the distance between the tubeplates slightly to 13ft. 11½in. from 13ft. 11⅞in.

The firebox casing was constructed of 9/16in. steel plate, except for the throat plate which was ⅝in. (increased to 11/16in. from July 1947). The overall length of the casing, measured at the bottom, was 9ft. 0in. The throat plate sloped back so that the extreme overall length was 10ft. 1½in. The overall length of 9ft. 7¼in. which appeared on the engine diagram is misleading, as it is the length measured from the rear of the outer casing to the front of the inner (copper) firebox. To improve fire cleaning at the sheds, Gorton records show that drop grates and hopper ashpans were fitted, starting in 1946. Records are incomplete and it is not known if the work was ever finished, or if rocking grates were afterwards fitted as a result of their successful employment on the B1's after 1947.

From November 1945 the number of small tubes was reduced by two to 141. This allowed space for wash-out plugs to be provided on either side of the blastpipe in place of the single one which was in an awkward position behind it.

The superheater elements were of the long return bend type, 1½in. outside diameter and 10 S.W.G. thick (inside diameter 1.244in.). From (officially) November 1944 the thickness was increased to 9 S.W.G. (inside diameter 1.212in.). The engine diagram was not altered. The element ends had ball-jointed (Melesco-type) ends, for which there were two methods of attachment, depending on the type of header fitted. The first ten boilers only, built at Doncaster, had the "V" bolt-type header. Four of these boilers were sent to Gorton: the first one was fitted to class B3 No. 6166 which was rebuilt in 1943, the other three were fitted to Nos. 6595, 6244 and 6334 when they were rebuilt in the early part of 1944. All the later Diagram 100A boilers had the "Through" bolt-type header. The two types were not interchangeable as the connections for the blower and anti-carboniser required different drilling in the smokebox tubeplate.

In 1951 Annesley acquired a large number of O1's, operating in an area notorious for bad water. In an attempt to alleviate the problem four engines were fitted experimentally during that year with chemical water treatment apparatus in the tender. This consisted of a cylindrical container inserted into the water space into which chemical briquettes were dropped. The addition of suitable chemicals to the boiler feed water prevented chemical solids already present from being deposited as scale on the interior surfaces of the boiler, thus improving the period between wash-outs and inhibiting corrosion of boiler tubes and plates. The treatment caused chemical solids either to remain in suspension or be deposited in the lower parts of the boiler as sludge. It was necessary to fit a blow down valve to the lower part of the boiler for periodic blowing off of sludge deposits before they could cause priming. During 1955-56 the remaining members of the class were all fitted with water treatment apparatus in their tenders and Everlasting pattern blow down valves on their boilers, with the exception of the five engines operating from Tyne Dock shed in the N.E. Region.

The chimney was 1ft. $7\frac{5}{16}$in. high with a traditional Doncaster appearance, similar chimneys being fitted to class O4/8. The proportions of chimney liner, cowl and blastpipe were identical on these two classes, and in fact very similar to those of class B1. Self-cleaning apparatus was fitted to class O1, commencing in 1948 and spread over the next six years.

The dome cover was the same height as on class B1, but differing in shape, Gorton favouring a more angular contour. Some class O1 engines later received B1-type dome covers, e.g. No. 63650. The cab was modelled on that of class B1, as indeed were the cabs of most of the Thompson classes, and had bucket-type seats for driver and fireman. An interesting omission was that of the glass sight screens, which were possibly thought unnecessary on a slow-moving goods engine. They were however fitted in the period 1953-55 (fig.83). At least two engines, Nos. 3592 and 3777, were at one time temporarily fitted with speed indicators driven from the right-hand trailing wheel coupling rod pin.

In 1952 Nos. 63712/55/60, 63856/74 were each equipped at Gorton Works with two 10in. diameter Westinghouse pumps, from ex-W.D. "Austerity" 2-8-0's, in connection with the working of block trains of 56-ton bogie iron ore wagons between Tyne Dock and Consett (fig. 82). The pumps were mounted side by side on the right-hand side of the firebox. The wagons had compressed air motors mounted on the chassis to operate the hopper doors. Compressed air was provided at 85 lb. per sq. in. in two independent systems, hence the need for two pumps. One system held the doors in the closed position and the other system opened them to discharge the iron ore whilst on the move over the bunker gantry at Consett. The block trains were vacuum-braked throughout for which purpose a vacuum ejector was fitted and the driver's steam brake valve was changed to the graduable type. To avoid confusion, the Westinghouse equipment in the cab was painted red with an accompanying notice reminding drivers that it was not part of the brake equipment. The whole venture was a joint project of B.R., Consett Ironworks Co. and Tyne Improvement Commission. The dates of fitting of the special equipment (which was retained to withdrawal) were:-

No.	*Fitted*
63712	5/1952
63755	7/1952
63760	6/1952
63856	5/1952
63874	10/1952

Screw couplings were generally fitted until 1947, with only one or two exceptions noted in 1946, but thereafter three-link couplings became standard (cf. figs. 84 and 80). However screw couplings were refitted to the five O1's which worked the block trains of bogie iron ore wagons from Tyne Dock to Consett and they also appeared towards the end on a number of other O1's also, in particular those fitted with A.W.S. equipment.

Brakes

All class O1 initially had steam brake only on the engine and tender and no provision for train braking. A $9\frac{1}{2}$in. diameter steam brake cylinder was located under the cab. In the case of the ex-G.C. engines, which previously had a vacuum ejector for the train, the equipment was removed on rebuilding, although provision for its retention was covered by a Doncaster drawing of a cab arrangement dated November 1943. The fitting of Nos. 63712/55/60, 63856/74 in 1952 with vacuum ejectors for the Tyne Dock—Consett iron ore traffic has already been mentioned.

At the very end of their career a few engines (including Nos. 63712/80, 63838/68/90) were fitted with the B.R. A.W.S. system, for which purpose they were fitted with a B.R. standard vacuum ejector on the left-hand side of the smokebox and through train pipes (fig. 83). In all cases the battery box was mounted on the left-hand side of the engine under the cab and the usual plates were fitted at the front end behind the coupling to protect the A.W.S. receiver. In the case of No. 63712 (in the N.E. Region), which already had an L.N.E.R. type vacuum ejector in connection with the iron ore

Fig. 76 Class O4/8 No. 63823 on down steel carrying empties near Beningbrough, about 1958.

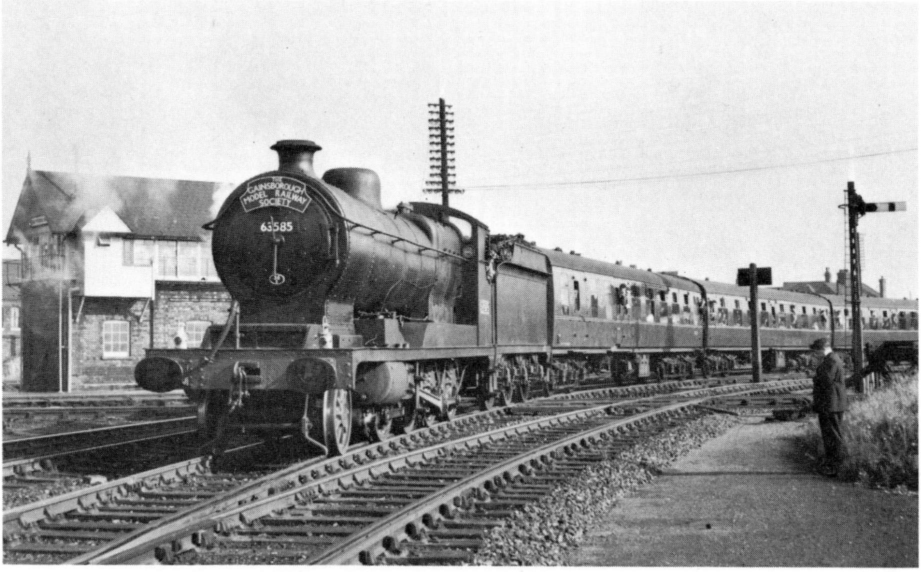

Fig. 77 Class O4/1 No. 63585 on "The Gainsborough Model Railway Society" special at Retford, 12th October 1963.

Three-link coupling replaced by screw type.

Fig. 78 Class O1 No. 6595 at Gorton Works, February 1944.

First rebuild from class O4, in grey livery for official photograph. Wakefield mechanical lubricator for cylinders and valves, central lubricator above second pair of coupled wheels for axleboxes, G.C. pattern buffers.

Fig. 79 Class O1 No. 3901 at Darnall shed, 1947.

Buffers with stepped shanks.

Fig. 80 Class O1 No. 3780 at Mexborough shed, June 1947.

Three-link coupling.

Fig. 81 Class O1 No. 63663 at Darnall shed, September 1949.

Gorton's angular style of dome cover, tender with front plate extended upwards.

Fig. 82 Class O1 No. 63755 at Tyne Dock shed, September 1953.

Westinghouse pump for operating hopper doors on bogie iron ore wagons, vacuum brake standpipe at front.

Fig. 83 Class O1 No. 63780 at March shed, June 1963.

Vacuum ejector fitted in connection with A.W.S. apparatus, glass sight screens.

Fig. 84 Class O1 No. 3687 on up class C goods at Nottingham Victoria station, April 1947.
Screw coupling.

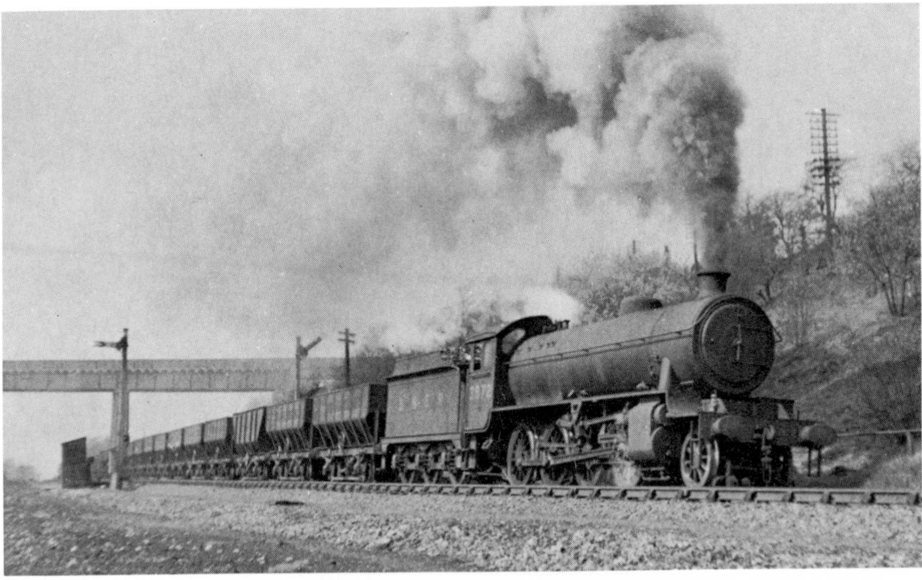

Fig. 85 Class O1 No. 3872 on up class C train of hopper wagons near Mottram, about 1947.

Fig. 86 Class O1 No. 63773 on down class A goods with dynamometer car leaving Acton for Severn Tunnel Junction during Interchange Trials, 31st August 1948.

Fig. 87 Class O1 No. 63591 on up class H goods leaving Barnston tunnel north of Loughborough, September 1959.

Fig. 88 Class O1 No. 63571 on up class H goods leaving Littlebury tunnel, May 1957.

Fig. 89 Class O1 No. 63712 on a Tyne Dock – Consett iron ore train at Washington, August 1955.

Fig. 90 Class O1 No. 63687 on up class H goods near Barnwell, October 1957.

Fig. 91 U.S. Army Class S160 No. 2108 at Doncaster Works, September 1944.

Sandbox on top of boiler in front of steam dome, Westinghouse pump on smokebox front plate, one-piece pony truck wheels with no separate tyres, double-bogie tender. Repainted glossy light grey prior to embarkation to the Continent after loan to L.N.E.R.

workings, this was changed to the B.R. pattern. Two months later this particular engine was withdrawn.

Tenders

Standard G.C. 4,000-gallon tenders were used with the rebuilds, the main variation being that the ex-R.O.D. engines did not have water pick-up gear, whereas the G.C. engines were so fitted. No. 6328 on rebuilding retained its tender with extended front plate (see class O4 p. 61), which was afterwards attached to No. 63663 (fig. 81). From March 1946 authority was given for the removal of water pick-up gear from classes O1 and O4, but photographic evidence suggests that few, if any, O1's prior to this date ever had tenders with water pick-up.

Maintenance

The class was normally maintained at Gorton prior to 1962, the only exception during this period being odd visits to Darlington Works by the Tyne Dock engines for light repairs. In 1962 Doncaster took over the maintenance and at least sixteen engines received repairs there in that year, whilst additionally Gorton still carried out occasional repairs including two general repairs in September and October of that year. After Doncaster ceased the repair of steam engines towards the end of 1963, Darlington took over responsibility for the survivors. No. 63768 appears to have been the last member of the class to receive a works repair, at the end of 1964. This was described as "a heavy motion repair".

Liveries

As befitting goods engines introduced in wartime conditions the engines were painted unlined black with the letters "N E" on the tender, which were changed to "L N E R" from January 1946. After nationalisation the tender inscription changed to "BRITISH RAILWAYS", followed later by the two versions of the emblem.

British Railways

All fifty-eight engines in due course had 60,000 added to their numbers. Meanwhile, Nos. 3579, 3646, 3752 and 3865 had the letter E added to the number before the renumbering scheme was introduced. No. 63752 after being renumbered in November 1948 even ran for a while with the letter E over the number.

B.R. Interchange Trials 1948

Freight engine trials took place towards the end of the summer of 1948 and the O1's were chosen to represent the L.N.E.R. In June No. 3865 was transferred to New England to give G.N. crews experience of the class, which at that time was not allocated to the G.N. section. On 2nd July Nos. 63773/89, 63872 were transferred to Hornsey for pre-test running. The last-mentioned engine was sent as spare and did not participate in the trials. On the dynamometer car tests the O1's worked as follows:-

Week commencing	*Regions*	*Section of line*
20th July	L.M.R.	Brent-Toton
27th July	E.R.	Ferme Park-New England
17th August	W.R.&S.R.	Bristol-Eastleigh
31st August	W.R.	Acton-Severn Tunnel Junction

The other classes were G.W.R. 28XX, L.M.S. Stanier 8F and ex-W.D. "Austerity" classes of 2-8-0 and 2-10-0. The G.W.R. engine had to burn hard steam coal, to which it was unaccustomed, and arrangements were made for additional tests to be carried out after the completion of the main Interchange Trials, using Welsh coal which suited its firegrate and smokebox arrangements.

Coal consumption was related to work done and the overall average figures for the competing engines in the main Interchange Trials, and for No. 3864 in the Additional Tests with Welsh coal, were as follows:-

Class	*Coal consumption* (lb./DBHP hr.)
G.W.R. 28XX	2.64*
L.N.E.R. O1	3.37
G.W.R. 28XX	3.42
L.M.S. 8F	3.52
W.D. 2-8-0	3.52
W.D. 2-10-0	3.77

* With Welsh coal (higher calorific value).

The wide range of results obtained from individual test runs suggests that the comparison was by no means straightforward. For example whilst Stanier 8F No. 48189 put up the best performance on the L.M.R. (3.14 lb.), class O1 No. 63773 was the best on the W.R. (3.14 lb. also) and class 28XX No. 3803 the best on the Eastleigh-Bristol run (3.22 lb.). Rather surprisingly, W.D. 2-10-0 No. 73774, which came last in the overall averages, achieved the lowest figure in any individual test in the

Interchange Trials proper, with 2.80 lb. on both down runs on the E.R.

The disparity in the results was to be expected from tests in which the competing engines worked scheduled goods trains, with varying loads and traffic stops, encountering permanent way checks, signal delays and stops to detach crippled wagons. The longest test runs were between Toton and Brent, over which section all competing engines had at least one run in excess of ten hours, with an adverse effect on coal consumption – 84 lb. per mile in the case of No. 63789.

Brief details are given in the accompanying table of the best performance of each competing engine working the 11-20 a.m. Acton-Severn Tunnel Junction, chosen so that the results may be compared with the performance of the G.W.R. engine burning Welsh coal in the Additional Tests. In each case the load was the same leaving Acton, 808 tons, though crippled wagons were afterwards detached en route at various points, except in the case of No. 48189 which kept its train intact to Stoke Gifford. In each case the load was reduced at Stoke Gifford to 700 tons for the Severn Tunnel.

The report of the trials credited the O1's with the lowest overall coal consumption of all the competing freight engines in the Interchange Trials proper. This was despite the poor performance of No. 63789 on the E.R. where its steaming was described as fair, with a tendency to lose pressure or water-level when working hard. On the first test run from Ferme Park, on 27th July, steaming suffered because of a jammed damper and at one point pressure dropped to 113 lb. per sq. in. On the second down run, on the 29th, it primed badly at one point. No. 63773 put up a better performance on the W.R. (fig. 86), highlights of which included recorded drawbar horsepowers of 1,038 at Hullavington on the first test run on 31st August and 1,000 on the following day at Patchway on the return trip.

Type	*L.M.S.* *Stanier* 8*F*	*G.W.R.* 28*XX*	*W.D.* 2-10-0	*W.D.* 2-8-0	*L.N.E.R.* O1	*G.W.R.* 28*XX*
Engine No.	48189	3803	73774	77000	63773	3864
Date	29/7/48	12/8/48	19/8/48	26/8/48	2/9/48	9/12/48
Train miles (actual)	118.8	118.9	119.8	118.9	118.8	119.3
Running time (mins.)*	339.7	351.3	364.9	346.9	351.7	364.8
Average speed (m.p.h.)*	20.90	20.31	19.70	20.57	20.27	19.60
Work done (h.p. hrs.)	1,714	2,138	1,792	1,880	2,230	2,274
Coal consumed:						
(lb./mile)	54.8	64.1	53.8	59.5	59.0	47.0
(lb./d.b.h.p.hr.)	3.80	3.57	3.59	3.76	3.14	2.46
Water used:						
(gall./mile)	43.5	44.4	40.9	45.2	44.2	45.2
(lb./d.b.h.p.hr.)	30.15	24.71	27.37	28.60	23.54	23.70
(lb./lb. coal)	7.94	6.93	7.62	7.60	7.49	9.62

* Exclusive of intermediate stops.

Allocation and Work

The earliest O1's had extended trials in all the L.N.E.R. areas and the first nine rebuilds were distributed as follows: Nos. 6595 (Gorton); 6244 (New England); 6334 (Tyne Dock); 6507 (Gorton); 6630 (Heaton, later Tyne Dock); 5385, 6601 (Thornton); 6283, 6624 (March). The pioneer engine No. 6595 visited Liverpool Street station on 17th February 1944 to be shown to officers of the Company. Afterwards it performed trials on the cross-Pennine route via Woodhead in competition with Stanier class 8F 2-8-0 No. 8511, though it was observed working a coal train on the G.N. main line towards the end of April 1944. The New England O1 No. 6244 performed trials between here and Ferme Park, with class 8F No. 8513, until both engines were eventually transferred together to Gorton in June 1945. The Thornton engines were employed (like the O4's before them) on the Fife—Aberdeen coal trains, though they also worked goods trains to Edinburgh. The March engines worked on the Whitemoor-Temple Mills goods services along with the O2's.

Up to November 1946, when the initial order for fifty conversions was completed, the later O1's in the Southern Area generally went to Gorton where they were put to good use on the cross-Pennine route. The only exceptions were No. 6324 to Retford until January 1946 and Nos. 6356, 6636, 3796 (ex-6596) to Frodingham for a brief period until May 1946. Later in 1946 eleven Gorton engines were transferred to Colwick and two to Woodford in exchange for W.D. "Austerity" 2-8-0's, though two months later they changed back again. The later O1's in the N.E. Area were at first distributed between Dairycoates, Springhead and Tyne Dock, but by August 1946 all were concentrated at the latter shed. The allocation of the class at the end of 1946 was then as follows: Gorton (40), March (2), Tyne Dock (6), Thornton (2). The only change during 1947 was the rebuilding of a further engine, No. 3594 (ex-5333), towards the end of the year and this returned to Doncaster, its shed prior to rebuilding.

One of the last improvements made by the L.N.E.R. on the G.C. Section was the introduction in 1947 of a better service of goods trains between Annesley and Woodford, with a tightening up of running times and booked water stops, whereas previously water had been taken at the driver's discretion en route. A similar scheme had been operated in the thirties on the G.C. main line which, with its few junctions and little conflicting traffic, was ideally suited for such methods of operation. The pre-war special workings affected only four trains each way per day and this scheme was completely eclipsed by the one introduced in 1947 which covered thirty-one trains. The down workings were all booked to take water at Loughborough, whilst nine of the up trains took water at Rugby and the remainder at Loughborough. These workings were covered entirely by Annesley men and in consequence Woodford lost some of its work. This caused some resentment, but there is no doubt that as far as loose-coupled goods workings were concerned, the Annesley-Woodford "runners", as they were nick-named, had no equal in Britain. The service was at first booked for class O4 engines, but the speeds necessary to keep time were such that hot axleboxes became prevalent and "Austerity" 2-8-0's were drafted in as replacements. The enginemen complained that the latter were unsuitable and rode badly, consequently trials were conducted using class O1 and O2 engines. In February 1948 class O1 Nos. 3687 and 3752 were sent to Annesley together with two O2's, for comparative trials with the "Austerity" 2-8-0's. The outcome of the trials was in favour of the O1's as they could keep time with the trains as well as requiring only one water stop. The O2's and the "Austerities" were both found to be deficient in braking at the speeds required. However, the O1's returned to Gorton two months later and it was not until the following year that eleven O1's were transferred to Annesley (including the two from March and the two from Thornton). In 1950 no fewer than forty more were transferred there, thus concentrating the entire Eastern Region stud of fifty-one O1's at Annesley shed.

Meanwhile in the N.E.R. the six Tyne Dock engines were transferred away in 1949, first to Darlington and then to Dairycoates, where they were joined by No. 63856, the last engine to be converted to class O1, in October of that year. These seven Hull engines also had a short spell at Springhead shed during 1950; otherwise their next move came in mid-1951 when Nos. 63712/55/60, 63856/74 were sent to Tyne Dock and Nos. 63676, 63740 were transferred to the E.R. to join the remainder of the class at Annesley. The position therefore at the end of 1951 was that the class was divided between two sheds: Annesley (53) and Tyne Dock (5).

The Tyne Dock engines were to remain there until all five were withdrawn in 1962. In 1952 as already related they were fitted with continuous vacuum brake and Westinghouse pumps for operating the iron ore trains from Tyne Dock to Consett, a duty on which the class will perhaps be best remembered (fig. 89). The O1's worked as train engines with banking assistance from Pelaw South to South Medomsley over gradients as steep as 1 in 35. In 1956 the O1's were replaced on this duty by B.R. Standard class 9F 2-10-0's and then took over the role of banking engines, although they were occasionally pressed into service as train engines. On two days running, 29th and 30th November 1959, No. 63760 was observed at Northallerton on an up parcels train, returning north on the second day on a train of condemned coaching stock.

In July 1956 No. 63725 of Annesley was sent on loan to Wellingborough, a former Midland shed, in exchange for Stanier class 8F 2-8-0 No. 48678. The purpose was to ascertain the comparative amount of boiler tube corrosion in the two classes due to the different water at each depot. It had been previously noted that the corrosion in the 8F class was greater at Wellingborough than in the O1's at Annesley, using similar water treatment methods. The exchange was concluded in December of the same year.

The Annesley engines virtually monopolised the Woodford workings and remained on these duties until 1957. In that year a major reshuffle of freight engines took place in the E.R., which sent twenty-five O1's to March and five to Colwick, to be replaced at Annesley by B.R. 2-10-0's. Twenty-three O1's were however retained at Annesley for coal traffic in the Nottingham area. As a result of a change in Regional boundaries in February 1958, Annesley passed to London Midland Region ownership and these O1's became part of L.M.R. book stock. They survived on these duties until withdrawn in 1962.

The March engines worked south to Temple Mills, whilst in March 1958 No. 63795 was even seen at Colchester. During 1960-61 March had an interesting goods turn, hauled sometimes by an O1, to Norwich and Lowestoft, then to Ipswich via the East Suffolk line and finally back direct to March. The local goods duty from March to Newmarket and back was also occasionally hauled by an O1. Meanwhile in 1959 five March O1's went to Staveley, followed in 1960 by a further nine. On the cessation of steam working at March in November 1963, only six O1's still remained there, several having been withdrawn earlier in the year. These six went to Staveley, which was to be the last home for many of the class.

At the end of 1963 the last eighteen engines of the class were all at Staveley engaged mainly on trip workings to Annesley and the Sheffield area, but also working to York. The end came for Staveley shed in 1965 by which time further withdrawals had reduced the O1's to ten; seven were transferred for a few weeks to Langwith, whilst three went to the Midland shed at Barrow Hill, although it is thought that they did little work from that depot. The last survivors all went in July of that year.

Engine Diagrams

1944. Class O4 Rebuild.

1947. Class O1. New engine diagram showing reduction in the number of tubes.

Classification: Southern Area load class 8; Route availability 6; B.R. power class 8F.

Summary of O1 Class

Original L.N.E.R. No.	*Built as O4*	*Final O4 Part*	*Rebuilt to O1*	*No. when Rebuilt*	*Subsequent Nos.* 1946		1947		*B.R.*		*With-drawn*
5333	11/1911	1	11/47	3594	—		—		63594	4/49	4/64
5408	5/1912	1	12/44	5408	3529	9/46	3678	2/47	63678	9/48	7/63
6195	9/1912	1	10/44	6195	3542	10/46	3711	3/47	63711	7/49	11/62
6213	8/1912	1	4/46	6213	3560	11/46	3773	3/47	63773	4/48	10/64
6214	9/1912	1	11/46	3561(a)	—		3777	3/47	63777	4/49	10/62
6216	9/1912	1	1/46	6216	3563	12/46	3789	2/47	63789	5/48	11/62
6220	10/1912	1	6/45	6220	3567	11/46	3803	3/47	63803	10/49	3/63

Original L.N.E.R. No.	*Built as O4*	*Final O4 Part*	*Rebuilt to O1*	*No. when Rebuilt*	*Subsequent Nos.* 1946		*B.R.*		*With-drawn*
6224	10/1912	1	8/49	63571(b)	—		—		12/64
6231	11/1912	1	10/45	6231	3578	11/46	63578	1/50	11/62
6232	11/1912	5	3/48	63579(b)	—		—		11/62
6242	12/1912	5	4/49	63589(b)	—		—		7/65
6243	12/1912	1	12/44	6243	3590	11/46	63590	1/49	7/65
6244	12/1912	1	4/44	6244	3591	12/46	63591	7/48	11/62
6245	12/1912	1	10/46	6245	3592	11/46	63592	7/48	7/63
6249	12/1912	7	7/49	63596(b)	—		—		8/63
5385	12/1913	1	7/44	5385	3610	10/46	63610	4/49	11/62

Summary of O1 Class (continued)

Original L.N.E.R. No.	*Built as* O4	*Final* O4 *Part*	*Rebuilt to* O1	*No. when Rebuilt*	*Subsequent Nos.* 1946		*B.R.*		*With-drawn*
5394	4/1914	1	3/45	5394	3619	6/46	63619	8/49	10/63
6555	2/1918	1	6/45	6555	3630	11/46	63630	6/48	7/65
6374	2/1918	1	9/45	6374	3646	12/46	63646	5/49	7/65
6545	3/1918	1	5/45	6545	3650	11/46	63650	9/49	6/65
6371	3/1918	4	12/45	6371	3652	11/46	63652	4/48	11/63
6359	8/1918	1	6/45	6359	3663	11/46	63663	8/49	11/64
6356	9/1917	1	3/46	6356	3670	9/46	63670	9/48	6/64
6350	11/1917	1	1/45	6350	3676	11/46	63676	4/49	11/62
6324	2/1918	1	12/45	6324	3687	11/46	63687	6/49	10/63
6341	3/1918	1	8/45	6341	3689	11/46	63689	10/49	11/62
6334	1/1919	1	5/44	6334	3712	9/46	63712	2/49	11/62
6328	8/1919	1	3/45	6328	3725	6/46	63725	8/49	7/65
6566	10/1917	1	8/45	6566	3740	5/46	63740	4/48	11/62
6571	10/1917	1	11/48	63746(b)	—		—		2/64
6575	12/1917	1	11/45	6575	3752	4/46	63752	11/48	11/62
6578	12/1917	1	10/44	6578	3755	7/46	63755	8/49	11/62
6579	2/1918	1	8/46	3760(a)	—		63760	6/49	11/62
6513	3/1918	1	12/45	6513	3768	6/46	63768	5/48	7/65
6505	5/1918	1	4/45	6505	3780	6/46	63780	9/48	7/63
6507	5/1918	1	6/44	6507	3784	7/46	63784	8/48	8/63
6515	6/1918	1	11/44	6515	3786	7/46	63786	2/49	9/64
6283	2/1918	1	9/44	6283	3792	6/46	63792	2/49	10/62
6595	2/1918	1	2/44	6595	3795	4/46	63795	12/48	10/63
6596	3/1918	1	4/46	3796(a)	—		63796	12/48	10/62
6601	5/1918	1	8/44	6601	3806	8/46	63806	12/48	11/62
6519	5/1918	1	2/45	6519	3808	7/46	63808	11/49	11/62
6263	7/1918	1	4/45	6263	3817	10/46	63817	1/49	11/62
6261	11/1918	1	6/49	63838(b)	—		—		10/62
6526	6/1919	1	6/46	6526	3854	12/46	63854	6/48	11/62
6617	6/1919	1	10/49	63856(b)	—		—		11/62
6533	8/1919	1	9/45	6533	3863	7/46	63863	5/50	6/65
6535	8/1919	1	2/46	6535	3865	7/46	63865	8/50	11/62
6624	8/1919	1	9/44	6624	3867	6/46	63867	10/48	11/62
6625	8/1919	1	2/45	6625	3868	4/46	63868	11/49	7/65
6626	8/1919	1	12/44	6626	3869	4/46	63869	6/48	11/62
6525	5/1919	1	5/46	3872(a)	—		63872	4/48	1/64
6630	6/1919	1	6/44	6630	3874	6/46	63874	2/49	11/62
6288	7/1919	1	11/44	6288	3879	6/46	63879	1/49	7/65
6635	9/1919	1	8/46	3886(a)	—		63886	11/48	10/62
6636	9/1919	1	3/46	6636	3887	6/46	63887	9/48	3/63
6639	5/1919	1	7/46	3890(a)	—		63890	6/48	3/63
6642	12/1919	1	10/45	6642	3901	4/46	63901	2/50	11/62

(a) Nos. 3561, 3760/96, 3872/86/90 received their new L.N.E.R. numbers when they were rebuilt.
(b) Nos. 63571/9/89/96, 63746, 63838/56 received their B.R. numbers when they were rebuilt.

U.S. ARMY

CLASS S160
4ft. 9in. ENGINES

Engines received 1942-43 on loan: U.S.A. 1616/9/23, 1771, 1835/6/77, 1900, 2100/2/12/35-8/64/5, 2244/5, 2314/5/26/7/39/49/54/8/75/7, 2400/1/7/8/10/9/21/3/7/8/9/33/4/9. Total 43. Transferred to G.W.R., L.M.S. and S.R. 1943.

Engines received 1943-44 on loan: U.S.A. 1697/8/9, 1700/3-10/2/3/4/20-3/7-31/68/9/72/3/80/8/92, 1827-34/6/9/40/2-50/79/82/5-90, 1903/4/8/11/2/9/22-6, 2032/3/41/3/5/7-51/7/83/5/6/94/7/9, 2101/4-8/11/3/4/5/7/9/20/1/3-8/46, 2242/6/7/50-3/73/4/82-7/9/91/3/5-9, 2300-11/6/7/28/9/48/55/61-7/70/1/3/4, 2418/20/36/7/44-7. Total 168. Handed over to U.S. Army 1944-45.

Towards the end of World War I the Baldwin Locomotive Works produced in large numbers a highly successful general purpose 2-8-0. The design subsequently figured in the U.S. Army's contingency plans for any future national emergency, suitably modified to take into account modern locomotive practice such as the wide firebox. Nothing concrete came of this proposal until April 1941 when at last the U.S. Army ordered eight improved engines (class S159), in order to use up available funds before the end of the fiscal year. The United States was still a neutral country so there was no military urgency, which was just as well because Lima Locomotive Works was unable to build to specification and had to spend some time making design changes and the engines were not turned out until 1942. These were the only S159's built, but it probably meant that more care was taken over its successor, class S160, which was *really* needed by the U.S. Army.

Class S160 was designed in May 1942 to the specification of Major J.W. Marsh of the Corps of Engineers (Railway Branch), afterwards part of the Transportation Corps. Where possible the 2-8-0 incorporated details from the class S200 2-8-2's which were designed and built for British Army use, under the Lend-Lease arrangement. Certain features were however changed in the interests of mass production, such as the retrograde fitting of axlebox grease lubricators. The 2-8-0's were built to Austerity standards, quantity taking precedence over quality, to produce engines which would help to win the War but be expendable afterwards. Castings were only used where it was impractical to employ rolled shapes or plates.

The locomotives were built in vast quantities by the three leading locomotive manufacturers in the U.S.: American Locomotive Co., Baldwin and Lima. Almost 800 were shipped to the United Kingdom in readiness for the allied invasion of Europe. Although intended for operation by U.S. Army Transportation Corps personnel, agreement was reached whereby the first 400 were put into immediate use by either the main line companies or the War Department.

No. 1623 was the first engine of the class to be taken into L.N.E.R. Operating Stock, on 30th December 1942, followed shortly afterwards by Nos. 1616/9, 1835/6. It was then decided to concentrate the class in and around South Wales for the time being and these five engines were transferred to the G.W.R. during the last week of January 1943.

A further thirty-eight engines were overhauled by the L.N.E.R. before being handed over to one of the other main line companies. These forty-three engines figured in the L.N.E.R. official transfer sheets and are accordingly included in the Summary for completeness, though their period of running-in from L.N.E.R. sheds was in some cases a matter of a few days only. Between March 1943 and January 1944 168 were acquired by the L.N.E.R. and retained by them on loan until after D-Day (fig. 91).

By January 1944 the full complement of 400 was at work in the United Kingdom, distributed as follows: G.W.R. 174, L.M.S. 50, L.N.E.R. 168, S.R. 6, W.D. 2. These engines were taken from the following batches:-

U.S. Army Nos.	*Maker*	*Works Nos.*	*Date*
1600-24	A.L.Co.	70431-55	1942
1625-49	,,	70278-302	1942
1650-76	,,	70457-83	1942
1677-1701	Baldwin	67661-85	1943
1702-26	,,	64641-65	1942
1727-1826	,,	67561-660	1942
1827-1926	Lima	8058-8157	1942-43
2032-2151	A.L.Co.	70514-633	1942-43
2152-2241	Lima	8158-8247	1943
2242-2331	Baldwin	69485-574	1943
2333-82	,,	69590-639	1943
2400-59	A.L.Co.	70749-808	1943
2590-2639	Baldwin	69818-67	1943

Further arrivals in Britain were prepared for service by U.S. Army personnel at Ebbw Junction, run-in by the G.W.R., greased and put into store in South Wales.

On the L.N.E.R. the engines were concentrated at six main sheds, unlike the contemporary W.D. 2-8-0's which were more widely distributed (see class O7). The U.S. engines worked a considerable proportion of the heavy goods traffic in certain areas, particularly the East Coast main line between Newcastle and Edinburgh, the G.C. main line south of Annesley, and the G.E. main line from March to Temple Mills. However, the incidence of failures was high due to hot axleboxes, firebox arch tubes leaking, fractured tubeplates and dropped lead plugs.

Immediately following the D-Day landings in Normandy on 6th June 1944, a start was made shipping the engines stored in South Wales, followed by the engines on loan to the main line companies. The L.N.E.R. returned their engines in August and September 1944, except for No. 1707 which had been damaged in a mishap in August 1944 and was not officially taken out of Operating Stock until February 1945. In fact it then entered Doncaster Works for a heavy repair and was not sent overseas until after the War had ended in Europe, by which time the military usefulness of these engines was on the decline. During 1946-47 they were disposed of by the U.S. Army Transportation Corps to a number of European countries.

Standard Dimensions*

Cylinders (2 outside)	19″×26″
Motion	Walschaerts with 10″ piston valves
Boiler:	
Max. diam. outside	5′ 10″
Barrel length	12′ 11¾″
Firebox length outside	7′ 9$\frac{11}{16}$″
Pitch	9′ 3″
Heating surface:	
Firebox	136 sq.ft.
Arch tubes (3×3″)	15 sq.ft.
Tubes (150×2″)	1055 sq.ft.
Flues (30×5⅜″)	567 sq.ft.
Total evaporative	1773 sq.ft.
Superheater	480 sq.ft.
Total	2253 sq.ft.
Grate area	41 sq.ft.
Boiler pressure	225 lb./sq.in.
Leading wheels	2′ 9″
Coupled wheels	4′ 9″
Tender wheels	2′ 9″
Tractive effort (85%)	31,490 lb.
Length over buffers	61′ 0¼″
Wheelbase:	
Engine	7′9″+5′2″+5′2″+5′2″ =23′3″
Tender	5′6″+5′10″+5′6″ =16′10″
Total	51′ 7¾″
Weight (full):	
Engine	72T 10C
Tender	52T 2C
Total	124T 12C
Adhesive	62T 18C
Max. axle load	15T 15C
Water capacity	5,400 gallons
Coal capacity	8T 0C

* No engine diagram issued by L.N.E.R. Dimensions based on Alco specification, published sources and G.W.R. diagrams.

Details

The frames were made of cast steel, 4½in. wide, set up 2ft. 10½in. apart. The coupled wheels had cast steel spoked centres with 3in. wide steel tyres. Before the engines could run in the United Kingdom, ⅜in. had to be turned off the inside of the flange to bring them into profile for the British gauge. The axle journals were 8in. diameter by 11in. long, lubricated by grease lubricators which proved to be inadequate and led to frequent overheated axleboxes. The spring gear was compensated between the first and second pairs of coupled wheels and also between the third and fourth pairs, to provide smooth riding on inferior permanent way. As a result the engines rode well in this country. However the flanges on the tyres were thin by British standards, only $\frac{15}{16}$in., as a result of which the engines sometimes took the wrong turning at points. This was particularly the case when running tender first through cross-overs having small radius curves, due to the large distance between the front tender wheels and the rear coupled wheels, which was 11ft. $6\frac{3}{4}$in. The drive was on to the third pair of coupled wheels. The leading pony truck had cast steel frames, whilst the pony truck wheels were constructed in one-piece rolled steel without separate tyres.

The cylinders were made of cast-iron with the smokebox saddle attached, the whole assembly serving to brace the front of the engine frames. The piston valves were 10in. diameter inside admission, with a maximum travel of $6\frac{1}{2}$in. A Nathan DV-4 eight-feed mechanical lubricator was mounted on the right-hand rear steam chest extension to feed oil to the valves and cylinders. A similar lubricator was mounted on the opposite side of the engine for the guide bars, valve rod crosshead guides and coupled wheel horn wedges.

The valves were operated by a lightweight design Walschaerts valve gear, which was unorthodox in that the die blocks worked in the upper half of the radius links for forward gear and in the lower half for reverse – this being contrary to usual British practice.

The boiler barrel was constructed of two telescopic rings: the rear one was 5ft. 10in. outside diameter and the front ring 5ft. $8\frac{3}{4}$in. The distance between the tubeplates was 13ft. $4\frac{15}{16}$in. The dome for the regulator valves was located on the rear ring, the cover for which was broad at the front to match the sandbox cover. The safety valves were located immediately behind the dome, mounted off-centre towards the fireman's side, presumably to clear the 12ft. 11in. load gauge. The larger of the two valves, a muffled type, was set to blow off first at 225 lb. per sq. in. The smaller valve, an open type, was set to blow off at 228 lb. The whistle was located to the left of the dome cover.

The inner firebox was welded from $\frac{3}{8}$in. thickness steel plate except for the tubeplate which was $\frac{1}{2}$in. The crown was supported by wrought iron stay bolts, screwed through the outer firebox plate, then the inner firebox crown with their ends finally riveted over on the fire side. The front end of the firebox was supported by two rows of flexible expansion stays instead. The brick arch was supported on three 3in.-diameter arch tubes, which added a further 15 sq. ft. to the direct heating surface but were a source of weakness and had to be omitted altogether from later engines. The firegrate was the wide type, approximately 7ft. long and 5ft. 10in. wide, giving a grate area which was quite close to that of the Gresley Pacifics. The firegrate had two rocking sections, one on each side of the centre line, and the ashpan had two hoppers, one on each side of the trailing coupled wheels. No dampers were provided, but secondary air was admitted to the firebox through hollow firebox stays, which was normal American practice. Light was reflected down these hollow stays, which at night were said to look like stars.

Two Nathan non-lifting injectors were provided, one at each side of the engine under the cab, with the water fed into the sides of the boiler through clack valves on the front barrel ring. The injectors were very powerful and required careful manipulation as steam pressure would quickly drop when both were working. Only one water gauge was provided, of the "Reflex" type, on the firebox backplate at the fireman's side. A remote control stop valve was provided, though it was located in a misleading position on the driver's side of the cab above the regulator handle at the end of an extension rod which was about 2ft. 3in. long and led down from the manifold. Trouble was experienced with firebox crown fusible plug failures due to the gauge glass registering a false water level. This was usually caused by the driver closing the stop valve in error – some thought it was "the manifold control valve". In the light of experience, the extension rod and its handwheel were painted red on some engines, and a plate fitted reading "This valve not to be touched".

Low water above the crown of the firebox not only risked the dropping of a lead plug but also gradually built up a dangerous condition with the roof stay bolts. This was because an undue rise in temperature of an individual bolt caused metal fatigue in the screw threads, which then deformed or broke, so that the bolt then pulled out of the crown. The problem was made worse by the formation of scale on the crown, resulting from inadequate boiler wash-outs for whatever reason. This caused a weakening of the firebox crown and its eventual collapse, with dire consequences. There were three such mishaps in the United Kingdom within the space of ten months.

The first failure was on the G.W.R. in November 1943 involving No. 2403 which fatally injured the fireman. As a result Nos. 2403 (no boiler or cab) and 1688 (damaged frames) were cannibalised at Swindon to provide one serviceable engine and a quantity of spare parts. The second failure occurred at Thurston in the early hours of 12th January 1944, whilst No. 2363 was working the 11-15 p.m. Ipswich – Whitemoor goods train. The enginemen were injured and the force of the explosion blew the fireman off the footplate. The third mishap occurred in South Harrow tunnel on 30th August 1944 whilst No. 1707 was working the 2-45 a.m. Neasden – Woodford goods train. Both driver and fireman received fatal injuries. By this date the engines were being handed over to the U.S. Army and it was too late for the L.N.E.R. to investigate further. The repairs to No. 1707 were heavy and, as mentioned earlier, it was not shipped to France until after the end of the War in Europe. It arrived at Neasden shed on 26th May 1945 en route to the Southern Railway for shipment. The Neasden men refused to keep it in steam and it was hauled away dead later that day. Unhappily, firebox collapses continued to occur abroad, with cases reported in six other European countries, as well as in both North Africa and the sub-continent of India. One such case, at Louvain (Belgium) about October 1945, involved No. 1829 which had been on loan to the L.N.E.R.

The smokebox rested on the saddle which was integral with the cylinders. A small chimney was fitted, well within the load gauge, and there was a half-round beading around the rim. The blastpipe had cross pattern steam dividers to split the exhaust. The blast was therefore considered to be heavy with coal consumption high. The smokebox door was off-centre to the left, facing, and was small by British standards. To the right of the door was the Westinghouse 9in. air compressor for the brakes.

The cab was 8ft. 10in. wide, outside, with large sliding glass windows. The roof was made of steel, wood lined, with the rearward extension over the cab entrance detachable for shipment purposes. (A requirement of the specification was that the engine could be lowered fully erected through a 35ft. 0in. ship's hatch). The cab side sheets were shallow but the vertical handrail extended well below and entrance was afforded by means of ladder steps on the tender frames. A door was provided in the front plate on the fireman's side which led to the running plate alongside the firebox, a standard American feature which could also be used for ventilation purposes. The driver's controls were on the right-hand side and presented a bewildering array at first sight. The reversing mechanism was a simple lever, but was in front of the seat with no room to obtain good leverage. To the left of the reversing lever was the Westinghouse brake valve with the Gresham & Craven solid jet vacuum ejector (fitted in the United Kingdom) just above it. High up above the regulator handle, where it was out of reach unless the driver stood up, was the Gresham & Craven air and vacuum graduable steam brake valve (again fitted in Britain).

Steam-operated sanders were provided in front of the leading coupled wheels for forward running and behind the driving coupled wheels for reverse running. The solitary sandbox was mounted on top of the boiler barrel in front of the steam dome.

Brakes

Steam brakes were provided for engine and tender, with both Westinghouse and vacuum for train operation. The steam brake cylinder was located towards the front of the engine, contrary to usual British practice, and was unsatisfactory in that it took a while to warm up and was slow-acting. The steam pipe from the driver's application valve to the brake cylinder was over twenty feet long, and in the temperate British climate was bound to be affected by condensation. The water which thus condensed in the pipe had to be expelled before a brake application could take effect. A hand brake was provided for the tender, on the fireman's side, which was fitted after arrival in the United Kingdom to conform to British requirements.

Tenders

The tender was large by normal British standards, with a carrying capacity of 5,400 Imperial gallons of water and 8 tons of coal. The tank body was of riveted construction with ¼in. thickness steel plate. The outline was similar to that of the contemporary British "Austerity" 2-8-0, with the coal bunker inset above the top of the tank to give better vision when running tender first. The tender frame comprised two steel channels about 23ft. 9in. long, supported on two centre bearing bogie trucks. The wheelbase of the bogies was 5ft. 6in. with their centres 11ft. 4in. apart. The wheels were 2ft. 9in. diameter cast-iron and the axle journals were 5in.

diameter by 9in. long. The bogie wheels had helical bearing springs and the general opinion was that these tenders rode extremely well.

The tenders that were attached to the Baldwin engines numbered between 1768 and 1792, at least, had cast-iron dragboxes. As these particular engines passed through Doncaster Works for acceptance they were fitted with intermediate rubbing plates.

Maintenance

The engines were received through a number of ports. At Hull, for example, they were unloaded at the King George Dock by means of the floating crane. The lifting gear was secured by fitting staff from Dairycoates shed and the lift was supervised by a shop foreman from Doncaster Works. The engine was then coupled to its tender and hauled to Dairycoates shed to await disposal instructions to one of the main line works. Usually four engines and tenders were received at a time though occasionally a ship would dock with five or sometimes six.

Before entering service in the United Kingdom the engines visited one or other of the main line works for acceptance as certain modifications were needed to allow them to run in this country. As far as the engines on loan to the L.N.E.R. were concerned, this work was carried out at Stratford, Doncaster, Gorton, Darlington, Cowlairs, Eastleigh, Swindon, Wolverhampton, Danygraig, Derby, Crewe and St. Rollox.

The engines spent about a week or so in works where the coupling rods, connecting rods and part motion were assembled, these having been stored during shipment inside the tenders. Other modifications were carried out including the fitting of standard brake gear. One engine, No. 2291, was fitted with a speed indicator at Doncaster Works.

Engines frequently returned to works for repair. No. 1722 for example, to traffic on the L.N.E.R. in April 1943 after initial overhaul at Wolverhampton Works, went into Doncaster Works a month later for its right-hand cylinder to be patched and a liner fitted. The situation on 10th June 1944, just after the allied landings in Normandy was that twenty-three out of the 168 engines on loan to the L.N.E.R. were either in or awaiting works. Four engines had broken cylinders (Nos. 1888, 2125, 2298, 2309), one had a broken frame (No. 1924) and others had defects with tubeplates, tubes, reversing gear, pony truck and lead plugs dropped. The mileage run up to this date ranged between 5,336 (No. 2446) and 34,377 (No. 2307).

Arrangements were made for the engines to be overhauled before being sent to France. Twelve engines were sent to Ebbw Junction in August 1944 for repairs by personnel of the U.S. Army's 756th Railway Shop Battalion. These included ten engines from Woodford, apparently chosen at random, and two March engines held up in Stratford Works for boiler repairs.

During September 1944 a further 155 engines were returned after loan. Only a small proportion of these passed through L.N.E.R. works, the majority apparently having to make do with a shed examination. At Woodford for example, the cylinders and steam chests were opened up, a fitter cleaned all the port ways and a woman labourer cleaned the carbon from the piston heads and piston valves. The parts were then inspected for damage and the cylinders were gauged for wear by a shop foreman sent from Doncaster Works. In the N.E. Area Darlington Works dealt with twelve out of the fifty engines operating in this Area. A further six were recommended to be sent to Ebbw Junction for overhaul but of these only No. 2105 has been traced there, No. 2120 being dealt with at Gorton, No. 2289 at Doncaster and Nos. 2303/10 at Eastleigh.

The last engine to be returned to U.S. Army control was No. 1707, which was not shipped to France until 5th June 1945, in the S.R. train ferry *Twickenham Ferry*.

Liveries

Most of the engines ran on the L.N.E.R. in light grey livery with matt finish and silver lettering and numbers, though No. 2373 in particular was subsequently painted glossy black for a press exhibition. The early engines simply had "U.S.A." on their tenders but later ones had "TRANSPORTATION CORPS" also. In many cases the running number also appeared on the back of the tender. Prior to handing back to the U.S. Army after D-Day, some engines were repainted glossy light grey at one of the L.N.E.R. main works (fig. 91).

Allocation and Work

On the Great Central Section, twenty-five U.S. Army 2-8-0's were allocated to Woodford (Nos. 1704/6/7/9/10/29/30/1, 1829/32/3/4/6/9/40/4/6-9, 2048-51/7), and comprehensive instructions regarding their rostering were issued. They were to be used on certain specified goods and coal trains, preference to be given to the Woodford – Mansfield service (including

Warsop and Langwith) and the Woodford – Neasden service. They could also be employed on a number of duties to Annesley (together with Markham, Heath, Hucknall and Awsworth Junction). At the same time, they were permitted to run to Staveley and Marylebone, but prohibited from use elsewhere, and they were to be returned to Woodford "promptly". Due to the circumstances prevailing at the time, with traffic congestion resulting in long hours for the enginemen, the Woodford "Yankees" were handled regularly by men from other depots, such as Neasden, Annesley, Leicester and Langwith. Despite the foregoing instructions, these engines were regularly employed on Woodford duties to Banbury with through traffic for the G.W.R., and they also appeared on L.N.E.R.-worked trips to Hayes on the G.W.R. They were usually loaded to capacity and sometimes the maximum for a class 7 engine was exceeded, in which case an assisting engine would be provided. For example, on 19th August 1943, two successive goods trains noted in the vicinity of Leicester were double-headed with Nos. 1709 and 1846 on the first, and class B7 No. 5469 (of Annesley) and No. 1829 on the other, both trains consisting of seventy wagons. A remarkable accident befell No. 1730 in March 1944 at Banbury (G.W.R.) shed; with a boilerful of water, it would not move when an attempt was made by the shed enginemen. Then suddenly and unexpectedly the engine did set off and before it could be stopped it had passed over rail-end chocks, across the yard, through a shed full of brick arch blocks, and nose-dived into the Oxford Canal! On 6th March it was seen being lifted from the canal by crane and later hauled back into Banbury shed.

In addition to the engines allocated to Woodford, a number of U.S. 2-8-0's which had been dealt with at Gorton Works on arrival in this country were used on goods work to Sheffield, before despatch to other sections of the L.N.E.R. or elsewhere.

The U.S. 2-8-0's were not used to any great extent on the G.N. Section, although Nos. 1768/9/72/80, 2287/96 and 2316 were very briefly shedded at Doncaster before re-allocation to other L.N.E.R. sheds. Colwick also had an allocation of these engines when Nos. 1710/29/31, 1832/48 were moved there from Woodford in 1944, but their duties continued to be chiefly on the G.C. Section line south of Nottingham. They were seldom seen at the southern extremity of the G.N. main line; No. 2033 of March worked a special goods to Finsbury Park in September 1943, whilst No. 2121 of Neville Hill lay at Hitchin for several weeks in May – June 1944.

The Great Eastern Section had a total of seventy-one U.S. 2-8-0's, fifty at March (Nos. 1703/5/8/12/3/4/20-3/7/8, 1827/8/30/1/42/3/5/50/79/82/5-90, 2032/3/41/3/5/7/83/5/6/94/7/9, 2101/8/11/3/4, 2242/6/7/73/4) and twenty-one at Stratford (Nos. 1699, 1700/68/9/72/3/80/8/92, 2361-4/73/4, 2436/7/44-7). The March engines were employed on heavy goods and coal traffic to Doncaster, Lowestoft, Peterborough and London via Cambridge. The Stratford engines usually worked to Whitemoor, but sometimes to Ipswich via Chelmsford, whilst No. 2437 was seen on 14th December 1943 passing through March on a special passenger train. A great deal of heavy traffic went from Whitemoor to London via Ely, Bury St. Edmunds and Ipswich. Cross-country traffic was also worked by "Yankees" from Bury St. Edmunds and Haughley to Ipswich, and local traffic from March to Wisbech and King's Lynn. They were very often seen at Cambridge shed and, apart from their employment on short-distance trips in that neighbourhood, they were said to have been used on local passenger, troop and empty coaching stock trains. No. 1843 of March spent a few weeks at Ipswich in June and July 1943, during which time it was noted on the East Suffolk line at Lowestoft. The engines worked special passenger trains conveying workers engaged in constructing airfields for the U.S. in Suffolk. One particular working from Whitemoor was to Lowestoft with a train load of bombs. Here the engine ran round its train and worked to Beccles. The bomb trains were then worked to airfields on the Waveney Valley line beyond Beccles by class J15 0-6-0's. Very strict orders were given that under no circumstances was the boiler pressure to exceed 200 lb. per sq. in. on the "Yankees", to avoid a firebox mishap. One of the authors also saw one of these engines performing some dramatic shunting on the 1 in 43 rising gradient of the first half-mile of the Mid-Suffolk Light Railway at Haughley, which was specially strengthened to take heavier engines, again in connection with serving U.S. air bases in the area. In the London district they were seen on a variety of duties including oil tank traffic from the Tilbury line, short-distance goods workings (for example, on the North Woolwich line) and empty carriages.

In the North Eastern Area, fifty U.S. 2-8-0's were divided equally between Heaton (Nos. 1903/4, 2119, 2282-5/9/91/3/7, 2300-11/6/7) and Neville Hill (Nos. 2104-7/15/7/20/1/3-8/46, 2250-3/7/86/95/6/8/9). The Heaton engines worked chiefly on the Newcastle to Edinburgh goods service, enabling ten Southern Railway class N15 4-6-0's to be returned from loan. The Heaton "Yankees" were handled also by Gateshead, Tweedmouth, St. Margaret's and Haymarket men, and they appeared on southbound goods trains as far as York. Although officially confined to goods work, it is believed that one of these engines was once called upon to work a passenger train from somewhere in the vicinity of Alnmouth to Newcastle when the booked engine failed. At Neville Hill, the American engines displaced class Q6 0-8-0's, and they had quite a wide sphere of operation from Leeds and Harrogate to York, Scarborough, Tees-side and Tyneside, being seen regularly at Starbeck, York, Darlington, Newport and Tyne Dock sheds. Sometimes they were utilised for local or branch line duties, such as to Masham from Starbeck. To relieve main line congestion, many East Coast goods trains south of Newcastle were routed via Leamside, rejoining the main line at Ferryhill, and so the "Yankees" were regularly seen passing through Pelaw, Washington and Penshaw. During wartime engines often strayed far from home and an occasional U.S. 2-8-0 from Neville Hill would turn up at Edinburgh, and one was recorded as far south on the G.N. Section as Hitchin. On 24th June 1944 No. 2251 was observed at Hartford (C.L.C.) on a westbound oil tank train assisted by a class J10 0-6-0.

Twenty-two U.S. 2-8-0's were allocated to the Scottish Area throughout their sojourn in the United Kingdom. These were Nos. 1697/8, 1908/11/2/9/22-6, 2328/9/48/55/65/6/7/70/1, 2418/20, all of which were shedded at St. Margaret's A further twenty-two engines of this class spent a short time working in the Scottish Area before transfer to other areas of the L.N.E.R. (Nos. 1710, 1829/32/3/4/6/44, 2101/11/3/4) or to the G.W.R. (Nos. 1616/9/23, 1835/77, 2314/5/54, 2419/21/8). The foregoing "temporary" Scottish Area engines, together with Nos. 1911/2, 2355 and 2420 of the "permanent" St. Margaret's engines were prepared for service at Cowlairs Works, and ran the customary short trip by way of steam trial before handing over to the Running Department. In addition, Nos. 1625/31, 1756/97/8, 1805, 2180/1/93/4, 2256/7/72/5/6/8, 2337/40/3/4, 2601/3/4/5/15/6, 2838/40/1/2/58/68 were dealt with at Cowlairs Works on arrival from America, but these engines were despatched to South Wales to be stored until required by the U.S. authorities for service on the Continent of Europe.

The first three of these engines to arrive at St. Margaret's, in December 1942 and January 1943 (Nos. 1623 and 1616/9 respectively), were used initially on the 10-15 a.m. Niddrie – Thornton goods, a short distance out-and-home duty, which ensured the engines' return to St. Margaret's each day. Inspector A. Black travelled with the engines at the outset, and Senior Spare Link men were the first crews to be instructed in their handling. These in turn were intended to instruct the other men, but in practice many drivers and firemen stepped on to these engines and worked booked trains with no special tuition whatever. One St. Margaret's crew was sent to Banbury with one of these engines to hand over to the Great Western.

The next U.S. engine to leave Cowlairs Works, in January 1943, was No. 1835 which was sent to Thornton, where it was used on a goods turn to Dundee, again to ensure its safe return daily, as at that time most goods workings over moderate or long distances were operated on the "changeover" principle, or the men left the engine at their destination and came home "on the cushions". Thus goods engines were liable to use by other sheds, with consequent extended absence from their home depot.

Early in May 1943, the U.S. 2-8-0's began to settle down to the normal main line goods workings at St. Margaret's, chiefly on the East Coast Route to Heaton, the Waverley Route to Carlisle, and to Glasgow, all usually change-over jobs. From January 1944, the class was banned from the Carlisle line because of their braking deficiencies, and after a derailment at a diamond crossing in Princes Street Gardens they were officially prohibited from going through the Waverley station, although this prohibition does not appear to have been rigidly enforced.

When the "Yankees" came, traffic was extremely heavy, and due to wartime difficulties many of the L.N.E.R.'s own engines were in a rundown condition. The newcomers were therefore most welcome, and their performance was considered astonishing, For example, one St. Margaret's driver had his first trip on a "Yankee" on 6th May 1943, No. 1844 on an East Coast goods with the full O4 load permitted to these engines. From Dunbar to Grantshouse the time taken was 30 minutes, as against the 42 booked, and the 1 in 96 of Cockburnspath, was climbed with full regulator, the reversing lever well notched up. The next night, the same crew with a K3 in poor condition took 60 minutes for this part of the journey with the reverser in full forward gear and "full throttle" up the bank.

Although the pulling power of the U.S. 2-8-0's left nothing to be desired, their braking was unsatisfactory by British standards. In American practice, it was customary to fit engines with Westinghouse brake for engine and train, and all goods trains had continuous brakes. However the S160's, although equipped with Westinghouse and vacuum brakes for the train, had a steam brake on the engine, and this had grave deficiencies, due principally to the long distance between the driver's valve and the brake cylinder. As far as the Scottish Area was concerned, another difficulty arose in the control of heavy slack-coupled trains on falling gradients. It had always been customary to use the tender hand brake for this purpose, but when this was tried on the "Yankees" it was found that the tender wheels (with which the tyres were integral) soon became overheated, and the "tyres" having been badly cast began to disintegrate.

Whilst the Scottish engines were actually stationed at St. Margaret's, they were frequently worked by Haymarket men on similar duties, and on the East Coast and Waverley Routes the Edinburgh men changed over with Heaton and Carlisle men respectively. The U.S. engines from Heaton shed also participated in the Newcastle-Edinburgh goods workings. In the Scottish Area, the U.S. 2-8-0's were prohibited from passenger train operation, and they were subject to a general speed restriction of 35 m.p.h. However, the latter was not strictly observed and much higher speeds were regularly attained, especially on the descent of Cockburnspath bank and on the favourable gradients between Dunbar and Monktonhall Junction.

The "Yankees" were regarded as very competent engines, free-steaming on all grades of coal, and easy to fire. They had very good injectors and they were very free-running. The enginemen and disposal staff greatly appreciated the rocking grate. However, there were several features which were not popular with British crews. For instance, the usual American position of the sandboxes on top of the boiler was quite unsuited to our laborious methods of hand-filling from ground level. The single boiler water-level gauge compared very unfavourably with the standard L.N.E.R. pair of easily-read gauge glasses and, due to the unfortunate arrangement of the shut-off valve some distance away, it was easily possible for this to be closed inadvertently causing a false water reading which could have disastrous consequences. The pole-type reversing lever was regarded as archaic, although it had fine notches in the quadrant, giving twenty-four positions of the gear on either side of centre. The worst feature of the reverser was that the quadrant was secured to the firebox. As a result of continuous vibration, the securing nut could work loose, and there were two cases on the East Coast main line where St. Margaret's drivers and firemen were badly scalded in such mishaps. If the safety valves, which were off-centre, lifted when passing through tunnels, the force of the steam hit the wall and disturbed soot and wet slime which settled on the rail surfaces. To prevent this happening, instructions were issued to Woodford shed, at least, that the engines were not to be allowed to "blow off" in tunnels.

The engines were fully equipped with a good set of tools on arrival in the United Kingdom. The firing shovel was the standard American type "scoop" with very wide mouth, and D-shaped handle instead of the usual British T-shaped one. The footplate brush was of excellent quality, superior to its L.N.E.R. counterpart, but this item of equipment had a tendency to "disappear" for office or domestic use! A complete set of fireirons was provided, and oilcans and feeders. The oil feeders ("pouries" in Scotland) were rather large and cumbersome as compared with the usual British types, and they were not very well liked. There was one other feature of the tool kit not normal on L.N.E.R. engines, a pinchbar. There were cases of reversing links seizing up on the "Yankees" and it was jokingly said that the pinchbar was for assisting in reversing the engine! These pinchbars were liable to be appropriated by the fitters and remained in use at some sheds long after the "Yankees" had left!

Preservation

Polish State Railways No. 474 (origin uncertain) was acquired by the Keighley & Worth Valley Railway in November 1977 and is now known as U.S.A.T.C. 5820. Hellenic State Railways No. 575 (Baldwin 70340/1944) was acquired by the Mid Hants Railway in 1981 and is now known as U.S.A.T.C. 3383.

Engine Diagram

Not issued.

Classification: Southern Area load class 7 (understood to have been reduced to class 6 on the G.E. Section).

Summary of S160 Class Engines on Loan

U.S.A. No.	*On Loan to L.N.E.R. From*	*To* (a)	*U.S.A. No.*	*On Loan to L.N.E.R. From*	*To* (a)
1616	1/43	1/43 (b)	1847	3/43	8/44
1619	1/43	1/43 (b)	1848	4/43	9/44
1623	12/42	1/43 (b)	1849	4/43	8/44
1697	8/43	9/44	1850	5/43	9/44
1698	9/43	9/44	1877	5/43	6/43 (b)
1699	10/43	9/44	1879	5/43	9/44
1700	1/44	9/44	1882	6/43	9/44
1703	5/43	9/44	1885	7/43	9/44
1704	4/43	8/44	1886	6/43	9/44
1705	4/43	9/44	1887	4/43	9/44
1706	5/43	9/44	1888	4/43	9/44
1707	4/43	2/45	1889	5/43	9/44
1708	4/43	9/44	1890	7/43	9/44
1709	4/43	8/44	1900	5/43	6/43 (b)
1710	4/43	9/44	1903	7/43	9/44
1712	5/43	9/44	1904	7/43	9/44
1713	5/43	9/44	1908	8/43	9/44
1714	4/43	9/44	1911	7/43	9/44
1720	4/43	9/44	1912	7/43	9/44
1721	4/43	9/44	1919	10/43	9/44
1722	4/43	9/44	1922	8/43	9/44
1723	4/43	8/44	1923	9/43	9/44
1727	5/43	9/44	1924	10/43	9/44
1728	5/43	9/44	1925	9/43	9/44
1729	5/43	9/44	1926	9/43	9/44
1730	5/43	9/44	2032	5/43	9/44
1731	5/43	9/44	2033	5/43	9/44
1768	9/43	9/44	2041	5/43	9/44
1769	8/43	9/44	2043	5/43	9/44
1771	7/43	9/43 (d)	2045	5/43	9/44
1772	8/43	9/44	2047	6/43	9/44
1773	9/43	9/44	2048	5/43	9/44
1780	9/43	9/44	2049	5/43	8/44
1788	9/43	9/44	2050	5/43	9/44
1792	8/43	9/44	2051	5/43	9/44
1827	4/43	9/44	2057	5/43	9/44
1828	4/43	9/44	2083	5/43	9/44
1829	4/43	8/44	2085	6/43	9/44
1830	5/43	9/44	2086	5/43	9/44
1831	5/43	9/44	2094	5/43	9/44
1832	4/43	9/44	2097	5/43	9/44
1833	4/43	9/44	2099	6/43	9/44
1834	5/43	8/44	2100	6/43	6/43 (b)
1835	1/43	1/43 (b)	2101	5/43	8/44
1836	1/43	9/44 (e)	2102	5/43	5/43 (b)
1839	5/43	8/44	2104	6/43	9/44
1840	5/43	8/44	2105	6/43	9/44
1842	4/43	9/44	2106	6/43	9/44
1843	5/43	9/44	2107	7/43	9/44
1844	5/43	8/44	2108	6/43	9/44
1845	4/43	9/44	2111	5/43	9/44
1846	4/43	9/44	2112	5/43	5/43 (b)

2113	5/43	9/44
2114	5/43	9/44
2115	7/43	9/44
2117	7/43	9/44
2119	8/43	9/44
2120	7/43	9/44
2121	8/43	9/44
2123	6/43	9/44
2124	7/43	9/44
2125	6/43	9/44
2126	6/43	9/44
2127	6/43	9/44
2128	6/43	9/44
2135	6/43	7/43 (b)
2136	6/43	7/43 (b)
2137	7/43	7/43 (b)
2138	6/43	7/43 (b)
2146	5/43	9/44
2164	9/43	10/43 (b)
2165	9/43	10/43 (b)
2242	6/43	9/44
2244	5/43	5/43 (c)
2245	5/43	5/43 (c)
2246	6/43	9/44
2247	6/43	9/44
2250	6/43	9/44
2251	6/43	9/44
2252	6/43	9/44
2253	6/43	9/44
2273	6/43	9/44
2274	6/43	9/44
2282	7/43	9/44
2283	8/43	9/44
2284	6/43	9/44
2285	8/43	9/44
2286	6/43	9/44
2287	7/43	9/44
2289	8/43	9/44
2291	6/43	9/44
2293	7/43	9/44
2295	6/43	9/44
2296	7/43	9/44
2297	7/43	9/44
2298	6/43	9/44
2299	6/43	9/44
2300	7/43	9/44
2301	7/43	9/44
2302	8/43	9/44
2303	7/43	9/44
2304	7/43	9/44
2305	7/43	9/44
2306	6/43	9/44
2307	8/43	9/44
2308	6/43	9/44
2309	7/43	9/44
2310	6/43	9/44
2311	6/43	9/44
2314	6/43	6/43 (b)
2315	6/43	10/43 (b)
2316	6/43	9/44
2317	6/43	9/44
2326	7/43	7/43 (b)
2327	7/43	7/43 (b)
2328	8/43	9/44
2329	8/43	9/44
2339	8/43	9/43 (b)
2348	7/43	9/44
2349	8/43	9/43 (b)
2354	7/43	7/43 (b)
2355	8/43	9/44
2358	8/43	9/43 (b)
2361	8/43	9/44
2362	9/43	9/44
2363	9/43	9/44
2364	9/43	9/44
2365	7/43	9/44
2366	9/43	9/44
2367	9/43	9/44
2370	8/43	9/44
2371	8/43	9/44
2373	8/43	9/44
2374	9/43	9/44
2375	9/43	9/43 (b)
2377	9/43	9/43 (b)
2400	7/43	7/43 (c)
2401	7/43	7/43 (c)
2407	8/43	8/43 (b)
2408	7/43	7/43 (b)
2410	8/43	9/43 (b)
2418	9/43	9/44
2419	7/43	7/43 (c)
2420	8/43	9/44
2421	7/43	7/43 (c)
2423	8/43	9/43 (b)
2427	8/43	8/43 (c)
2428	7/43	7/43 (c)
2429	8/43	9/43 (c)
2433	8/43	8/43 (b)
2434	8/43	8/43 (b)
2436	9/43	9/44
2437	8/43	9/44
2439	8/43	9/43 (b)
2444	9/43	9/44
2445	10/43	9/44
2446	10/43	9/44
2447	10/43	9/44

(a) Unless otherwise indicated, the engines were handed over to U.S. Army on the dates shown.
(b) Transferred to G.W.R.
(c) Transferred to L.M.S.
(d) Transferred to S.R.
(e) No. 1836 was transferred to G.W.R. 1/1943 and returned to L.N.E.R. 3/1943.

CLASS O6

STANIER 4ft. 8½in. ENGINES

Engines received 1943-45 on loan: L.M.S. 8500-59. Total 60. Handed over to L.M.S. 1946-47.

ENGINES BUILT AFTER GROUPING (1944-46): 3125-67, 7651-75. TOTAL 68.

In November 1939 the War Department adopted the Stanier 2-8-0 as its standard goods engine and large orders were placed with private contractors. At the same time an earlier decision to transfer 300 Robinson 2-8-0's to Government use was rescinded (see class O4).

In 1941 discussions took place between the Ministry of War Transport and the four main line companies with a view to having them construct a considerable number of Stanier 2-8-0's in their own workshops, though the G.W.R., L.N.E.R. and the S.R. expressed unwillingness to take them into their own stocks at the end of Government control. Between June 1943 and September 1945 sixty of these engines were built by the L.N.E.R. (fig. 92). Lettered "L M S" and numbered 8500-59 in that company's series, they were treated as being on loan to the L.N.E.R. until such time as the appearance of sufficient numbers of "Austerity" 2-8-0's (class O7) facilitated their eventual release in 1946-47. In the N. E. Area the engines on loan were referred to as "WD (R) 2-8-0". The construction of these L.M.S. engines is summarised in the accompanying table.

L.M.S. Nos.	*Maker*	*Order No.*	*Date ordered*	*Works Nos.*	*No. built*	*Date*
8500-9	Darlington	—	July 1943*	1924/32/7-43/5	10	1944
8510-9	Doncaster	371	May 1942	1956-9/61/2/4-7	10	1943-44
8520-9	,,	373	December 1942	1968-72/4-7/9	10	1944-45
8530-9	,,	374	,,	1980-3/5-8/90/89	10	1945
8540-59	Darlington	—	January 1943	1946-9/51-66	20	1944-45

* Originally ordered from Gorton in May 1942, then from Doncaster in December 1942 (E.O. 372).

Meanwhile, in February 1943 the L.N.E.R. informed the Ministry that in the national interest it was prepared to absorb and pay for up to 100 of this type of engine, subject to the right to cancel any not actually under construction at the end of the War. A firm order was placed for sixty-eight engines, made up of twenty-five from the S.R. works at Brighton and forty-three from Darlington. The latter appear to have been straight substitutions for forty-three engines which were to have been built at Crewe, then cancelled and, it is believed, the material diverted to the L.N.E.R. The sixty-eight engines were numbered in the L.N.E.R. series. The Brighton engines were delivered first, between June and September 1944 (fig. 93). Initially they were not given an L.N.E.R. classification and were simply referred to as "W.D.". However the classification O6 was introduced for these engines in September 1945, during which month No. 3125, the first of the Darlington-built engines, appeared. Meanwhile part of the Darlington order had been transferred to Doncaster for completion and O6's were turned out from both works simultaneously until well into 1946 (fig. 94). They differed from the

Fig. 92 L.M.S. Class 8F No. 8510 at Doncaster Works, May 1943.

Built by and on loan to L.N.E.R. In L.M.S. livery, tender with disc wheels.

Fig. 93 Class O6 No. 7652 at Brighton Works, June 1944.

Built by S.R. for L.N.E.R. Wakefield mechanical lubricators, welded tender tank, spoked tender wheels.

Fig. 94 Class O6 No. 3144 at Darlington Works, about August 1946.

Built at Darlington Works for L.N.E.R. Silvertown mechanical lubricators, riveted tender tank, spoked tender wheels.

Fig. 95 Class O6 No. 3146 on up class B goods passing Torside, September 1946.

Fig. 96 Class O6 No. 3518 on up class B goods at York station, August 1947.

Fig. 97 W.D. "Austerity" Class No. 7177 at Doncaster Works, January 1945.

Prepared at Doncaster for despatch to Continent after loan to L.N.E.R. Scottish Area. Note diameter of smokebox less than that of boiler clothing plate, 8in. numerals on cab side, 2in. letters on tender.

Fig. 98 W.D. "Austerity" Class No. 7337 at Cambridge shed, 11th June 1944, shortly after being involved in the ammunition train explosion at Soham.

On loan to L.N.E.R. before despatch to Continent.

Fig. 99 W.D. "Austerity" Class No. 78711 at Haymarket shed, July 1946.

On loan to L.N.E.R. after return from Continent and subsequently purchased as L.N.E.R. No. 3175. Large painted W.D. number on smokebox door as applied in Belgium.

Fig. 100 Class O7 No. 3085 at Stratford Works, June 1947.

Original shallow anti-vacuum valve behind chimney, vacuum reservoir cylinder on running plate alongside firebox.

Fig. 101 Class O7 No. 63183, 1948.

Westinghouse brake equipment removed, smokebox door numberplate.

Fig. 102 W.D. 2-8-0 Class No. 90001 at Darlington shed, September 1959.

Formerly class O7 No. 3001. L.N.E.R.-type anti-vacuum valve behind chimney, boiler rebuilt with new firebox showing altered arrangement of hand holes, handrails and vacuum ejector exhaust pipe.

L.N.E.R. Nos.	*Maker*	*Order No.*	*Date ordered*	*Works Nos.*	*No. built*	*Date*
7651-75	Brighton	—	March 1943	—	25	1944
3125-47	Darlington	—	March 1943	1967-89	23	1945-46
3148-57	Doncaster	375	February 1944*	—	10	1945-46
3158-67	,,	376	February 1944*	1991-9, 2001	10	1946

* Originally ordered from Darlington in March 1943.

engines on loan from the L.M.S. in minor details but from an operating point of view were identical. The construction of class O6 is summarised above.

Nos. 3148-57 were not allocated Doncaster works numbers in order to balance the cancellation of works numbers 1554-63 at the time of the Grouping, these numbers never subsequently being used (see Part 1 of this series, p.94). This was probably done to ensure that when Doncaster turned out its 2,000th locomotive (class A2 No. 500), it would correctly display works number 2000, as calculations could have shown that if Doncaster was not careful, this honour would fall upon an L.M.S. type locomotive!

After the War the L.N.E.R. took delivery of large numbers of W.D. "Austerity" 2-8-0's, resulting in the transfer of Nos. 8500-59 to the L.M.S. On the eve of nationalisation, in September 1947 the loan to the L.N.E.R. of a further sixty-eight "Austerities" was arranged to allow disposal of the O6's to the L.M.S., to be treated as on loan. All the O6's were sent to the L.M.S. before the end of the year, except for No. 3554 (ex-3154) which followed in January 1948, thus becoming a B.R. inter-regional transfer. The classification O6 was discontinued in May 1948 when the engines were deleted from Eastern Region book stock.

Withdrawal of Stanier class 8F 2-8-0's commenced in January 1964 and included Nos. 48508 and 48772 (ex-3567). August 1968 saw the withdrawal of the remaining standard gauge steam locomotives on B.R. and it was somewhat ironical that these should have included six former L.N.E.R. locomotives, Nos. 48715/23/7/30/52/65 (ex-3510/8/22/5/47/60), as well as No. 48519 which was one of the 8F's built at Doncaster for the L.M.S. Thus the L.N.E.R. was represented at the end of main line steam by locomotives which had been designed by a rival company, but which they had built.

Standard L.N.E.R. Dimensions

Cylinders (2 outside)	$18\frac{1}{2}'' \times 28''$
Motion	Walschaerts with 10" piston valves
Boiler:	
Max. diam. outside	5' $8\frac{3}{8}''$
Barrel length	11' $11\frac{5}{16}''$(a)
Firebox length outside	10' $9\frac{3}{8}''$(b)
Pitch	8' 11"
Diagram No.	114
Heating surface:	
Firebox	171 sq.ft.
Tubes ($202 \times 1\frac{3}{4}''$)	1134 sq.ft.
Flues ($21 \times 5\frac{1}{8}''$)	345 sq.ft.
Total evaporative	1650 sq.ft.
Superheater ($21 \times 1.1018''$)	215 sq.ft.
Total	1865 sq.ft.
Grate area	28.65 sq.ft.
Boiler pressure	225 lb./sq.in.
Leading wheels	3' $3\frac{1}{2}''$
Coupled wheels	4' $8\frac{1}{2}''$
Tender wheels	4' 3"
Tractive effort (85%)	32,438 lb.
Length over buffers	63' $0\frac{3}{4}''$
Wheelbase:	
Engine	8' 9" + 5' 6" + 5' 6" + 6' 3" = 26' 0"
Tender	7' 6" + 7' 6" = 15' 0"
Total	52' $7\frac{3}{4}''$
Weight (full):	
Engine	70T 10C
Tender	54T 13C
Total	125T 3C
Adhesive	62T 0C
Max. axle load	16T 0C
Water capacity	4,000 gallons
Coal capacity	9T 0C

(a) The engine diagram quoted the distance between tubeplates, 12' $2\frac{7}{8}''$. See under Details.

(b) The engine diagram quoted the length of the firebox casing at the bottom, 9' 3". See under Details.

L.N.E.R. and L.M.S. Renumbering

The L.M.S.-numbered engines, 8500-59, duplicated the numbers of fifty-three B12's, which was unfortunate but presumably caused little concern as during the war period there were many "foreign" engines running on L.N.E.R. lines. As a result of the 1946 renumbering, Thornton shed for a time housed both L.M.S. and L.N.E.R. 8504, the latter being a class J69 shunting engine.

The twenty-five engines which were built at Brighton in 1944 were numbered 7651-75 in the L.N.E.R. stock list. These numbers had been allotted in April 1943 and involved two class D16 4-4-0's, Nos. 7656/65, having to revert to their pre-1942 numbers. In the case of No. 7656 there was a six-weeks overlap: the new O6 with this number went into traffic on 6th July 1944 but the corresponding D16 was not renumbered 8786 until 16th August 1944 (see Part 3C p.20).

Meanwhile, in July 1943 the details of Thompson's general renumbering scheme for L.N.E.R. locomotives was worked out and, prior to its implementation in 1946, allocation of numbers to new locomotives was in accordance with this scheme and involved the temporary renumbering of some existing engines (see Part 1 of this series, p.38). As far as class O6 was concerned, in February 1945 the numbers 3125-67 were allotted to the engines on order at Darlington and Doncaster. This involved renumbering ten class J50 0-6-0T's, Nos. 3157-64/6/7, to 3180-9 to clear these numbers. When the general renumbering scheme was put into effect in January 1946, Nos. 7651-75 were renumbered 3100-24 between April and June of that year and, by the following October when the last engine was completed, the class was then numbered 3100-67.

In December 1946 the L.N.E.R. purchased 200 W.D. "Austerity" 2-8-0's (see class O7) and this caused an alteration to the general renumbering scheme which was then nearing completion. The numbers carried by the O6's were required for the "Austerity" 2-8-0's and Nos. 3100-67 therefore became 3500-67 between February and April 1947, which in turn entailed the renumbering of fifty-nine 2-8-0's of classes O1 and O4.

On transfer to the L.M.S. (or L.M. Region) between September 1947 and January 1948, Nos. 3500-67 were immediately renumbered 8705-72 in the L.M.S. series, following the similar engines built by the S.R. for the L.M.S. The engines were usually renumbered at the L.M.S. shed where they were first received, e.g. at Farnley Junction for engines received from the N.E. Area and at Canklow for engines received from Mexborough.

Details

The boiler was Type 3C in the L.M.S. classification list. The barrel had two rings, the first of which was parallel, 5ft. 0in. diameter, into which was recessed the smokebox tubeplate. The second ring tapered outwards to 5ft. 8⅜in. outside diameter at the firebox end. The boiler was fed by two under-footplate injectors (left side live steam, right side exhaust steam) delivering water through clack valves on the top of the second barrel ring on to feed trays in the boiler which de-aerated the water and assisted in the precipitation of scale-forming solids. The Belpaire firebox had a sloping throatplate and the overall length of the casing at the bottom was 9ft. 3in. The distance between tubeplates was 12ft. 2⅞in.

The superheater comprised three rows of seven elements each. These were of the bifurcated type, 1¼in. outside diameter and No. 11 S.W.G. thickness, with ball-jointed ends secured to the headers by means of "Through" bolts.

There were two mechanical lubricators on the right-hand running plate, that at the front having six feeds to each cylinder and the rear one having one feed to each coupled wheel axlebox. "Solid" oil was pumped to the undersides of the cylinder barrel and to the piston rod and piston valve rod glands. The oil to the steam chest for the piston valve liners was, however, first atomised to prevent carbonisation problems at the high temperature encountered. The main stop valve for the atomiser system was located high up on the left-hand side of the smokebox and was normally left open while the engine was in steam. This provided steam to the atomiser control valve, which was coupled to the cylinder cock gear in such a way that it closed when the cocks were opened. Leaving the cocks open whilst standing therefore prevented the gradual build up of pressure in the steam chests. The lubricators on Nos. 3125-67 (and L.M.S. 8500-59) were the Silvertown type, standard on the L.M.S., with twelve feeds (cylinders) and eight feeds (axleboxes), whilst those on Nos. 7651-75 (later 3100-24) were the Wakefield No. 7 pattern favoured by the L.N.E.R. (cf. figs. 94 and 93).

The maximum travel of the piston valves was 6$\frac{15}{32}$in. in full gear, with steam cut-off at 76 per cent of the piston stroke (front port) or 72½ per cent (back port). When coasting, the reversing gear was set at 55 per cent cut-off and the regulator handle placed in the drifting position.

The coupled wheel axle journals were 8½in. diameter and 11in. long, which were generous proportions considering that the maximum axle load was only 16 tons. The axleboxes were made of steel with brass inserts having a white metal bearing surface. They were exceptionally free of trouble from overheating according to a report issued in December 1945, which stated that up to the end of September of that year there had been only one such occurrence on a class O6 engine and this had been caused by a mechanical fault in the lubricating system, resulting in No. 7656 suffering a hot axlebox in September 1944. There had, however, been ten cases of hot axleboxes in the same period affecting the L.M.S. engines on loan, mainly due to leaking oil pipes.

Steam sanding was provided for forward running in front of the leading and driving coupled wheels and for reverse running behind the driving coupled wheels.

Brakes

The engines had steam brake with a vacuum ejector for train braking. There were two brake cylinders under the cab.

Tenders

The tender was the standard L.M.S. 4,000-gallon type. Those attached to Nos. 7651-75 had tanks of welded construction whilst those attached to the engines built at Doncaster and Darlington had riveted tanks (cf. figs. 93 and 94). A further point of difference was that those attached to the former had spoked wheels whilst those built by the L.N.E.R. generally had disc wheels (cf. figs. 93 and 92). There were however some exceptions among the later engines, in particular Nos. 3144 (built Darlington) and 3566 (built Doncaster) observed with spoked wheels, which could have been due to changes (see also under Maintenance).

Maintenance

The engines visited L.N.E.R. works for repairs. As far as the O6's were concerned, there were eleven recorded instances of general repairs undertaken at Darlington, as follows; 1946: Nos. 3104/7/11/8/23/4; 1947: Nos. 3503/12/30/48/9. In the same period Doncaster dealt with Nos. 3120/2, both ex-works in December 1946. The engines usually visited the nearest works to the home shed for light repairs but there were two notable exceptions. No. 3143, new in June 1946 and allocated to Dunfermline, almost immediately visited Darlington Works for a non-classified repair and its original tender was replaced by the new one intended for No. 3144 but which had not yet left works. (No. 3144 went into traffic with the tender allocated to No. 3145, whilst the latter acquired the repaired tender from No. 3143). The same engine No. 3543 (ex-3143) visited Gateshead Works in August 1947 for a selective repair, two months prior to being handed over to the L.M.S. in October 1947.

Liveries

The engines were painted unlined black with "L M S" or "N E" ("L N E R" from No. 3140 in April 1946) on the tender sides according to ownership. The L.M.S. engines had standard L.M.S.-style 10in. cab side numerals, 14in. tender lettering and smokebox door numberplates. Nos. 3125-47 were also fitted when new with smokebox door numberplates and similar plates were later noted on other engines after they had been through works. As recounted earlier, the L.N.E.R. engines were renumbered into the 35XX series early in 1947, mostly at the engines' home depots as a result of which the numberplates were at variance, whilst in some cases these were removed until they could be replaced at the next works visit.

British Railways

By nationalisation, Nos. 8500-59 had been handed over to the L.M.S. and in addition all but one of the class O6 engines were on loan to that company and had in fact been renumbered into the 87XX series. Only No. 3554 remained on the L.N.E.R. but this engine too was transferred to the L.M. Region in January 1948. The former L.N.E.R. engines were all permanently transferred to L.M.R. book stock in May 1948 and in due course were renumbered 48705-72. It should be remarked that No. 48729, thus renumbered in April 1948 whilst still in Eastern Region book stock, had carried five different numbers in just over three and a half years.

Allocation and Work

The first L.M.S. standard class 8F 2-8-0 built by the L.N.E.R., No. 8510, went into traffic in

June 1943 from Doncaster Works, running-in at the shed there before being allocated to Tyne Dock on the 7th of the month. Eight months elapsed before the second engine appeared in February 1944, No. 8500 from Darlington Works. Doncaster's second engine, No. 8511 appeared one month later whilst Darlington's second engine, No. 8501, appeared in the following June. Construction then proceeded steadily from the two works and by September 1945 the sixty loan engines were all in traffic.

Meanwhile the first class O6 engine, No. 7651, arrived from Brighton Works in June 1944, running-in at Neasden before being allocated to Mexborough later that month. Brighton built Nos. 7651-75 (later 3100-24) in the short space of fourteen weeks. There was then a gap of exactly one year before No. 3125 appeared from Darlington in September 1945. Construction eventually ceased in October 1946 when the class total stood at sixty-eight.

With the addition to stock of the last O6, the number of Stanier type 2-8-0's operating on the L.N.E.R. reached its peak of 128, and an immediate start was made handing over Nos. 8500-59 to the L.M.S. In October 1946 these engines were allocated as follows:-

	8F	O6
March	11	5
Mexborough	—	27
Immingham	16	—
Ardsley	—	5
Tyne Dock	4	—
Heaton	11	17
St. Margaret's	6	2
Dunfermline	4	11
Thornton	8	1

It will be noted that the engines were allocated to depots which had to cater for heavy wartime and post-war traffic flows. In addition to providing increased power their arrival enabled many L.N.E.R. engines to receive much needed overhauls.

Nos. 8510/4/5/6/8/9 were allocated to Doncaster for a short period whilst running-in in 1943-44. They could be seen working over the East Lincolnshire line through Louth on trains destined for Whitemoor Yard (March). This route was used to relieve congestion over the direct G.N. & G.E. Joint line through Lincoln and Spalding, the diversion being via Barnetby, Grimsby and Boston to join the normal route at Spalding. No. 8515 for example was so used on 23rd June 1944 prior to allocation to Scotland.

The sixteen engines at March remained there until leaving the L.N.E.R., working mainly between Whitemoor and Temple Mills alongside the normal L.N.E.R. types. No. 8501 was recorded at Stratford for the first time on 18th June 1944 and a year later Nos. 8534/54 were noted at Enfield Lock in a commendably clean condition – rather unusual for the period.

The engines were not commonly seen on the G.N. lines to London, apart from between May 1944 and June 1945 when No. 8513 was at New England shed for trials against class O1 No. 6244, and again in the early part of 1946 when No. 3150 spent a few weeks at this shed undergoing trials against the newly-rebuilt class K5 2-6-0. Isolated appearances were recorded in 1946 when No. 3153 (Mexborough) was seen at Hitchin on 31st July and No. 3123 (Heaton) appeared on a down empty wagon train on 8th August. The only other G.N. Section shed to house these engines was Ardsley, which acquired Nos. 3154-8 from Mexborough in August 1946 for an eight-month spell in connection with the relining of the Woodhead tunnels. During this period, commencing 25th August, certain L.N.E.R. trains were diverted via Standedge with L.N.E.R. crews. During the second week of September 1946, for example, Nos. 3156/8/5 were noted on the evening goods from Neville Hill via Leeds City and Huddersfield on the 10th, 12th and 13th respectively.

In March 1944 Gorton received No. 8511, which spent some time on trials against the first Thompson class O1 rebuild No. 6595 on the heavily graded route over Woodhead to Wath and Immingham, being seen passing Retford on 14th April 1944. Six engines were added later in 1944 and a further nine in the early part of 1945, and eventually the Gorton stud replaced Robinson O4's on the Woodhead line. In September 1945 six engines moved away to Mexborough, joined in December by one more, but three later returned to Gorton in March 1946. In May 1946 the whole Gorton allocation was transferred to Immingham, where they remained until transfer to the L.M.S. in 1947.

During the summer of 1944 fourteen out of the twenty-five O6's built by the Southern Railway were allocated to Mexborough, where they remained until handed over to the L.M.S. in 1947. Eighteen others built by the L.N.E.R. also went to this shed in 1945-46. Mexborough's large allocation was used extensively on duties normally handled by the O4's, working south to Annesley, Banbury or Woodford, east to Immingham or Whitemoor, as well as across the

Pennines to Manchester. Some reached Whitemoor via the East Lincolnshire line, where Nos. 7651/71 were noted in the autumn of 1944. No. 3153 was transferred from Mexborough to Thornton in October 1946 and was notable in being the only O6 to be transferred from one Area to another, apart from a small number of allocations made solely for running-in purposes.

At the southern end of the G.C. line, all the Brighton built engines were handed over to the L.N.E.R. at Neasden, where the first five, Nos. 7651-5, were initially allocated for a few days before passing on to their permanent sheds. At this time the class saw frequent use on this end of the G.C. Section.

In the N.E. Area, No. 8510 went into traffic in June 1943 at Tyne Dock. It soon commenced working mineral trains to both Newport and Leeds (Neville Hill). It was seen on the latter duty on 30th July, assisted over the final stage of the journey by class C7 No. 2194 and again on 9th August when the assisting engine was class D11 No. 6401 *James FitzJames*. No. 8510 was transferred to Heaton in February 1944 where it was joined shortly afterwards by the second engine, No. 8500. By June 1946 Heaton had an allocation of fifteen loan engines and seventeen O6's. Their chief duties were over the main line to Berwick and Edinburgh, with occasional trips to York, Hull or Leeds. On the goods workings to Edinburgh, crews changed at Tweedmouth or Marshall Meadows signal box (just north of Berwick). Sometimes the Heaton men were relieved at Tweedmouth and the train was worked to Marshall Meadows by Tweedmouth men who then handed over to St. Margaret's or Haymarket crews for the run to Edinburgh.

After being run-in at Doncaster, No. 8514 was sent to Tyne Dock in May 1944 for trials in the Durham coalfield area. Here it was joined shortly afterwards by Thompson class O1 No. 6334, newly rebuilt. No. 8512 was transferred from Heaton to Tyne Dock in July 1944 to take part in these trials after No. 8514 had been damaged in a collision. After the tests with the O1 had been completed, No. 8514 was transferred to Heaton and one month later No. 8512 was returned to that shed. Four loan engines were transferred from Heaton to Tyne Dock in July 1946, apparently in anticipation of their impending release to the L.M.S. as they had already run high mileages. The remaining loan engines at Heaton were subsequently handed over to the L.M.S. whilst the seventeen O6's were all transferred to York in April 1947.

In the Scottish Area the engines were known to the North British men as "Caleys", in accordance with local custom—even among the general populace—of calling the L.M.S. "The Caley" throughout the entire period of its existence. Coming brand new at a time when there was a shortage of engines and many of the existing stud were somewhat run-down, the Stanier type 2-8-0's were warmly welcomed and their standard of performance made a favourable impression. Eighteen loan engines and fourteen O6's were sent new to the Scottish Area during the years 1944-46. After early periods of running-in, the allocation settled down to St. Margaret's (5), Dunfermline (14), Thornton (10) and Aberdeen (3). Subsequently the Aberdeen engines moved to St. Margaret's in August and September 1945 whilst No. 3153 was transferred from Mexborough to Thornton in October 1946.

The Scottish Area engines were used principally on main line goods traffic between Edinburgh and Heaton, and on goods and coal trains from Edinburgh and the various Fife yards to Aberdeen, with occasional appearances on the Waverley Route, between Edinburgh and Carlisle. Occasionally they "filled in" with empty carriage working around Edinburgh whilst on 25th May 1946 No. 8540 (Thornton) was reported working the 4-13 p.m. relief passenger train Glasgow (Queen Street) – Thornton.

The last of the loan engines was handed over to the L.M.S. in July 1947. Two months later a start was made transferring the O6's to the L.M.S., on loan. At nationalisation only No. 3554 (ex-3154) remained to be transferred and this move was effected in January 1948.

At the time of writing, No. 48518 (built Doncaster 1944) is still at Barry and may be preserved.

Engine Diagram

1944. "Type W.D. LMS". Reclassified O6, 9/1945. Diagram deleted 12/1947.

Classification: Southern Area load class 7; Route availability 6; B.R. power class 8F.

Summary of O6 Class

B.R. No.		L.M.S. No.		L.N.E.R. Nos. 1947		1946		Original	Maker	Built	Sent to L.M.S.	With-drawn
48705	1/49	8705	11/47	3500	2/47	3100	4/46	7651	Brighton	6/1944	11/47	3/67
48706	3/49	8706	12/47	3501	2/47	3101	4/46	7652	,,	6/1944	12/47	3/66
48707	12/49	8707	11/47	3502	2/47	3102	4/46	7653	,,	6/1944	11/47	4/67
48708	11/48	8708	10/47	3503	2/47	3103	4/46	7654	,,	6/1944	10/47	4/67
48709	2/50	8709	10/47	3504	3/47	3104	4/46	7655	,,	6/1944	10/47	7/67
48710	6/49	8710	11/47	3505	3/47	3105	4/46	7656	,,	7/1944	11/47	9/67
48711	12/49	8711	11/47	3506	2/47	3106	4/46	7657	,,	7/1944	11/47	1/67
48712	1/50	8712	10/47	3507	3/47	3107	4/46	7658	,,	7/1944	10/47	6/67
48713	10/49	8713	12/47	3508	2/47	3108	4/46	7659	,,	7/1944	12/47	3/66
48714	7/49	8714	11/47	3509	2/47	3109	4/46	7660	,,	7/1944	11/47	11/67
48715	8/49	8715	11/47	3510	2/47	3110	4/46	7661	,,	7/1944	11/47	8/68
48716	12/48	8716	10/47	3511	3/47	3111	6/46	7662	,,	8/1944	10/47	8/65
48717	10/49	8717	10/47	3512	2/47	3112	4/46	7663	,,	8/1944	10/47	4/67
48718	1/49	8718	11/47	3513	3/47	3113	4/46	7664	,,	8/1944	11/47	4/66
48719	4/50	8719	11/47	3514	3/47	3114	5/46	7665	,,	8/1944	11/47	8/65
48720	1/50	8720	10/47	3515	3/47	3115	4/46	7666	,,	8/1944	10/47	6/68
48721	6/48	8721	11/47	3516	3/47	3116	5/46	7667	,,	8/1944	11/47	9/67
48722	5/49	8722	11/47	3517	3/47	3117	5/46	7668	,,	8/1944	11/47	5/68
48723	1/49	8723	10/47	3518	2/47	3118	6/46	7669	,,	8/1944	10/47	8/68
48724	8/48	8724	11/47	3519	3/47	3119	5/46	7670	,,	9/1944	11/47	10/67
48725	4/49	8725	11/47	3520	2/47	3120	5/46	7671	,,	9/1944	11/47	9/67
48726	9/49	8726	11/47	3521	3/47	3121	5/46	7672	,,	9/1944	11/47	9/66
48727	7/49	8727	11/47	3522	3/47	3122	5/46	7673	,,	9/1944	11/47	8/68
48728	3/50	8728	10/47	3523	2/47	3123	6/46	7674	,,	9/1944	10/47	3/67
48729	4/48	8729	10/47	3524	2/47	3124	4/46	7675	,,	9/1944	10/47	12/67

B.R. No.		L.M.S. No.		L.N.E.R. Nos. 1947		Original	Maker	Works No.	Built	Sent to L.M.S.	With-drawn
48730	6/48	8730	11/47	3525	2/47	3125	Darlington	1967	9/1945	11/47	8/68
48731	5/50	8731	9/47	3526	2/47	3126	,,	1968	9/1945	9/47	8/67
48732	8/50	8732	10/47	3527	2/47	3127	,,	1969	10/1945	10/47	11/65
48733	10/49	8733	10/47	3528	2/47	3128	,,	1970	10/1945	10/47	5/65
48734	9/49	8734	9/47	3529	3/47	3129	,,	1971	11/1945	9/47	10/64
48735	1/50	8735	10/47	3530	2/47	3130	,,	1972	11/1945	10/47	10/67
48736	6/49	8736	10/47	3531	2/47	3131	,,	1973	11/1945	10/47	8/66
48737	3/50	8737	10/47	3532	2/47	3132	,,	1974	11/1945	10/47	5/65
48738	4/50	8738	10/47	3533	3/47	3133	,,	1975	12/1945	10/47	12/66
48739	1/50	8739	10/47	3534	2/47	3134	,,	1976	12/1945	10/47	1/67

B.R. No.		L.M.S. No.		L.N.E.R. Nos. 1947		L.N.E.R. Nos. Original	Maker	Works No.	Built	Sent to L.M.S.	With-drawn
48740	1/50	8740	9/47	3535	2/47	3135	Darlington	1977	1/1946	9/47	3/68
48741	11/49	8741	9/47	3536	2/47	3136	,,	1978	2/1946	9/47	10/67
48742	2/50	8742	10/47	3537	2/47	3137	,,	1979	3/1946	10/47	9/67
48743	12/49	8743	10/47	3538	4/47	3138	,,	1980	3/1946	10/47	3/67
48744	5/50	8744	9/47	3539	2/47	3139	,,	1981	4/1946	9/47	3/68
48745	8/52	8745	10/47	3540	2/47	3140	,,	1982	4/1946	10/47	5/68
48746	3/50	8746	9/47	3541	2/47	3141	,,	1983	5/1946	9/47	5/68
48747	3/49	8747	10/47	3542	4/47	3142	,,	1984	5/1946	10/47	9/66
48748	10/48	8748	10/47	3543	2/47	3143	,,	1985	6/1946	10/47	4/66
48749	4/50	8749	10/47	3544	2/47	3144	,,	1986	8/1946	10/47	3/68
48750	10/49	8750	10/47	3545	4/47	3145	,,	1987	8/1946	10/47	1/68
48751	5/48	8751	11/47	3546	3/47	3146	,,	1988	9/1946	11/47	2/67
48752	3/49	8752	12/47	3547	4/47	3147	,,	1989	10/1946	12/47	8/68
48753	6/48	8753	10/47	3548	4/47	3148	Doncaster	—	10/1945	10/47	3/67
48754	2/49	8754	10/47	3549	2/47	3149	,,	—	10/1945	10/47	5/67
48755	7/48	8755	10/47	3550	3/47	3150	,,	—	10/1945	10/47	10/66
48756	1/50	8756	10/47	3551	2/47	3151	,,	—	11/1945	10/47	1/67
48757	5/50	8757	10/47	3552	2/47	3152	,,	—	11/1945	10/47	12/67
48758	10/48	8758	9/47	3553	3/47	3153	,,	—	12/1945	9/47	12/67
48759	3/50	8759	1/48	3554	3/47	3154	,,	—	12/1945	—*	11/65
48760	10/48	8760	10/47	3555	2/47	3155	,,	—	12/1945	10/47	3/66
48761	5/48	8761	11/47	3556	3/47	3156	,,	—	1/1946	11/47	1/65
48762	11/48	8762	10/47	3557	3/47	3157	,,	—	1/1946	10/47	2/66
48763	3/51	8763	10/47	3558	3/47	3158	,,	1991	2/1946	10/47	4/68
48764	9/50	8764	9/47	3559	2/47	3159	,,	1992	2/1946	9/47	12/67
48765	7/48	8765	10/47	3560	3/47	3160	,,	1993	3/1946	10/47	8/68
48766	8/48	8766	10/47	3561	4/47	3161	,,	1994	3/1946	10/47	2/67
48767	3/49	8767	10/47	3562	2/47	3162	,,	1995	3/1946	10/47	9/67
48768	6/48	8768	11/47	3563	3/47	3163	,,	1996	3/1946	11/47	8/67
48769	9/48	8769	10/47	3564	2/47	3164	,,	1997	4/1946	10/47	8/65
48770	5/48	8770	9/47	3565	3/47	3165	,,	1998	5/1946	9/47	4/67
48771	2/50	8771	9/47	3566	2/47	3166	,,	1999	5/1946	9/47	12/65
48772	9/48	8772	9/47	3567	4/47	3167	,,	2001	6/1946	9/47	1/64

* Transferred to L.M. Region 1/48.

Summary of L.M.S. 2-8-0 Engines on Loan

L.M.S. No.	Maker	On loan From*	To	L.M.S. No.	Maker	On loan From*	To
8500	Darlington	2/44	10/46	8530	Doncaster	4/45	3/47
8501	,,	6/44	10/46	8531	,,	4/45	1/47
8502	,,	8/44	3/47	8532	,,	4/45	3/47
8503	,,	9/44	10/46	8533	,,	5/45	1/47
8504	,,	9/44	5/47	8534	,,	5/45	5/47
8505	,,	10/44	10/46	8535	,,	6/45	6/47
8506	,,	10/44	1/47	8536	,,	6/45	6/47
8507	,,	10/44	5/47	8537	,,	7/45	6/47
8508	,,	10/44	7/47	8538	,,	8/45	7/47
8509	,,	11/44	2/47	8539	,,	9/45	4/47
8510	Doncaster	6/43	6/47	8540	Darlington	12/44	1/47
8511	,,	3/44	7/47	8541	,,	12/44	11/46
8512	,,	4/44	6/47	8542	,,	12/44	2/47
8513	,,	4/44	12/46	8543	,,	1/45	3/47
8514	,,	5/44	3/47	8544	,,	1/45	4/47
8515	,,	6/44	1/47	8545	,,	2/45	1/47
8516	,,	7/44	7/47	8546	,,	2/45	1/47
8517	,,	7/44	1/47	8547	,,	3/45	7/47
8518	,,	8/44	4/47	8548	,,	3/45	12/46
8519	,,	9/44	7/47	8549	,,	3/45	5/47
8520	,,	10/44	11/46	8550	,,	4/45	5/47
8521	,,	10/44	6/47	8551	,,	4/45	7/47
8522	,,	11/44	12/46	8552	,,	5/45	1/47
8523	,,	11/44	12/46	8553	,,	5/45	4/47
8524	,,	12/44	4/47	8554	,,	6/45	7/47
8525	,,	12/44	4/47	8555	,,	6/45	6/47
8526	,,	1/45	2/47	8556	,,	7/45	5/47
8527	,,	1/45	10/46	8557	,,	7/45	5/47
8528	,,	2/45	4/47	8558	,,	8/45	5/47
8529	,,	4/45	2/47	8559	,,	8/45	6/47

* Dates taken on loan are also dates built by L.N.E.R.

CLASS O7

MINISTRY OF SUPPLY AUSTERITY CLASS

RIDDLES 4ft. 8½in. ENGINES

Engines received 1943-44 on loan: W.D. 7000-10/2/3/4/6-41/65-99, 7100-28/30-49/62-7/9-94/6-9, 7200-22/4-40/2-62, 7300-9/24-68/70-99, 7400-21/50-71. Total 350. Transferred to G.W.R. or S.R. 1944, or handed over to W.D. 1944-45.

ENGINES PURCHASED BY L.N.E.R. (Added to stock 1946-47): 3000-3199. TOTAL 200. (Former W.D. 70800/4/10/3/5/6/18/21-4/6/7/8/30/1/2/7/40/1/2/4/7/8/52/4/8/70/2, 77002/9/21/33/83/91, 77100/10/3/31/6/46, 77211/3/20/3/33/6/43/50/1/4/65/72/6/7/9/81/4/90/8, 77300/16/8/22/36/9/43/54/7/60/3/7/9/70/3/82/5/97, 77410/2/20/3/7/30/5/7/48/73/4/86/7/91/6/8, 77501/2/4-7, 78513/5/6/20/7/8/34/40/50/62/5/70/7/82/4/91, 78603/8/25/7/8/30/3/4/5/9/41/2/5/6/8/51/3-6/61-5/8/70/3/4/6/7/9/80/6/7/90/1/2/6-9, 78702/3/6-13/6/8, 79177/80/5/7/91/2, 79200/11/6/36/40/1/5/7/51/3/85/8, 79305/8 received on loan 1945-46 and purchased 1946; W.D. 70846, 77046/93, 77112/33, 77391, 77422/93, 78649/67 added to stock 1947).

Engines received 1947 on loan: W.D. 70802/7/17/34/9/50/71/7, 77003/4/6/8/10/3/6-20/2/3/31/2/4-7/9/41/2/4/7/50/1/7/61/3/6/7/8/70/1/3/5/6/8/81/5/7/8/9/95/6, 77104/7/11/8-21/4/7/8/9/35/8/44/7/9/52/5/7/63/4/6/7/9/70/3-6/8/81/2/5/6/7/95/8/9, 77201/4/6-9/15/8/21/2/7/8/30/1/2/5/48/9/52/8/60/1/3/71/4/8/83/92, 77302/3/5/7/9/12-5/7/9/20/3/4/7/8/9/34/8/42/50-3/6/8/62/4/71/2/5/81/6/90/2/4/5. 77401/2/4/6/11/3-6/8/9/24/5/6/8/31-4/6/9-42/5/9/52-5/7/8/9/61/2/4/5/7-70/6/80/4/8/92/4/7/9, 77503, 78514/25/6/32/7/8/53/9/61/4/8/72/5/8/85/7/8/92/4/8/9, 78600/1/9/10/4/6/37/43/50/82/3/4, 78700/15, 79178/81/2/4/6/94/8, 79202/4/6/8/9/20/7/9/39/42/4/59/63/4/5/71/6/80, 79306/10/2. Total 270. Purchased by B.R. 1948.

At the outbreak of war in 1939 the Mechanical & Electrical Engineer (Scotland) on the L.M.S., R. A. Riddles, became Director of Transport Equipment at the Ministry of Supply. In 1941 he became Deputy Director-General of Royal Engineer Equipment. It is not surprising therefore that the Stanier class 8F 2-8-0 should be so quickly adopted as the standard goods engine for war needs. However in the summer of 1942 design work started on the "Austerity" 2-8-0, which took into account the limitations of materials and manpower at that time. Whilst the "Austerity" was based on the Stanier design, and indeed many parts were interchangeable, Riddles broke away from L.M.S. practice by adopting a parallel boiler with a round top firebox. Altogether 935 engines appeared in the short space of twenty-nine months from January 1943 to May 1945, and their construction is summarised in the accompanying table.

The engines were intended for deployment overseas by British Army personnel but when they first appeared there was no immediate requirement for them on active service. Large numbers were therefore loaned to the British main line companies to help with the movement of vital war supplies. By March 1944 there were 457 in service in the United Kingdom as follows: L.N.E.R. 350, L.M.S. 50, S.R. 50, W.D. 7. Later deliveries from the manufacturers were put into store to await despatch to the Continent.

After the Allied landings in Normandy in June 1944, a start was made shipping the engines to the Continent. Those in store were the first to go followed by the ones from the main line companies. During August and September 1944 the L.N.E.R. transferred sixty-three to the G.W.R. to ease the loss of that company's American 2-8-0's. During November and December a further eight went to the G.W.R. and twenty-three to the S.R. Between November 1944 and February 1945 the remaining 256 "Austerities" on the L.N.E.R. were withdrawn from Operating Stock, overhauled in the company's own shops and sent to the Continent.

W.D. Nos. (a)	*Maker*	*Order No.*	*Date ordered*	*Works Nos.*	*No. built*	*Date*
800-79	N.B. Loco.(b)	L943	July 1943 (d)	24891-970(f)	80	1944
7000-49	,, (c)	,,	May1943 (e)	24971-25020(f)	50	1943
7050-9	Vulcan Foundry	2289	– 1942	4866-75	10	1943
7060-7109	,,	2290	– 1942	4876-4925	50	1943
7110-49	,,	2291	– 1942	4926-65	40	1943
7150-7299	N.B. Loco.(c)	L943	August 1942	25021-170	150	1943-44
7300-7449	,, (b)	,,	,,	25171-320	150	1943-44
7450-9	Vulcan Foundry	2291	– 1942	4966-75	10	1943
7460-7509	,,	2292	– 1942	4976-5025	50	1943-44
8510-30	N.B. Loco.(b)	L943	July 1943	25321-41(f)	21	1944
8531-59	,, (c)	,,	,,	25342-70(f)	29	1945
8560-8624	,, (c)	,,	,,	25371-435(f)	65	1944-45
8625-71	Vulcan Foundry	2299	– 1943	5026-72	47	1944
8672-8718	,,	2300	– 1943	5073-5119	47	1944
9177-9219	,,	2307	– 1944	5120-62	43	1944
9220-62	,,	2308	– 1944	5163-5205	43	1944-45
9263-9312	,,	2313	– 1944	5206-55	50	1945

(a) Engines built after September 1944 had 70000 added to these numbers.
(b) Queen's Park Works.
(c) Hyde Park Works.
(d) Originally ordered March 1942 (L942) as L.M.S. type 2-8-0.
(e) Originally ordered July 1942 as L.M.S. type 2-8-0.
(f) Works plates not fitted in sequence.

Altogether 932 engines were sent overseas and only Nos. 77223, 77369 and 79250 remained in the United Kingdom. The engines operated from sheds in France, Belgium, Holland and Germany, whilst for a few months in 1945 211 were borrowed by the U.S. Army Transportation Corps. After the war in Europe ended, large numbers became surplus to Army requirements and were put into store on the Continent. In November 1945 the engines started to return home and the main line companies between them agreed to take 460 on loan. The L.N.E.R. had the greatest need for them and by the end of 1946 had acquired 190, of which all but two had been abroad. (The exceptions were Nos. 77223 and 77369 from military establishments in Scotland).

In November 1946 the L.N.E.R. decided to purchase 200 "Austerities" (for £4,500 each) in advance of the 1948 Building Programme, and the 190 engines already on loan were accordingly transferred from Operating to Running Stock from 28th December 1946. The remaining ten engines, Nos. 70846, 77046/93, 77112/33, 77391, 77422/93, 78649/67, were taken straight into Running Stock in the early part of 1947. The classification O7 was introduced in January 1947 to cover these 200 engines, which were then renumbered 3000-3199.

In addition to the engines which they purchased, the L.N.E.R. also agreed to receive on loan a further 210 engines. This number was increased to 278 in September 1947 to facilitate the transfer of the sixty-eight Stanier class O6 2-8-0's to the L.M.S.

During 1947 270 "Austerities" were repaired and put into service in L.N.E.R. Operating Stock, out of the authorised total of 278. Some of these engines were in a really bad condition and, to facilitate repairs to engines needing less attention, Nos. 77024/80, 77162, 77225, 77306/65, 77456 were utilised at Darlington Works from May 1947 to provide a pool of serviceable parts. At nationalisation the eight nominated engines still to enter service comprised these seven engines and No. 77253 under repair at Stratford Works. It was not until July 1948 that the last of these, No. 77024, was overhauled and put into service.

At 31st December 1947 there were 409 "Austerity" 2-8-0's on loan to the main line companies, including eighty-nine on the G.W.R. and fifty on the S.R. In December 1948 the

British Transport Commission decided to purchase an additional 533 "Austerity" 2-8-0's, for £2,929 each. The engines were taken into Running Stock at the year end, including those still in store awaiting overhaul. The purchase was back-dated to October 1948 for book keeping purposes. The classification O7 was discontinued from 26th January 1949 after which date they were officially referred to as W.D. 2-8-0. At first all 733 engines of the class were included in the joint Eastern and North Eastern Regions book stock, but in June 1950 the engines operating in the other Regions were transferred within book stock to the operating Region. It was not until October 1959 that the Eastern and North Eastern Regions operated independent book stocks.

Withdrawals from British Railways stock commenced in December 1959 and were completed in September 1967. As this work is primarily concerned with the history of L.N.E.R. locomotives, no attempt will be made to provide a complete coverage of the entire class. The "Summary" is divided into three sections: (i) Dates for engines on loan to the L.N.E.R. during the war, with post-1949 British Railways numbers where applicable to identify which of these completed their careers on main line service in the United Kingdom; (ii) Full data for L.N.E.R. class O7; (iii) Data for engines which were still on loan to the L.N.E.R. at nationalisation, with their British Railways numbers.

Standard L.N.E.R. Dimensions

Cylinders (2 outside)	19″×28″
Motion	Walschaerts with 10″ piston valves
Boiler:	
Max. diam. outside	5′ 8½″
Barrel length	11′ 7½″(a)
Firebox length outside	10′ 3″
Pitch	9′ 0″
Diagram No.	119 (b)
Heating surface:	
Firebox	168 sq.ft.
Tubes (193×1¾″)	1061 sq.ft.
Flues (28×5⅛″)	451 sq.ft.
Total evaporative	1680 sq.ft.
Superheater (28×1.087″)	298 sq.ft.(c)
Total	1978 sq.ft.
Grate area	28.6 sq.ft.
Boiler pressure	225 lb./sq.in.
Leading wheels	3′ 2″
Coupled wheels	4′ 8½″
Tender wheels	3′ 2″
Tractive effort (85%)	34,215 lb.
Length over buffers	63′ 6″
Wheelbase:	
Engine	8′7″+5′3″+5′3″+5′9″ =24′10″
Tender	5′3″+5′3″+5′3″ =15′9″
Total	53′ 1¾″
Weight (full):	
Engine	70T 5C
Tender	55T 10C
Total	125T 15C
Adhesive	61T 5C
Max. axle load	15T 12C
Water capacity	5,000 gallons
Coal capacity	9T 0C

(a) The engine diagram quoted the distance between tubeplates (12′ 0″). See under Development and Details.

(b) B.R. standard class BR10 from July 1950.

(c) This figure appeared on the engine diagram after September 1947. For earlier variations of superheating surface see p. 121.

Numbering

The engines were allocated W.D. numbers commencing at 7000 except that a batch ordered initially as L.M.S. type 2-8-0's, Nos. 800-79, retained these numbers. Engines completed after 5th September 1944 had 70,000 added to their numbers to prevent possible confusion with engines on other systems. The existing engines at W.D. establishments were quickly renumbered but those on loan to the main line companies retained their four-figure numbers for the time being. The engines recalled towards the end of 1944 were overhauled in one or other of the main line works, then despatched to Longmoor where they were renumbered before being sent to the docks. From early 1945 they were sent instead direct to the ports of embarkation, by-passing Longmoor, so that arrangements then had to be made for them to be renumbered in the main line works. The earliest officially recorded examples were Nos. 77248 (Cowlairs, 20th January) and 77194 (Darlington, 24th). In addition Nos. 77021, 77197/8 were observed at Stratford on 28th January and No. 77214 at Gorton on 3rd February.

In the immediate post-war period 237 "Austerity" 2-8-0's were loaned to the Netherlands State Railways and numbered 4301-4537 in their stock. Fifty-two were transferred back to the War Department in 1946 and subsequently returned to England still bearing their N.S. numbers though their W.D. numbers were later restored. Of these, the following later passed into L.N.E.R. stock:-

W.D. No.	*N.S. No.*	*L.N.E.R. No.*
77009	4528	3000
77021	4318	3002
77410	4370	3034
78677	4504	3156

Many engines were loaned to the main line companies and they continued to carry their W.D. numbers. The L.N.E.R. afterwards purchased 200 of these engines and they were renumbered into L.N.E.R. stock between February and April 1947. Nos. 3000-3100 were allocated to the engines built by N.B. Loco. Co. and 3101-99 to those built by Vulcan Foundry. As far as the N.B. Loco. series engines were concerned, they were renumbered according to their months of construction, as recorded at Doncaster, regardless of whether built at Hyde Park or Queen's Park. There were however two anomalies: No. 77002 (3001) was placed after No. 77009 (3000) although both were built in February 1943; No. 70852 (3071) was shown as built in July 1944, instead of June, which then placed it after No. 77265 (3070). No. 3109 entered traffic in February 1947 bearing its new number and thus never ran in L.N.E.R. ownership as No. 77133.

Development and Details

Boilers

The boiler barrel was constructed of two telescopic rings: the rear one was 5ft. 8½in. outside diameter and the front one 5ft. 7⅛in. The dome for the vertical slide type regulator valves was located on the rear ring with the two Ross pop safety valves mounted side by side behind. The barrel was not lagged, relying instead on the 2in. air space under the clothing plates as insulation against heat loss. However the L.N.E.R. started lagging the boilers on the O7's and this was extended after nationalisation to the engines on loan. Asbestos mattresses were used at first, then fibre glass from about 1949.

Two Davies & Metcalfe live steam injectors were provided, one at each side of the engine below the cab, though both were the right-hand pattern to facilitate interchange. They were the No. 11 Monitor pattern with No. 10 size cones. Water was fed into the boiler through two clack valves on the front ring. The feed pipes originally passed over the outside of the clothing plate, and over the vacuum ejector exhaust pipe on the left-hand side with the boiler handrail on this side bent over the feed pipe. This arrangement was quickly altered and on later engines the feed pipes ran out of sight under the clothing plate in the air space. However when boiler insulation was applied after the war, the feed pipes generally reverted to the original positioning, though not in all cases. In B.R. days the top feed clack valves on engines repaired at Cowlairs Works were sometimes modified and lowered; engines noted altered included Nos. 90020 (ex-3020), 90468/89 (ex-3147/68). (Swindon Works fitted higher clack valves but this feature did not appear on the former L.N.E.R. O7's).

The earlier engines had a continuous blow down valve which operated whilst either injector was in use. Water was discharged on to the ballast at the rear of the tender after passing first through a length of copper pipe located inside the tank. Later engines had a manual "Ever-lasting" blow-off cock instead, which was operated from the right-hand side of the cab. This discharged water and sludge on to the ballast below the ashpan. With the Vulcan engines, the change was made with No. 7482.

The diameter of the smokebox was 5ft. 7⅞in., i.e. noticeably less than that of the boiler clothing plate which was 6ft. 0⅝in. (fig. 97). The door was secured by the usual two-handle and centre dart fastening method. The rim of the door fitted conically against the front plate with no asbestos sealing ring. In February 1947 the L.N.E.R. considered substituting their own type of door but then decided that this was not necessary as the existing door was standard with class O6 for which flanging blocks were available in their own works. The chimney was 9⅛in. high and the height above rail level to the top was only 12ft. 7in., compared with 12ft. 10 9/16in. to the top of the dome cover. The anti-vacuum valve behind the chimney (fig. 100) had a shallow cover and both valve and cover frequently broke. From December 1947 a strengthened valve of L.N.E.R. design became standard (fig. 102). The blastpipe top had a 5⅛in. diameter orifice, originally pitched 11in. below the centre line of the boiler but lowered by 4in. from March 1943 to improve steaming. The diameter of the orifice was reduced to 4⅞in. from June 1954, two years after dynamometer car tests had been held between Carlisle (Durran Hill) and Kilmarnock (Hurlford) from 26th March to 7th May 1952 with No. 90464 (ex-3143). During these tests three blastpipe orifice diameters were tried out: 5⅛in. (original setting), 4 15/16in. and finally 4⅞in.

The superheater was the Melesco type with long-loop elements and ball-jointed ends secured to the header by the "Through" bolt method. The elements were $1\frac{3}{8}$in. outside diameter and originally 10 S.W.G. thickness (inside diameter 1.119in.), whilst the distance from the ends of the elements to the firebox tubeplate was 2ft. $4\frac{3}{4}$in. This gave a heating surface figure of 310 sq. ft., which appeared on the L.M.S., L.N.E.R. and Ministry of Supply engine diagrams. (The L.M.S. diagram however showed the elements as 11 S.W.G. which corresponded to an inside diameter of 1.143in. The L.N.E.R. diagram showed the inside diameter as 1.107in. which did not correspond to any recognised gauge thickness). The G.W.R. engine diagram showed the heating surface figure as 338 sq. ft., which was the original proposal before it was decided in October 1942 to shorten the elements by 10in. at the firebox end to prevent the ends burning: this diagram was later corrected to show 310 sq. ft. From September 1947 new elements were 9 S.W.G. thickness (inside diameter 1.087in.) and the revised heating surface figure was 298 sq. ft.

The smokebox tubeplate was flanged all round and recessed into the front ring of the barrel. The upper part, which had no tubes to restrain it from bulging outwards, had four gusset plates riveted to both the tubeplate itself and the inside of the front ring to form a rigid joining. Bracing the tubeplate in this manner was afterwards considered unsatisfactory. The gusset plates fractured under stress and had either to be welded up or renewed. Sometimes the tubeplate itself buckled outwards and had to be straightened: there were two such recorded cases dealt with at Doncaster Works in 1947. From April 1951 these gusset plates were replaced by four diagonal (fork) stays, which provided adequate non-rigid bracing. From February 1953 replacement smokebox tubeplates had their thickness increased from $\frac{3}{4}$in. to $\frac{7}{8}$in., which reduced the distance between the tubeplates slightly from 12ft. 0in. to 11ft. $11\frac{7}{8}$in.

The outer firebox casing was the round topped type in contrast to L.M.S. practice though the same method of direct roof staying was employed, whereas in contemporary L.N.E.R. practice with round topped fireboxes two rows of expansion sling link stays were provided towards the front where the effect of expansion and contraction was most felt. At the sides of the firebox, throatplate and backplate, the upper (rigid) stays were copper, riveted over on the fire side, whilst the lower (flexible) stays were steel, secured with nuts on the fire side. This arrangement also conformed to L.M.S. practice. In the hottest part of the firebox it was therefore easy to replace a burnt nut without having to scrap the stay itself. The upper part of the casing backplate was braced by six gusset plates in the manner described earlier for the smokebox tubeplate.

The inner firebox was constructed from $\frac{5}{8}$in. thick copper plate, except for the tubeplate which was 1in. The firegrate was of the narrow type: 8ft. $7\frac{7}{16}$in. long and 3ft. $3\frac{5}{8}$in. wide, giving a grate area of 28.6 sq. ft. with a drop of 1ft. 4in. over its length. Some of the fireboxes on the early engines had drop grates. Their bars were not at the extreme front as in L.N.E.R. practice, but further back, and they were hinged at the front so that they dropped away from the ashpan door. Thus whereas on L.N.E.R. engines the ashes tended to fall out of the ashpan, provided the door was already open, on the "Austerities" the ashes simply accumulated further back in the ashpan. The mechanism for operating the drop grate was in the ashpan itself which meant that ashes and clinker were deposited on the rodding, causing it to warp and even burn through. The L.N.E.R. removed the drop grate gear post-war and afterwards the drop bars themselves were replaced by continuous bars.

As far back as 1942 the L.N.E.R. criticised the firebox design as being too rigid. Sir William Stanier agreed that this was true but in view of the war urgency he said it was too late to do anything about it. In the early post-war period the boilers started to give a lot of trouble. In particular the firebox tubeplate serrated or fractured in the radius of the crown flange. Depending on the severity, the engine was either sent straight to works or kept under observation. No. 77318 (later 3007) for example was found to have some serrations at a shed examination in September 1946 but remained in traffic for a further nine months before being sent to Doncaster Works where a new copper tubeplate was fitted. Whilst the usual remedy was to fit a new tubeplate, Vickers-Armstrongs welded up the trouble spots in less severe cases. Welding copper was not practised at that time in the L.N.E.R. works but they adopted this method after nationalisation. From August 1948 replacement copper tubeplates had 1in. radius flanges instead of $\frac{3}{4}$in. to reduce the incidence of cracking at the edges.

Three "Austerities" on loan to the L.N.E.R. during the War were reboilered before being sent abroad. No. 7095 was under repair at Stratford Works in 1944 when two fractures were discovered in the firebox steel throatplate. The boiler was returned to Vulcan Foundry for repairs. One fracture was rewelded before a Ministry of Supply inspector saw the boiler and condemned it in October 1944. Vulcan sent a new boiler to Stratford where it was fitted to No. 7095. Afterwards quite a number of boilers developed similar fractures, all apparently in steel plate from the same supplier, Colville's. Tests carried out by the Ministry's Research Department confirmed Colville's insistence that the steel was according to specification. The Works Manager at Vulcan Foundry said this was most fortunate as otherwise a lot of boilers would have had to be scrapped as they had kept no records of which boiler plates had come from which batch.

No. 7337 was severely damaged in the ammunition train explosion at Soham in June 1944 (fig. 98) and it was rebuilt with a new boiler at N.B. Locomotive Co.'s Queen's Park Works in September 1944. Finally, No. 77406 received a new boiler in May 1945 at Stratford Works and its old one, with a damaged firebox, was returned to N.B. Locomotive Co.

The Ministry of Supply provided seven spare boilers in 1947 to facilitate repairs to their loaned engines: one to Swindon, two to Brighton and four to Scotswood (Vickers-Armstrongs). The L.N.E.R. purchased seventeen boilers for the O7's: one from N.B. Locomotive Co. (originally fitted to No. 7406), one from Vulcan Foundry (originally fitted to No. 7095), six from Longmoor and nine from Belgium (including two originally fitted to Nos. 78633/57). The boiler purchased from N.B. Locomotive Co. was fitted to No. 3133 at Stratford Works in May 1947. The boiler obtained from Vulcan Foundry had been left out of doors and was purchased as scrap for £400. After being repaired at Gorton in November 1947 it was fitted to No. 3040 in March 1948. Two boilers from Belgium were fitted in August 1947 to Nos. 3003 (at Doncaster) and 3041 (at Cowlairs). The remaining boilers, thirteen provided for O7's and four for engines on loan, were concentrated at Scotswood.

In October 1947 the L.N.E.R. commenced paying for some of the boilers they had acquired from Longmoor and Belgium. The originally agreed price had been £2,000 each, which probably assumed that they were all in sound condition. The L.N.E.R. for example now offered to pay only £1,300 for the damaged boiler which had originated in No. 78633. Agreement was reached whereby the L.N.E.R. paid for the four sound boilers provided by the Ministry at Scotswood for their loaned engines as already mentioned. To balance this, the four worst purchased boilers standing at Scotswood were sent to Vulcan Foundry for repairs in December 1947, charged no doubt to the Ministry.

At first Vickers-Armstrongs carefully segregated the boilers on the O7's from those on the "Austerities" on loan. The four boilers received from the Ministry for the loaned engines were correctly fitted to Nos. 77018, 77315, 77457, 78682 in August-September 1947, though as mentioned earlier these boilers were afterwards purchased by the L.N.E.R. Six spare O7 boilers were then fitted to Nos. 3056, 3111/28/38/46 and 77071 in September-October 1947. Fitting an O7 boiler to No. 77071 was apparently a mistake, partly offset for book-keeping purposes by then fitting its old boiler to an O7, No. 3147 in October 1947. However, Vickers complicated matters by giving both boilers the same number, 10355 in the L.N.E.R. series, whereas that on No. 3147 should have been given the number 20194. The latter engine then passed to Cowlairs maintenance who seem to have been unaware of the duplication, although it was recorded at both Doncaster and Darlington. Because of this, Cowlairs afterwards renumbered this boiler BR10-748 in May 1951, in accordance with the September 1949 boiler renumbering scheme, whereas it should have become BR10-540.

The "Austerity" was designed with a view to easy conversion to oil-firing if desired, without the boiler having to be removed from the frames. In the post-war fuel crisis the L.N.E.R. included 111 class O7's in its short-lived scheme to convert 450 engines to burn oil fuel. No. 78670 was converted at Doncaster Works in January 1947, with the Weir type burner. The superheater elements were shortened by 1ft. 6in. to prevent burning at the firebox end due to the hotter flue gases, and the riveted ends of the copper stays inside the firebox were fitted with steel caps to protect them from the more intense local heat. After running-in at Doncaster, by which time the engine had been renumbered 3152, it was sent to March shed for trials, where it was tested on the fairly flat stretch of road between Whitemoor and Peterborough with loads of around 400 tons. The engine worked well on the level but on reaching a speed of 35 m.p.h. the steam pressure fell to 165 lb. per sq. in. and could not be restored to 225 lb. The burner was subsequently lifted above the level of the fire door peep-hole and the brick arch lengthened, after which on trials pressure rarely fell below 215 lb. per sq. in. The engine was converted back to coal burning at Swindon Works in October 1948.

The second engine nominated for conversion to oil burning was No. 3012 which entered Vickers-Armstrongs Works in June 1947 for heavy repairs and boiler change. The instruction was subsequently cancelled and the engine was returned to traffic in the following October still coal-fired. No further "Austerities" were considered for oil burning by the main line companies.

There were complaints in the N.E. Region of tube corrosion due to sediment accumulating on the palm stays. Replacement copper tubeplates fitted after August 1948 therefore had four fewer tube holes in the vicinity of these stays, in order to improve the circulation of water which was thought to have been the trouble. The corresponding holes in the smokebox tubeplate were simply plugged. This practice was only employed at Darlington Works and by Vickers-Armstrongs, and led to such anomalies as engines operating in the Eastern Region also having this 189-tube variety of boiler because they had been shopped at Darlington and conversely engines operating in the N.E. Region having the original 193-tube variety at the time of their withdrawal because they had been shopped at either Crewe or Gorton. The 189-tube variety was not recognised on any of the engine diagrams and the following details have been taken from the corresponding boiler diagram:-

Firebox	168 sq.ft.
Tubes (189 × $1\frac{3}{4}$in.)	1039 sq.ft.
Flues (28 × $5\frac{1}{8}$in.)	451 sq.ft.
Total evaporative	1658 sq.ft.

In 1951 the firebox was redesigned to overcome numerous difficulties encountered chiefly in the N.E. Region. New casings had the following features. The gusset plates supporting the upper part of the backplate were replaced by six diagonal stays. The front four rows of direct roof stays were replaced by two rows of expansion sling stays. Instead of ten transverse stays above the crown of the inner firebox, eleven were provided. The steel stays at the sides of the firebox were replaced by stays of Monel, a cupro-nickel alloy having a high tensile strength and resistance to corrosion. The ordinary wash-out plugs above the crown of the inner firebox were replaced by inspection hand holes, spaced unevenly apart in the same manner as in the Thompson Diagram 100A boiler. The $1\frac{3}{4}$in. diameter smoke tubes were replaced by 161 2in. diameter tubes, which also necessitated the provision of a new smokebox tubeplate. These alterations were incorporated in fifty-three boilers built at Crewe in 1951-54, the last one of which was put into service on No. 90493 (ex-3172) in January 1955 at Cowlairs Works. Again, this 161-tube variety was not recognised on any of the engine diagrams, but the corresponding boiler diagram provided the following details:-

Firebox	168 sq.ft.
Tubes (161 × 2in.)	1012 sq.ft.
Flues (28 × $5\frac{1}{8}$in.)	451 sq.ft.
Total evaporative	1631 sq.ft.

Between 1952 and 1962 approximately a third of the original boilers were rebuilt with the new style firebox. Most of these were rebuilt at Darlington Works with only a handful dealt with at Crewe and Gorton. The alterations were drastic and involved the removal for scrap of the complete firebox and smokebox tubeplate, and starting afresh with the original barrel. There was one recorded instance at Darlington where, after a discarded back end had been cut up in November 1957, the barrel disappeared too! The whole boiler was written off in November 1959 after a thorough search failed to reveal it. The post-1951 new and rebuilt boilers were easily identified by their unevenly spaced firebox hand holes, as previously mentioned. In addition, their covers were pitched slightly lower than the former wash-out seatings, so that the handrails and vacuum ejector exhaust pipe had to be repositioned to clear them (fig. 102).

General

The frames were 34ft. $10\frac{3}{4}$in. long, $1\frac{1}{8}$in. thick and spaced 4ft. $1\frac{1}{2}$in. apart. L.M.S. style drawgear was provided, with the shackles pinned to the hook. The buffers were the Turplat weldless type, 1ft. $8\frac{1}{4}$in. long with plain cylindrical shanks and square bases.

Walschaerts valve gear was provided, fitted throughout with plain bearings. Contrary to usual British practice, the radius rod was suspended from the reversing crank by a swing link instead of the reversing crank being attached directly to an extension of the radius rod. Both the reversing rod, running back to the cab, and the reversing shaft between the frames, were made of tubular steel.

The cylinders were made of cast-iron, 19in. diameter by 28in. stroke, inclined at 1 in 36 from the horizontal. The piston valves were 10in. diameter with narrow rings and were designed for inside admission. The maximum travel of the valves was $6\frac{5}{8}$in. at 75 per cent cut-off. Lubrication was provided by a Detroit pattern 32A four-feed sight feed lubricator inside the cab on the fireman's side. Two feeds supplied oil to the cylinder barrels and the other two supplied oil to the steam chests.

As a wartime expediency and to speed up delivery, many parts were fabricated to reduce the number of steel castings and forgings to a minimum. The centres of the driving wheels (third coupled pair) were made of cast steel whilst those of the remaining coupled wheels were high duty cast-iron. Rolled steel tyres were fitted in the usual manner. There was no provision for balancing the reciprocating masses, which was perhaps considered unimportant in a slow moving goods engine where there was a need to save weight. In B.R. days Darlington Works did rebalance the wheels on one engine (No. 90527, ex-77056, and not one of the engines formerly operating on the L.N.E.R.) to include 40 per cent of the reciprocating masses. There was considerable fore and aft motion as a result, so the experiment was concluded. The springs comprised nine plates, 5in. wide by $\frac{5}{8}$in. thick, at 3ft. 6in. centres. Although the engines were intended for use on lines laid on temporary road beds, the spring gear was not compensated (unlike the tender springs), nor was there any provision for adjustment after assembly. The axleboxes were steel castings with pressed-in white metalled bronze bearings. The journal surfaces were $8\frac{1}{2}$in. diameter and 11in. long ($11\frac{1}{8}$in. in the case of the leading and trailing coupled wheels which had additional side play) and were lubricated by oil syphon feed.

The pony truck wheels were originally made from chilled cast-iron, afterwards from rolled steel, with tyres in one piece having a generous rim section to permit re-turning after wear had taken place. The springs comprised seven plates, 4in. wide by $\frac{1}{2}$in. thickness, at 2ft. 6in. centres. The axleboxes were bronze castings with white metal inserts. The truck had three-pin swing link control and the total side play was 7in., enabling the engine to negotiate curves down to 5 chains, or $4\frac{1}{2}$ chains dead slow.

Steam sanding was provided, for forward running in front of the leading and driving coupled wheels and for reverse running behind the driving coupled wheels.

The cab was plain and offered little in the way of comfort for the crew. The overall width across the side sheets was 8ft. 6in. and the sides themselves stopped short at running plate level. Access to the cab was by means of ladder steps at the front of the tender, with the assistance of vertical handrails on both the tender and cab sides. The single side window was just an opening with no glass, but an arm rest was provided on the lower ledge. There was no ventilator in the cab roof but presumably this was not considered essential with unglazed side windows. There was no entrance door between engine and tender to prevent the enginemen from falling out, but padded tip-up seats were provided. The engines were designed for left-hand drive. The reversing gear was a horizontal screw, the quadrant type regulator handle had an extension to it on the fireman's side and there were two water gauge glasses. The driver had a Gresham & Craven steam brake valve, Westinghouse air brake valve and a solid jet type combination vacuum brake ejector (see also under Brakes).

In February 1946 Doncaster prepared drawings for the provision of roof ventilators, entrance doors and sliding glass windows. The various works were instructed to modify the engines as opportunity occurred, though few engines appear to have been altered at that time. As soon as the 200 "Austerities" were taken into Running Stock in class O7, steps were taken to bring certain features into line with L.N.E.R. practice. Once more the works were instructed in February 1947 to fit roof ventilators, entrance doors and sliding windows, whilst other approved modifications included: regulator handle to have the extension removed at the fireman's side, fitting of anti-glare plate at the side of the fire door, replacement of the original water gauge glasses (which were inferior and always breaking) by the L.N.E.R. type, removal of carriage warming apparatus from those engines fitted, substitution of Group Standard drawgear when renewals were needed (this modification was never carried out) and the fitting of steel tyres to the pony truck and tender wheels when the treads and flanges had become sufficiently worn to justify renewal.

In general these modifications were not carried out to engines on loan, but in May 1947 it was agreed to fit roof ventilators, entrance doors and sliding windows. However, these loaned engines were usually passing through works for acceptance only, when modifications were not normally carried out. Thus the distinction between the O7's and the engines on loan gradually became obvious. Matters came to a

Fig. 103 W.D. "Austerity" class No. 7206 on a Fort William – Maryhill No. 2 express goods near Garelochhead, about 1944.

On loan to L.N.E.R. prior to despatch to the Continent.

Fig. 104 W.D. "Austerity" Class No. 77230 on down class A goods at Ruislip, 1947.

On loan to L.N.E.R. after return from Continent and purchased by B.R. after nationalisation.

Fig. 105 W.D. "Austerity" Class No. 77298 on up class C goods near Ruddington, May 1946.

On loan to L.N.E.R. after return from Continent and subsequently purchased as L.N.E.R. No. 3082. Large painted W.D. number on smokebox door as applied in Belgium.

Fig. 106 Class O7 No. 3094 on down class B goods near Ashley (C.L.C.), April 1947.

Westinghouse pump still fitted, retaining W.D. No. 78584 on bufferbeam.

Fig. 107 W.D. 2-8-0 Class No. 90000 on up class F goods near Great Ponton, May 1953.

Formerly class O7 No. 3000.

Fig. 108 W.D. 2-8-0 Class No. 90085 on up class F goods near Mountnessing (G.E.), September 1951.

Formerly class O7 No. 3085.

Fig. 109 W.D. "Austerity" 2-10-0 Class No. 3651 at Doncaster Works, December 1943.

Run-in by L.N.E.R. but not taken on loan. Subsequently despatched to Longmoor Military Railway and not sent overseas. Later named *Gordon* and at present on the Severn Valley Railway.

head in July 1947 when enginemen at New England and Colwick threatened not to take the loaned engines off shed until something was done to improve the cab comfort. After some delay it was agreed in November 1947 "as a gesture of goodwill" to fit one or two of these engines with roof ventilators, sliding windows and anti-glare plates. In December 1947 two Colwick engines, Nos. 77209 and 78514, were sent specially to Gorton works for these alterations to be carried out.

In January 1948 the Ministry of Transport gave permission for alterations to be made to their engines on loan. As this cleared up the matter of who paid for them, the former L.N.E.R. works were instructed that the modifications being carried out to the O7's could also be made to the engines on loan, except that for the time being the latter were not to receive boiler lagging.

About 1959-61 glass sight screens were fitted to the cabs of the engines operating in the L.M. Region, including nine former class O7 engines at Woodford: Nos. 90033/46/65/6/95, 90448/86, 90504/9.

The axle weights shown on the L.N.E.R. engine diagram (and incidentally on the one issued by the L.M.S.) were the same as appeared in "The Railway Gazette" for 10th September 1943. However, the engine diagram issued by the G.W.R. was prepared from the Ministry of Supply diagram and therefore showed what were simply the original estimated weights in working order before the first engine was completed. After nationalisation it appears that for the sake of uniformity between each Region's records, the weights on both the Doncaster and Derby engine diagrams were amended to agree with the Swindon issue, the latter being the one with the heaviest weights. The revised weights were as follows:-

Engine	72T 0C
Tender	56T 0C
Total	128T 0C
Adhesive	62T 0C
Max. axle load	15T 10C

On the L.N.E.R. the wartime maximum loadings taken by the "Austerities" were class 7 and post-war class 8. However, in 1948 it was reported that a number of engines repaired by Vickers-Armstrongs displayed class 7. In November 1956 the Eastern Region Running Department reported that whilst these engines could take class 8 loads over the G.N. and G.C. routes, a class 7 load only was allowable on the G.E. Section. Tests held shortly before this date had also confirmed that no reasonable improvement could be made and in fact suggested that tests might be needed on some of the G.N. and G.C. routes to confirm whether or not present loadings were satisfactory. The outcome of the matter is not recorded.

Brakes

Steam brakes were provided for engine and tender, with both vacuum and air for train braking. On the engine a 12in. diameter brake cylinder was located under the cab, whilst the 10½in. diameter brake cylinder for the tender was at the front end. A Westinghouse type K.L.2A 10in./10⅞in. steam driven air compressor was mounted on the fireman's side of the smokebox. From March 1943 the pump was lowered 9in. so as not to restrict the forward view from the cab, possibly commencing with new engine No. 7027. Two air reservoirs were located out of sight between the frames. The vacuum ejector exhaust pipe ran along the outside of the boiler on the left-hand side to the smokebox. The vacuum reservoir cylinder was mounted on the left-hand running plate alongside the firebox (fig. 100).

The Westinghouse air pumps were removed from the engines as they passed through shops after July 1946 and stored pending a decision on the ultimate ownership of the engines. Following purchase by the L.N.E.R., the entire air brake equipment was removed from the O7's as they passed through shops and the process was eventually completed after nationalisation (cf. figs. 106 and 101). The equipment was similarly removed from the remaining loaned engines in B.R. days. The vacuum reservoir cylinder was removed from the left-hand running plate and relocated out of sight between the frames. The air pumps and reservoirs from some of these engines were fitted to the class Q7 0-8-0's and selected class O1 2-8-0's in connection with the Tyne Dock – Consett iron ore workings (see page 92).

Five "Austerities" loaned to the L.N.E.R. in 1947 were fitted with A.T.C. equipment in 1949-50. These were Nos. 90169, 90253, 90659/65, 90730, allocated to New England shed. The fitting of B.R. standard A.W.S. equipment commenced in January 1959. By September 1960, for example, the Eastern Region reported having fitted fifty-eight engines operating on the G.N. Section.

Tenders

The frames were 24ft. 4in. long, spaced 5ft. 9½in. apart and devoid of any lightening holes. The tank was of welded construction, 22ft. 7in. long outside, 8ft. 6½in. wide and held 5,000 gallons of water. The bunker was the self-trimming type with sloping sides and held 9 tons of coal. Above the top of the tank the bunker was only 6ft. 9in. wide, which gave reasonable visibility when running tender first. A ladder was provided at the back of the tender to provide access to the water filler hole.

The rigid wheelbase had eight wheels, 3ft. 2in. diameter, with their axles equally spaced. On the early engines they were made from chilled cast-iron with ample thickness to allow for turning. The flange profile of the rear wheels was different from that of the other six wheels, so that they were not interchangeable. Care was taken to paint the rear axle red, on which were stencilled the words "TRAILING AXLE". It was soon discovered that the practice of running down gradients with the tender hand brake partially applied produced flats on the treads, whilst tender first running through crossover roads caused pieces to flake off. From September 1943 new tenders had rolled steel wheels, again with ample allowance for turning. These wheels were interchangeable on all four axles. The earlier tenders were scheduled to have their cast-iron wheels changed for the new type when spares became available, though priority had to be given first of all to changing the rear pair. Gorton Works for example recorded changing the rear wheels on the tenders attached to Nos. 7162/5/71/3/4, 7333. A scheme was in hand in February 1947 to fit tyres to the wheels when the treads and flanges had become sufficiently worn to warrant the expense. To what extent this was carried out is not known and the only instance recorded is that of No. 90111 (ex-77013, one of the engines loaned to the L.N.E.R.) which received new tender tyres in October 1952.

The axleboxes were made of cast-iron with white metal lined brass inserts. The springs comprised sixteen plates, 4½in. wide at 3ft. 0in. centres. (The top plate was ½in. thickness whilst the remainder were $\frac{7}{16}$in.). The springs on the first and second pairs of wheels had compensated beams to give better riding on inferior track, and likewise the springs on the third and fourth pairs. Compensated springing is beneficial on uneven straight track, but it can give rise to trouble on curves when the wheelbase is rigid, as the first pair of wheels entering the curve tend to ride up and it was soon found that these wheels were prone to derailment when running tender first. In the N.E. Area this was particularly so in the Thornaby and Bishop Auckland areas, possibly aggravated by poor track maintenance, and Darlington Works altered the tender springs on one or two engines in the belief that the trouble arose from inadequate spring compensation. However, fitting more flexible springs did not solve the problem. Another possibility considered at the time was that the intermediate buffers between engine and tender were too stiff and therefore restrained the tender from taking the curves correctly, though nothing could be done about this. As it was, slight fore and aft motion was causing the built-up intermediate buffers to collapse, and eventually even stronger springs had to be fitted. From about January 1944 the rubbing blocks for these intermediate buffers were stiffened to prevent them fracturing too.

The N.E. Area was particularly concerned about these matters and arranged in August 1943 to adapt two old N.E.R. tenders from withdrawn Atlantics, so that they could be attached to "Austerities" to provide a float of spare tenders enabling the modifications to be carried out without the engines themselves being laid up. The tender from class C7 No. 2170 was prepared in August 1943 and suitably painted khaki with no lettering. The second tender came from class C6 No. 532 and was prepared in October 1943. These tenders were only noted attached to Nos. 7071 and 7204. On 2nd December 1944 No. 7071 was transferred to the Southern Railway and as late as 13th January 1945 it was noted on Eastleigh shed still attached to its N.E.R. tender. The engine sailed from Southampton Docks to the Continent on 11th March and four days later its old tender arrived back at Darlington Works. The other reconditioned tender, after standing spare at York shed for a while, had already arrived back at Darlington Works in January 1945.

Reports of tenders being derailed whilst running tender first were still prevalent after nationalisation though the exact causes were usually hard to find. One instance reported in November 1955 was attributed by the Eastern Region to insufficient clearance for the intermediate buffers between engine and tender. Meanwhile more flexible bearing springs were being tried out on the third and fourth pairs of wheels. These comprised nineteen plates, 4½in. wide at 3ft. 0in. centres. (The top plate was ½in.

thick as before, whilst the remainder were $\frac{3}{8}$in.). Two engines received these modified springs and also modified axlebox guides: Nos. 90184 (ex-77208, one of the engines loaned to the L.N.E.R. in 1947) and 90473 (ex-63152), in June 1953 and March 1954 respectively. This experiment was concluded in March 1955 but then taken up by the L.M. Region in May 1956 who decided to fit their 310 "Austerities". This final experiment was concluded in September 1963, after withdrawals had commenced, with the comment that it had been proved that the new arrangement overcame derailments.

The tenders were BR 5 in the B.R. standard tender classification.

Liveries

The "Austerities" were originally painted in khaki-brown livery, with 2in.-high cab side numerals, tender letters and broad arrow motif, all painted in matt golden yellow. From March 1943 the cab numerals became 6in. for clarity whilst operating in the United Kingdom, and finally 8in. from the end of December 1943 (fig. 97). From March 1944 the livery became khaki-green, whilst at a later date "W D" appeared on the tender in 12in. letters with a 10in. broad arrow motif.

Engines repaired in Belgium displayed the engine number on the smokebox door, in large painted numerals astride the twin-handles, in addition to the usual position on the front bufferbeam. This feature was retained for a while on those engines concerned which afterwards ran on the L.N.E.R., including Nos. 77298, 78711 and 79241 (figs. 99 and 105).

The various L.N.E.R. works were instructed on 15th January 1947 to letter the tenders "L N E R" on the 200 O7's as they passed through and, if they required repainting, to treat them in all respects as L.N.E.R. stock. The existing five-figure numbers were retained for a few weeks before a start was made renumbering the engines into the 3XXX series. Engines known to have run for a short time with "L N E R" on the tenders and W.D. numbers on the cab sides include Nos. 77093, 77112, 77316 and 78649.

The rapid renumbering of the O7's between February and April 1947 brought yet another variety: No. 3165 at least ran as such with the letters "W D" still on the tender. It also had the 21st Army Group badge painted on the cab side and between the letters on the tender.

The engines were gradually renumbered into the 60,000 series after nationalisation and smokebox numberplates were generally applied (fig. 101). The work was not completed before the decision was taken to renumber all the B.R.-owned "Austerities" into the 90,000 series.

Names

Several engines acquired unofficial names whilst abroad, including one which had been previously on loan to the L.N.E.R., this being No. 77138 *Lisa.* After the War, No. 77337 became *Sir Guy Williams* on the Longmoor Military Railway. In addition, the last "Austerity" 2-8-0 to be built, No. 79312, was named *Vulcan* with the plates affixed to the cab sides. This engine was loaned to the L.N.E.R. in 1947 and became No. 90732 after nationalisation, and continued to carry its plates.

Maintenance

The engines on loan during the War visited L.N.E.R. works for occasional light repairs. When they were recalled by the War Department towards the end of 1944 they were first of all reconditioned at whichever was the most convenient works. The Carlisle engines for example travelled south to Doncaster and Gorton (to avoid light running to Cowlairs), and then to the south of England.

In the immediate post-war period the 184 engines acquired by the L.N.E.R. between November 1945 and July 1946 were put straight into traffic – except for six engines (Nos. 70826/42, 78641/98, 78703, 79240) needing minor attention first at Ashford Works. The last sixteen engines to become class O7 were overhauled at Stratford (Nos. 70846, 77422/93, 78516, 78649/67/76), Darlington (Nos. 77100, 77254, 77391, 78603/77), R. Stephenson Hawthorns (Nos. 77093, 7112/33) and Eastleigh (No. 77046) before entering service, between October 1946 and February 1947. By 1947 the majority of the O7's were in need of general repair, which would have stretched the resources of the company's own works. To ease the situation thirty-five engines were repaired at the Scotswood Works of Vickers-Armstrongs during 1947, with a further seventeen under repair there at the end of the year. Meanwhile the L.N.E.R. continued to deal with light repairs in their own shops: Gateshead Works for example out-shopped fourteen during 1947. After nationalisation Vickers-Armstrongs continued for a while to carry out general repairs and between June 1947 and April 1949 no fewer than 167 O7's were overhauled at Scotswood.

In addition to the class O7 engines, the L.N.E.R. accepted a further 278 "Austerities" on loan, of which all but the final eight were in service by the end of 1947. These engines all needed repairs before being put into service and no fewer than 111 were specially overhauled in Belgium before being repatriated, though some of these still needed some slight attention on arrival at sheds on the L.N.E.R. The remaining engines visited one or other of the main works, including Brighton, Eastleigh and Crewe, or else were repaired by R. Stephenson & Hawthorns or Vickers-Armstrongs.

After nationalisation general repairs to the former L.N.E.R. engines were mainly carried out at Gorton, Darlington and Cowlairs, though they were occasionally dealt with elsewhere. No. 90049 (ex-3049) for example visited St. Rollox Works in 1953 for a general repair. In addition there were ten recorded visits to Inverurie Works for non-classified repairs by former O7's at Aberdeen (Ferryhill). The first appearance was No. 90498 (ex-63177) in August 1952 and the last was No. 90020 (ex-63020) in February 1965. Between these dates Nos. 90041 (ex-63041) and 90455 (ex-3134) each made three visits whilst No. 90097 (ex-63097) made two.

Life mileages are recorded for several former O7's, ranging from 359,968 for No. 90424 (ex-63103) to 527,536 for No. 90500 (ex-63179).

British Railways

At nationalisation 200 O7's were taken into British Railways Running Stock. In addition 409 "Austerities" on loan were taken into Operating Stock, including 270 from the L.N.E.R. From March 1948 60,000 was added to the running numbers of the O7's though the process was not completed: thirty were renumbered at main works (Doncaster, Gorton, Darlington), 100 by Vickers-Armstrongs, three on shed (Carlisle Canal 2, Old Oak Common 1), whilst sixty-seven were not renumbered. No. E63197 ran for a while thus, both with the temporary E prefix to denote the Eastern Group and its new B.R. number. From 1st February 1949 the engines were gradually renumbered into a new series commencing at 90000. Nos. (6)3000-3100 and (6)3101-99 became 90000-100 and 90422-520 respectively. The remaining engines built by N. B. Loco. Co., became 90101-421 and the engines built by Vulcan Foundry became 90521-732.

Shortly after nationalisation locomotive interchange tests were initiated as a means of producing in as short a time as possible indications of the most desirable features to incorporate in future standard designs. As far as the goods engines were concerned, the following 2-8-0's were tested working the 7-30 a.m. Ferme Park – New England: "Austerity" No. 63169, Thompson class O1 No. 63789, Churchward "28XX" class No. 3803, Stanier 8F No. 48189, together with W.D. "Austerity" 2-10-0 No. 73774. It will suffice here to give brief details of the best performance of the various competing engines. No. 63169 provided the lowest coal and water consumption figures and it was shortly after these tests that the British Transport Commission decided to purchase a further 533 of these locomotives.

Type	*L.N.E.R.* O1	*W.D.* 2-10-0	*L.M.S.* 8*F*	*G.W.R.* "28*XX*"	*L.N.E.R.* O7
Engine No.	63789	73774	48189	3803	63169
Date	27/7/48	12/8/48	17/8/48	24/8/48	2/9/48
Max. train load (tons)	575	575	575	575	575
Average speed (m.p.h.)	23.8	25.7	26.5	22.9	26.1
Average d.b.h.p.	546	486	505	415	425
Coal consumed (lb./mile)	61.7	50.3	51.2	51.5	47.1
Water used (gall./mile)	50.6	41.8	43.2	44.9	37.7

Allocation and Work

350 "Austerity" 2-8-0's were loaned to the L.N.E.R. in 1943-44 to help with the movement of raw materials and war supplies. Those built by the North British Locomotive Co. were run-in from Eastfield shed, where their duties consisted of main line goods workings though they were also seen on passenger trains, particularly between Clydebank East and Springburn. The engines received from Vulcan Foundry were run-in from Gorton shed, whence they worked over the G.C. main line at least as far south as Woodford.

For the engines built by the N.B. Locomotive Co. and run-in from Eastfield, the date received by the L.N.E.R. was taken as the building date in all later records. Prior to February 1944 the engine was taken into Operating Stock the next day and this date was taken as the commencement of the period of loan to the L.N.E.R. The only exception here was No. 7306, received on 18th April 1943 but returned to the makers for repairs before being taken into stock on 24th April. Due to the one day lapse, seven engines were officially built in the month preceding the loan date shown in the Summary table (Nos. 7024/38, 7172, 7204/22, 7331/68). During the period of running-in, several engines were inevitably returned to the makers for attention. Nos. 7341/78 were particularly troublesome and were returned three times. Engines were not always returned to the factory of origin: Nos. 7002/4/5/7/12/3/8 for example were built at Hyde Park works but went back to Queen's Park works.

After the engines had been run-in the majority were transferred to other sheds on the L.N.E.R. system where they generally settled down. However Nos. 7006/12/20 were returned to the makers shortly after their arrival at New England shed, and all three arrived back at New England in the first week of April 1943. In addition Eastfield despatched six engines to the War Department (Nos. 7015 Longmoor, 7168 Faslane then Longmoor, 7195 Melbourne then Longmoor, 7223 Faslane then Cairnryan, 7241 Cairnryan, 7369 Faslane) and twenty-four to the Southern Railway (Nos. 7422-45); as these engines were in L.N.E.R. Operating Stock for only about a week, they are not included in the "Summary".

From 27th February 1944 the 169 "Austerity" 2-8-0's that were run-in from Eastfield on behalf of the War Department were excluded from L.N.E.R. statistical returns. Summarised, Eastfield ran-in 443 "Austerity" 2-8-0's between February 1943 and March 1945, including the pioneer No. 7000. This engine was completed on 16th January 1943, worked first of all on the L.M.S., returned to the makers on 27th February for reconditioning and was finally handed over to the L.N.E.R. on 6th March. Of this total, 244 remained on the L.N.E.R. until after D-Day, twenty-four went to the Southern Railway and 175 to the War Department. For completeness it should be noted that the engines built by N.B. Locomotive Co., and not run-in from Eastfield, were dealt with by the L.M.S. at either Balornock (Hyde Park engines) or Polmadie (Queen's Park engines).

Similar arrangements applied to the Vulcan Foundry engines, these being run-in from Gorton. They were first of all delivered new to the L.M.S. at Warrington, from which shed they were usually worked in pairs to Gorton. The date received by the L.N.E.R. (rather than the slightly earlier date handed over to the L.M.S.) was taken as the building date for all future records. Prior to March 1944 this date was also taken as the date on loan to the L.N.E.R., which consequently avoided discrepancies when they arrived on the last day of the month.

After a period of running-in, 106 were despatched to other sheds on the L.N.E.R. system. Gorton also despatched a further twenty-six to the Southern Railway (Nos. 7472-97), followed by fourteen to the War Department for storing (Nos. 7498-7501/8/9, 8625/6 to Longmoor and Nos. 7502-7 to Melbourne); again, as these engines were in L.N.E.R. Operating Stock for only about a week, they are not included in the Summary. From 26th March 1944 the "Austerities" that were run-in from Gorton on behalf of the War Department, were excluded from L.N.E.R. statistical returns. The exact total is not known, as many engines were dealt with instead by the L.M.S., at Springs Branch and Patricroft sheds.

The sheds to which these 350 "Austerities" on loan to the L.N.E.R. were allocated at the end of February 1944, after the last engine (No. 7413) had completed its trials, are shown in the table on page 132. Transfers between sheds were generally few, until September 1944 when there was a major reshuffle to replace the American 2-8-0's which were being sent overseas first. Sixty-three "Austerities" were transferred to the G.W.R. followed two months later by a further eight, whilst twenty-three were transferred to the Southern Railway in November and December. Meanwhile a start had been made withdrawing engines from stock, reconditioning them and sending them overseas. These withdrawals were spread over three months, to some extent being delayed by the limited capacity in the L.N.E.R.'s own workshops to handle this quantity.

The engines returned to the W.D. towards the back end of 1944 were sent to Longmoor to await their turn for shipment, whilst preference was given to new engines. From 6th January 1945 reconditioned engines were sent direct to Dover. Here they were stabled by S.R. staff, their tenders filled to capacity with coal, their tanks and boilers emptied of water, and finally tools, lamps and fireirons were removed and returned to the owning company. Army personnel then took over. Tenders were uncoupled, the detachable portion of the cab roof extension was removed to facilitate storage on ship, and a complete set of W.D. tools, lamps and fireirons was provided. The engines were shipped across the channel aboard one or other of the S.R. train ferries, *Hampton Ferry* or *Twickenham Ferry*.

The official date of return to the W.D. after wartime loan, shown in the Summary, is the date entering works for reconditioning. In many cases the engine was ex-works some time later and could therefore be seen still on the L.N.E.R. an appreciable time after its official date of return. For example, No. 77304 was observed shunting at Enfield Lock on 11th April 1945, three months after its return date, whilst No. 77406 was observed at Stratford shed on 26th May 1945, fresh ex-works after a boiler change, four months after its return date. Finally No. 77145 was ex-Darlington Works on 14th June 1945, five months after its return date – and six weeks after the war had ended in Europe.

After the War, of the 350 engines originally on loan to the L.N.E.R. in 1943-44, 287 eventually came under British Railways ownership. The remaining engines are accounted for as follows. Nos. 77125 and 77238 were scrapped after a head-on collision near Kleve (W.Germany) on 16th August 1945. No. 77183 (as N.S. 4485) was involved in a collision near Kraneburg (W.Germany) on 6th November 1945 whilst on loan to the Netherlands State Railways, and was eventually scrapped in January 1947. No. 77337 returned to England and operated on the Longmoor Military Railway until 1965, latterly as W.D. 400. No. 77450 also returned to England, but after overhaul at Woolwich Arsenal was shipped to Hong Kong where it survived until 1957 as Kowloon-Canton Railway No. 30. The remaining fifty-eight engines were purchased by the Dutch Government towards the end of 1946, but fourteen were withdrawn in 1949 following a major electrification scheme whilst the others survived until 1953-58.

It was in November 1945 that a start was made returning the "Austerity" 2-8-0's to England. The first batch, comprising Nos. 70818/48, 77279, 77504, 78645/51/61, 78716, arrived at Dover on the 17th of the month, and these were then followed by further regular shipments. The earliest arrivals back were in reasonable condition and the Southern Railway was able to despatch the majority of these to the L.N.E.R. within a few days of their arrival at the port. For a while they were sent in batches of four at a time destined to a particular shed. Later arrivals from the Continent were not in such good condition and they could not always be made up into orderly batches. Most of the engines were handed over via Canonbury Junction on the North London line, though engines for March shed travelled instead via the Tottenham & Hampstead Junction line. (Later, engines for G.C. sheds were handed over at Neasden). The engines were taken straight into L.N.E.R. Operating Stock on the dates they were handed over, except that during November and December 1945 only, the Scottish Area did not record their allotment into stock until they actually received them, usually a week or so later. Thus, for example, the batch for Dundee that left the Southern Railway on 29th November 1945, straggled down in December with No. 77277 arriving first (2nd), followed by Nos. 78654, 79251 (6th). Finally No. 77505, which had been derailed at Canonbury, arrived on the 12th of the month. Another exception involved No. 78635 (New England) which was handed over on 16th December but not taken into stock until 31st December, and presumably only then to balance the year-end totals. It spent a while longer laid up at New England awaiting boiler repairs after an incident in which the water level had dropped too low and uncovered the crown of the firebox. By the end of the year there were 105 on loan, allocated to: New England (20), Colwick (20), March (16), York (13), Newport (16), St. Margaret's (12), Thornton (4), Dundee (4).

From 1st January 1946 all engines were taken into L.N.E.R. Operating Stock on the day that they were handed over, provided that they were in a serviceable condition when they left the Southern Railway. Early in the new year Canonbury was the scene of another derailment, on 12th January, when No. 77486 (for York) mounted the platform ramp after demolishing a signal post. It was re-railed later in the day by class J52 No. 4257. The mishap had occurred early on the 12th and the engine concerned was recorded in the North Eastern Area's records as being added to stock on the 11th.

During 1946 large numbers of "Austerities" were in store up and down the country. They were not generally taken into stock until after the necessary repairs had made them fit for service. However the following engines were taken into stock prematurely and their book entries cancelled whilst repairs were carried out:-

W.D. No.	*Original date to stock*	*Amended date to stock*
78516	5/46	24/8/46
78649	5/46	18/1/47
78667	5/46	11/1/47
78676	5/46	2/11/46
77100	30/8/46	23/10/46
77254	30/8/46	2/11/46
78603	30/8/46	5/10/46
78677	30/8/46	11/10/46
77051	28/2/47	9/4/47
77327	28/2/47	11/4/47
79264	28/2/47	19/4/47
77459	15/3/47	18/4/47

Fresh sheds to acquire "Austerities" during 1946 were Woodford, Gorton, Springhead, Heaton, Eastfield and Aberdeen. Thus the 200 engines purchased by the L.N.E.R. in December 1946 were spread throughout the system at the main sheds, for use on heavy duties on both main and secondary lines. Only 190 of these were actually in service at the end of the year (see table on p. 132 for allocations). During January and February 1947 the last ten were put into traffic, at New England 3, Immingham 2, March 2, Heaton 3. Changes during 1947 brought fresh venues for the owned engines (class O7) at Doncaster (the oil-fired engine on trials), Mexborough, Annesley and Tweedmouth. The allocations at the end of the year are given in the table on p. 132.

In addition, the L.N.E.R. took a further 270 engines during 1947, on loan only. Many were housed at the same sheds as the O7's so that their work became inextricably mixed, though for statistical purposes they were kept separate. Fresh sheds for these loaned engines were Barnsley, Staveley, Retford, Neville Hill, Dairycoates, Stockton and Dunfermline. Both Barnsley and Retford lost their allocations in October 1947 when a major reshuffle sent twenty-nine "Austerities" from the Southern Area to the North Eastern Area, without exchange. The position at the end of 1947 regarding these loaned engines is also summarised in the accompanying table.

During 1948 the last eight engines of the L.N.E.R. quota were put into traffic at former L.N.E.R. sheds: Mexborough 1, Eastfield 5, Aberdeen 2. The Scottish Region engines had originally been allocated to the N.E. Area and one of these, No. 77225, spent about a week at Dairycoates before going to Eastfield. In addition to these eight engines, a further three "Austerities" were allocated to ex-L.N.E.R. sheds in the Scottish Region during 1948, these being Nos. 77237, 77374/99, which will not appear in the Summary but are included here for completeness. The situation in Scotland was further complicated during 1948 by movements to and from ex-L.M.S. sheds and the transfer of Carlisle (Canal) to L.M. Region control.

In March 1948 No. 78522 was transferred on a temporary basis from the Western Region to the Eastern Region, in exchange for the oil-fired O7, No. 3152, which then went to Old Oak Common shed. The engines were transferred back again after about seven months. Towards the end of 1948 a large scale movement of "Austerities" took place to provide a proportionate balance of engines on loan from the Ministry of Supply. The N.E. Region transferred twenty-seven to the Eastern Region and a further two to the Scottish Region, receiving in exchange a similar number of O7's. Within the Eastern Region, the Western Section transferred seven to the Eastern Section in exchange for a similar number of O7's. The engines concerned had hardly time to settle down at their new sheds when all the "Austerities" formerly on loan were purchased by British Railways. The classification O7 was quickly dropped and a new number series were allocated to all the "Austerities". Within a short time the distinction was lost between the former O7's, the engines that had been on loan to the L.N.E.R. at nationalisation and the engines that were put into service by British Railways. For this reason the following description of the work undertaken by the engines that were owned by or on loan to the L.N.E.R. in general covers the period 1943 to 1948 only.

It may be mentioned that four former O7's remained at the same sheds to which they were allocated in 1945-46, when they returned from the Continent after the War, until they were withdrawn in 1962-63. These were Nos. 90058 (Thornton), 90455 (Aberdeen), 90472 (Thornton) and 90504 (Woodford), formerly L.N.E.R. Nos. 3058, 3134/51/83.

Allocation at:	23/2/44 *(on loan)*	31/12/46 (O7)	31/12/47 (O7)	31/12/47 *(on loan)*
New England	35	29	26	10
Colwick	30	14	33	13
Woodford	—	26	17	8
Staveley	—	—	—	3
Mexborough	10	—	10	48
Gorton	—	10	—	—
Immingham	—	—	2	—
March	55	37	30	31
York	30	10	—	10
Neville Hill	—	—	—	28
Dairycoates	20	—	—	12
Springhead	—	7	—	11
Newport	45	20	16	17
Stockton	—	—	—	9
Tyne Dock	20	—	—	10
Heaton	—	6	28	—
Tweedmouth	—	—	7	4
Carlisle	10	—	—	—
St. Margaret's	15	9	11	14
Haymarket	4	—	—	—
Eastfield	18	3	3	7
Parkhead	10	—	—	—
Dunfermline	10	—	—	11
Thornton	18	9	9	23
Dundee	11	5	5	1
Aberdeen	9	5	3	—
	350	190	200	270

Southern Area

No. 7006 was allocated to New England shed on 28th February 1943 and was quickly followed by nineteen others from N.B. Loco. Co. over the ensuing three months. All were put to work on duties hitherto undertaken by Gresley 2-8-0's of classes O1 and O2, which were then transferred away from New England, mainly to Colwick where the work was less onerous. In mid-April 1943 Nos. 7006/7/8/12/20/1/2 were all seen on coal trains working up the G.N. main line to Hornsey whilst on 22nd April No. 7300 hauled a goods over the Hertford loop. Other duties took them northwards from Peterborough to Colwick, Grimsby and Doncaster.

Tests were conducted with No. 7035 hauling sixty loaded coal wagons over the seventy-three miles from New England to Ferme Park (Hornsey), returning with seventy empties. The timing allowed 2 hrs. 55 mins. southbound and 2 hrs. 43 mins. northbound. As a result of these trials five regular return workings were introduced in July 1943 of which the quickest southbound timing was 2 hrs. 57 mins. and 2 hrs. 54 mins. return. One stop for water was made at Hitchin in each direction. (Shortly after this, Nos. 7080-94 from Vulcan Foundry were allocated new to New England). The 1944 timetable contained eight such workings on weekdays, all worked on an out and home basis: five by New England men and three by Hornsey men. On Sundays there were three up and four down trains. Similar schedules were operated between Colwick and New England with four return trips on weekdays taking just over two hours each way.

A sighting of an "Austerity" on an express passenger train occurred on 11th January 1944 when the train from Leeds due into King's Cross at 2-46 p.m. arrived at 4-0 p.m. in charge of No. 7084 which had replaced a failed engine at Offord. An unusual combination seen on an up goods passing Brookmans Park on 22nd April 1944 was class N2 No. 2589 + No. 7090.

After the War, the O7's became a familiar sight on the New England – Ferme Park coal trains, many of which were upgraded to class A speed at an average of 3 hrs. 50 mins. overall with one stop at Hitchin for water. Returning empty wagon trains were allowed 3¼ hours. There were also some through engine workings between Hornsey and Doncaster, changing crews at Peterborough and taking 7 hrs. 35 mins. overall. Certain unusual workings are on record, as on 30th November 1945 when No. 79180, a new arrival at New England, was noted at Hornsey on an up coal train piloted by class C1 No. 4458. On 21st August 1946 No. 70826 arrived in King's Cross at about 9-0 a.m. with a local passenger train from Hatfield. On 24th April 1947 the 6-53 a.m. King's Cross – Cambridge stopping train was observed at Welwyn North 45 minutes late with class N2 No. 9540 + No. 77034.

It is noticeable that Doncaster did not have a permanent allocation of "Austerities", other than the oil-fired No. 78670 (later 3152) whilst it was on trials there, but retained instead a stud of older 2-8-0's, Gresley classes O1 (later O3) and O2 with some Robinson O4's.

Colwick received thirty engines between October 1943 and January 1944. Their main duties took them southwards over the Great Central lines to Woodford, Banbury and even Neasden, as well as to Peterborough and March. On 3rd August 1944 No. 7111 traversed the new Bounds Green – Palace Gates connection at Wood Green (opened the previous month for two-way working in replacement of the original 1930 siding connection which needed a shunting movement) with a goods for Temple Mills, whilst No. 7115 was at Ipswich on August Bank Holiday that year.

Colwick received twenty "Austerities" towards the end of 1945 though for a short time in the autumn of 1946 they were exchanged for class O1 Thompson rebuilds from Gorton, in order to give increased tractive effort on the intensive coal train services from Nottinghamshire pits. This scheme was short-lived, the O1's departed and Colwick once more acquired a stud of "Austerities".

Woodford had no wartime allocation of "Austerities", acquiring instead a large number of the American 2-8-0's. However by mid-1946 the shed had an allocation of thirty for working over the southern end of the G.C. main lines. As in the case of Colwick, several were exchanged for class O1 Thompson 2-8-0's shortly afterwards on a two-month trial. In June 1947 twelve "Austerities" were transferred from Woodford to Annesley, which was another former G.C. shed previously without "Austerities". Again this proved to be a short-lived experiment and Annesley exchanged all its "Austerities" for O4's before the end of the year.

Mexborough acquired ten engines, Nos. 7452-61, from March shed in January and February 1944, whilst another former G.C. shed, Neasden acquired nine engines, Nos. 7075-9/96-9, from March shed in May and June 1944 at the height of activity on the southern end of the G.C. main line around D-Day. As described later the G.C. lines saw many workings from distant sheds, especially in the months preceding D-Day, when prodigious amounts of supplies and materials were moved southwards to reception areas close to the points of embarkation.

Stratford received fifteen engines in July and August 1943 but they were soon transferred to March, though not before No. 7337 had been observed working the 2-14 p.m. Ipswich – Yarmouth express on 31st July 1943, the Saturday before the August Bank Holiday. Further engines were sent direct to March, which by January 1944 had the greatest concentration of the class (sixty-four engines) to assist with the movement of traffic to and from the numerous airfields in East Anglia, as well as to London Docks and Temple Mills. The March allocation dropped to fifty-four by the end of February 1944, with the transfers to Mexborough mentioned earlier.

On 14th December 1943 No. 7117 worked the 8-5 p.m. Ely – March passenger train, losing one hour on the sixteen mile run due to traffic congestion. On 1st June 1944 No. 7337 was working the 11-40 p.m. goods from Whitemoor to Ipswich, comprising 51 open wagons loaded with U.S. aircraft bombs and components. The leading wagon, which held ten tons of unfused bombs, caught fire and the driver stopped the train at Soham. The fireman and a signalman uncoupled the wagon from the rest of the train and the driver then drew forward. The wagon exploded killing instantly fireman J. W. Nightall and fatally injuring signalman F. Bridges. Driver B. Gimbert escaped with injuries. Their heroic action prevented what would have been an even worse disaster had the whole train blown up, and undoubtedly saved this small Cambridgeshire town from utter destruction. Thirty-seven years later, in a ceremony at March on 28th September 1981, the action of the train crew was again recognised when two Stratford class 47 diesels

Nos. 47577 and 47579 were formally named *Benjamin Gimbert G.C.* and *James Nightall G.C.,* respectively.

In the immediate post-war period, March was the only G.E. Section shed to receive an allocation of "Austerities", which it utilised on its heavy duties northwards to Doncaster and Colwick, across the East Anglian lines to Norwich and Lowestoft, as well as to Ipswich via Bury St. Edmunds, and of course southwards to London via Cambridge and Bishops Stortford. (Stratford shed did not acquire any until after nationalisation, and then only in small numbers). On one occasion in July 1946 class J39 No. 2951 failed at Angel Road whilst working the 10-0 p.m. Liverpool Street – Peterborough mail. It was replaced by No. 78651 of March, which lost a further 17 minutes in running over the next 19 miles to Sawbridgeworth.

North Eastern Area

The North Eastern Area acquired 115 engines in 1943-44. The first twenty-three all went to York shed, between April and August 1943, and later arrivals increased this total to thirty by the middle of November. In May 1943 York engines Nos. 7023/8/33, 7301 were observed passing through Penistone in the Manchester direction, whilst No. 7034 was seen at Stockport and No. 7027 on the Fallowfield line. Dairycoates received twenty engines during 1943. Nearby Springhead shed acquired three from Dairycoates in March 1944 (to allow three class Q6 0-8-0's to be transferred to Cudworth), followed by nine further "Austerities" from York two months later. Tyne Dock received thirty-one engines by January 1944, though within two months of their arrival eleven of these were transferred to Newport to replace Q6's. By February 1944 Newport shed had the largest concentration of the class in the N.E. Area, with forty-five engines. In July 1944 seven Newport engines were noted at work on the Saltburn line, marked on both engine and tender buffer beams "Local Traffic Only". (At this time a number of class Q5 0-8-0's were in store). This period saw many workings from the N.E. Area southwards over the G.C. lines as exemplified by the appearances of No. 7235 (Tyne Dock) at Banbury on 6th March 1944, No. 7239 (York) at Woodford on 14th March and Nos. 7025/68 (York), 7203 (Newport) all at Woodford on 30th June. In September 1944 twenty-five "Austerities" were transferred from Newport to the G.W.R. and a further five to New England. At the same time seven were transferred from Tyne Dock to the G.W.R. and a further eleven to Heaton. In November and December twenty-three were transferred to the Southern Railway; the remaining engines were reconditioned by the L.N.E.R. and returned to the War Department.

In the immediate post-war period, the "Austerities" allocated to the North Eastern Area were initially divided between Newport and York, though for a time Springhead also had a small allocation. In November 1946 eight engines were transferred from the N.E. Area to March to replace the "Austerity" 2-10-0's which had been returned to the War Department. (The N.E. Area received back in exchange eight class J25 0-6-0's on loan to the G.W.R. since 1939-40). As on the other Sections, the "Austerities" became the mainstay of heavy goods and mineral haulage, continuing until replaced by dieselisation.

Scottish Area

The Scottish Area received 105 engines, shared between nine sheds ranging from Carlisle to Aberdeen. They were generally employed on main line goods workings: Edinburgh – Newcastle (changing men at Tweedmouth), Edinburgh – Carlisle (changing men at or near Hawick), Edinburgh – Glasgow (via Polmont and via Bathgate), and Edinburgh to Fife and Aberdeen. When going through to Aberdeen there was a change of men en route. The "Austerities" also worked from Glasgow to Fort William, again with the men changing en route (fig. 103). The turntable at Fort William was too short to accommodate these engines, which had to be uncoupled from their tenders before being turned separately. However it is believed that the turntable rails were eventually extended so that engine and tender could be turned in the normal way. In June 1943 one of these engines was noted at Craigendoran working the 2-56 p.m. Fort William – Glasgow passenger train, having apparently replaced a failed class K4 2-6-0. On 17th July No. 7165 (Eastfield) was noted at Dalmeny on a passenger train and No. 7005 (also Eastfield) was similarly noted at Kinghorn. On the 25th of the month No. 7170 (Eastfield) was noted at Castlecary on an eastbound troop train whilst three days later No. 7176 (Dundee) was seen working the 3-30 p.m. Aberdeen – King's

Cross express somewhere north of the border. On 10th September 1943 another engine, believed to be No. 7162 (Eastfield) worked the 4-55 p.m. Glasgow – Edinburgh and returned with the 7-55 p.m. stopping train to Glasgow. From time to time the class was seen on empty stock trains around Edinburgh and on occasional military specials like the one recorded at Castlecary. Five engines were transferred to the G.W.R. in September 1944 followed by eight more in November, during which month six were transferred to the Southern Area. The remaining engines were returned to the War Department by early 1945.

Between December 1945 and May 1946 thirty-five "Austerities" were put to work in the Scottish Area. Four were transferred to March shed in November 1946, to replace 2-10-0's leaving thirty-one to become class O7. They were put to use on similar main line goods duties as when they were on loan during the War, but additionally they were used on the Perth main line. Other duties included "conditionals" on the main lines in Central Scotland, the St. Margaret's breakdown train and occasionally on passenger trains, e.g. Edinburgh – Leven, as well as empty stock to and from Craigentinny carriage sidings.

The O7's in the Scottish Area were booked to take the same loads as class O4, and a notice dated January 1944 imposed a speed restriction of 35 m.p.h. However many of their duties (particularly in the post-war period) were hardly appropriate for engines with coupled wheels of only 4ft. 8½in. diameter, especially on the East Coast main line. Many of the goods trains on this route were fully or partially vacuum braked, even including some in the No. 1 express category. To keep time on such trains they had to be driven hard, so their condition deteriorated and they became rough and noisy. This was aggravated by the tendency of the tender to bump against the engine incessantly, especially when running fast downhill. An O7 in full cry at about 60 m.p.h. was certainly a stirring spectacle, passing through places like Longniddry on the Berwick main line, or Stonehaven northbound. It was small wonder that numerous complaints were made by the men; nevertheless their use on this type of duty continued until the fifties.

The Aberdeen engines worked southwards over the N.B. Section and there were no recorded observations on the G.N. of S. Section until after nationalisation, which is strictly outside the period that this survey is intended to cover. However their appearance on this Section, noted for its employment of smaller engines in general than on the other Sections on account of the special characteristics to be found, cannot pass without comment – particularly as the engines concerned were mostly former class O7 engines. On 19th August 1949 for example No. 63142 (Dundee) was seen on a down goods at Kittybrewster, having possibly worked through from Dundee where it had been seen earlier that day. During the night of 20th/21st August 1953 three Bertram Mills' Circus special trains were run from Fraserburgh to Huntly, with a reversal at Dyce. Special No. 600, 620 tons, left Fraserburgh behind class B1 Nos. 61307/46, which were changed at Dyce for class B12 No. 61502 and No. 90041 (ex-63041). For operating reasons at Huntly, the special ran forward to Grange Junction, where it was hauled round the triangle to Grange North Junction by the Keith pilot, and ran back to Huntly. Special No. 601, 635 tons, left Fraserburgh behind class B1 Nos. 61347/51, which were changed at Dyce for class K2 No. 61779 and No. 90455 (ex-3134). The same procedure was adopted round the Grange triangle. The third special was lightly loaded and handled throughout by class B1 No. 61350 unassisted.

During October 1953, shortly after the Bertram Mills episode, Kittybrewster shed found itself short of B1's, with nine out of traffic on one occasion. Ferryhill shed loaned a few engines to help out, including two "Austerities", Nos. 90097 (ex-63097) and 90455 (ex-3134). Whilst on loan, these latter both worked the 7-35 a.m. Kittybrewster – Keith goods train.

An unusual visitor to the Deeside line in 1955 was No. 90489 (ex-63168), an Eastfield engine which appeared on the 8-45 a.m. Aberdeen – Banchory goods on 26th June. "Austerities" continued to appear on the G.N.S. Section though published reports of sightings diminished. One of the present authors noted two on Kittybrewster shed on 13th September 1956: Nos. 90041 (ex-63041) of Ferryhill and 90441 (ex-3120) of Thornton.

Mention should also be made of workings over ex-L.M.S. lines, in particular the Highland section where a number of former O7's were sighted in the early part of 1949 working goods trains, including Nos. 63020 (Eastfield), 63071 (Dundee), 3134 (Ferryhill) and 63192 (Thornton).

Withdrawals commenced in December 1959 with No. 90083 (ex-3083), followed one month later by No. 90062 (ex-3062). Thus the first two

"Austerity" 2-8-0's to be withdrawn had both been O7's. The next one to be withdrawn was No. 90191 in February 1960. As W.D. No. 77221 this had been one of the engines on loan to the L.N.E.R. in 1947. There were no further withdrawals until 1962, when scheduled withdrawals began. The last engines were withdrawn during September 1967, including five former O7's, Nos. 90009/74/6 (ex-3009/74/6), 90430/78 (ex-3109/57).

Engine Diagrams

1944. "W.D. 2-8-0 Class".
1946. Reissued. Diagram reclassified "Austerity O7", 1/1947. Reverted to "W.D. 2-8-0", 1/1949.

Classification: Southern Area load class 8; Route availability 6; B.R. power class 8F.

Summary of W.D. 2-8-0 Engines on Loan 1943-45

W.D. No.	*On loan From*	*To*(a)	*B.R. No.*
7000	3/43	12/44	90101
7001	2/43	12/44	90102
7002	2/43	12/44	90001
7003	2/43	12/44	90103
7004	2/43	12/44	90104
7005	2/43	12/44	90105
7006	2/43	1/45	90106
7007	2/43	1/45	90107
7008	2/43	12/44	90108
7009	2/43	1/45	90000
7010	4/43	1/45	90109
7012	3/43	12/44	90110
7013	3/43	12/44	90111
7014	3/43	12/44	90112
7016	3/43	12/44	90114
7017	3/43	12/44	90115
7018	3/43	12/44	90116
7019	3/43	1/45	90117
7020	3/43	1/45	90118
7021	3/43	1/45	90002
7022	3/43	1/45	90119
7023	3/43	12/44	90120
7024	4/43	12/44	90121
7025	4/43	12/44	90122
7026	4/43	12/44	90123
7027	4/43	12/44	90124
7028	4/43	12/44	90125
7029	4/43	1/45	90126
7030	4/43	1/45	90127
7031	4/43	12/44	90128
7032	4/43	12/44	90129
7033	4/43	12/44	90004
7034	4/43	12/44	90130
7035	4/43	1/45	90131
7036	4/43	1/45	90132
7037	4/43	1/45	90133
7038	5/43	1/45	—
7039	5/43	1/45	90134
7040	5/43	11/44(b)	90135
7041	5/43	11/44(b)	90136
7065	6/43	12/44	—
7066	6/43	1/45	90536
7067	6/43	1/45	90537
7068	6/43	11/44(c)	90538
7069	7/43	12/44(c)	—
7070	7/43	1/45	90539
7071	7/43	12/44(c)	90540
7072	7/43	12/44(c)	90541
7073	7/43	11/44(c)	90542
7074	7/43	2/45	90543
7075	7/43	1/45	90544
7076	7/43	12/44	90545
7077	7/43	12/44	90546
7078	7/43	12/44	90547
7079	8/43	11/44	90548
7080	8/43	12/44	90549
7081	8/43	1/45	90550
7082	8/43	12/44	—
7083	8/43	12/44	90422
7084	8/43	12/44	—
7085	8/43	12/44	90551
7086	8/43	1/45	90552
7087	8/43	9/44(b)	90553
7088	8/43	9/44(b)	90554
7089	8/43	9/44(b)	90555
7090	8/43	1/45	90556
7091	8/43	9/44(b)	90423
7092	8/43	1/45	90557
7093	8/43	12/44	90424
7094	9/43	9/44(b)	90558

Summary of W.D. 2-8-0 Engines on Loan 1943-45 (continued)

W.D. No.	*On loan From*	*To*(a)	*B.R. No.*
7095	9/43	11/44	90559
7096	9/43	11/44	90560
7097	9/43	11/44	90561
7098	9/43	12/44	90562
7099	9/43	11/44	90563
7100	9/43	2/45	90425
7101	9/43	11/44	90564
7102	9/43	1/45	90565
7103	9/43	1/45	90566
7104	9/43	2/45	90567
7105	9/43	1/45	—
7106	9/43	11/44	90568
7107	9/43	1/45	90569
7108	9/43	12/44	90570
7109	9/43	12/44	—
7110	10/43	11/44	90426
7111	10/43	9/44(b)	90571
7112	10/43	1/45	90427
7113	10/43	9/44(b)	90428
7114	10/43	9/44(b)	—
7115	10/43	11/44	90572
7116	10/43	9/44(b)	90573
7117	10/43	1/45	—
7118	10/43	1/45	90574
7119	10/43	2/45	90575
7120	10/43	12/44	90576
7121	10/43	11/44	90577
7122	10/43	11/44	90578
7123	10/43	11/44	90579
7124	10/43	11/44	90580
7125	10/43	11/44	—
7126	10/43	11/44	90581
7127	11/43	11/44	90582
7128	11/43	11/44	90583
7130	11/43	11/44	90585
7131	11/43	2/45	90429
7132	11/43	2/45	—
7133	11/43	11/44	90430
7134	11/43	12/44	—
7135	11/43	9/44(b)	90586
7136	11/43	9/44(b)	90431
7137	11/43	9/44(b)	—
7138	11/43	9/44(b)	90587
7139	11/43	12/44(c)	—
7140	11/43	9/44(b)	—
7141	11/43	9/44(b)	90588
7142	11/43	9/44(b)	90589
7143	11/43	12/44(c)	—
7144	12/43	9/44(b)	90590
7145	12/43	1/45	90591
7146	12/43	9/44(b)	90482
7147	12/43	12/44(c)	90592
7148	12/43	9/44(b)	90593
7149	12/43	11/44	90594
7162	6/43	12/44	90149
7163	6/43	12/44	90150
7164	6/43	12/44	90151
7165	6/43	1/45	90152
7166	6/43	12/44	90153
7167	6/43	12/44	90154
7169	6/43	1/45	90155
7170	6/43	1/45	90156
7171	6/43	12/44	90157
7172	7/43	1/45	—
7173	7/43	1/45	90158
7174	7/43	2/45	90159
7175	7/43	12/44	90160
7176	7/43	12/44	90161
7177	7/43	12/44	—
7178	7/43	12/44	90162
7179	7/43	12/44	90163
7180	7/43	12/44	90164
7181	7/43	12/44	90165
7182	7/43	12/44	90166
7183	7/43	1/45	—
7184	7/43	12/44	90167
7185	8/43	12/44	90168
7186	8/43	12/44	90169
7187	8/43	1/45	90170
7188	8/43	11/44	—
7189	8/43	12/44	—
7190	8/43	12/44(c)	—
7191	8/43	12/44	—
7192	8/43	12/44(c)	90171
7193	8/43	12/44(c)	—
7194	8/43	12/44	—
7196	8/43	12/44(c)	90173
7197	8/43	1/45	—
7198	8/43	1/45	90174
7199	9/43	11/44	90175
7200	8/43	1/45	90176
7201	8/43	1/45	90177
7202	8/43	1/45	90178
7203	8/43	1/45	90179
7204	9/43	1/45	90180
7205	9/43	1/45	90181
7206	9/43	12/44	90182
7207	9/43	1/45	90183
7208	9/43	12/44	90184
7209	9/43	12/44	90185
7210	9/43	12/44(c)	90186
7211	9/43	1/45	90012

Summary of W.D. 2-8-0 Engines on Loan 1943-45 (continued)

W.D. No.	On loan From	On loan To(a)	B.R. No.
7212	9/43	1/45	90187
7213	9/43	2/45	90013
7214	9/43	1/45	90188
7215	9/43	11/44(b)	90189
7216	9/43	11/44(b)	—
7217	9/43	11/44(b)	—
7218	9/43	11/44(b)	90190
7219	9/43	11/44(b)	—
7220	9/43	11/44(b)	90014
7221	9/43	1/45	90191
7222	10/43	2/45	90192
7224	10/43	2/45	—
7225	10/43	2/45	90193
7226	10/43	1/45	90194
7227	10/43	1/45	90195
7228	10/43	1/45	90196
7229	10/43	9/44(b)	90197
7230	10/43	2/45	90198
7231	10/43	9/44(b)	90199
7232	10/43	12/44(c)	90200
7233	10/43	9/44(b)	90021
7234	10/43	2/45	90201
7235	10/43	12/44(c)	90202
7236	10/43	12/44	90022
7237	10/43	11/44(c)	90203
7238	10/43	12/44	—
7239	10/43	11/44(c)	90204
7240	10/43	9/44(b)	—
7242	11/43	1/45	90206
7243	11/43	9/44(b)	90027
7244	11/43	9/44(b)	—
7245	11/43	2/45	—
7246	11/43	2/45	—
7247	11/43	1/45	90207
7248	11/43	1/45	90208
7249	11/43	1/45	90209
7250	11/43	1/45	90028
7251	11/43	1/45	90029
7252	11/43	1/45	90210
7253	11/43	1/45	90211
7254	11/43	1/45	90030
7255	11/43	1/45	90212
7256	11/43	2/45	90213
7257	11/43	2/45	90214
7258	11/43	9/44(b)	90215
7259	12/43	9/44(b)	90216
7260	12/43	12/44	90217
7261	12/43	9/44(b)	90218
7262	12/43	9/44(b)	—
7300	3/43	1/45	90003
7301	4/43	11/44(c)	—
7302	4/43	12/44	90219
7303	4/43	12/44	90220
7304	4/43	1/45	—
7305	4/43	1/45	90221
7306	4/43	12/44	90222
7307	4/43	1/45	90223
7308	5/43	1/45	—
7309	5/43	1/45	90224
7324	6/43	1/45	90236
7325	6/43	1/45	90237
7326	6/43	1/45	90238
7327	6/43	1/45	90239
7328	6/43	1/45	90240
7329	6/43	1/45	90241
7330	6/43	1/45	90242
7331	7/43	2/45	—
7332	7/43	1/45	90243
7333	7/43	1/45	—
7334	7/43	1/45	90244
7335	7/43	1/45	90245
7336	7/43	1/45	90009
7337	7/43	1/45	—
7338	7/43	2/45	90246
7339	7/43	1/45	90010
7340	8/43	1/45	90247
7341	8/43	2/45	—
7342	8/43	2/45	90248
7343	8/43	1/45	90011
7344	8/43	12/44(c)	—
7345	8/43	1/45	—
7346	8/43	1/45	—
7347	8/43	1/45	—
7348	8/43	2/45	90249
7349	8/43	1/45	—
7350	8/43	1/45	90250
7351	8/43	12/44	90251
7352	9/43	2/45	90252
7353	9/43	1/45	90253
7354	9/43	9/44(b)	90015
7355	9/43	1/45	90254
7356	9/43	1/45	90255
7357	9/43	2/45	90016
7358	9/43	12/44(c)	90256
7359	9/43	12/44(c)	90257
7360	9/43	1/45	90017
7361	9/43	2/45	—
7362	9/43	12/44	90258
7363	9/43	2/45	90018
7364	9/43	2/45	90259
7365	9/43	2/45	90260
7366	9/43	9/44(b)	—

Summary of W.D. 2-8-0 Engines on Loan 1943-45 (continued)

W.D. No.	*On loan From*	*To*(a)	*B.R. No.*
7367	9/43	1/45	90019
7368	10/43	2/45	90261
7370	10/43	1/45	90024
7371	10/43	12/44	90262
7372	10/43	2/45	90263
7373	10/43	2/45	90025
7374	10/43	2/45	90264
7375	10/43	2/45	90265
7376	10/43	2/45	—
7377	10/43	9/44(b)	—
7378	10/43	12/44	90266
7379	10/43	12/44	90267
7380	10/43	12/44(c)	90268
7381	10/43	1/45	90269
7382	10/43	12/44(c)	90026
7383	10/43	9/44(b)	—
7384	10/43	2/45	—
7385	11/43	9/44(b)	90031
7386	11/43	9/44(b)	90270
7387	11/43	1/45	—
7388	11/43	1/45	90271
7389	11/43	2/45	—
7390	11/43	2/45	90272
7391	11/43	1/45	90032
7392	11/43	1/45	90273
7393	11/43	2/45	90274
7394	11/43	2/45	90275
7395	11/43	1/45	90276
7396	11/43	2/45	—
7397	11/43	2/45	90033
7398	11/43	12/44	90277
7399	11/43	9/44(b)	90278
7400	11/43	9/44(b)	—
7401	12/43	9/44(b)	90279
7402	12/43	11/44	90280
7403	12/43	9/44(b)	—
7404	12/43	9/44(b)	90281
7405	12/43	11/44	—
7406	12/43	1/45	90282
7407	12/43	11/44	90283
7408	12/43	9/44(b)	90284
7409	12/43	9/44(b)	—
7410	12/43	1/45	90034
7411	12/43	12/44	90285
7412	12/43	9/44(b)	90035
7413	12/43	9/44(b)	90286
7414	12/43	9/44(b)	90287
7415	12/43	9/44(b)	90288
7416	12/43	9/44(b)	90289
7417	1/44	12/44	—
7418	1/44	9/44(b)	90290
7419	1/44	9/44(b)	90291
7420	1/44	9/44(b)	90036
7421	1/44	9/44(b)	90292
7450	12/43	9/44	—
7451	12/43	9/44(b)	90595
7452	12/43	12/44	90596
7453	12/43	9/44(b)	90597
7454	12/43	9/44(b)	90598
7455	12/43	9/44(b)	90599
7456	12/43	9/44(b)	90600
7457	12/43	9/44(b)	90601
7458	12/43	9/44(b)	90602
7459	12/43	9/44(b)	90603
7460	12/43	9/44(b)	90604
7461	12/43	9/44(b)	90605
7462	12/43	12/44	90606
7463	12/43	11/44	90607
7464	12/43	12/44	90608
7465	1/44	9/44(b)	90609
7466	1/44	11/44	90610
7467	1/44	11/44	90611
7468	1/44	12/44	90612
7469	1/44	11/44	90613
7470	1/44	12/44	90614
7471	1/44	11/44	90615

(a) Unless otherwise indicated, the engines were withdrawn from Operating Stock on the dates shown, then overhauled by the L.N.E.R. prior to being sent overseas.

(b) Transferred to G.W.R.

(c) Transferred to S.R.

Summary of O7 Class

Second B.R. No.	First B.R. No.	L.N.E.R. No.	W.D. No.	Maker	Works No.	Built	On loan (a)	With-drawn
90000 10/50	63000 6/48	3000 3/47	77009 (c)	N.B. Loco. Co.	24980	2/1943	7/46	6/65
90001 4/49	63001 4/48	3001 2/47	77002	,,	24973	2/1943	3/46	4/66
90002 6/50	63002 5/48	3002 3/47	77021 (c)	,,	24992	3/1943	7/46	4/66
90003 12/49	63003 10/48	3003 2/47	77300	,,	24990	3/1943	3/46	6/64
90004 3/49	(63004)	3004 2/47	77033	,,	25004	4/1943	3/46	12/63
90005 4/49	63005 6/48	3005 2/47	77046	,,	25017	5/1943	1/47 (b)	4/65
90006 5/49	(63006)	3006 2/47	77316	,,	25181	5/1943	3/46	9/63
90007 9/49	63007 10/48	3007 2/47	77318	,,	25183	5/1943	3/46	7/65
90008 3/49	63008 1/49	3008 3/47	77322	,,	25192	6/1943	4/46	4/67
90009 10/50	63009 3/48	3009 2/47	77336	,,	25204	7/1943	3/46	9/67
90010 7/49	63010 5/48	3010 4/47	77339	,,	25207	7/1943	3/46	2/65
90011 5/51	63011 6/48	3011 2/47	77343	,,	25213	8/1943	3/46	6/66
90012 3/50	63012 4/48	3012 2/47	77211	,,	25082	9/1943	3/46	2/64
90013 4/49	63013 5/48	3013 2/47	77213	,,	25084	9/1943	12/45	4/66
90014 12/50	(63014)	3014 2/47	77220	,,	25091	9/1943	12/45	4/67
90015 1/50	63015 7/48	3015 2/47	77354	,,	25224	9/1943	12/45	5/63
90016 9/50	63016 4/48	3016 2/47	77357	,,	25222	9/1943	12/45	6/67
90017 6/51	63017 9/48	3017 2/47	77360	,,	25227	9/1943	3/46	9/63
90018 4/51	63018 4/48	3018 2/47	77363	,,	25231	9/1943	3/46	4/66
90019 2/50	63019 4/48	3019 2/47	77367	,,	25238	9/1943	12/45	12/63
90020 9/50	63020 12/48	3020 2/47	77223	,,	25094	10/1943	5/46	4/67
90021 6/49	(63021)	3021 3/47	77233	,,	25104	10/1943	12/45	11/62
90022 8/50	(63022)	3022 3/47	77236	,,	25107	10/1943	12/45	10/62
90023 11/50	63023 8/48	3023 2/47	77369	,,	25240	10/1943	5/46	9/62
90024 7/50	63024 12/48	3024 2/47	77370	,,	25241	10/1943	3/46	2/66
90025 10/49	(63025)	3025 3/47	77373	,,	25244	10/1943	12/45	8/65
90026 6/49	63026 7/48	3026 3/47	77382	,,	25255	10/1943	3/46	12/63
90027 6/50	(63027)	3027 2/47	77243	,,	25114	11/1943	12/45	5/63
90028 4/49	63028 4/48	3028 2/47	77250	,,	25121	11/1943	3/46	12/62
90029 5/50	63029 9/48	3029 2/47	77251	,,	25122	11/1943	3/46	7/65
90030 9/50	63030 8/48	3030 2/47	77254	,,	25125	11/1943	11/46	4/67
90031 7/50	(63031)	3031 3/47	77385	,,	25257	11/1943	7/46	5/63
90032 3/49	(63032)	3032 2/47	77391	,,	25261	11/1943	1/47 (b)	2/66
90033 10/50	63033 8/48	3033 3/47	77397	,,	25267	11/1943	3/46	5/63
90034 9/49	63034 5/48	3034 3/47	77410 (c)	,,	25281	12/1943	7/46	9/62
90035 2/51	63035 8/48	3035 2/47	77412	,,	25283	12/1943	3/46	2/66
90036 10/49	(63036)	3036 3/47	77420	,,	25290	1/1944	5/46	12/65
90037 10/50	63037 5/48	3037 2/47	77422	,,	25292	1/1944	1/47 (b)	4/66
90038 7/50	63038 7/48	3038 2/47	77423	,,	25293	1/1944	3/46	8/65
90039 10/49	(63039)	3039 3/47	77427	,,	25155	1/1944	3/46	9/66
90040 7/50	(63040)	3040 4/47	77430	,,	25157	1/1944	1/46	7/65
90041 4/49	63041 12/48	3041 2/47	77435	,,	25162	2/1944	3/46	12/66
90042 10/50	63042 10/48	3042 2/47	77437	,,	25295	2/1944	1/46	1/65
90043 3/51	63043 7/48	3043 2/47	77448	,,	25306	3/1944	1/46	12/65
90044 6/49	(63044)	3044 2/47	70800	,,	25308	3/1944	12/45	12/66
90045 11/50	63045 6/48	3045 2/47	70804	,,	25312	3/1944	3/46	10/65
90046 7/49	(63046)	3046 4/47	70810	,,	25318	3/1944	1/46	3/63
90047 8/50	63047 7/48	3047 2/47	70813	,,	24891	3/1944	12/45	6/67
90048 10/50	63048 5/48	3048 2/47	70815	,,	24893	3/1944	12/45	5/63
90049 12/49	(63049)	3049 2/47	70816	,,	24894	4/1944	12/45	9/63
90050 5/50	63050 6/48	3050 2/47	70818	,,	24896	4/1944	11/45	5/63
90051 4/49	63051 4/48	3051 2/47	70821	,,	25163	4/1944	12/45	10/65
90052 4/50	63052 5/48	3052 2/47	70822	,,	25164	4/1944	1/46	3/64
90053 5/49	63053 6/48	3053 2/47	70823	,,	25165	4/1944	11/45	7/65
90054 5/49	(63054)	3054 2/47	70824	,,	25166	4/1944	11/45	1/67

Fig. 110 Class P1 No. 2393 at New England shed, about 1926.

Fitted with ordinary superheater and single anti-vacuum valve behind chimney, booster fitted, Westinghouse pump on side of boiler for booster clutch control, two sight-feed lubricator pipes alongside boiler to cylinders (with further two on left-hand side, cf. fig. 111).

Fig. 111 Class P1 No. 2394, 1926.

Fitted with "E" type superheater and twin anti-vacuum valves behind chimney, booster fitted, booster throttle at side of smokebox in steam pipe for booster, substantial footsteps at front of tender and none below cab.

Fig. 112 Class P1 No. 2394 at Doncaster shed, May 1932.

"E" type superheater replaced by ordinary type, reversing rod with a set in it above the trailing coupled wheel (cf. fig. 110), leading sanders changed from steam operation to gravity feed with rodding alongside firebox (cf. fig. 110).

Fig. 113 Class P1 No. 2394, 1926.

Smokebox showing "E" type superheater, with large number of elements. Note also vacuum ejector exhaust pipe leading to cowl of chimney, blower pipe connected to blastpipe top, three main steam pipes leading to steam chests with additional steam pipe for booster, exhaust steam pipe from the middle steam chest leading to side of blastpipe (connection from booster out of sight behind), tall blastpipe top, front plate with asbestos door sealing ring.

Fig. 114 Class P1 No. 2394, 1926.

View of booster below cab showing cylinder covers with drain cocks below, inlet steam (left-hand) and exhaust steam (right-hand) pipes to a central manifold, ball and socket flexible joints in steam pipes, three control pipes on the right which respectively provided air from the reverse lever pilot valve to the clutch mechanism to mesh the gears, air from the clutch (when fully engaged) to open the booster throttle at the left-hand side of the smokebox (fig. 111) and air to open the cylinder cocks.

Fig. 115 Class P1 No. 2393 at New England shed, June 1939.
Booster removed, footsteps provided below cab, cab sides built up and longer vertical handrail fitted (cf. fig. 111).

Fig. 116 Class P1 No. 2393 at Doncaster Works, September 1945 after withdrawal.
Diagram 94HP boiler (with round dome).

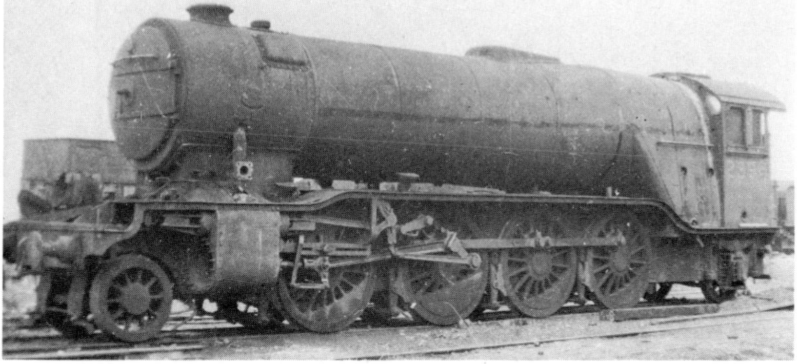

Fig. 117 Class P1 No. 2394 at Doncaster Works, September 1945 after withdrawal.
Diagram 94A boiler (with steam collector dome).

Fig. 118 Class P1 No. 2394 on down class A empty wagon train approaching Potters Bar, February 1926.

Fig. 119 Class P1 No. 2393 on up 100-wagon coal train approaching Potters Bar, probably 1927.

Hole in fall plate below smokebox for access to 2 to 1 gear motion levers.

Fig. 120 Class P1 No. 2394 on up coal train approaching Hadley North tunnel, about 1937.

Hinged cover for the 2 to 1 lever access aperture.

Fig. 121

Class P2 No. 2001 under construction, March 1934.

Alfol corrugated aluminium insulating foil placed over boiler and cylinders.

Fig. 122

Class P2 No. 2001 under construction, March 1934.

Boiler clothing plates and cab added, coupled wheels in position, Spencer double case buffers.

Fig. 123 Class P2 No. 2001 completed, May 1934.

Smokebox door open showing Kylchap cowls, Crosby tri-note whistle.

Fig. 124 Class P2 No. 2001 completed, May 1934.

Layout of cab showing large reversing hand wheel on left-hand side, hinged heat shield in front of firehole door.

Fig. 125 Class P2 No. 2001 *Cock o' the North* at Doncaster Works, May 1934.

Footsteps at front.

Second B.R. No.		*First B.R. No.*		*L.N.E.R. No.*		*W.D. No.*	*Maker*	*Works No.*	*Built*	*On loan* (a)	*With-drawn*
90055	6/51	63055	3/48	3055	2/47	70826	N.B. Loco. Co.	25168	5/1944	12/45	3/65
90056	11/49	(63056)		3056	2/47	70827	,,	25169	5/1944	12/45	5/67
90057	9/50	63057	3/48	3057	3/47	70828	,,	25170	5/1944	11/45	6/67
90058	2/50	(63058)		3058	2/47	70830	,,	24900	5/1944	1/46	12/63
90059	9/50	(63059)		3059	2/47	70831	,,	24901	5/1944	11/45	4/65
90060	11/50	(63060)		3060	2/47	70832	,,	24902	5/1944	12/45	6/62
90061	1/50	63061	7/48	3061	2/47	70837	,,	24907	5/1944	12/45	6/67
90062	10/50	63062	6/48	3062	2/47	70840	,,	24910	5/1944	12/45	1/60
90063	3/50	63063	9/48	3063	2/47	70841	,,	24911	5/1944	12/45	4/66
90064	1/51	63064	4/48	3064	3/47	70842	,,	24914	5/1944	12/45	1/64
90065	6/50	63065	8/48	3065	2/47	70844	,,	24917	6/1944	1/46	3/64
90066	7/51	63066	11/48	3066	2/47	70846	,,	24919	6/1944	1/47 (b)	5/63
90067	7/49	63067	5/48	3067	2/47	70847	,,	24920	6/1944	12/45	10/64
90068	11/50	63068	7/48	3068	2/47	70848	,,	24921	6/1944	11/45	7/66
90069	9/50	(63069)		3069	2/47	70854	,,	24915	6/1944	1/46	1/66
90070	8/50	63070	4/48	3070	2/47	77265	,,	25136	6/1944	12/45	2/65
90071	11/49	63071	5/48	3071	2/47	70852	,,	24924	6/1944 (d)	1/46	4/67
90072	7/50	63072	5/48	3072	2/47	70858	,,	24928	7/1944	5/46	12/65
90073	10/49	63073	6/48	3073	2/47	70870	,,	25412	8/1944	5/46	2/66
90074	9/49	63074	4/48	3074	3/47	70872	,,	24940	8/1944	12/45	9/67
90075	2/50	63075	11/48	3075	2/47	77272	,,	25143	7/1944 (d)	12/45	4/66
90076	7/50	63076	7/48	3076	2/47	77276	,,	25147	8/1944	11/45	9/67
90077	6/50	63077	7/48	3077	2/47	77277	,,	25148	8/1944	12/45	5/63
90078	9/50	63078	8/48	3078	2/47	77279	,,	25150	8/1944	11/45	11/66
90079	10/50	63079	6/48	3079	2/47	77281	,,	24952	8/1944	11/45	1/64
90080	10/49	(63080)		3080	3/47	77284	,,	24955	8/1944	3/46	2/66
90081	1/50	63081	4/48	3081	2/47	77290	,,	24961	8/1944	12/45	6/67
90082	11/50	63082	4/48	3082	3/47	77298	,,	24969	9/1944	11/45	7/66
90083	5/49	63083	7/48	3083	2/47	78513	,,	24950	9/1944	12/45	12/59
90084	3/51	63084	9/48	3084	2/47	78515	,,	25414	9/1944	12/45	6/65
90085	2/49	(63085)		3085	2/47	78516	,,	25415	9/1944	8/46	5/65
90086	8/49	(63086)		3086	2/47	78520	,,	25418	9/1944	1/46	8/63
90087	12/50	63087	9/48	3087	2/47	78562	,,	25323	9/1944	12/45	10/62
90088	8/50	(63088)		3088	3/47	78565	,,	25326	9/1944	12/45	7/65
90089	5/49	63089	4/48	3089	2/47	78527	,,	25426	9/1944	12/45	1/67
90090	10/50	(63090)		3090	2/47	78528	,,	25427	10/1944	12/45	5/63
90091	10/50	(63091)		3091	3/47	78570	,,	25331	10/1944	12/45	6/67
90092	10/50	63092	4/48	3092	2/47	78577	,,	25338	10/1944	12/45	10/65
90093	12/50	63093	7/48	3093	2/47	78582	,,	25343	11/1944	5/46	8/62
90094	5/50	63094	6/48	3094	2/47	78584	,,	25345	11/1944	12/45	6/67
90095	10/49	(63095)		3095	2/47	78591	,,	25352	11/1944	12/45	6/63
90096	12/51	63096	11/48	3096	2/47	78603	,,	25364	12/1944	10/46	9/65
90097	3/49	63097	6/48	3097	2/47	78608	,,	25369	12/1944	1/46	8/63
90098	7/49	(63098)		3098	2/47	78534	,,	25389	1/1945	11/45	11/64
90099	4/49	63099	3/48	3099	2/47	78540	,,	25395	2/1945	3/46	6/67
90100	12/51	63100	11/48	3100	4/47	78550	,,	25405	3/1945	3/46	1/64
90422	3/50	63101	9/48	3101	3/47	77083	Vulcan Foundry	4899	8/1943	5/46	6/65
90423	4/51	63102	7/48	3102	3/47	77091	,,	4907	8/1943	3/46	12/65
90424	11/49	63103	8/48	3103	2/47	77093	,,	4909	8/1943	1/47 (b)	12/63
90425	11/49	63104	7/48	3104	3/47	77100	,,	4916	9/1943	10/46	12/62
90426	11/50	63105	6/48	3105	4/47	77110	,,	4926	10/1943	3/46	3/65
90427	12/50	63106	10/48	3106	3/47	77112	,,	4928	10/1943	1/47 (b)	6/67
90428	10/50	63107	5/48	3107	3/47	77113	,,	4929	10/1943	3/46	1/66
90429	8/50	63108	7/48	3108	4/47	77131	,,	4947	11/1943	4/46	4/67
90430	6/51	63109	10/48	3109	2/47	77133	,,	4949	11/1943	2/47 (b)	9/67

Second B.R. No.		*First B.R. No.*		*L.N.E.R. No.*		*W.D. No.*	*Maker*	*Works No.*	*Built*	*On loan* (a)	*With-drawn*
90431	6/49	63110	6/48	3110	2/47	77136	Vulcan Foundry	4952	11/1943	12/45	12/62
90432	2/49	(63111)		3111	3/47	77146	,,	4962	12/1943	11/45	10/65
90433	10/50	(63112)		3112	2/47	77473	,,	4989	1/1944	1/46	4/64
90434	8/50	(63113)		3113	3/47	77474	,,	4990	1/1944	3/46	6/67
90435	1/50	63114	5/48	3114	3/47	77486	,,	5002	2/1944	1/46	9/63
90436	7/50	(63115)		3115	3/47	77487	,,	5003	2/1944	1/46	6/62
90437	10/49	63116	6/48	3116	3/47	77491	,,	5007	2/1944	1/46	4/66
90438	6/49	(63117)		3117	4/47	77493	,,	5009	2/1944	1/47 (b)	10/65
90439	1/51	63118	8/48	3118	3/47	77496	,,	5012	3/1944	5/46	11/65
90440	3/49	(63119)		3119	3/47	77498	,,	5014	3/1944	12/45	8/63
90441	6/49	63120	4/48	3120	2/47	77501	,,	5017	3/1944	12/45	10/66
90442	12/50	(63121)		3121	3/47	77502	,,	5018	3/1944	12/45	4/65
90443	2/51	63122	4/48	3122	4/47	77504	,,	5020	3/1944	11/45	6/65
90444	6/50	63123	3/48	3123	2/47	77505	,,	5021	3/1944	12/45	1/67
90445	8/50	(63124)		3124	3/47	77506	,,	5022	3/1944	12/45	7/66
90446	9/49	63125	4/48	3125	2/47	77507	,,	5023	3/1944	11/45	11/63
90447	12/49	63126	9/48	3126	2/47	78625	,,	5026	3/1944	12/45	11/63
90448	1/51	63127	6/48	3127	3/47	78627	,,	5028	3/1944	1/46	12/65
90449	4/49	(63128)		3128	3/47	78628	,,	5029	3/1944	11/45	1/66 (e)
90450	11/49	(63129)		3129	4/47	78630	,,	5031	3/1944	12/45	6/67
90451	5/50	63130	4/48	3130	3/47	78633	,,	5034	4/1944	12/45	12/66
90452	4/49	(63131)		3131	3/47	78634	,,	5035	4/1944	12/45	6/65
90453	3/49	(63132)		3132	3/47	78635	,,	5036	4/1944	12/45	10/63
90454	8/51	63133	10/48	3133	3/47	78639	,,	5040	4/1944	11/45	6/65
90455	11/49	(63134)		3134	2/47	78641	,,	5042	4/1944	1/46	9/62
90456	10/50	(63135)		3135	3/47	78642	,,	5043	4/1944	11/45	2/66
90457	5/50	(63136)		3136	3/47	78645	,,	5046	5/1944	11/45	1/66
90458	6/50	63137	8/48	3137	2/47	78646	,,	5047	5/1944	12/45	6/67
90459	5/50	(63138)		3138	4/47	78648	,,	5049	5/1944	11/45	6/67
90460	4/49	(63139)		3139	3/47	78649	,,	5050	5/1944	1/47 (b)	6/65
90461	3/49	63140	4/48	3140	2/47	78651	,,	5052	5/1944	11/45	9/63
90462	2/49	63141	6/48	3141	3/47	78653	,,	5054	5/1944	11/45	1/67
90463	9/50	63142	4/48	3142	4/47	78654	,,	5055	5/1944	12/45	11/63
90464	4/50	(63143)		3143	2/47	78655	,,	5056	5/1944	12/45	3/64
90465	6/50	63144	6/48	3144	2/47	78656	,,	5057	5/1944	1/46	1/67
90466	12/50	63145	6/48	3145	4/47	78661	,,	5062	5/1944	11/45	12/65
90467	9/50	(63146)		3146	3/47	78662	,,	5063	5/1944	12/45	11/63
90468	10/49	(63147)		3147	4/47	78663	,,	5064	6/1944	12/45	4/67
90469	10/49	(63148)		3148	4/47	78664	,,	5065	6/1944	12/45	11/64
90470	11/49	63149	5/48	3149	2/47	78665	,,	5066	6/1944	12/45	12/66
90471	4/49	(63150)		3150	3/47	78667	,,	5068	6/1944	1/47 (b)	4/66
90472	6/50	63151	5/48	3151	2/47	78668	,,	5069	6/1944	12/45	12/63
90473	12/49	63152	4/48	3152	3/47	78670	,,	5071	6/1944	12/45	9/62
90474	10/50	(63153)		3153	4/47	78673	,,	5074	6/1944	12/45	7/65
90475	6/49	(63154)		3154	3/47	78674	,,	5075	6/1944	12/45	8/63
90476	11/50	63155	6/48	3155	2/47	78676	,,	5077	6/1944	11/46	7/65
90477	4/49	(63156)		3156	3/47	78677 (c)	,,	5078	6/1944	10/46	3/66
90478	11/49	(63157)		3157	4/47	78679	,,	5080	6/1944	12/45	9/67
90479	5/49	(63158)		3158	4/47	78680	,,	5081	6/1944	11/45	9/66
90480	3/49	63159	4/48	3159	2/47	78686	,,	5087	7/1944	11/45	8/65
90481	6/49	(63160)		3160	3/47	78687	,,	5088	7/1944	1/46	10/66
90482	11/50	(63161)		3161	4/47	78690	,,	5091	7/1944	1/46	7/67
90483	2/51	63162	5/48	3162	3/47	78691	,,	5092	7/1944	12/45	3/64
90484	9/49	63163	4/48	3163	4/47	78692	,,	5093	7/1944	3/46	3/66
90485	11/50	63164	6/48	3164	2/47	78696	,,	5097	8/1944	12/45	8/64

Summary of O7 Class (continued)

Second B.R. No.	First B.R. No.	L.N.E.R. No.	W.D. No.	Maker	Works No.	Built	On loan (a)	With-drawn
90486 9/51	63165 7/48	3165 3/47	78697	Vulcan Foundry	5098	8/1944	1/46	4/65
90487 12/50	63166 6/48	3166 3/47	78698	,,	5099	8/1944	1/46	8/63
90488 12/50	63167 4/48	3167 4/47	78699	,,	5110	8/1944	11/45	12/64
90489 2/50	63168 4/48	3168 2/47	78702	,,	5103	8/1944	12/45	4/67
90490 5/50	63169 4/48	3169 2/47	78703	,,	5104	8/1944	12/45	2/64
90491 9/49	63170 6/48	3170 2/47	78706	,,	5107	8/1944	3/46	9/65
90492 11/49	(63171)	3171 2/47	78707	,,	5108	8/1944	12/45	10/65
90493 1/50	(63172)	3172 2/47	78708	,,	5109	8/1944	12/45	2/66
90494 8/50	63173 3/48	3173 3/47	78709	,,	5110	8/1944	12/45	9/62
90495 7/50	63174 4/48	3174 2/47	78710	,,	5111	8/1944	11/45	12/62
90496 10/49	(63175)	3175 2/47	78711	,,	5112	8/1944	12/45	4/65
90497 9/50	63176 6/48	3176 2/47	78712	,,	5113	8/1944	11/45	3/63
90498 6/49	63177 4/48	3177 2/47	78713	,,	5114	9/1944	3/46	2/66
90499 7/50	63178 3/48	3178 2/47	78716	,,	5117	9/1944	11/45	12/63
90500 8/49	63179 3/48	3179 2/47	78718	,,	5119	9/1944	11/45	8/63
90501 9/49	(63180)	3180 2/47	79177	,,	5120	9/1944	12/45	11/65
90502 3/49	(63181)	3181 3/47	79180	,,	5123	9/1944	11/45	5/63
90503 11/50	63182 7/48	3182 2/47	79185	,,	5128	9/1944	11/45	1/67
90504 9/50	63183 5/48	3183 3/47	79187	,,	5130	9/1944	3/46	5/63
90505 11/49	(63184)	3184 2/47	79191	,,	5134	10/1944	12/45	6/62
90506 5/51	63185 11/48	3185 2/47	79192	,,	5135	10/1944	3/46	1/66
90507 9/50	(63186)	3186 2/47	79200	,,	5143	10/1944	1/46	6/63
90508 10/50	63187 1/49	3187 2/47	79211	,,	5154	11/1944	3/46	12/62
90509 9/50	63188 6/48	3188 3/47	79216	,,	5159	11/1944	3/46	8/65
90510 11/50	(63189)	3189 2/47	79236	,,	5179	12/1944	12/45	7/65
90511 2/50	63190 6/48	3190 2/47	79240	,,	5183	12/1944	1/46	6/64
90512 2/51	63191 6/48	3191 2/47	79241	,,	5184	12/1944	1/46	9/62
90513 9/50	63192 7/48	3192 3/47	79245	,,	5188	1/1945	4/46	7/62
90514 8/50	63193 5/48	3193 3/47	79247	,,	5190	1/1945	5/46	1/66
90515 10/49	63194 4/48	3194 2/47	79251	,,	5194	1/1945	12/45	11/65
90516 12/49	63195 6/48	3195 3/47	79253	,,	5196	1/1945	3/46	11/65
90517 10/50	63196 9/48	3196 2/47	79285	,,	5228	3/1945	12/45	5/66
90518 10/51	63197 4/48	3197 2/47	79288	,,	5231	3/1945	11/45	2/66
90519 2/51	63198 1/49	3198 2/47	79305	,,	5248	4/1945	5/46	9/64
90520 3/49	(63199)	3199 3/47	79308	,,	5251	5/1945	3/46	2/65

(a) Unless otherwise indicated, the engines were taken into Operating Stock on the dates shown, then transferred to Running Stock in 12/1946.

(b) Taken direct into Running Stock on the dates shown.

(c) W.D. Nos. 77009/21, 77410, 78677 also ran in Holland for a few months in 1945-46 as N.S. Nos. 4528, 4318/70, 4504, respectively.

(d) W.D. Nos. 70852, 77272 appeared in L.N.E.R. records as built 7/1944, 8/1944 respectively.

(e) No. 90449 was withdrawn in 6/1964, reinstated to stock in 9/1964 and finally withdrawn in 1/1966.

Summary of W.D. 2-8-0 Engines on Loan 1947

W.D. No.	*On loan from*	*B.R. No.*	*W.D. No.*	*On loan from*	*B.R. No.*
70802	8/47	90313	77087	9/47	90553
70807	9/47	90314	77088	10/47	90554
70817	2/47	90319	77089	2/47	90555
70834	6/47	90323	77095	2/47	90559
70839	8/47	90326	77096	9/47	90560
70850	10/47	90330	77104	3/47	90567
70871	3/47	90340	77107	9/47	90569
70877	7/47	90344	77111	10/47	90571
77003	2/47	90103	77118	5/47	90574
77004	3/47	90104	77119	9/47	90575
77006	3/47	90106	77120	3/47	90576
77008	10/47	90108	77121	3/47	90577
77010	2/47	90109	77124	4/47	90580
77013	10/47	90111	77127	8/47	90582
77016	3/47	90114	77128	3/47	90583
77017	3/47	90115	77129	3/47	90584
77018	3/47	90116	77135	10/47	90586
77019	9/47	90117	77138	3/47	90587
77020	11/47	90118	77144	10/47	90590
77022	2/47	90119	77147	6/47	90592
77023	10/47	90120	77149	3/47	90594
77024	7/48 (b)	90121	77152	11/47	90144
77031	3/47	90128	77155	8/47	90145
77032	9/47	90129	77157	11/47	90146
77034	3/47	90130	77162	4/48 (b)	90149
77035	8/47	90131	77163	11/47	90150
77036	3/47	90132	77164	3/47	90151
77037	9/47	90133	77166	11/47	90153
77039	9/47	90134	77167	3/47	90154
77041	8/47	90136	77169	3/47	90155
77042	2/47	90137	77170	5/47	90156
77043	3/47	90138	77173	11/47	90158
77047	6/47	90139	77174	3/47	90159
77050	2/47	90521	77175	2/47	90160
77051	4/47	90522	77176	11/47	90161
77055	6/47	90526	77178	9/47	90162
77057	5/47	90528	77181	9/47	90165
77061	1/47	90532	77182	11/47	90166
77063	3/47	90534	77185	3/47	90168
77066	8/47	90536	77186	7/47	90169
77067	3/47	90537	77187	3/47	90170
77068	11/47	90538	77195	4/47	90172
77070	2/47	90539	77198	9/47	90174
77071	9/47	90540	77199	4/47	90175
77073	9/47	90542	77201	1/47	90177
77075	3/47	90544	77204	3/47	90180
77076	8/47	90545	77206	3/47	90182
77078	3/47	90547	77207	1/47	90183
77080	5/48 (b)	90549	77208	7/47	90184
77081	6/47	90550	77209	9/47	90185
77085	4/47	90551	77215	10/47	90189

Summary of W.D. 2-8-0 Engines on Loan 1947 (continued)

W.D. No.	*On loan from*	*B.R. No.*	*W.D. No.*	*On loan from*	*B.R. No.*
77218	3/47	90190	77364	5/47	90259
77221	3/47	90191	77365	5/48 (b)	90260
77222	8/47	90192	77371	4/47	90262
77225	2/48 (b)	90193	77372	2/47	90263
77227	11/47	90195	77375	8/47	90265
77228	11/47	90196	77381	8/47	90269
77230	4/47	90198	77386	11/47	90270
77231	9/47	90199	77390	2/47	90272
77232	3/47	90200	77392	2/47	90273
77235	1/47	90202	77394	11/47	90275
77248	8/47	90208	77395	8/47	90276
77249	11/47	90209	77401	6/47	90279
77252	3/47	90210	77402	3/47	90280
77253	1/48 (b)	90211	77404	3/47	90281
77258	10/47	90215	77406	8/47	90282
77260	2/47	90217	77411	1/47	90285
77261	3/47	90218	77413	3/47	90286
77263	2/47	90346	77414	4/47	90287
77271	5/47	90348	77415	11/47	90288
77274	3/47	90349	77416	10/47	90289
77278	2/47	90350	77418	2/47	90290
77283	2/47	90352	77419	4/47	90291
77292	3/47	90358	77424	2/47	90293
77302	9/47	90219	77425	8/47	90294
77303	2/47	90220	77426	3/47	90295
77305	7/47	90221	77428	10/47	90296
77306	2/48 (b)	90222	77431	9/47	90298
77307	6/47	90223	77432	11/47	90299
77309	8/47	90224	77433	3/47	90300
77312	9/47	90227	77434	5/47	90301
77313	8/47	90228	77436	10/47	90302
77314	5/47	90229	77439	2/47	90303
77315	3/47	90230	77440	8/47	90304
77317	9/47	90231	77441	2/47	90305
77319	10/47	90232	77442	9/47	90306
77320	8/47	90233	77445	2/47	90309
77323	2/47	90235	77449	10/47	90311
77324	8/47	90326	77452	10/47	90596
77327	4/47	90239	77453	1/47	90597
77328	6/47	90240	77454	1/47	90598
77329	10/47	90241	77455	9/47	90599
77334	4/47	90244	77456	4/48 (b)	90600
77338	3/47	90246	77457	9/47	90601
77342	3/47	90248	77458	1/47	90602
77350	11/47	90250	77459	4/47	90603
77351	5/47	90251	77461	5/47	90605
77352	10/47	90252	77462	9/47	90606
77353	3/47	90253	77464	11/47	90608
77356	4/47	90255	77465	2/47	90609
77358	3/47	90256	77467	2/47	90611
77362	3/47	90258	77468	2/47	90612

Summary of W.D. 2-8-0 Engines on Loan 1947 (continued)

W.D. No.	*On loan from*	*B.R. No.*	*W.D. No.*	*On loan from*	*B.R. No.*
77469	3/47	90613	78616	7/47	90405
77470	3/47	90614	78637	7/47	90634
77476	9/47	90616	78643	10/47	90636
77480	6/47	90618	78650	10/47	90638
77484	1/47	90621	78682	9/47	90646
77488	7/47	90623	78683	9/47	90647
77492	2/47	90625	78684	10/47	90648
77494	3/47	90626	78700	11/47	90653
77497	2/47	90627	78715	10/47	90657
77499	10/47	90628	79178	10/47	90659
77503	10/47	90629	79181	6/47	90660
78514	9/47	90365	79182	3/47	90661
78525	5/47	90368	79184	8/47	90662
78526	10/47	90369	79186	8/47	90663
78532	9/47	90409	79194	10/47	90665
78537	3/47	90410	79198	6/47	90668
78538	10/47	90411	79202	7/47	90670
78553	8/47	90418	79204	9/47	90672
78559	3/47	90421	79206	7/47	90674
78561	4/47	90371	79208	5/47	90676
78564	3/47	90373	79209	8/47	90677
78568	5/47	90374	79220	2/47	90683
78572	5/47	90376	79227	3/47	90688
78575	4/47	90377	78229	3/47	90690
78578	8/47	90378	79239	8/47	90695
78585	9/47	90382	79242	3/47	90696
78587	6/47	90383	79243	8/47	90697
78588	8/47	90384	79259	4/47	90700
78592	6/47	90386	79263	7/47	90703
78594	3/47	90387	79264	4/47	90704
78598	10/47	90391	79265	9/47	90705
78599	8/47	90392	79271	10/47	90709
78600	7/47	90393	79276	10/47	90714
78601	2/47	90394	79280	10/47	90717
78609	5/47	90400	79306	9/47	90727
78610	2/47	90401	79310	9/47	90730
78614	9/47	90403	79312 (c)	11/47	90732

(a) Unless otherwise indicated, the engines were all taken into B.R. Running Stock, 12/1948.

(b) Nos. 77024/80, 77162, 77225/53, 77306/65, 77456, all allocated to the L.N.E.R., were taken into B.R. Operating Stock on the dates shown.

(c) Named *Vulcan*.

2-10-0 CLASS

There was also a 2-10-0 version of the ubiquitous "Austerity" 2-8-0, 150 being built in 1943-45. Again, the L.N.E.R. had use of some of these engines at that period. In 1948 twenty-five were bought by British Railways and put into service mainly on former L.M.S. lines in Scotland. A number of these particular engines had seen earlier service on the L.N.E.R. They were withdrawn in 1961-62.

MINISTRY OF SUPPLY AUSTERITY CLASS

RIDDLES 4ft. 8½in. ENGINES

Engines received 1943-44 on loan: W.D. 3650/61/7-71/3/5/6/9/80/1. Total 13. Transferred to L.M.S. 1944.

Engines received 1945 on loan: W.D. 73774-93. Total 20. Handed over to W.D. 1946.

The design of the "Austerity" 2-10-0 was developed from its 2-8-0 counterpart and many parts were interchangeable. 150 engines were built, in two batches, and their construction is summarised in the accompanying table.

The engines were intended for use overseas by British Army personnel but when the first batch appeared, between December 1943 and June 1944, there was no immediate requirement on active service for the majority of them (fig. 109). However, twenty were sent to the Middle East after they had been run-in by the L.N.E.R., though even in their case sixteen were put into store on arrival. Thirteen engines, as listed above, were loaned to the L.N.E.R. but all were transferred to the L.M.S. by May 1944. The disposition at June 1944 when the first batch was complete, was as follows: L.M.S. 79, Longmoor 1, Egypt 16, Syria 4. The seventy-nine engines on loan to the L.M.S. were subsequently sent to the Continent where they were later joined by twenty-four from the batch built in 1945. During 1946 the 2-10-0's in service on the Continent were purchased by the Netherlands State Railways, whilst those that had been in store in Egypt were transferred to Greece.

At home, Nos. 73774-93 from the second batch were loaned to the L.N.E.R. in 1945 but were handed over to the War Department towards the end of 1946. At nationalisation there were no 2-10-0's on the L.N.E.R. In December 1948 the British Transport Commission decided to purchase twenty-five 2-10-0's, including Nos. 73774-93, the transaction being back-dated to the previous October. The engines were all added to Running Stock at the end of December 1948, although the majority were at the time in store and not put into service until 1949-50. The engines operated from former L.M.S. sheds, mostly in Scotland, and survived until 1961-62.

W.D. Nos. (a)	*Maker*	*Order No.*	*Date ordered*	*Works Nos.*	*No. built*	*Date*
3650-3749	N.B. Loco. Co. (b)	L945	June 1943	25436-535 (c)	100	1943-44
3750-99	,, (b)	L948	March 1944	25596-645	50	1945

(a) Engines built after September 1944 had 70,000 added to these numbers.

(b) Hyde Park Works.

(c) Originally allocated 25321-420, afterwards changed to allow consecutive numbering of the 2-8-0 engines.

Standard W.D. Dimensions

Cylinders (2 outside)	19″×28″
Motion	Walschaerts with 10″ piston valves
Boiler:	
Max. diam. outside	5′ 9⅞″
Barrel length	16′ 1⅜″ (a)
Firebox length outside	10′ 10¼″
Pitch	9′ 3″
Diagram No.	— (b)
Heating surface:	
Firebox	192 sq. ft.
Tubes (152×1⅞″)	1170 sq. ft.
Flues (28×5¼″)	589 sq. ft.
Total evaporative	1951 sq. ft.
Superheater (28)	423 sq. ft.
Total	2374 sq. ft.
Grate area	40 sq. ft.
Boiler pressure	225 lb./sq. in.
Leading wheels	2′ 9″
Coupled wheels	4′ 8½″
Tender wheels	3′ 2″
Tractive effort (85%)	34,215 lb.
Length over buffers	67′ 6¼″
Wheelbase:	
Engine	8′ 8″+5′ 3″+5′ 3″ +5′ 3″+5′ 3″ =29′ 8″
Tender	5′ 3″+5′ 3″+5′ 3″ =15′ 9″
Total	57′ 1″
Weight (full):	
Engine	78T 6C
Tender	55T 10C
Total	133T 16C
Adhesive	67T 3C
Max. axle load	13T 9C
Water capacity	5,000 gallons
Coal capacity	9T 0C

(a) The engine diagram quoted the distance between tubeplates (15′ 8″). See under Details.

(b) B.R. standard class BR11 from July 1950.

Numbering

The engines on loan to the L.N.E.R. in 1943-44 had 70,000 added to their original four-figure numbers after their transfer to W.D. ownership, to avoid possible confusion with other engines. Those loaned to the L.N.E.R. in 1945-46 already had their five-figure numbers when received.

Details

The boiler barrel was constructed of three parallel rings: the rear ring was 5ft. 9⅞in. outside diameter, the middle ring 5ft. 8½in. and the front ring 5ft. 7⅛in. The smokebox tubeplate was flanged all round and recessed into the front ring of the barrel. The distance between the tubeplates was 15ft. 8in. The dome for the regulator valve was located on the middle ring and the safety valves on the rear ring.

The superheater was the Melesco type with long loop elements and ball-jointed ends secured to the header by the "Through" bolt method. At the rear the ends were 1ft. 11¾in. from the tubeplate.

As with the "Austerity" 2-8-0 class, the diameter of the smokebox door was 5ft. 7⅞in. whilst that over the boiler clothing plate at the front was 6ft. 0⅝in. (However the clothing plate tapered over the rear ring of the barrel and was 6ft. 2½in. outside diameter over the front of the firebox). The chimney was the same pattern, 9⅛in. high, and the height to the top above rail level was 12ft. 10in. on account of the higher boiler pitch. The dome cover was noticeably flattened in appearance and the height to the top was 12ft. 11in.

The overall length of the firebox casing was 10ft. 10¼in. whilst at the foundation ring it was only 7ft. 3½in., the difference being accounted for by the long combustion chamber at the front end. The inner firebox was of all-welded steel construction, being also welded to the outer casing at the firehole door ring. The firegrate was 6ft. 7½in. wide and 6ft. 0¾in. long, providing an area of 40 sq. ft. The grate itself was the Hulson rocking type, with five rocking sections on each side of the firebox, similar to the type fitted to the U.S. Army class S160 2-8-0's. The brick arch was supported on three 3in. diameter longitudinal tubes, which ran from the backplate to the throat plate. The hopper ashpan had two doors, fore and aft of the trailing axle; no dampers were provided.

The arrangement of cylinders, valve motion and reversing gear was similar to that employed in the "Austerity" 2-8-0 class. The drive was on to the middle pair of coupled wheels, which were flangeless to help in negotiating curves. The springs on the coupled wheels comprised seven plates, 5in. wide by ⅝in. thickness, at 3ft. 6in. centres, whilst those for the pony truck wheels had ten plates, 4in. wide by ½in. thickness, at 2ft. 9in. centres. The total sideplay of the pony truck was 10in. Whilst operating on the L.N.E.R., the engines were not allowed to use cross-over roads between station platforms nor use sidings alongside loading banks, on account of their throw-over on curves. As with the 2-8-0 "Austerities", steam sanding for forward running was provided in front of the leading and driving coupled wheels and for reverse running behind the driving coupled wheels.

Brakes

Steam brakes were provided for engine and tender with vacuum and Westinghouse for train braking. The fitting and arrangement were as employed in the "Austerity" 2-8-0 engines (see p. 125). There were no brake blocks applied to the trailing coupled wheels.

Tenders

The 8-wheel tenders were the same type as attached to the "Austerity" 2-8-0 engines and described under class O7. Exchanges between the two classes did take place; for example No. 90763's original tender was transferred to No. 90128 in January 1954 and No. 90767's original tender was transferred to No. 90004 in December 1955.

Liveries

The first batch of engines on loan to the L.N.E.R. were painted in khaki-brown livery with 8in.-high cab side numerals (6in. in the case of No. 3650), and with 2in.-high letters "W D" on the tender and a broad arrow motif. The second batch of engines were painted in khaki-green livery, with 8in.-high cab side numerals and 12in.-high letters on the tender, and a 10in. broad arrow motif.

Names

Several engines at one time or another carried either official or unofficial names, including two which had previously been on loan to the L.N.E.R.: Nos. 73669 *Major Constant Mertens* and 73681 *Flying Dutchman*. It is worth noting that No. 73755 was named *Longmoor,* in recognition of it being 'THE 1000TH BRITISH BUILT FREIGHT LOCOMOTIVE FERRIED TO EUROPE SINCE "D" DAY', and the last two engines built, Nos. 73798/9, were both named *North British*.

British Railways

The twenty engines loaned to the L.N.E.R. in 1945-46 were afterwards purchased by British Railways and put into Running Stock in 1949-50. Together with the five other engines purchased at the same time, these 2-10-0's were renumbered 90750-74 in order of their former W.D. numbers. Renumbering was not completed until September 1952 when No. 73788, which had spent some time at Rugby Testing Station, became 90764.

Allocation and Work

Between December 1943 and March 1944 fifty-one "Austerity" 2-10-0's, Nos. 3650-61/7-3705, were delivered new to Eastfield shed where they were run-in on main line goods workings, principally Glasgow – Edinburgh (via Polmont and via Bathgate). Afterwards they were retained for a while, until alternative employment was found elsewhere, in contrast to the "Austerity" 2-8-0's which generally left Eastfield a week or so after being received from the makers. Two photographs of these engines appeared in the "L.N.E.R. Magazine". One showed No. 3671 in the newly-opened light tunnel at Thornton shed, whilst the other depicted No. 3690 passing Saughton Junction on a goods train, stated to be the 2-30 p.m. Niddrie – Thornton. There is a record in a Haymarket fireman's diary of No. 3680 working the 2-55 p.m. Meadows – Heaton goods train. During the period they worked on the L.N.E.R., these engines were included in Operating Stock.

By the middle of March 1944 thirty 2-10-0's had been despatched as follows: Longmoor (No. 3651), Middle East (Nos. 3652-60/72/4/7/8/82-5), Stratford (Nos. 3661/7), New England (Nos. 3668-71/3/5/6/9/80/1), leaving No. 3650 at Eastfield. Whilst at New England the 2-10-0's worked on the G.N. main line to Ferme Park and all were recorded in the London area.

After experience with Nos. 3662-6, received direct from the makers, the L.M.S. then agreed to accept the remaining engines, on loan until they were required to be sent overseas. Between 26th March and 2nd April Nos. 3686-3705 were transferred to the L.M.S. from Eastfield shed, and all subsequent new engines were delivered direct to the L.M.S. from the makers. On 28th March the two Stratford engines were similarly transferred to the L.M.S. followed the next day be eight out of the ten New England engines. This left No. 3650 still at Eastfield, ultimately transferred on 7th April, and Nos. 3669/70 under repair at New England, eventually transferred on 3rd May and 25th April respectively. The engines on loan to the L.M.S. were subsequently sent to the Continent and only No. 73651 remained in the United Kingdom, at Longmoor.

The second batch of 2-10-0's, Nos. 73750-99, appeared between March and September 1945 and were all delivered initially to Eastfield shed. However unlike the first batch, these later engines were excluded from L.N.E.R. statistical returns and were not taken into Operating Stock whilst being run-in. The first twenty-four were sent to the Continent, by which time the ending of hostilities in Europe had reduced the need for the class on active service. The remaining engines accordingly stayed in the United Kingdom, Nos. 73774-93 being loaned to the L.N.E.R. whilst the final six were put into store at Longmoor.

The engines loaned to the L.N.E.R. were allocated to March shed, where they were used in particular on goods trains to Temple Mills. They appeared elsewhere too on the G.E. Section, for example during September 1945 Nos. 73774/6/7/9/81 were noted at Ipswich. Towards the end of 1946 they were sent to Longmoor via Feltham, for storage. On 27th September 1946, for example, Nos. 73782/9 were observed being towed away dead by class J39 No. 4963 of Stratford. At Longmoor they joined Nos. 73794/5/6 in store, having been replaced by repatriated "Austerity" 2-8-0's which were more versatile. The three other 2-10-0's that had been in store at Longmoor were put into service in 1946: No. 73797 at Longmoor, Nos. 73798/9 at Cairnryan. The latter two were loaned to the L.M.S. in March 1947.

In September 1947 the Southern Railway commenced overhauling the twenty-three engines stored at Longmoor, Nos. 73774-96, most of which were in a decrepit condition. Eastleigh Works dealt with the first batch, Nos. 73774/6/81/4/94/5, which were afterwards generally run-in on goods trains to Portsmouth and Salisbury though they were not officially taken on loan. Afterwards they were stored at sheds on the Southern Region of British Railways, in a serviceable condition. Later, Nos. 73774/6 were temporarily restored to traffic to allow them to take part in the 1948 Locomotive Interchange Trials, so that once more the class made a brief appearance on the G.N. main line south of Peterborough.

In the second half of 1948 Ashford Works dealt with the second batch from Longmoor, Nos. 73777/9/83/5/6/92, with the intention of storing them afterwards in a serviceable condition. At the end of 1948 the British Transport Commission decided to purchase twenty-five "Austerity" 2-10-0's, including Nos. 73798/9 which were already in service on loan to the Scottish Region. The serviceable engines were brought out of store on the Southern Region towards the end of January 1949 and despatched to the Scottish Region. No. 73788 however was noted in Crewe Works in March 1949 and afterwards spent some time at Rugby Testing Station, to test all the brake rollers simultaneously, so did not enter traffic effectively in the Scottish Region until March 1951.

The remaining nine engines awaiting overhaul on the Southern Region at the time of their purchase were put into service in the Scottish Region gradually, between June 1949 and July 1950, after repairs at Eastleigh (Nos. 90751/8/63/7/9/72), Ashford (Nos. 90754/6) and Brighton (No. 90766).

Whilst in the Scottish Region, the 2-10-0's operated from former L.M.S. sheds, Kingmoor, Carstairs, Hamilton, Motherwell and Grangemouth. In May 1952 No. 90763 (ex-73787) was transferred on loan to Doncaster, presumably in connection with the introduction of the new B.R. standard class 9F 2-10-0 class. No. 90763 was exchanged for No. 90757 (ex-73781) at the beginning of August 1952. No. 90757 was shortly afterwards transferred to the Western Region at Banbury, then to the Southern Region at Ashford, before returning to Scotland at the end of October 1952.

Preservation

After the Longmoor Military Railway closed down on 31st October 1969, No. AD600 *Gordon* was retained in working order on loan from the Ministry of Defence to the Severn Valley Railway. As No. 3651 (later 73651, then 600) this engine spent practically its entire working life at Longmoor, being the only one of the 1943-44 batch that never went overseas.

In 1946 the Netherlands State Railways acquired 103 2-10-0's, which they renumbered 5001-5103 in order of their former W.D. numbers. These were all withdrawn in 1948-52 as a result of the rapid electrification of the system. One member of the class, No. 5085 withdrawn in May 1951, is preserved at Utrecht as W.D. No. 73755 *Longmoor.*

In 1946 the Hellenic State Railways acquired the sixteen 2-10-0's which had been stored in Egypt. These became Nos. 951-66 in order of the former W.D. numbers. Nos. 951/60 (Ex-W.D. Nos. 3652/72) were purchased after their withdrawal by the Mid Hants Railway and shipped to England in 1981.

Engine Diagram
Not issued by L.N.E.R.

Summary of W.D. 2-10-0 Engines on Loan 1943-46

W.D. No.	*On loan From*	*On loan To (a)*	*B.R. No.*
3650	12/43	4/44 (b)	—
3661	12/43	3/44 (b)	—
3667	2/44	3/44 (b)	—
3668	2/44	3/44 (b)	—
3669	3/44	5/44 (b)	—
3670	2/44	4/44 (b)	—
3671	3/44	3/44 (b)	—
3673	2/44	3/44 (b)	—
3675	2/44	3/44 (b)	—
3676	2/44	3/44 (b)	—
3679	2/44	3/44 (b)	—
3680	3/44	3/44 (b)	—
3681	2/44	3/44 (b)	—
73774	6/45	9/46	90750
73775	6/45	10/46	90751
73776	6/45	9/46	90752
73777	6/45	10/46	90753
73778	6/45	10/46	90754
73779	6/45	10/46	90755
73780	6/45	9/46	90756
73781	6/45	10/46	90757
73782	6/45	9/46	90758
73783	6/45	11/46	90759
73784	6/45	9/46	90760
73785	7/45	11/46	90761
73786	7/45	10/46	90762
73787	7/45	10/46	90763
73788	7/45	10/46	90764
73789	7/45	9/46	90765
73790	7/45	10/46	90766
73791	7/45	9/46	90767
73792	8/45	11/46	90768
73793	8/45	9/46	90769

(a) Unless otherwise indicated, the engines were transferred to the W.D. on the dates shown.
(b) Transferred to L.M.S.

2-8-2 CLASSES

SUMMARY OF CLASS TOTALS

Class	31st December																				
	1925	1926	1927	1928	1929	1930	1931	1932	1933	1934	1935	1936	1937	1938	1939	1940	1941	1942	1943	1944	1945
P1	2	2	2	2	2	2	2	2	2	2	2	2	2	2	2	2	2	2	2	2	
P2										2	2	6	6	6	6	6	6	6	5		
Total	2	2	2	2	2	2	2	2	2	4	4	8	8	8	8	8	8	8	7	2	Nil

Although used extensively abroad, the 2-8-2 tender wheel arrangement was adopted only by the L.N.E.R. on the standard gauge lines in Great Britain. Two classes were introduced by Gresley, one for heavy goods work and the other for express passenger duties, totalling only eight engines. Difficulties were experienced with both classes and the type disappeared finally from use after a relatively brief existence of twenty years.

Following the introduction of his Pacific locomotives in 1922, Gresley turned his attention to the provision of a goods engine capable of hauling even greater loads than his three-cylinder 2-8-0's. A 2-8-2 with 5ft. 2in. coupled wheels was eventually chosen and carried his Pacific boiler and cylinders. Two engines were turned out during 1925 and were classified P1. Both were equipped with boosters which could be cut in to drive the trailing wheels, but this equipment was later discarded. The considerable power of these fine-looking locomotives caused problems to the Operating Department and no more were built. Both were withdrawn during 1945.

When an express passenger locomotive more powerful than the class A3 Pacifics was mooted for the Edinburgh – Aberdeen services, Gresley again turned to the 2-8-2 wheel arrangement. Class P2 No. 2001 *Cock o' the North* was completed in 1934. It had 6ft. 2in. coupled wheels (a new wheel diameter for the L.N.E.R. and soon to be repeated in the class V2 2-6-2 design) and incorporated a number of other features new to Doncaster designs, such as a Kylchap double blastpipe, smoke deflectors, vee-shaped cab front and chime whistle. In addition, No. 2001 was fitted with Lentz poppet valves driven by rotary cams and was equipped with an A.C.F.I. feed water heater.

To afford a comparison, a second engine, No. 2002 was turned out later the same year and this had Gresley's standard arrangement of Walschaerts valve gear and derived motion driving piston valves. The feed water heater was omitted.

Four more P2's were constructed in 1936, similar to No. 2002 but with streamlined front ends like the A4 class, and there were also a number of differences between the engines of this batch.

The first two engines were later given the streamlined front end, whilst No. 2001 also received new cylinders with piston valves in place of the Lentz gear and had its feed water heater removed.

When Thompson succeeded Gresley as Chief Mechanical Engineer he had all six P2's rebuilt as Pacifics during 1943-44. The further history of these controversial engines will be found in Part 2A of this series.

CLASS P1

GRESLEY 5ft. 2in. ENGINES

ENGINES BUILT AFTER GROUPING (1925): 2393/4. TOTAL 2.

In 1922 Gresley contemplated the possibility of designing a mineral engine more powerful than his latest class O2 2-8-0. The new design would carry his Pacific boiler. His first idea was for a 2-10-2 with 4ft. 8in. diameter coupled wheels. The wheel spacing would have been 7ft. 7in. + 5ft. 0in. + 5ft. 0in. + 5ft. 0in. + 5ft. 0in. + 8ft. 2in., i.e. giving a total engine wheelbase of 35ft. 9in., exactly as in the new class A1 Pacific. This would certainly have been a powerful machine but there must have been some doubts about the wisdom of introducing a ten-coupled design. The alternative proposal was for a 2-8-2, which allowed the coupled wheels to be spaced further apart and increased to 5ft. 2in. diameter.

In April 1923 the wheelbase and axle weight distribution was submitted to the Civil Engineer, who agreed to the engine working between London and Shaftholme on all lines which had been passed for the Pacifics. Doncaster drawing office was instructed on 29th May "to lose no time in getting on with the drawings" for the new design. The proposal was then put before the Locomotive Committee in August 1923 and it was stated that two 2-8-2's would cost £8,000 each and be able to haul 25 per cent more wagons per train than the 2-8-0's currently used between Peterborough and London, and could also be used between Wath Yard and Immingham via the Doncaster Avoiding Line. In the original submission it was stated that "full loads can be found for them", but rather significantly these particular words were omitted in the notes of the meeting.

Meanwhile in July 1923 Gresley was looking into the provision of a booster engine on the trailing carrying axle under the cab. The Superheater Co., New York, was handling the design work and they attempted to work out a scheme with a radial truck, but then eventually admitted in May 1924 that Gresley's arrangement of a Cartazzi truck was acceptable and "undoubtedly about the lightest form of suspension that could be worked out for booster application to these Mikado engines". The Superheater Co. also recommended fitting the boiler with a type "E double" superheater. No. 2394 was fitted with one of these superheaters whilst No. 2393 had the conventional Robinson type.

Other unusual features for a Doncaster design were the steam reversing gear, the steam brakes on the engine and tender with vacuum ejector for train working and a high-capacity six-wheeled tender carrying 7 tons of coal and 4,700 gallons of water.

No. 2393 was completed in June 1925 just in time to take part in the Stockton & Darlington Centenary celebrations which commenced on 1st July. No. 2394 appeared five months later. The actual cost for the pair of these engines was £20,986. The engines could only be usefully employed on coal trains running between New England and Ferme Park, but the prodigious loads they were capable of hauling proved to be an embarrassment to the Operating Department. However at a joint meeting of the Superintendents and Locomotive Running Superintendents held on 5th October 1926, it was recommended that four 0-8-0's should be withdrawn and replaced by "four G.N. type three-cylinder 2-8-2 coal engines", suggesting that at this date the Operating Department still looked on these engines with favour. The recommendations were not accepted and on 23rd November 1926 the Chief General Manager stated that the justification for the Mikado type goods engines was being dealt with departmentally in the Southern Area.

Results from the "E" type superheater were disappointing and No. 2394 was altered to the conventional Robinson type in November 1931. The boosters were not put to much use and the equipment was eventually removed from both engines in 1937-38. The final modification came in November 1942 when No. 2394 received an

A3-type boiler. Class Part 2 was intended to cover this variety but as No. 2393 was also in works at the year-end awaiting similar treatment, the subdivision was unnecessary and both engines remained simply class P1. By then the writing was on the wall for this non-standard class which had no place in Thompson's schemes. Both engines were withdrawn in July 1945 though this was not quite the end of the story. The frames from No. 2393 were retained for a while as a boiler carrier at Doncaster Works (thus noted on 1st September 1946), the boilers were used to rebuild class A1 Nos. 2557/65 to class A3 in December 1945, whilst the tenders after suitable modification were employed again with class B2.

The construction of the class is summarised in the accompanying table.

Engine Nos.	*Maker*	*Order No.*	*Date ordered*	*Works Nos.*	*No. built*	*Date*
2393/4	Doncaster	303	November 1923	1619/20	2	1925

Standard L.N.E.R. Dimensions

	180 *lb.* *boiler*	220 *lb.* *boiler*
Cylinders (3)	20″ × 26″	19″ × 26″
Motion	Walschaerts/Gresley with 8″ piston valves	
Boiler:		
Max. diam. outside	6′ 5″	6′ 5″
Distance between tubeplates	19′ 0″ (a)	18′ 11¾″
Firebox length outside	9′ 5½″	9′ 5¾″
Pitch	9′ 4½″	9′ 4½″
Diagram No.	94	94HP/94A

	Robinson super.	*E Double super.*	*43-element super.*
Heating surface (sq. ft.):			
Firebox	215	215.0	215.0
Tubes	1880	503.6	1354.2
Flues	835	2158.8	1122.8
Total evaporative	2930	2877.4	2692.0
Superheater	525	1104.0	706.0 (b)
Total	3455	3981.4	3398.0
Tubes	168 × 2¼″	45 × 2¼″	121 × 2¼″
Flues	32 × 5¼″	124 × 3½″	43 × 5¼″
Elements	32 × 1¼″	62 × $\frac{15}{16}$″	43 × 1.244″
Grate area (sq. ft.)	41.25	41.25	41.25
Boiler pressure (lb./sq. in.)	180	180	220
	With booster	*Booster removed*	
Tractive effort (85%)	38,500 lb.	38,500 lb.	42,466 lb.
Booster cylinders (2)	10″ × 12″	—	—
Booster tractive effort	8,500 lb.	—	—

Weight (full):			
Engine	100T 0C	91T 14C	94T 16C
Tender	51T 8C	51T 8C	51T 8C
Total	151T 8C	143T 2C	146T 4C
Adhesive (coupled)	71T 10C	66T 18C	69T 5C
Adhesive (booster)	18T 4C	—	—
Max. axle load	18T 13C	17T 9C	17T 15C

	Common particulars
Leading wheels	3′ 2″
Coupled wheels	5′ 2″
Trailing wheels	3′ 8″
Tender wheels	3′ 9″
Length over buffers	69′ 10″
Wheelbase:	
Engine	8′ 8″ + 6′ 6″ + 6′ 0″ + 6′ 0″ + 9′ 0″ = 36′ 2″
Tender	6′ 6″ + 6′ 6″ = 13′ 0″
Total	59′ 8″
Water capacity	4,700 gallons
Coal capacity	7T 0C

(a) Altered to 18′ 11¾″, 12/1939.

(b) The figure of 703 sq. ft. appeared on the engine diagram with a corresponding discrepancy in the total.

L.N.E.R. Renumbering

Under the 1943 scheme the numbers 3990/1 were allocated but both engines were withdrawn before the scheme was implemented in 1946.

Development

The layout of the valve gear was based on that of the contemporary class O2 2-8-0's, with 1¼in. lap valves and 5½in. full travel at 75 per cent cut-off. A departure from Doncaster practice was the provision of steam reversing gear as an aid to the driver when starting a heavy load, particularly useful when having to set back to ease the couplings. The 7in. diameter steam reversing cylinder and 5in. diameter oil cataract cylinder were located between the frames on the right-hand side of the engine over the driving axle. The reversing handle in the cab was connected to the steam valve on the reversing cylinder by means of rodding which was visible on the right-hand side of the engine as it passed along the underside of the running plate. On No. 2393 the rodding was straight, whilst on No. 2394 the rodding had a noticeable set in it above the trailing coupled wheels where it crossed over the booster exhaust steam pipe (cf. figs. 110 and 112. The piston in the cataract cylinder followed the movement of the piston in the reversing cylinder, thereby lifting or lowering the radius rod as required. When the desired setting was reached the driver operated the clutch, which was vacuum-powered and held the reversing shaft firmly in position.

The steam reverse was of course quicker in action than the standard screw reverse and it helped to avert a near disaster when No. 2393 was brand new. It was standing in the works yard on steaming tests outside the weigh house when the Assistant Works Manager, G. A. Musgrave, opened wide the regulator – which promptly stuck. The driver immediately put the engine into mid-gear and a column of water and steam shot out of the chimney! Long travel valve gear was never fitted to the class and the steam reversing gear was retained to the end.

The locomotive booster was introduced in 1919 on the New York Central Railroad. It was a supplementary steam engine adapted to drive the trailing carrying axle through an idler gear which could be engaged when extra power was needed, i.e. when starting or climbing a gradient. As described in Part 3A of this series on page 26, a booster was ordered by the G.N.R. shortly before Grouping and fitted in July 1923 to class

C1 No. 1419 (later 4419). This was the standard Type C-1 booster, a 10in. by 12in. double-acting engine with cranks set at 90 degrees. The gear ratio between the engine crankshaft and the trailing axle was 14 to 36. Similar boosters were provided for the P1's and, although the boiler pressure in their case was higher, the engine diagram showed the same booster tractive effort that applied in the case of No. 4419 when it was first fitted.

The booster (fig. 114) was connected to the trailing carrying wheels by means of gears and when not in use was held out of gear by a spring. The booster could only be operated in full fore gear and automatically cut out when the reversing gear was notched up. The booster had to be cut in before speed exceeded 10 m.p.h. and had to be cut out when 21 m.p.h. was reached. This operation was controlled by compressed air for which purpose a Westinghouse 8in. by 8½in. air compressor was located on the right-hand side of the boiler (fig. 110). The live steam pipe to the booster passed along the left-hand side of the engine. The exhaust steam passed along the right-hand side of the engine to the smokebox, where it was then delivered into an annular ring which circled the top of the blastpipe. A separate 1ft. 2½in. tall plain top was fitted to the blastpipe, with a 5in. diameter orifice, so that the exhaust from the booster mixed with the main exhaust some distance below the orifice (fig. 113). At a later date a 4⅝in. shorter blastpipe top was provided for No. 2394 and it is recorded that No. 2393 was brought into line in October 1931.

When the P1's eventually appeared in 1925, the booster on No. 4419 had already been modified. The gear ratio had been reduced to facilitate safe operation at higher speeds, a new pilot valve permitted its use when notched up to 50 per cent cut-off and the operation was now steam controlled to give a more rapid response. These new features were not considered essential in the case of the P1's which were of course employed on a totally different type of work.

On 6th September 1925 No. 2393 worked a special 1,575-ton train from New England to Ferme Park, comprising dynamometer car, 101 loaded mineral wagons and 20-ton brake van. Owing to the maximum capacity of the dynamometer car spring being only 18 tons, the booster was not used for the start out of New England and the maximum effort required to start the train was only 12 tons. A stop was made at Offord and on restarting an attempt was made to employ the booster, but three-quarters of a mile was covered before it was properly in gear. The pressure in the booster steam chest was then only 100 lb. per sq. in., as the regulator was only partly open. After the booster had been cut out, speed rose to 30 m.p.h. and the next 1½ miles to Biggleswade were run at 45 per cent cut-off and the regulator wide open. This was a compromise between the Test Engineer's desire to work the engine at 35 per cent with fully open regulator and the accepted practice of operating this engine at 50 per cent with partly open regulator to avoid running hot. The maximum draw-bar horsepower exerted on this stretch was 1,210 h.p.

On arrival at Cambridge Junction the axleboxes were checked and the right-hand leading coupled one was found to be hot. The horn gap wedge was eased slightly to allow the train to proceed. The train was restarted with the booster in, the safety catch on the dynamometer car having first been put on as a precaution. About half a mile from the start, when speed was 9 m.p.h., the booster was disengaged and the dynamometer car spring put into action, the pull recorded being 14 tons. The remainder of the journey was uneventful though the offending axlebox was still very hot on arrival at Ferme Park.

This test had been the first occasion on which the engine had been given an adequate load and it had been within its capability. Coal consumption was high: 150 lb. per mile or 4.56 lb. per draw-bar horsepower hour. It was concluded from the tests that whilst the current method of working with partly open regulator persisted, the best use could not be made of the booster. Far better results could be obtained from the main engine, only, by simply operating with a wide open regulator. It was recommended that drivers should be trained to operate trains of 1,600 tons weight at about 35 per cent cut-off with a more open regulator, though this would be hard to institute because of the fear of overheating an axlebox.

The booster was only really of value when working maximum loads of about 1,600 tons but for operating considerations loads fell far short of this. There were also technical difficulties. The steam pipe connections to the booster under the cab had articulated couplings to permit vertical movement and side play. This arrangement resulted in the cast-iron pipes frequently breaking close to the ball and socket joints, with an almost endless flow of replacement castings being sent from Doncaster Works to New England shed. The trouble may have been caused by over-tightening the joints to ensure a steamtight fit, with not enough slack left

Fig. 126 Class P2 No. 2001 *Cock o' the North* at Doncaster Works, May 1934.

Fitted with Lentz rotary cam poppet valve gear. Tubular reversing shaft alongside boiler, horizontal running plate above cylinders and coupled wheels, drive for mechanical lubricators taken from a crank on the third coupled wheel, four wash-out plugs in view above boiler handrail (fifth one out of sight in cab), firebox handrail on left-hand side raised clear of reversing gear shaft, 3ft. 7in. vertical cab handrail, vacuum ejector exhaust pipe sloping down in front of cab, tender with spoked wheels.

Fig. 127 Class P2/2 No. 2002 *Earl Marischal* at Doncaster Works, October 1934.

Walschaerts/Gresley valve gear. Reverse curve in running plate behind cylinders, outside steam pipe cover protruding through boiler casing, firebox handrail at normal height, drive for mechanical lubricators taken from radius link, tender wheels with disc centres.

Fig. 128 Class P2/2 No. 2002 *Earl Marischal* at Doncaster Works, April 1935.

Additional smoke lifting plates alongside boiler casing with nameplates repositioned, boiler handrails cut back clear of smoke lifting plates, Teloc speed recorder bracket alongside trailing coupled wheel.

Fig. 129 Class P2/2 No. 2002 *Earl Marischal* at Ferryhill shed (Aberdeen), August 1935.

Tablet catcher in position on tender.

Fig. 130 Class P2/1 No. 2001 *Cock o' the North* at Dundee shed, September 1935.

Tandem pump for A.C.F.I. feed water heater on running plate, four wash-out plugs above boiler handrail (all in view), cab cut-out altered and vertical handrail 4ft. 3in.

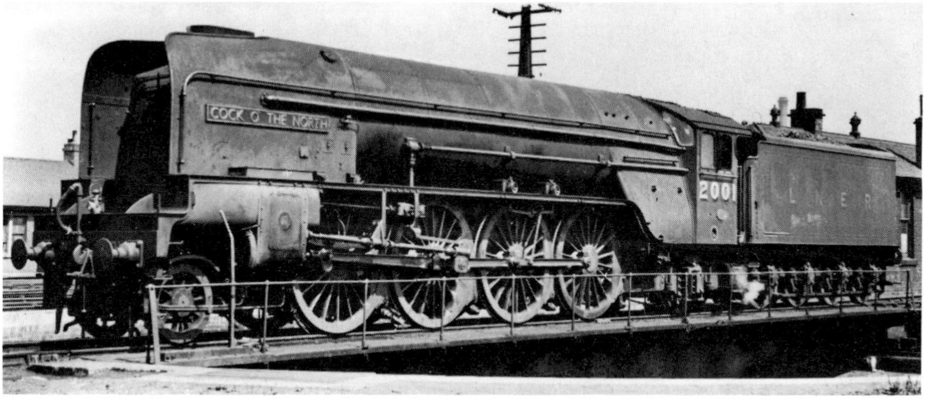

Fig. 131 Class P2/1 No. 2001 *Cock o' the North* at Haymarket shed, August 1937.

Hole cut in tender side sheet for tablet catcher.

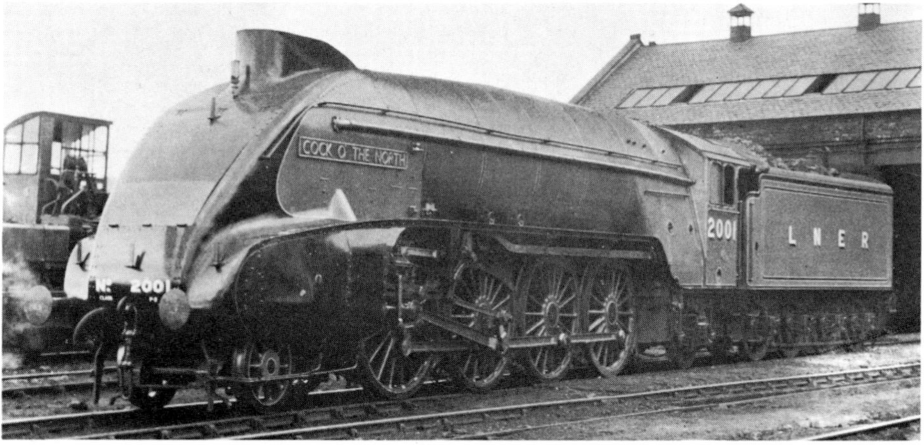

Fig. 132 Class P2/2 No. 2001 *Cock o' the North* at Haymarket shed, 1938.

Fully streamlined with poppet valves removed. New buffers, front footsteps removed, retaining raised handrail alongside firebox.

Fig. 133

Class P2/2 No. 2002 *Earl Marischal* at Doncaster Works, October 1936.

Fully streamlined. Cab cut-out altered and vertical handrail 4ft. 3in., front footsteps removed.

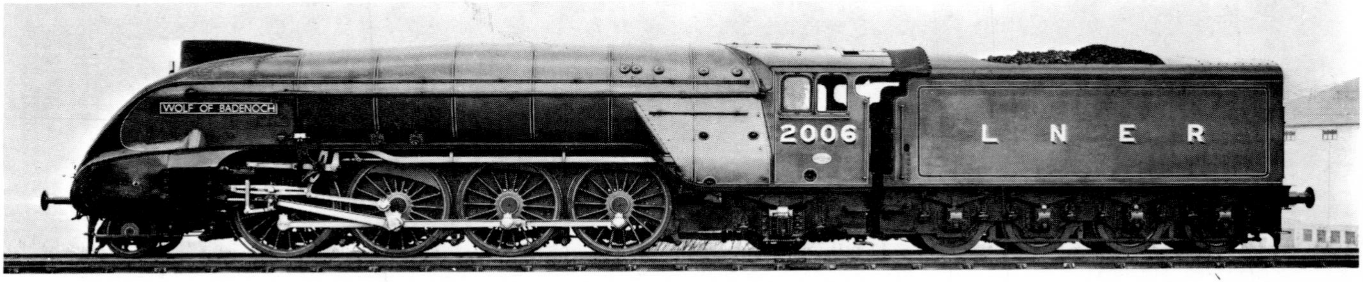

Fig. 134

Class P2/3 No. 2006 *Wolf of Badenoch* at Haymarket shed, November 1936.

Longer combustion chamber, five firebox hand holes (inspection doors) in view above boiler handrail, vacuum ejector exhaust pipe horizontal throughout, additional cab roof ventilators, vertical cab handrail 4ft. 6in., streamlined non-corridor tender with rubber sheeting across gap above cab entrance.

Fig. 135 Class P2/2 No. 2003 *Lord President* at Doncaster Works, May 1936 before entering service.

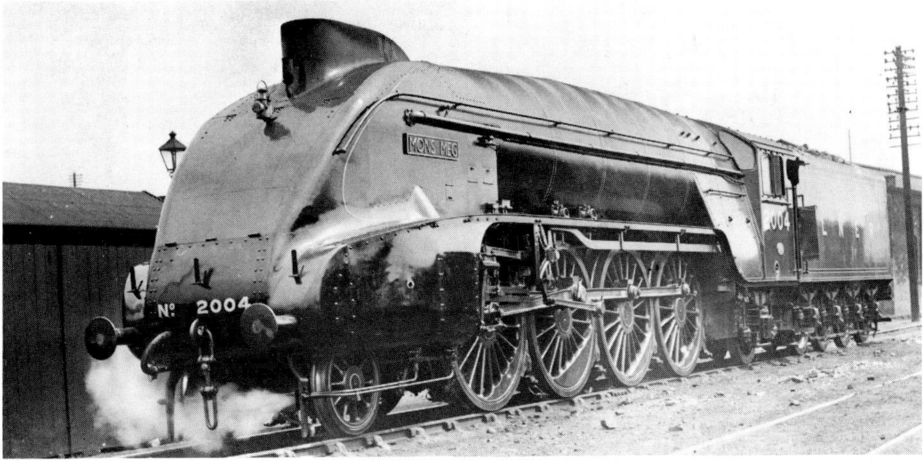

Fig. 136 Class P2/2 No. 2004 *Mons Meg* at Grantham shed, July 1936.

Fig. 137 Class P2/2 No. 2005 *Thane of Fife* at Ferryhill shed (Aberdeen), about 1937.
With single chimney and whistle mounted further from upper hinge of casing.

Fig. 138 Class P2/1 No. 2001 *Cock o' the North* arriving at King's Cross station with an up express, 1934.

Fig. 139 Class P2/2 No. 2002 *Earl Marischal* on the 4-0 p.m. King's Cross – Leeds express between Hadley North and Potters Bar tunnels, November 1934.

Prior to fitting of smoke lifting plates and showing effect of unsatisfactory exhaust clearance.

Fig. 140 Class P2/1 No. 2001 *Cock o' the North* on an Edinburgh – Aberdeen express at Inverkeithing, 1936.

Fig. 141 Class P2/2 No. 2002 *Earl Marischal* on the 1-45 p.m. fish Aberdeen – King's Cross at Ferryhill (Aberdeen), May 1938.

Fig. 142 Class P2/2 No. 2003 *Lord President* on the 7-8 a.m. Leeds – King's Cross stopping passenger train at Newark station, July 1936.

Fig. 143 Class P2/2 No. 2003 *Lord President* on the 9-0 a.m. Aberdeen – Edinburgh express at Kirkcaldy station, 1936.

to take the sharp curves of the New England turning triangle. Whatever the cause, the problems were never cured. The booster equipment was eventually removed completely from No. 2394 in April 1937.

The booster on No. 2393 was kept going for a while longer by fitting it in February 1937 with the cylinders from the booster which had been taken off class C1 No. 4419 in November 1935. No. 2393 ran in traffic for three months with, it is understood, the booster out of use while Doncaster tried to work out a satisfactory method of converting the control to steam operation. Towards the end of May 1937 No. 2393 returned to the works to have the booster removed, modified and refitted, though apparently still with air control as the Westinghouse pump was retained, and was back in service in the first week of June. No. 2393 ran in this condition for a further eleven months before the entire equipment was at last removed in May 1938 (fig. 115). For some time the P1's had been handling reduced loads and the boosters were not missed, except perhaps by the fitting staff at New England shed!

The Superheater Co., New York, recommended the fitting of a type "E double" superheater to improve the steaming capacity of the Pacific boiler. Gresley was given a reasonable assurance that with this type a steam temperature of 700 degrees Fahr. could be expected, as against 575 degrees which The Superheater Co. considered to be the upper limit with the existing A1 boiler. Two sets of "E" type superheaters were ordered on 23rd December 1924 for the new P1's, though later it was decided to fit one of them instead to a class A1 Pacific then on order, No. 2562. The other set was fitted to No. 2394.

The boiler had 45 small tubes and 124 flue tubes, $2\frac{1}{4}$in. and $3\frac{1}{2}$in. diameter respectively, and 62 elements. There were 29 "2 element" superheater units. Each unit branched into two elements near to the front tubeplate. Each branch element then traversed two adjacent flue tubes, one above the other. The two branch elements reunited prior to entering the superheated side of the header. In addition there were 4 "single element" units, which each traversed two adjacent flue tubes. (See fig. 113). The elements were $1\frac{3}{16}$in. outside diameter and No. 10 S.W.G. thickness. This gave an internal diameter of 0.9315in., which was approximated to $\frac{15}{16}$in. on the engine diagram.

Tests were conducted with class A1 No. 2562 in March 1926 (see Part 2A of this series, pp. 11 and 12), during which the average steam temperature was only 31 degrees higher than with the standard Robinson superheater, though the highest temperature recorded was 650 degrees Fahr. The results were not sufficiently impressive to justify the general adoption of the "E" type superheater and No. 2394 was fitted with a standard Robinson 32-element superheater in November 1931.

Nos. 2393/4 retained their original boilers until 1934, which was a far longer association of engine and boiler than was found in the class A1 Pacifics. During this period the engines had been kept to one sphere of operation and, whether or not this was a contributory factor, the condition of the boilers at the end of nine years left something to be desired. The boiler out of No. 2393 was badly pitted and F. H. Eggleshaw, Works Manager, said it was in "the worst condition of any Pacific boiler I have ever seen". He sought permission to rivet a copper plate over the worst area but after deliberation he was instructed to renew completely the parallel ring. This boiler was duly repaired and put back into service on class A1 No. 4481. The condition of the boiler taken out of No. 2394 is not recorded but was probably worse, as it was simply scrapped in August 1934. Both engines received second-hand Pacific boilers in 1934 from Nos. 4475 and 2568 respectively. No. 2394 was reboilered again in 1937, this time acquiring the boiler from No. 2561.

Since 1927 only A3-type boilers had been built for Pacifics and the A1's were progressively rebuilt to class A3. In November 1942 class P1 No. 2394 acquired a second-hand boiler previously carried by class A3 No. 2507, whilst No. 2393 was similarly altered in January 1943 when it received the boiler off class A3 No. 2573. These A3-type boilers were pressed to 220 lb. per sq. in. as compared with 180 lb. per sq. in. of the A1 type. The cylinders were lined up from 20in. to 19in. diameter and the tractive effort was increased from 38,500 to 42,466 lb., giving a rather low factor of adhesion (see later).

The A3-type boiler had a 43-element Robinson superheater in place of the 32-element pattern in the A1 boiler. The header was wider on account of the two extra columns of flues and the ends protruded through the sides of the smokebox. These openings had noticeable cover plates, which readily distinguished the A3 boiler from the A1-type. No. 2394, reboilered first, received the Diagram 94A type, which had the "banjo" shaped dome casting, whilst No. 2393 was given the Diagram 94HP type, which had the round dome casing (cf. figs. 117 and 116). After the

P1's were withdrawn in 1945, their A3-type boilers were used again on Pacifics.

A dimension which appeared on L.N.E.R. engine diagrams was the adhesive factor, arrived at by dividing the weight on the coupled wheels by the nominal tractive effort. With the P1's this produced the rather low figure of 4.16, hence the value of the booster engine to aid starting. After the booster equipment had been dismantled in 1937-38, the resulting redistribution of weight significantly reduced the weight on the coupled wheels from 71 tons 10 cwt. to 66 tons 18 cwt., thereby lowering the adhesive factor to 3.89, though by this time the P1's were handling much lighter loads than their designer had intended. Finally, the adhesive factor was lowered still further, to 3.65, after the A3-type boilers were fitted in 1942-43.

Details

Frames and Running Gear

The main frames consisted of 1⅛in. thick steel plates, spaced 4ft. 1½in. apart except under the firebox where they bent inwards, followed by a parallel section under the cab, 3ft. 5in. apart. Separate outside frames, 1in. thick and 6ft. 0½in. apart at the rear end, were bolted to the main frames close to the frame stay supporting the front of the firebox. Strengthening plates, 1in. thick and about 6ft. long, were bolted and welded to the inside faces of the main frames at this joint. The rear end provided a substantial double-frame support for the firebox. The frames were supported ahead of the firebox by the frame stays, motion plates and inside cylinder casting. Six 1ft.-diameter circular lightening holes were cut in each frame, two between each adjacent pair of coupled wheel horn gaps. There is no record of the frames giving any trouble, unlike those of the contemporary Pacifics.

The front buffer plate was 8ft. 7in. wide by 1ft. 4in. deep. Curved pieces 6½in. deep by 10in. wide were cut away from the bottom corners for clearance purposes if operating away from the G.N. Section. Spencer double case buffers were provided and the Group Standard type were never fitted.

Because of the proximity of the booster pipes below the cab there was no room for footsteps in the usual position. These had to be fitted ahead of the vertical run of the pipes and suspended from a bracket bolted to the frames just clear of the spring hanger. The overall width across the footsteps was 8ft. 8in. The treads were narrower than normal and too far forward to be of much use. The footsteps at the front of the tender, sited below the cab entrance, were in fact better placed (fig. 111). In January 1934 the Running Department complained that there had been two or three cases where enginemen had slipped when climbing down from the cab and asked for an improvement to be made. As a result the tender steps were widened by a further 4in. No. 2393 was altered in May 1934 followed two months later by No. 2394. When the boosters were removed in 1937-38 substantial footsteps were provided below the cab handrail (fig. 115). Footsteps were never provided at the front end although they were fitted to the class A1 and A3 Pacifics after 1935.

The pony truck incorporated Gresley's patent swing link suspension. The truck itself had ⅞in. thick frames spaced 2ft. 11½in. apart, with helical bearing springs on the outside of them. The radius arm was 6ft. 6in. long and the pony truck wheels were 3ft. 2in. diameter. The journals were 6½in. diameter and 9in. long. The minimum radius curvature which the engines could negotiate was 6 chains. Guard irons were fitted to the pony truck frames in addition to the main frames.

The coupled wheels had laminated springs, comprising nine plates 5in. wide and ⅝in. thick, at 3ft. 6in. centres, as in the Gresley 2-8-0 classes. Equalising beams connected these springs to attain a more even weight distribution: these beams were removed in 1940 from No. 2393 (May) and No. 2394 (April). The axlebox journals were 8½in. diameter and 9in. long and were lubricated by means of a Hulburd eight-feed mechanical lubricator, mounted on the right-hand side running plate.

The trailing carrying wheels had the type of laminated springs which were fitted to class C1 No. 4419, with booster. These comprised fourteen plates, 5in. wide and ⅝in. thick at 4ft. 6in. centres. Lighter springs, having eleven plates instead of fourteen, as fitted to the Pacifics, were substituted when the booster equipment was dismantled in 1937-38 as there was an appreciable reduction in the axle load from 18 tons 4 cwt. to 14 tons 14 cwt. The axlebox journals were 6in. diameter and 11in. long as in the Pacifics.

The outside cylinders were inclined at 1 in 40 whilst the inside one was inclined at 1 in 8 to enable the connecting rod to clear the leading coupled axle. All three connecting rods were 7ft. 0in. between their centres, with the drive on the second coupled axle, so that the three cylinders were approximately in line – unlike in the A1 arrangement which had longer outside connecting rods. The three steam chests were positioned in the same horizontal plane, with that for the inside cylinder situated to the left of it. The piston valves were 8in. diameter. The inside cylinder was operated by means of Gresley's 2-to-1 derived gear, which is described in detail and illustrated in Part 2A of this series on page 36. The middle cylinders of Nos. 2393/4 were renewed in May 1934 and April 1940 respectively, but the original outside pairs were retained to the end.

The main cylinder and valve lubrication was by means of a Detroit sight-feed hydrostatic lubricator mounted in the cab on the fireman's side. Four feeds passed along the outside of the boiler at a slight slope to the smokebox (fig. 110). Cylinder and valve lubrication for the booster engine was by means of a small sight-feed lubricator, also on the fireman's side of the cab, which delivered oil into the booster steam pipe.

Sanding was provided for forward running only, in front of the leading coupled and driving coupled wheels (and in front of the booster wheels prior to this equipment being dismantled in 1937-38). The sanding gear was steam operated at first, but the leading sanders were changed to gravity feed in November 1927 (No. 2394) and September 1928 (No. 2393). With the altered arrangement, the rodding was visible where it passed along the outside of the firebox cladding on the right-hand side (cf. figs. 110 and 112).

Boilers

The boilers were interchangeable with those of the Gresley Pacific classes A1 and A3, and are described more fully in Part 2A of this series. The barrel was constructed in two sections, the front one being parallel and the rear one coned. The front section was 5ft. $7\frac{3}{4}$in. inside diameter whilst the coned or taper section was 6ft. 5in. outside diameter at the firebox end.

A 5in. diameter Lockyer regulator valve was provided at first. This was located in the dome casing on the parallel ring and the main steam pipe connecting it to the saturated side of the header was 5in. diameter (or $6\frac{1}{2}$in. in the case of No. 2394 with the "E" type superheater). The steam pipes in the smokebox which carried the steam from the superheated side of the header to the cylinders were $4\frac{1}{2}$in. internal diameter (or 5 in. in the case of No. 2394). The Lockyer valve was subsequently replaced by a similarly-acting balanced regulator valve, which had a loose top seating to counter the difficulty of ensuring steam tightness at both top and bottom valves. When reboilered in November 1942 with an A3-type boiler No. 2394 had a combined regulator and perforated steam collector, located on the taper section of the barrel. The steam collector, which had seventeen rows of $\frac{5}{8}$in. diameter holes, was introduced to prevent priming.

The smokebox tubeplate was $\frac{3}{4}$in. thick with a $\frac{1}{2}$in. radius flange (1in. for renewals from October 1930). The firebox tubeplate was 1in. thick with a 1in. flange. The distance between the tubeplates was 19ft. 0in. From May 1938 the thickness of the tubeplate in replacement fireboxes was increased to $1\frac{1}{4}$in. while at the same time four smoke tubes which overlapped the flange were dispensed with, and the distance between tubeplates was reduced to 18ft. $11\frac{3}{4}$in. It is not known if this particular alteration affected either of the P1's. In the A3-type boilers the smokebox tubeplates were $\frac{3}{4}$in. thick with a 1in. radius flange, but the firebox tubeplates were $1\frac{1}{4}$in. thick, also with a 1in. radius flange. The distance between the tubeplates was 18ft. $11\frac{3}{4}$in.

The Diagram 94 boiler fitted to No. 2393 when new and to No. 2394 from November 1931, had a standard Robinson 32-element superheater, with half return bend (or short loop) elements. The elements were $1\frac{1}{2}$in. outside diameter, No. 9 S.W.G. thickness, which gave an internal diameter of 1.212in., though this was approximated on the engine diagram as $1\frac{1}{4}$in. From December 1932 the gauge was reduced to No. 10 S.W.G., thus increasing slightly the internal diameter and from December 1937 the engine diagram showed the exact dimension of 1.244in.

The anti-vacuum valve fitted to the P1's was of the same type as that first provided for the K3's built in 1920. A $4\frac{1}{2}$in. diameter valve lifted under pressure of steam from the saturated side of the header, sealing the air inlet. When the regulator was closed, the valve dropped, thus admitting air into the header and superheater elements. Prior to November 1931 No. 2394 had twin anti-vacuum valves in association with its "E"-type superheater (cf. figs. 110 and 111).

The engines had a Davies & Metcalfe No. 10 exhaust steam injector under the footplate on the fireman's side of the cab, with the steam and delivery valve on the firebox faceplate. Also on the faceplate, but on the driver's side, was a Gresham & Craven No. 10 combination live steam injector (No. 11 size in the case of No. 2394 with the "E"-type superheater). The live steam injectors were changed to the under-footstep type when A3-type boilers were fitted.

In August 1927 No. 2394 was fitted with a Diamond auto-gyroidal-type soot blower. This was mounted on the back of the firebox and directed a jet of steam on to the tubeplate by manual operation of a control handle. The high velocity steam combined with the firebox gases to sweep through the tubes and into the smokebox the accumulation of soot and ashes. In March 1936 the Locomotive Running Superintendents stated that they saw no advantage in retaining soot blowers and it was decided to remove them from all engines which had them at their next repair. No. 2394 was next shopped in August 1936 and the soot blower was probably removed then.

General

The cabs were identical with those fitted to the contemporary A1's. The side sheets, which had twin windows, were spaced 8ft. 2in. apart and their rear ends curved inwards. Each side sheet was cut away at window level by a further 10in. The centres of the pillars for the vertical handrails were 3ft. 7in. apart. Hinged glass sight screens were fitted between the two side windows, about 1934. Seat backs were provided for these two engines in February and April 1937 respectively, and at the same time a reduction of 11in. was made in the rear side sheet cut-out and 8in. longer vertical handrails were fitted (cf. figs. 111 and 115). The engines were arranged for right-hand drive, with the steam reverse and booster controls, combination vacuum ejector with steam brake valve, on that side of the cab. Gresley pull-out regulator handles were provided at both sides of the cab.

The overall width of the running plate was 8ft. 9in., except alongside the cab where it was 9ft. 0in. There was a footstep half way up the reverse curve in the running plate in front of the firebox. An inspection hole was provided in the vertical platform plate at the front end below the smokebox for access to the middle cylinder motion (fig. 119). A small cover hinged near to the left-hand frame was provided for this hole to keep out ash (fig. 120), in 1934 to Nos. 2393 (May) and 2394 (July).

The handrails which ran the full length of both sides of the boiler were positioned 1ft. $2\frac{13}{16}$in. above the boiler centre line, though latterly No. 2394 had a Diagram 94A boiler with handrails 1ft. 1in. above centre line. At the front end they curved round towards the front of the smokebox and were matched by the smokebox door handrail. Additional handrails, 4ft. 6in. long, were located on the sides of the firebox. These were pitched 4in. higher than the horizontal handrails on the cab sides, except that on No. 2393 they were pitched at the same height as the cab handrails from May 1934 (first boiler change) to January 1943 (fitted with high pressure boiler). The vacuum ejector exhaust pipe ran horizontally alongside the boiler, on the right-hand side, and was pitched 6in. above the boiler centre line.

The smokebox door was 5ft. 1in. diameter and on No. 2393 when new fitted flat against a steel sealing ring, which was the only aid towards preserving an airtight fit. The door was locked by the standard crossbar and dart arrangement, with the rear handle on the centre boss in the vertical position and then tightened by screwing up the outer handle. A new style of joint ring was introduced in November 1925 in time to be applied to No. 2394 when new. This had a $\frac{3}{4}$in. wide recess all the way round, packed with asbestos. The edge of the door was rounded and provided a more satisfactory fit when pressed against this packing. No. 2393 was probably brought into line at its March 1927 repair.

The chimney was the same $8\frac{1}{2}$in.-high pattern fitted to the A1's conforming to the L.N.E.R. Composite Load Gauge. Similar chimneys were afterwards fitted to classes A3 and V2.

Brakes

Steam brakes were provided for engine and tender with a vacuum ejector for train braking. Two $7\frac{1}{2}$in. diameter steam brake cylinders were mounted side by side between the frames just in front of the firebox throatplate. On the tender there was a 9in. brake cylinder mounted vertically between the frames just in front of the leading axle.

Tenders

Two high-capacity six-wheel tenders, Nos. 5293/4, were provided for the P1's. They were designed and built at Doncaster and incorporated some of the features of the Pacific-type eight-wheel tenders, such as same tank width and depth, sloping front plate with a slot on the fireman's side to take the fire irons, rounded corners at the back of the tender, same height above rail level to the top at the sides and same overall height (12ft. 0in.). Certain Darlington features which had meanwhile been adopted for the 4,200-gallon Group Standard tenders were also incorporated, including double-framed chassis with no rear guard irons, double-case buffers (also fitted to the Pacific tenders) and 3ft. 9in. diameter wheels. New features included the flush back and sides, anticipating their standardisation on the Group Standard tenders by some three years.

The outside frames were 23ft. 5$\frac{3}{8}$in. long, 1in. thick and 6ft. 1$\frac{1}{2}$in. apart, whilst the inside frames were 20ft. 7$\frac{1}{4}$in. long, $\frac{1}{2}$in. thick and 4ft. 1in. apart. The width over the side sheets was 8ft. 0$\frac{1}{2}$in. – that over the running plate was 8ft. 9in. – and at the front end the side sheets curved inwards so that the distance between their ends was 6ft. 11in. The bunker was of the self-trimming type, whilst the tank incorporated a large well between the frames. Water pick-up gear was provided. The coping plates were "solid", without flare or coal rails, and overlapped the tank side sheets – the joint being clearly visible – otherwise presenting a flush appearance. The vertical handrails fitted on the curved ends at both front and rear were 4ft. 3in. between pillar centres.

The overhang at the front of the tender was extra long, to provide adequate clearance for the steam pipes at the back of the booster. The front footsteps were supported from a bracket which was bent outwards to clear these pipes. The axle bearings were outside the frames, with the Group Standard fifteen-plate springs at 3ft. 6in. centres.

After the P1's were withdrawn their tenders were reconditioned at Darlington prior to their subsequent employment with class B2 Nos. 2815 (later 1615) and 1632 (see Part 2B, p. 162).

Maintenance

The P1's were shopped at Doncaster Works and prior to their booster equipment being dismantled used to run about 45,000 miles between general repairs, which fell far short of the 60,000 which was expected of them. After 1937-38 matters improved and mileages between 60,000 and 65,000 were easily attained between general repairs, which were at approximately 2$\frac{1}{2}$ year intervals. Between May 1940 and December 1942 when it entered shops for reboilering, No. 2393 ran 67,638 miles. The best performance by No. 2394 was 63,270 from rebuilding in November 1942 to entering shops for the last time in June 1945. Total life mileages are not recorded but in both cases would be somewhere between 350,000 and 400,000.

Liveries

As befitted their status as goods engines they were painted black with red lining, though the latter was omitted after 1928. Small brass number plates were fitted to the cab sides at first. On No. 2393 the plates were pitched rather high up, off centre in relation to the handrail above, whereas on No. 2394 they were fitted lower down and more or less central with the handrail. These plates were transferred to a position inside the cabs when the numbers were applied to the cab sides in 1931. The tender lettering was changed from "L N E R" to plain "N E" when they acquired A3-type boilers in 1942-43.

Exhibitions

As mentioned earlier, No. 2393 when new took part in the Stockton & Darlington Centenary celebrations in July 1925. No. 2394 was exhibited at Cambridge on 7th and 8th May 1936 whilst No. 2393 was on view to the public at New Barnet on 5th and 6th June 1937.

Allocation and Work

After No. 2393 made its public debut at the Darlington Centenary parade it was allocated to New England shed on 29th July 1925. Trial running took place on loaded coal trains between New England and Ferme Park (Hornsey), including the trial with the dynamometer car described on p. 156. The second P1, No. 2394, was allocated new to Doncaster shed on 18th November 1925 before joining No. 2393 at New England on 2nd December, afterwards sharing a diagram evolved for this class exclusively. The working timetables set out instructions for the working of these trains and the following extracts have been taken from the July 1926 issue.

Following trains are worked by Mikado engines and convey 100 wagons between New England and London.

UP

328 (9.25 a.m. New England to Ferme Park), Mondays to Saturdays inclusive.

DOWN

116 (5.30 a.m. Ferme Park to New England), Tuesdays to Saturdays inclusive.

70 (5.0 a.m. Ferme Park to New England), Sundays.

Approximate length of trains is 670 yards. Must be worked in both directions with 20 ton brake.

UP

Trains should not pass on to Up Main line at either Westwood or Spital Junctions until they can be dealt with by Crescent Junction.

In the event of the Up Home signals at Connington being at danger, drivers must draw well up to them before bringing the trains to a stand, so as to clear safety catch 701 yards north of Up Home signals.

Trains must be run on Up Goods line Connington to Abbotts Ripton or Leys; Huntington North No. 1 to Offord or beyond; and Arlesey to Cambridge Junction. They must also run on Up Slow or Goods lines Hitchin South to Knebworth or Woolmer Green.

Engines to take water Cambridge Junction.

No. 5 Reception Road at Ferme Park to be cleared in readiness.

DOWN

Trains to leave Ferme Park with equivalent of 20 or more empties next engine which must be detached Fletton Junction for use in Brick Yards, except in case of 70 down, Sundays, when wagons must be detached Holme.

Water to be taken at Biggleswade and the trains must be run on the Goods line from Arlesey. If absolutely necessary for water to be taken at Hitchin drivers must give two crows at Langley, where the signalman must pass the information forward to Stevenage North and Hitchin South, and trains must be turned Slow line from Stevenage.

Engine of 70 down (Sundays) to take water Hitchin.

IF NECESSARY TO DIVERT MIKADO ENGINE FROM ITS BOOKED WORKING (116 DOWN 5.30 A.M. EX FERME PARK), YARDMASTER AT FERME PARK MUST ARRANGE FOR TRAIN WORKED BY MIKADO ENGINE TO BE MADE UP TO 100 EMPTY WAGONS, AND RUN AS "100 WAGON SPECIAL".

SPECIAL TO BE TELEGRAPHED FORWARD "100 WAGON SPECIAL" AND INSTRUCTIONS SHOWN ABOVE APPLY. STAFF TO BE PREPARED TO DEAL WITH TRAIN ACCORDINGLY.

From the foregoing it will be clear that a great deal of the southbound journey was run on slow or goods lines. From Peterborough North the 9-25 a.m. class C goods ex-New England followed the 9-12 a.m. "Mark Lane" express (8-30 a.m. ex-Grantham) and 9-15 a.m. semi-fast passenger trains to London. It was passed by the 7-50 a.m. Leeds – King's Cross "Breakfast Train" at Leys before entering the two-track section beyond at 10-43. Huntingdon was passed at 10-58, followed by a five-minute halt at Offord (11-8 to 11-13) for locomotive purposes where it was passed by the 7.0 a.m. Leeds – King's Cross. At St. Neots it was passed by the 10-55 a.m. Peterborough – Hitchin stopping train, which it followed at 11-45. After negotiating the Sandy bottle-neck the goods line was used to allow passage of the 9-0 a.m. ex-Leeds, 9-5 a.m. ex-Hull and 8-0 a.m. ex-Newcastle expresses, eventually passing Arlesey at 1-5 p.m. Ten minutes were booked at Hitchin (1-40 to 1-50) for locomotive purposes, then Hatfield was passed at 2-40 and finally Potters Bar at 3-15, after the passage of the up Leeds Pullman and 3-10 p.m. local passenger from Potters Bar. After that the train was due at Ferme Park at 3-50 p.m.

In practice heavy delays could occur when several of these express trains were duplicated or when excursion trains were run. In the winter months, when coal traffic into London was extremely heavy, congestion occurred in the yards at Ferme Park and Hornsey, causing trains to be held at places along the line waiting for the yards to be cleared. After Grouping a reception road, capable of holding three 80-wagon trains, had been installed between Cemetery Box and New Southgate. It was customary to see a P1 and its train standing on this line behind others for several hours. On such occasions the New England crew was relieved by men sent out from Hornsey shed. (By 1932 the difficulty in obtaining a path for the up 100-wagon train had worsened. Nine passenger trains were then booked to pass it en route and the overall time allowed had been extended to 6 hours 42 minutes).

Better conditions obtained for the down empties on weekdays. This train was timed at class A speed throughout and was able to run on the fast line for much of the journey. Hatfield was passed at 6-25 and Hitchin at 7-28 (after following the 7-3 a.m. Knebworth – Baldock passenger train from Hitchin South). Water was taken at Biggleswade after which the train was held at Sandy until 8-25 for both the 6-30 a.m.

milk empties to Stafford and 7-15 a.m. Leeds express to pass. There was a further stop for locomotive purposes, at Offord 8-55 to 9-0, and Huntingdon was passed at 9-10. A stop was made at Fletton Junction to detach wagons, departing at 10-20 after the passage of the 7-45 a.m. King's Cross – Doncaster stopping train and reaching New England at 10-40 a.m., in 5 hours 10 minutes overall.

Thus it will be appreciated that operation of 100-wagon trains presented certain difficulties, mainly arising from the physical limitations of the route between Peterborough and London. At the time of building the P1 class there were expectations that the bottle-necks caused by two-track sections at some half a dozen places would be eliminated, thus easing the working of slow-moving trains. Mainly on account of financial stringency these hindrances were not eased until fifty years passed and one of them, at Welwyn, seems destined to remain for ever. Further difficulties arose from 1932 onwards when accelerations were made in most express passenger train schedules, coupled with introduction of colour-light signalling at selected locations which entailed shorter block sections. In 1932, therefore, the first steps were taken towards speeding up coal trains as described under class K3 in Part 6A. In that year only the 9-15 a.m. from New England was designated for 100-wagon loads and a Mikado engine, whilst the down empties had been reduced to 80 wagons with no specified locomotives.

During the early stages of design work on the new class P2 express passenger engines, No. 2394 was tried out on the 7-45 a.m. King's Cross – Doncaster stopping passenger train as far as Peterborough, and attained speeds of 65 m.p.h.

There were probably occasions when a P1 had to be pressed into passenger service in an emergency. One observer reported seeing, in the late thirties, a down express running into Peterborough station behind a P1 assisting a Pacific, but dated reports have not been traced.

In the war years both P1 Mikados continued to work regularly on the G.N. main line between Peterborough and Hornsey, sometimes appearing on pick-up trains on which unwary drivers were known to overlook the increased power under their control and cause broken couplings whilst shunting in wayside station yards. Towards the end of their lives a P1 was seen at least once leaving Ashburton Grove, Holloway, on the well-known rubbish train.

In their early years the two Mikados were handled by two selected sets of men at New England who worked through to Hornsey, lodged and returned with the down empties train, thereby working up and down on alternate days. It was inevitable that coal consumption reached high levels in view of the numerous stops and effort involved in re-starting 1,600-ton loads. Possibly some improvement would have ensued had these engines been given long travel gear like the Pacifics, but this was not to be. Taking into account circumstances prevailing at the end of the war in 1945 it was hardly surprising that the P1's had the doubtful distinction of being the first Gresley-designed class to be withdrawn from service.

Engine Diagrams

Section L.N.E., 1925. Fitted with booster; composite diagram for Robinson and "E" Type superheater details. "E" details deleted, 12/1934.

Section L.N.E., 1937. Booster removed. Length between tubeplates altered from 19ft. 0in. to 18ft. 11¾in., 12/1939. Height to the top of safety valves above rail level altered from 13ft. 2in. to 13ft. 1in., 12/1940.

Section L.N.E., 1942. With Diagram 94A boiler; height to the top of the safety valves above rail level 13ft. 0 15/16in. Alternative details for small dome of Diagram 94HP boiler added, 12/1943.

Classification: Southern Area load class 7 (with 220 lb. boiler class 9); Route availability 7.

Summary of P1 Class

1943 No.	Orig. No.	Maker	Works No.	Built	Booster removed	220 lb. boiler	With-drawn
(3990)	2393	Doncaster	1619	6/1925	5/38	1/43	7/45
(3991)	2394	,,	1620	11/1925	4/37	11/42	7/45

CLASS P2

GRESLEY 6ft. 2in. ENGINES

ENGINES BUILT AFTER GROUPING (1934-36): 2001-6. TOTAL 6.

The main line between Edinburgh and Aberdeen abounds in severe gradients and twisting curves over which it was not permitted to double-head the Pacifics, so that the heaviest loads had to be handled by two smaller engines. Gresley sought to avoid double-heading on this route by providing a locomotive which was capable of handling unaided loads of up to 530 tons, so he chose the Mikado, or 2-8-2 type, wheel arrangement. The extra pair of coupled wheels provided additional adhesion and allowed a substantial increase in tractive effort to be provided over class A3. The pony truck at the front end instead of a bogie helped to keep down the overall length.

The first scheme for such a locomotive was produced in Gresley's office at King's Cross on 30th March 1932 (drawing 1) and depicted an engine with 6ft. 2in. diameter coupled wheels, A3-type boiler, dual chimney (as fitted to class A3 No. 2751 *Humorist* at about that time), three cylinders 21in. diameter by 26in. stroke (with the outside pair arranged horizontally) and tractive effort 43,500 lb. This was followed almost immediately by the first of a series of schemes from the Doncaster drawing office (drawing 2), which showed 3in. saved between engine and tender, normal chimney, outside cylinders inclined slightly and no dip in the running plate towards the front. In April 1932 a weight and wheelbase diagram was submitted to the Engineers of the Southern, North Eastern and Scottish Areas. This showed that by then a further 3in. had been saved between the pony truck and leading coupled wheels. The total weight in working order (engine only) was estimated as 103 tons 14 cwt., with a maximum axle load of 20 tons. Nine months elapsed before an outline drawing was prepared from these revised details, in January 1933 (drawing 3), which showed the running plate raised clear of the coupled wheels with a dip restored behind the cylinders.

In February 1933 construction of two engines was authorised and the necessary order was issued shortly afterwards, though the design had not in fact by then been finalised. On 31st March the order was reduced to one engine only. During that month the design had been revised so as to incorporate a longer firebox. This increased the overall length by 1ft. 3¼in. and the estimated weight by 3 tons 9 cwt. At the same time Gresley decided that a double blastpipe was essential. A scheme was worked out similar to the arrangement which had been introduced in 1924 on the Belgian State Railways to reduce excessive back pressure in the cylinders. This was however rejected in favour of the French Kylala-Chapelon arrangement. Smoke deflectors were incorporated, reminiscent of the arrangement employed in class W1 No. 10000. Gresley also decided to fit A.C.F.I. feed water heater equipment. A new outline diagram was prepared in June 1933 (drawing 4) which took account of the latest developments.

In July 1933 Associated Locomotive Equipment Ltd. provided some drawings for the new locomotive covering the two technical features which this firm was supervising. These were the Kylchap double blastpipe arrangement and a scheme to employ Lentz rotary cam poppet valve gear. An outline diagram was prepared at the same time (drawing 5), which also showed the running plate raised over the cylinders and the incorporation of a perforated steam collector in the dome.

The next outline diagram appeared in October 1933 (drawing 6). This showed the smoke deflector plates extended well forward of the smokebox and sloping forward to trap the maximum amount of air to assist in clearing the smoke and exhaust steam, with the cab front plate sloping in a similar manner to match. During later wind tunnel experiments with a scale model, it was found that it would be an improvement if the smoke deflector plates were vertical. The outline diagram which appeared in March 1934 (drawing 9) showed this new feature, and also a vee-shaped cab front.

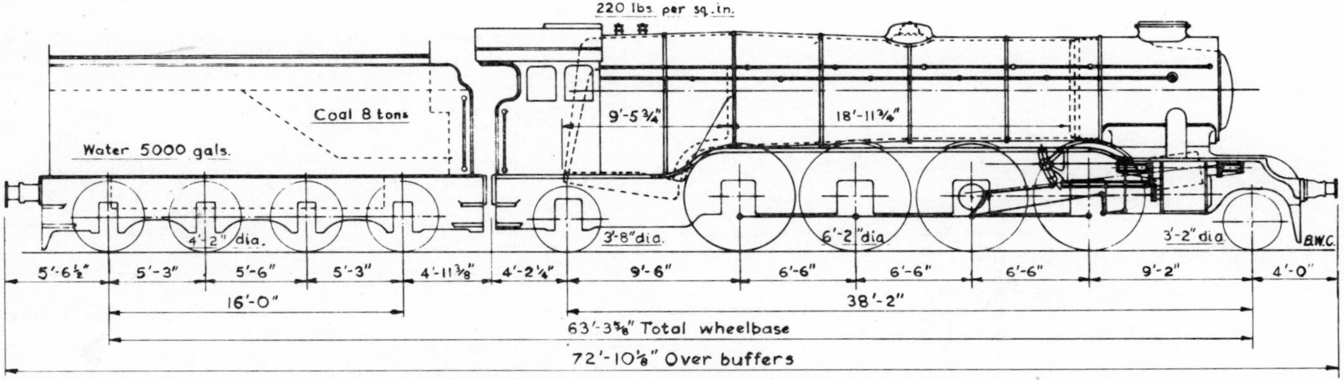

PROPOSED 2-8-2 TYPE – MARCH 1932

1

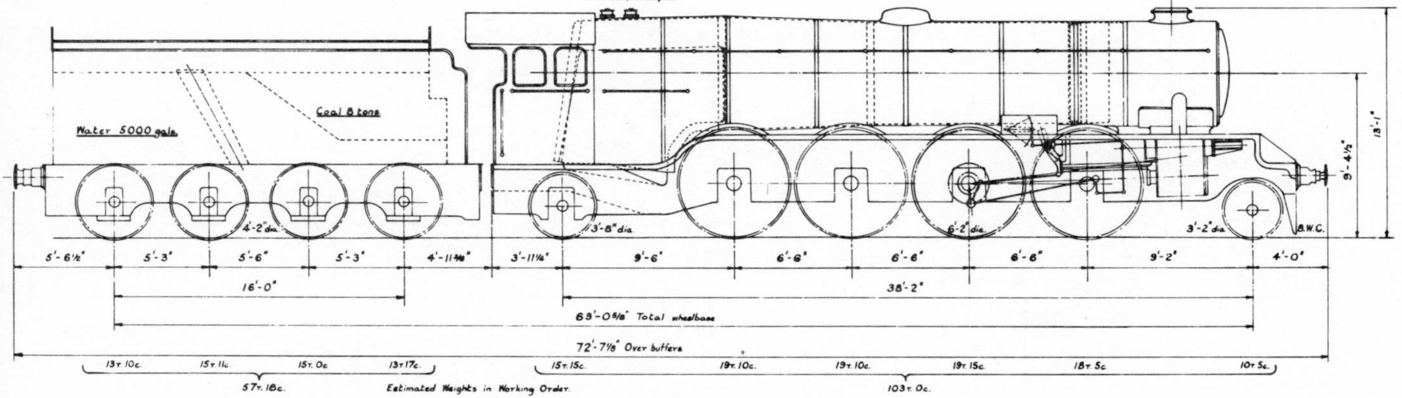

PROPOSED 2-8-2 TYPE - APRIL 1932

2

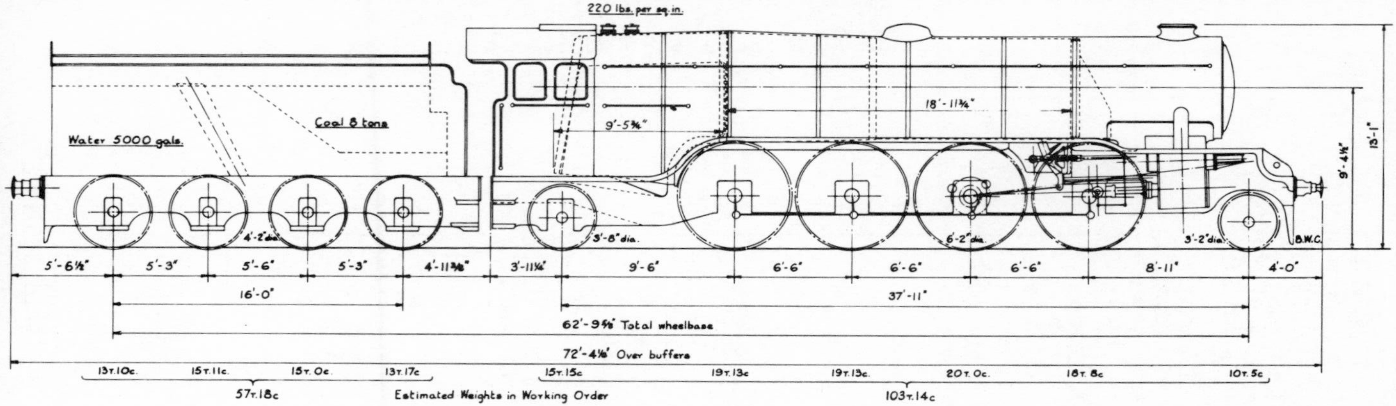

PROPOSED CLASS P2 — JANUARY 1933

3

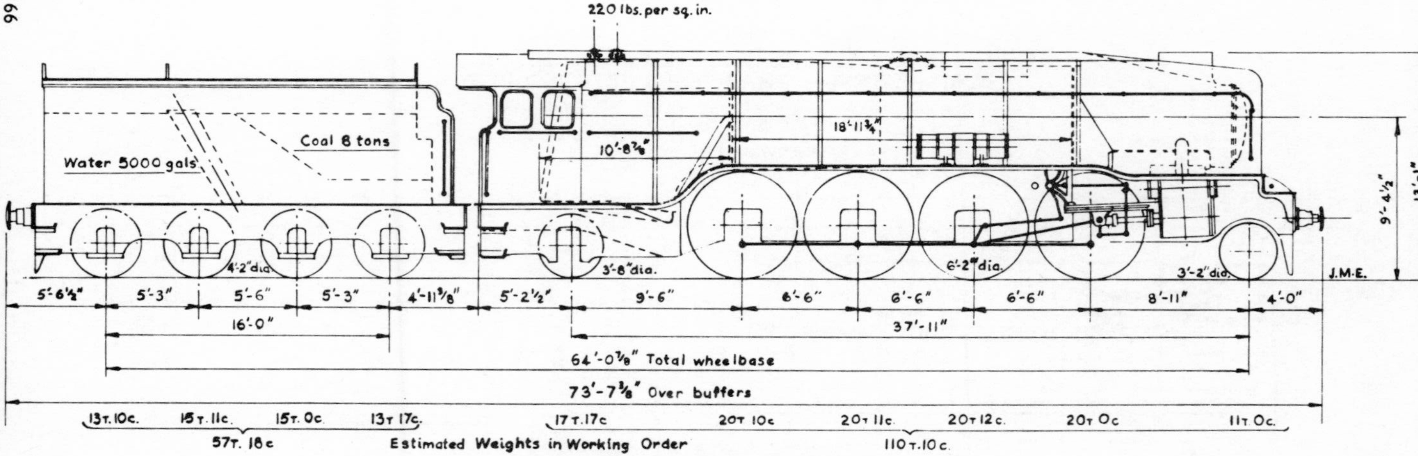

PROPOSED CLASS P2 — JUNE 1933

4

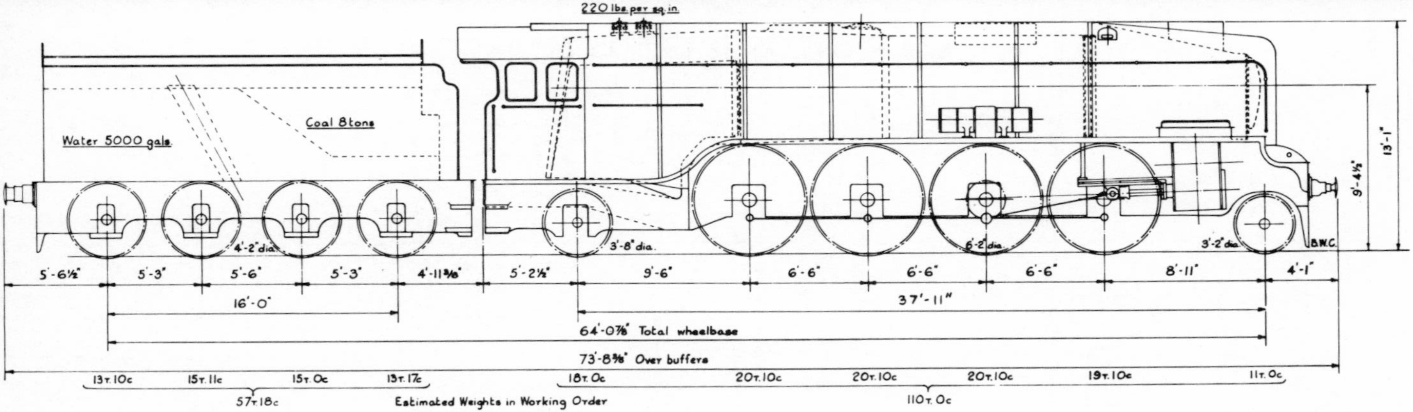

PROPOSED CLASS P2 — JULY 1933

5

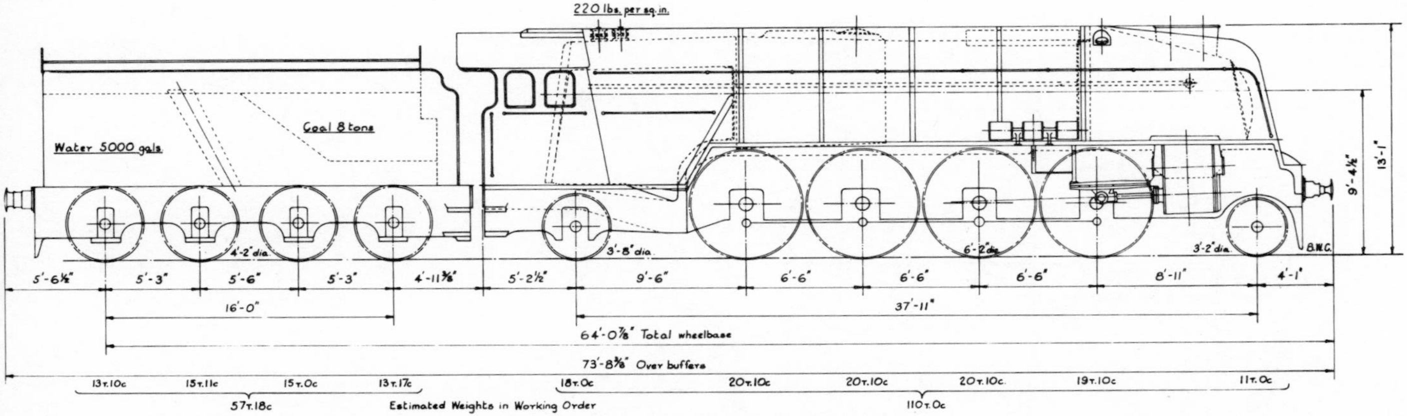

PROPOSED CLASS P2 — OCTOBER 1933

6

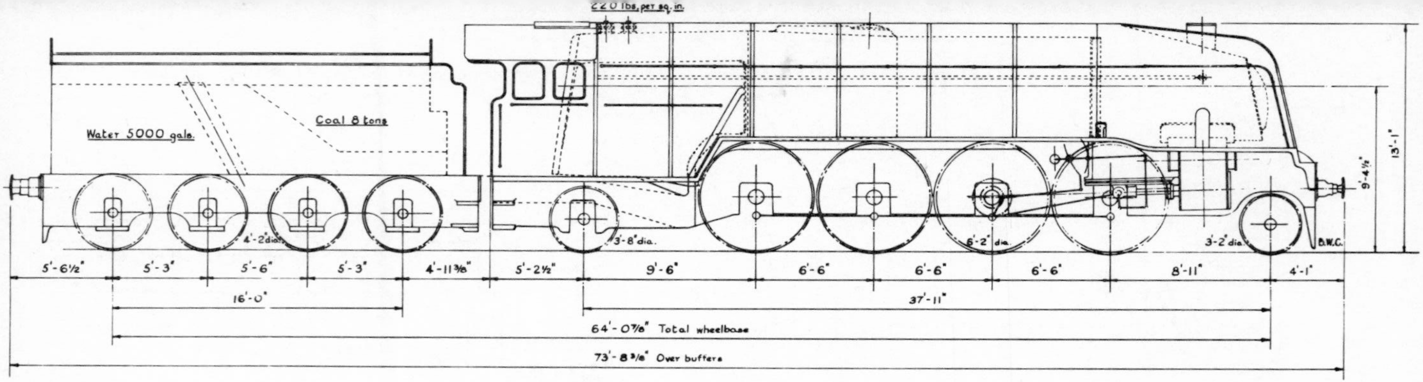

PROPOSED CLASS P2-OCTOBER 1933

7

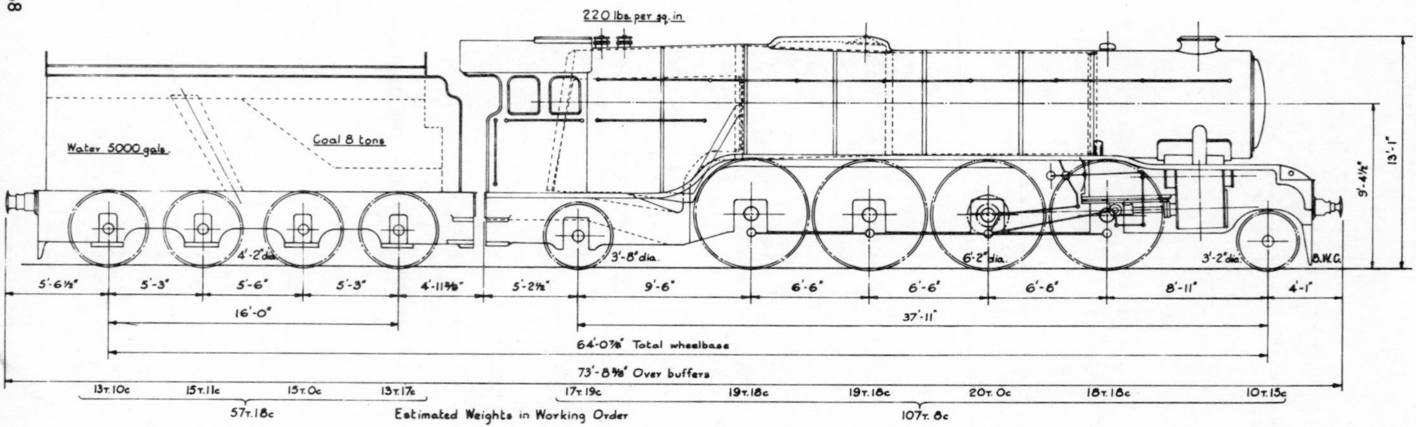

PROPOSED CLASS P2 – DECEMBER 1933

8

Engine Nos.	Maker	Order No.	Date ordered	Works Nos.	No. Built	Date
2001	Doncaster	330	March 1933(a)	1789	1	1934
2002	,,	332	November 1933	1796	1	1934
2003-6	,,	334	November 1933	1836/9/40/2	4	1936

(a) Two engines ordered initially, but reduced to one later.

No. 2001 *Cock o' the North* was completed on 22nd May 1934. In December of that year it left for the locomotive testing station at Vitry-sur-Seine, near Paris, returning to England two months later. Further tests were conducted and modifications were made before the engine eventually went into service in Scotland.

Meanwhile in November 1933 a further five P2's were ordered. The first of these (No. 2002) was to have piston valves and Walschaerts/Gresley valve gear, but a decision respecting the last four engines (Nos. 2003-6) was left in abeyance for the time being. An outline diagram had been prepared in October 1933 for the piston valve version (drawing 7). This showed a single chimney but Gresley almost immediately afterwards said he wanted this engine to be identical to the first one in all respects except for cylinders and motion (see drawing 8, prepared December 1933). In the event, there were other detail differences, in particular the omission of the A.C.F.I. feed water heater. No. 2002 *Earl Marischal* was completed in October 1934, but it was not until June 1935 that it too went into everyday service in Scotland.

Nos. 2003-6 (all of which also carried names – see p. 189) appeared in 1936, with piston valves and Walschaerts/Gresley valve gear like No. 2002, but steamlined at the front to resemble the A4 class. It had also been intended at first to provide side valances (drawing 10), but these were dispensed with and the running plate over the coupled wheels was similar in appearance to that of the first two P2's. There were three important differences: No. 2004 had a by-pass valve which diverted part of the exhaust away from the blastpipe, No. 2005 had a plain single chimney and No. 2006 had a longer combustion chamber in its firebox.

Three class parts were introduced to cover the main variations: Part 1 for No. 2001 with poppet valves, Part 2 for Nos. 2002-5 with piston valves and Part 3 for No. 2006 with piston valves and longer combustion chamber. Construction of the class is summarised in the accompanying table.

In October 1936 at its first heavy repair at Doncaster Works, the front end of No. 2002 was streamlined to conform to the later engines. When No. 2001 entered Doncaster Works in September 1937 for a heavy repair it was decided to rebuild it with conventional piston valves and Walschaerts valve gear to bring it into line with the other P2's. The A.C.F.I. feed water heater was also removed and the engine was streamlined. The engine returned to traffic in April 1938, reclassified Part 2.

The P2's were not without their faults and in particular they suffered from an abnormal incidence of damaged driving crank axles, the result of overheated big-ends which usually scored the crank-pin and made replacement necessary. In some cases the crank axle actually broke in traffic as a result of this weakening. This factor probably contributed to the eventual downfall of the P2's, which came after Gresley's death in 1941 when Thompson succeeded to the post of C.M.E. All six engines were rebuilt to class A2 (later A2/2) between January 1943 and December 1944, and their subsequent history is described in Part 2A of this series.

L.N.E.R. Numbering

The class was originally allotted Nos. 2981-6 following on after a batch of J39's for the Scottish Area, but in April 1934 Gresley agreed to number the engines from 2001 upwards. By this time *Cock o' the North* was in an advanced stage of construction and upon completion its original motion was noted with 2981 stamped on it.

Under the 1943 complete renumbering scheme the engines were allotted 990-5, but at the time the scheme was formulated in July 1943 rebuilding had begun of the engines to class A2 and the process was complete before the scheme was implemented in January 1946. Therefore these six engines were renumbered in the 500 series of 4-6-2's, although No. 2005 carried number 994 for three weeks in April and May 1946 before becoming 505.

Standard L.N.E.R. Dimensions

Cylinders (3)	21″ × 26″	
	No. 2001 *(orig.)*	*Remainder* (a)
Motion	Lentz R.C.	Walschaerts/Gresley
Valves:		
Steam	8″ poppet	9″ piston
Exhaust	9″ poppet	9″ piston
	Nos. 2001-5	*No.* 2006
Boiler:		
Max. diam. outside	6′ 5″	6′ 5″
Distance between tubeplates	18′ 11¾″	17′ 11¾″
Firebox length outside	10′ 9″(b)	11′ 9″
Pitch	9′ 4½″	9′ 4½″
Diagram	106	108
Heating surface:		
Firebox	237.0 sq.ft.	252.5 sq.ft.
Tubes (121 × 2¼″)	1354.2 sq.ft.	1281.4 sq.ft.
Flues (43 × 5¼″)	1122.8 sq.ft.	1063.7 sq.ft.
Total evaporative	2714.0 sq.ft.	2597.6 sq.ft.
Superheater (43 × 1.244″)	776.5 sq.ft.(c)	748.9 sq.ft.
Total	3490.5 sq.ft.	3346.5 sq.ft.
Grate area	50 sq.ft.	
Boiler pressure	220 lb./sq.in.	
Leading wheels	3′ 2″	
Coupled wheels	6′ 2″	
Trailing wheels	3′ 8″	
Tender wheels	4′ 2″	
Tractive effort (85%)	43,462 lb.	
Length over buffers:		
Nos. 2001/2 (orig.)	73′ 8⅜″	
Remainder (d)	74′ 5⅜″	
Wheelbase:		
Engine	8′11″ + 6′6″ + 6′6″ + 6′6″ + 9′6″ = 37′11″	
Tender	5′3″ + 5′6″ + 5′3″ = 16′0″	
Total	64′ 0⅞″	

	Part 1	*Part* 2 (orig.)	*Parts* 2,3 (streamlined)
Weight (full):			
Engine	110T 5C	109T 8C	107T 3C
Adhesive	80T 12C	80T 10C	78T 19C
Max. axle load	20T 10C	20T 14C	20T 0C

Leading particulars applicable to tenders fitted:

	New Type (welded)	*New Type (riveted)*	*Streamlined*
Engine Nos.	2001	2002	2003-6
Weight (full)	55T 6C	57T 18C	60T 7C(e)
Water capacity	5,000 gallons	5,000 gallons	5,000 gallons
Coal capacity	8T 0C	8T 0C	8T 0C(f)

(a) No. 2001 also, from April 1938.
(b) Shown as $10' \, 8\frac{7}{8}''$ on original engine diagram for No. 2001, by a different method of calculation. See under Details on p. 182.
(c) For a short time No. 2001 ran with sine wave elements with reduced heating surface. See under Details on p. 183.
(d) Nos. 2001/2 also, after being streamlined.
(e) Originally shown in error as 57T 18C. Corrected in December 1937.
(f) Altered to 9T 0C in December 1937.

Development

ROTARY CAM VALVE GEAR

Following early satisfaction with the D49's fitted with Lentz rotary cam equipment (see Part 4 of this series), Gresley arranged for the Associated Locomotive Equipment Ltd. (formerly Lentz Patents Ltd.) to design and supply similar equipment for the first P2. The arrangement consisted of two camshafts which obtained their rotary motion by means of suitable skew gears and a driving (propeller) shaft so designed that the rotation of the camshafts was synchronised with that of the driving axle. The camshafts were placed above the cylinders with their axes at right angles to the horizontal centre line of the locomotive. Mounted on the camshafts were six scroll cams which controlled admission and exhaust.

The steam inlet cams provided pre-admission and cut-off for an infinite variation of cut-off positions between 10 and 70 per cent in forward gear and 31 and 70 per cent for reverse running. The exhaust cams provided suitable points of compression and release in all cut-off positions.

The valves were placed with their axes in the horizontal plane. There were four valves for each cylinder, two for admission and two for exhaust. The spring-loaded valve spindles were kept in contact with intermediate levers which in turn had rollers that followed the cam profile. In the mid-gear position the admission valves were kept closed and the exhaust valves kept open.

The reversing gear consisted of a handwheel in the cab (fig. 124), which was connected to a tubular shaft running along the left-hand side of the boiler (fig. 126) to a bevel gearbox, then by means of a vertical shaft to a mitre gearbox just below the running plate. A cross shaft ran from there to the corresponding mitre gearbox under the right-hand running plate. Operating shafts passed forward from these mitre gearboxes into the cylinder casting. A pinion on the end of each operating shaft meshed into a rack on one of the two camshafts. By operating the handwheel in the cab, the twin camshafts moved transversely relative to the locomotive centre line. This brought different points on the cams into contact with the rollers on the intermediate levers.

An advantage of the cam-operated poppet valves was their slow opening followed by quick movement, then rapid closing followed again by slow movement at the actual point of closure. Operation was clean and smooth with no throttling of steam through partly-open ports. The advantage of the cams was that they could be designed to give perfect valve events throughout the full working range of cut-offs. The rotary valve gear meant that identical valve events applied to both forward and return strokes of the piston, whereas with radial valve gears such as Walschaerts it was necessary to compensate for the angular effect which tended to cut off steam earlier on the forward stroke. However there was one flaw in the arrangement. The effective area of the pistons was less on the forward stroke than on the return to the extent of the cross-sectional area of the piston rod. Whereas this disproportion of power was compensated for in the Walschaerts valve gear fitted to the Pacifics, it had been overlooked in the case of No. 2001 until after the Lentz gear parts had arrived at Doncaster. Gresley asked the makers to bear this point in mind in any future development.

A spare set of cams was ordered at about the time No. 2001 first appeared in May 1934. Then on 31st of that month Gresley asked the makers if they could be modified to give a longer cut-off in full gear and also for the steam valves to be kept slightly open in mid-gear for the middle cylinder only. However, their manufacture was too far advanced for any alteration to be made affecting the maximum cut-off, but the alteration was made to the mid-gear setting. These new cams were probably fitted sometime during June.

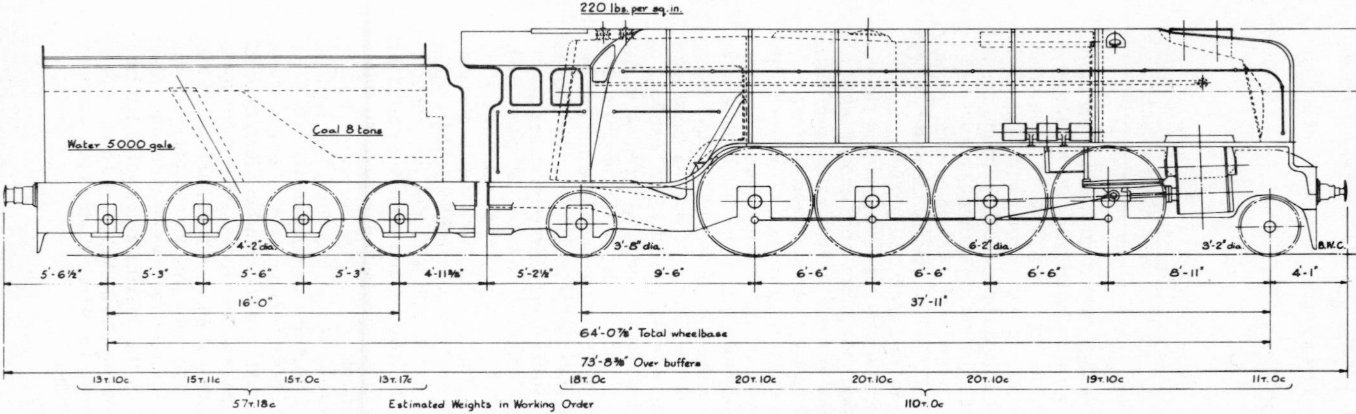

PROPOSED CLASS P2 – MARCH 1934

9

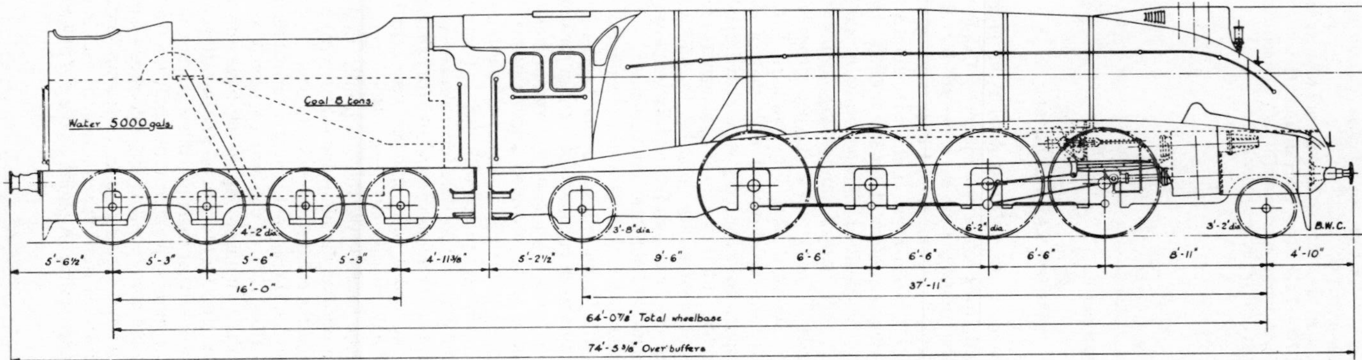

PROPOSED CLASS P2-MARCH 1936

10

Fig. 144 Class P2/2 No. 2004 *Mons Meg* leaving King's Cross station with the 4-0 p.m. Leeds express, 21st August 1936.

Fig. 145 Class P2/2 No. 2004 *Mons Meg* on the 5-15 p.m. Edinburgh – Aberdeen express at Leuchars Junction station, September 1938.

Fig. 146 Class P2/2 No. 2005 *Thane of Fife* leaving Stonehaven on an Edinburgh – Aberdeen express (with sleeping cars), 1937.

Fig. 147 Class P2/2 No. 2005 *Thane of Fife* at Kirkcaldy on an Edinburgh – Dundee semi-fast, 1936.

Fig. 148 Class P2/3 No. 2006 *Wolf of Badenoch* on an Edinburgh – Aberdeen express at Princes Street Gardens, Edinburgh, August 1937.

Fig. 149 Class P2/3 No. 2006 *Wolf of Badenoch* approaching Aberdour on the 2-0 p.m. Edinburgh – Aberdeen express, 1937.

Fig. 150 Class P2/3 No. 2006 *Wolf of Badenoch* on an Edinburgh – Aberdeen express near Stonehaven, August 1943.

In wartime with white painted patches behind buffers and white outline of buffer heads to aid visibility during blackout conditions.

The valve events initially chosen were found, after indicator tests had taken place, to give too low a final compression pressure for the best cylinder efficiency. The cause was the over-large clearance spaces resulting from the layout of the poppet valves. To correct this a new exhaust cam was fitted to the left-hand cylinder, and the point at which the exhaust valves closed and compression commenced was advanced from 65 per cent of the stroke to 50 per cent. Further indicator trials showed that the alteration was successful in raising the final compression pressure by the desired amount, and new matching cams were fitted to the other two cylinders a month later.

The scroll cams and rollers suffered from heavy wear because contact between their surfaces was a point. It was decided to substitute stepped cams, which had parallel surfaces presenting a line of contact, and these were fitted in November 1934 whilst the engine was being prepared for its trials in France. It is interesting to observe that the D49 which came out new on October 1932 with scroll cams, No. 282 *The Hurworth,* had these replaced by stepped cams in April 1934, one month before No. 2001 appeared. The stepped cams which were fitted to No. 2001 had six settings in forward gear: 12, 18, 35, 45 and 75 per cent, and in backward gear there were just two: 35 and 75 per cent, so the advantages of having infinite variations of cut-off were lost. However, the maximum cut-off had been increased from 70 to 75 per cent as an aid to starting heavy trains. Valve opening and closing positions for the different cam arrangements when working in an early cut-off position are set out in the accompanying table.

No. 2001 Valve Settings

Date	5/1934	8/1934	11/1934
Percentage of piston stroke:			
Steam valve opens (pre-admission point)	97	97	96.4
Steam valve closes (cut-off point)	10	10	12
Exhaust valve opens (release point)	85	85	80
Exhaust valve closes (compression point)	65	50	50

During the Vitry tests it was noticed that the exhaust beats at the chimney were uneven. No fault was found but the unequal clearance volumes were suspected. These were significantly different for the outside and inside cylinders and slightly different for the front and back strokes. This meant that there was quite a difference in the various expansion ratios. On the return of No. 2001 to Doncaster, modifications were made to the steam passages which reduced the clearance volumes slightly, though doing nothing to alleviate the problem of the inequalities. The various clearance volumes, expressed as percentages of the cylinder volume, are set out in the accompanying table for No. 2001 before and after this alteration, and also for No. 2002 with conventional cylinders, for comparison.

Cylinder Clearance Volumes

Engine No.	2001	2001	2002
Date	5/1934	3/1935	10/1934
Outside cyls. (front) (%)	12.40	10.88	7.74
,, ,, (back) (%)	11.78	10.26	7.19
Inside cyls. (front) (%)	16.10	14.35	7.83
,, ,, (back) (%)	15.80	14.05	7.62

The cams rollers and valves were subject to considerable wear and they frequently had to be ground down to profile. They were also affected by the high temperature found in the cambox and in March 1935 a circulating system for the oil in the cambox was tried out. This comprised small pumps fitted to the front ends of the driving shafts which protruded beyond the camshaft gearboxes, out of sight behind the lagging. The radiator was a series of copper pipes mounted on a frame under the bufferbeam. As far as is known, this fitting was removed at a later date.

Early Trials with No. 2001

The initial trials with No. 2001 were mainly concerned with its steaming, though its double blastpipe was just one of several new features incorporated in the design. This was not strictly the first occasion Gresley had met with the double blastpipe, for whilst serving under F. W. Webb as a Premium Apprentice, he helped construct L.N.W.R. No. 1502 which had such a fitting though, as Gresley afterwards commented, it was badly designed and a failure.

No. 2001 was the first L.N.E.R. engine to have the Kylala-Chapelon ("Kylchap") arrangement of *double* blastpipe and chimney (fig. 123). Each blastpipe was bisected by a "feather" which split the exhaust before it reached the orifice. A removable blastpipe top was fitted so that it was a relatively simple matter to fit a new one with a different diameter orifice, whilst in the top were fitted four wedge-shaped taper blocks ("Goodfellow tips") to split the exhaust further before passing through the cowls. Four sizes of taper blocks were provided, ranging from No. 0 (smallest) to No. 3 (largest). The cross-sectional area through each blastpipe top was reduced according to which size was fitted.

A number of variations were tried out on No. 2001, ranging from $5\frac{3}{16}$in. diameter orifice with No. 3 taper blocks when it was new, which produced a blast which was too keen, to 6in. diameter with no taper blocks at all, which severely reduced the smokebox vacuum and impeded steaming. It was eventually established at Vitry that the best combination for No. 2001, with its quick-acting poppet valves, was 6in. diameter with No. 1 taper blocks. It is convenient at this point to summarise the combinations which were actually tested and which are referred to in the following narrative.

Blastpipe top diam.	*Taper block size fitted*	*Area through each orifice*
$5\frac{3}{16}$in.	No. 3	16.4 sq. in.
$5\frac{1}{2}$in.	No. 3	19.1 sq. in.
,,	No. 1	20.8 sq. in.
$5\frac{3}{4}$in.	No. 3	21.3 sq. in.
,,	No. 0	23.9 sq. in.
,,	nil	26.0 sq. in.
$5\frac{5}{8}$in.	nil	24.9 sq. in.
6in.	No. 1	25.4 sq. in.
,,	No. 0	26.2 sq. in.
,,	nil	28.3 sq. in.

From 11th to 16th June 1934 and again on the 18th, the engine worked the 10-50 a.m. "Parly" King's Cross to Peterborough and back with the 2-48 p.m. express, due into King's Cross at 4-15 p.m., in the hands of King's Cross driver C. Peachey. On the 14th O.V.S. Bulleid (Gresley's assistant) rode on the footplate on the return trip (load 476 tons) and remarked that it was "really extraordinarily good".

The first dynamometer car test was held on the 19th, from King's Cross to Barkston and back, with Peachey who was by now quite at home on the footplate. The load was nineteen vehicles including the dynamometer car, totalling 649 tons. On the outward run a draw-bar pull of 6.1 tons was recorded at mile post 96 on the short level stretch before Stoke summit, where the cut-off had just been lengthened from 25 to 30 per cent. The speed was $57\frac{1}{2}$ m.p.h. and boiler pressure 210 lb. per sq. in. On the return journey a draw-bar pull of 5.9 tons was recorded on the 1 in 200 climb at mile post 31 after Hitchin with 30 per cent cut-off, when speed was 60 m.p.h., and the boiler and steam chest pressures were 210 lb. and 180 lb. per sq. in. respectively. This pull was equivalent to 2,100 horsepower at the draw-bar. The highest speed was 76 m.p.h., at New Barnet on the return trip.

The next day the engine was back on the 10-50 a.m. "Parly", this time with King's Cross driver W. A. Sparshatt. On the return trip with the 2-48 p.m. ex-Peterborough a 5 minute early arrival was made into King's Cross. On the 21st No. 2001 was on the 1-30 p.m. out of King's Cross, a Doncaster turn, and maximum speeds of 83 m.p.h. were recorded several times before Peterborough, where arrival was 3 minutes early, despite a permanent way check at Yaxley.

Another dynamometer car test was made on 27th June, from Doncaster to Grantham and back, with nineteen vehicles totalling 637 tons, with Doncaster driver F. Elms. The only interesting point occurred on the outward run, on the 1 in 200 climb just beyond Barkston. The engine accelerated from 37½ to 42 m.p.h. with 40 per cent cut-off, equivalent to a draw-bar horsepower on the level of 2,070.

Further dynamometer car tests took place during the first week in July, on the 11-4 a.m. Doncaster – King's Cross (around 420 tons) and back with the 4-0 p.m. from King's Cross (around 580 tons to Peterborough and 420 tons to Doncaster). The cylinders were indicated at the same time. The first run was on the 2nd and on the outward journey the fireman had difficulty maintaining steam between Doncaster and Peterborough, whilst the A.C.F.I. pump also gave trouble. Pressure was only 180 lb. on leaving Doncaster though it did recover to 210 lb. by Rossington. Low pressures were also recorded at mile post 130 after Tuxford (170 lb.), Newark (175 lb.), Barkston (150 lb.), Grantham (175 lb.) and Corby (165 lb.). The driver appears to have kept the regulator open almost continuously to Peterborough except for permanent way slacks. Down the bank from Stoke a maximum of 87½ m.p.h. was recorded at mile post 90, with 12 per cent out-off, with the regulator not eased until six miles further on, in readiness for the Peterborough stop. Gresley met the train at King's Cross and on seeing the record he instructed the engineer in charge of the test not to do it again, but to go fast up the banks and coast down them.

Similar tests were held the next day and the run down Stoke bank provided an interesting comparison, showing due regard to Gresley's orders. Speed reached 71 m.p.h. at Corby but here the regulator was closed and the engine put into mid-gear. Speed gradually dropped to 64 m.p.h. at Essendine where the regulator had to be partly opened with 12 per cent cut-off to maintain speed. Speed over Werrington troughs was 69 m.p.h. before steam was shut off and brakes applied for the Peterborough stop. On this occasion the fireman had had no difficulty maintaining steam and between Doncaster and Peterborough pressure only occasionally dropped below the 200 lb. mark. The remainder of the journey to King's Cross was uneventful, with 72 m.p.h. reached at both Tempsford, where the regulator was then eased, and at New Barnet, where steam was shut off and the engine put into mid-gear to coast the last nine miles into King's Cross in seven seconds under ten minutes, with the brakes applied entering Copenhagen Tunnel. Returning with the 4-0 p.m. the engine primed badly in the tunnels just leaving King's Cross, scouring the tunnel walls and covering the dynamometer car and front coaches with soot and grime. The observers in the indicating shelter at the front escaped the deluge! The blast was clearly too heavy and the engine was returned to the works to have its blastpipe tops opened out from the original 5 3/16in. diameter to 5½in., retaining the large (No. 3) taper blocks. The tests scheduled for the 4th were therefore cancelled whilst the necessary work was carried out, and the exterior of the dynamometer car was cleaned.

One more test was made that week, on the 5th, primarily to indicate the cylinders when working in 15 per cent cut-off, to investigate the compression pressures. The right-hand gudgeon pin overheated on the run up to King's Cross, turning it blue, and a fresh engine had to be found for the return trip whilst No. 2001 received attention on King's Cross shed.

The dynamometer car tests were resumed the following week, with one run on the 10th from Doncaster to King's Cross and a round trip on the 11th from King's Cross to Grantham and back. The blastpipe tops were still 5½in. diameter though now apparently with the smaller (No. 1) taper blocks. The engine still had trouble steaming. On the 11th, for example, the return trip departed from Grantham at 5-44 p.m., (evidently the 3-15 p.m. ex-Leeds running thirty-five minutes behind schedule). Boiler pressure at the start was 200 lb. but this rapidly dropped to 165 lb. per sq. in. passing Stoke Box. Down the bank the maximum speed was 73½ m.p.h. at Helpston. South of Peterborough the maximum speed was 76½ m.p.h. at Tempsford and two minutes were recovered to King's Cross.

Between 13th and 19th July four runs were made without the dynamometer car, trying out different combinations of blastpipe top diameter, taper block size and with or without Kylchap cowls. The results were summarised as follows:-

Blastpipe top 5½in. diameter, No. 1 taper blocks, no cowls: capable of dealing with any condition likely to be met with in the Southern Area.

Blastpipe top 5¾in. diameter, no taper blocks, no cowls: smokebox vacuum too low to steam the engine effectively in 12½ per cent cut-off, especially at low steam chest pressures.

Blastpipe top 5¾in. diameter, No. 3 taper blocks, no cowls: also capable of dealing with any condition likely to be met with in the Southern Area.

Blastpipe top 5¾in. diameter, No. 3 taper blocks, Kylchap cowls refitted: had an ample margin in reserve and was considered capable of covering any requirement demanded in the Scottish Area.

On 30th July the engine returned to Scotland in this latest condition, but on 23rd August it came back to Doncaster for its other two 50 per cent compression cams to be fitted. Examination in the works showed that the existing cams were badly pitted and grooved, and the rollers had deformations and flat surfaces. It was decided to replace these continuous cams by the stepped type and a set was immediately ordered (see later). The engine returned to traffic on 27th August with a full set of 50 per cent compression cams, still the continuous type, and resumed regular working between Edinburgh and Dundee. However, it was back in Doncaster Works from 9th to 16th September to have a new left-hand piston fitted.

No. 2001 was heavy on coal and a test was arranged from Edinburgh to Dundee and back on 1st October for the benefit of a draughtsman, E. Windle, sent from Doncaster to investigate this complaint. As was usual with coal consumption tests only the judged minimum amount of loose coal was put in the tender, after careful weighing, supplemented by a further quantity of coal loaded in bags and held in reserve. There seems to have been a serious miscalculation of the engine's likely consumption, because on the return journey the engine ran out of coal at Dalmeny! Coal from the signalbox bunker was taken on board to enable No. 2001 to proceed and the delay to the passenger train was recorded as 45 minutes. The Haymarket driver on this occasion was D. Macguire, whose methods were usually regarded as somewhat heavy-handed, and J. Bartholomew (Chief Locomotive Inspector in the Scottish Area) was also present on the footplate.

The test was repeated on 5th October, on the 2-0 p.m. Edinburgh – Aberdeen as far as Dundee and back with the 5-40 p.m. (the 3-45 p.m. Aberdeen – King's Cross). The blastpipe tops were now 6in. diameter with, apparently, the smallest (No. 0) taper blocks. The return journey from Dundee was recorded in detail. The load was 543 tons to Thornton, where the Glasgow portion was detached, and 465 tons forward. There was difficulty maintaining boiler pressure, which usually dropped to around 180 lb., though it quickly recovered each time the regulator was closed for one of the booked stops or a permanent way slack. The total amount of coal used on the round trip was 5 tons 9 cwt. Consumption worked out at 103.75 lb. per train mile or 0.1478 lb. per ton mile. After making due allowance for coal used for kindling before the start of the journey and the additional light engine mileage, the consumption could be expressed as 91.9 lb. per engine mile. These figures are of particular interest as they are the only ones which have been traced for No. 2001 when working on the L.N.E.R. No. 2001 returned to Doncaster shortly after this test and was in the works from 10th to 22nd October.

Gresley spoke on the telephone to Chapelon on 22nd October and mentioned that No. 2001 was steaming properly with 6in. diameter blastpipe tops and small taper blocks. Chapelon expressed his surprise as this meant that the total sectional area through which the steam passed was well in excess of French practice (250/270 sq. cm.) to obtain perfect evaporation. He recommended a return to a smaller orifice so that the engine could develop its power at all times. Gresley was not convinced, and No. 2001 spent most of the week on test with its smokebox vacuum recorded under different working conditions, still fitted with 6in. diameter blastpipe tops. The smallest taper blocks were also retained except on the 27th when they were removed altogether. The return trip on the 24th, working the 12-25 p.m. Grantham – Doncaster stopping passenger train, is of interest. The load was recorded as 24 pairs of wheels and Doncaster driver W. Sowden made a rapid acceleration after the Tuxford stop to 80 m.p.h. before braking for the Retford stop.

The tests were continued during the following week, with Doncaster driver G. Trower. On the 30th No. 2001 worked the 2-30 p.m. stopping passenger train to Grantham. The blastpipe tops were still 6in. diameter, with the taper blocks removed. On this occasion however the Kylchap cowls were also removed. On the 31st the engine worked the 2-0 p.m. Doncaster – King's Cross as far as Grantham. New $5\frac{5}{8}$in. diameter blastpipe tops had been fitted. The taper blocks and Kylchap cowls were still absent. This day's testing was the last before the engine was prepared for trials in France. The left-hand connecting rod big-end had run hot, as a result of which more sideplay was provided on the bushes.

Trials in France

No. 2001 entered Doncaster Works on 1st November to be made ready for its visit to France. The continuous cams were removed and in their place were fitted stepped cams. After this modification was carried out, No. 2001 was noted on 27th November working the 12-2 p.m.

Doncaster – King's Cross and back with the 5-45 p.m. It was in this condition that the engine was sent to France.

No. 2001 left Doncaster on the evening of 4th December 1934 for Parkeston under its own steam and hauling three loaded 40-ton bogie coal wagons, a van of spare material and a guard's van, all vacuum braked. It was observed working up the Cambridge main line between Tottenham and Copper Mill Junction, as presumably consideration of weight had precluded the route via Bury St. Edmunds. The fire was dropped on arrival on Parkeston shed and the engine and tender cleaned down prior to being loaded on board the night ferry from Harwich to Calais on the 5th. The train was unloaded at Calais shortly after noon on the 6th and steam was raised again. It ran under its own steam the next day to Vitry-sur-Seine, again hauling its train of coal and spares. Gresley's assistant, O.V.S. Bulleid, accompanied the engine with Doncaster driver G. Trower and fireman W. Gant.

A most ambitious programme was planned for No. 2001 at the testing station. First, tests would be carried out to determine the best combination of blastpipe top diameter and taper blocks size. Various combinations would be tried, each at different speeds and cut-off positions, in short tests of six minutes duration each, during which conditions would be held steady. After ascertaining the best combination of blastpipe top and taper blocks, coal consumption tests would be held at various speeds and in different cut-off positions. Finally, road tests to determine draw-bar horsepower under continuous operating conditions at 80, 100 and 120 kilometres per hour.

Unfortunately a series of misfortunes marred the tests. For one reason or another it was almost impossible to maintain full boiler pressure and during the first series of tests, pressure was usually around 205 – 210 lb. per sq. in. Overheated axleboxes and bearings were frequent whilst on the test bed, though they remained cold on road tests. It appeared that the absence of vibrations on the rollers, of the violent type associated with operating conditions, was preventing the occasional breaks in the oil film on the bearing surfaces from immediately sealing themselves.

The engine's first appearance on the rollers was on 13th December, for demonstration purposes when a top speed of 76 m.p.h. was achieved. The run was stopped when the right-hand driving axlebox ran hot and No. 2001 had to be sent to the nearby Paris-Orleans electric locomotive works where two new driving axleboxes had to be fitted.

Its next appearance on the rollers was on the 17th, when successful runs were made at 60 kilometres per hour in the 12, 18, 25 and 35 per cent cut-off positions. This was with the 6in. diameter blastpipe tops and smallest (No. 0) taper blocks. There was considerable smoke at the chimney top, especially in the shorter cut-off positions, and the fire was somewhat sluggish. Testing on the 18th was abandoned soon after starting when the left-hand crank pin ran hot and the rest of the day was occupied fitting a new coupling rod bush, but unfortunately this ran hot too on the 19th. However, successful tests were made on the 21st, at 80, 100 and 120 kilometres per hour in 12 per cent cut-off, before pausing for the Christmas break.

Tests were resumed on 2nd January 1935. The back plate of the ashpan had meanwhile been removed to increase the air flow through the grate to see if this would reduce the amount of smoke being emitted at the chimney top. It made no difference, but before test readings could be taken the plant was put out of action by a minor breakage. The opportunity was therefore taken to fit another blastpipe top.

Readings were taken on the 3rd running at 60 kilometres per hour in 12, 18, 25 and 35 per cent cut-off, and also in 12 per cent cut-off at 80, 100 and 120 kilometres per hour. With the $5\frac{1}{2}$in. diameter blastpipe tops and largest (No. 3) taper blocks, as now fitted, the amount of smoke emitted had been almost eliminated but this had resulted in an excessive amount of coal being thrown out of the chimney top instead. During these tests the left-hand leading coupled axlebox heated up and the engine was afterwards taken back to the electric locomotive works for attention.

Testing was resumed on the 7th. New blastpipe tops had meanwhile been fitted, $5\frac{3}{4}$in. diameter, with the smallest (No. 0) taper blocks. After three records had been taken the same axlebox ran hot again. Again on the 12th this axlebox ran hot after only three records had been taken.

The blastpipe tops were altered back to 6in. diameter, with however No. 1 taper blocks, before testing was resumed on the 15th at 60 kilometres per hour in 12, 18 and 25 per cent cut-off: and there were no overheating problems. Next day three tests were made at 80 kilometres per hour, in 12, 18 and 25 per cent cut-off. During the third test, the indicated horsepower was 2,278, the highest so far recorded. A fourth test was started at 100 kilometres per hour in 12 per cent cut-off, but abandoned after five minutes with the usual axlebox failure.

The engine returned to the electric locomotive works to have all its coupled wheels taken out and axleboxes completely remetalled. Because there was no suitable lathe there, the wheels and axles were sent by road to the Nord works at Ermont, twenty miles away, whilst the axleboxes were dealt with by a specialist firm at La Courneurve, to the north east of Paris. The work therefore took longer than anticipated, and it was the 26th of the month before a trial run was made to check the bearings, from Vitry to Etampes, a distance of about 60 kilometres. It had been intended to go through to Orleans but on arrival at Etampes the engine was pronounced too heavy to proceed and it was promptly returned to Vitry tender first. A fairly constant speed of 25 m.p.h. was maintained throughout and the bearings remained cool.

By now it had been established that the best blast arrangement was the present 6in. diameter blastpipe top with No. 1 taper blocks. This gave a sharper blast and cleared the smoke away more quickly than with the No. 0 taper blocks and although it reduced the drawbar horsepower slightly it was adopted as the best combination for the later tests.

It was decided to commence the coal consumption tests on 28th January. After running on the rollers for a short time the right-hand driving axlebox ran hot and the test was stopped. The axlebox was remetalled at the electric locomotive works and the engine was sent light on the 31st to the main works at Tours for a full inspection. The highest speed on this journey was 58 m.p.h. and as the bearings were entirely cold on arrival at Tours, Bulleid decided against doing anything further. However arrangements were made for some fast runs from Tours to Orleans and back to see how the axleboxes would stand up. Two round trips were made on 1st February. On the first one a maximum speed of 78 m.p.h. was recorded whilst on the second the maximum was 82.8 m.p.h. Another round trip was made the next day. After each run the bearings were checked and found to be cool. It was decided to bring forward the road tests, using the Paris – Orleans dynamometer car and three counter-pressure locomotives. These latter were four-cylinder compound 4-6-0's, dating from 1913-14, of which four examples were at that time available for this purpose: Alsace – Lorraine Railways Nos. 1157/9/60/1 (later becoming S.N.C.F. 230 D 1 to 4).

Three runs were made between St. Pierre des Corps and Orleans, a distance of just under 70 miles. One outward run was made on the 4th, returning on the 5th, and a final outward run on the 6th. The running during these tests was perfect, with all axleboxes and bearings remaining cool throughout. As far as power output was concerned the results were disappointing. The Doncaster draughtsman, E. Windle, who accompanied these tests, wrote at the time that there "was apparently only one point which prevented a really high horsepower being obtained and that was the steam falling to 150 lb.

ROAD TESTS BETWEEN ST. PIERRE DES CORPS AND ORLEANS

Date	4.2.35	5.2.35	6.2.35
Direction	Outward	Return	Outward
Distance (a) (miles)	63.7	63.5	62.4
Average speed (a) (m.p.h.)	44.7	55.9	68.0
Average boiler pressure (lb./sq. in.)	197.5	188.5	169.0
Cut-off (%)	18	25	35
Average d.b.h.p.	1,213	1,646	1,847
Corrected for gradient (b)	1,236	1,587	1,883
Coal consumption (c) (lb.)	4,680	5,800	5,721
Firing rate (a) (lb./min.)	56	88	107

(a) Whilst regulator was open.

(b) The ruling gradient was rising on the outward journey.

(c) After allowing for coal used for lighting up, wasted through the safety valves blowing off, and fire left on the grate at the end of the trip.

soon after the start of the main trial and failing to come up to 200 lb. throughout the run. As it was, the maximum horsepower was just under the 2,000 mark or rather less than the maximum we have had at home". The main features of these tests are set out in the table, based on the figures prepared by the L.N.E.R. which differ slightly from those published elsewhere.

The high firing rate will be noted. The French people commented at the time on the small size of the firehole door and the small firing shovel which was used. Bulleid afterwards recommended redesigning the firehole door on the lines of P.L.M. or Est practice but Windle thought it would be undesirable, stating that when he questioned the firemen they did not express any difficulty in carrying out their work in a satisfactory manner.

The engine returned to Vitry and the coal consumption tests were resumed on 8th February, with a two hours sustained run at 90 kilometres per hour in 18 per cent cut-off. The regulator was not opened fully in order to give the engine a little more running-in on the plant before coming to the high power test. As a result of this, the boiler pressure managed to stay at a constant 220 lb. per sq. in., for the first time since testing began in France. However at the end of the test the regulator was opened out to the full amount for a few minutes in order to determine the maximum horsepower possible at this speed and in this cut-off position. This was found to be about 1,600.

The second coal consumption test was held next day. The intention was to run the engine at 90 kilometres per hour producing 1,600 h.p., but in 25 per cent cut-off. The steam chest pressure necessary to provide this horsepower was 150 lb. The engine was only able to hold this condition for twenty minutes when the boiler pressure began to fall back steadily, with no chance of regaining it. The test continued for a further forty minutes so that the average horsepower for the full hour was under 1,300. Again the axleboxes and bearings remained cold, which was attributed to the test conditions of working at a lower steam chest pressure, 150 lb. per sq. in., than in the previous tests when pressures were usually around the 195 – 205 lb. mark.

It was clear that a considerable smokebox draught was essential during stationary testing, as on the road the movement of the engine and vibrations all helped to shake the fire. The smallest (No. 0) taper blocks were therefore refitted into the 6in. diameter blastpipe tops before the third coal consumption test was started, on the 11th. The engine rode well but the A.C.F.I. feed water equipment was losing too much water. For the first ninety minutes any slight variation in the boiler pressure was easily brought back to the blowing off point, but then there was some difficulty in maintaining pressure in the boiler above 150 lb., so much so that the test was stopped nine minutes short of the end of the two hour test. It was then found that the right-hand driving axlebox was slightly warm. This cooled down and a repeat run was started in the afternoon, which had to be abandoned after twenty-seven minutes when the left-hand leading coupled axlebox ran hot instead. This completed the tests in France.

The engine was cleaned at the Nord works at La Chapelle and prepared for exhibition at Paris (Gare du Nord) on 17th February, in company with one of the Nord super Pacifics and, in the afternoon, one of the new Maybach diesel electric streamlined trains. The engine left La Chapelle works on the 20th under its own steam for Calais, with its train of three (empty) coal wagons, van of spares and guard's van. The train was loaded on the 21st and the ferry left for Harwich later that evening.

Trials with No. 2002

No. 2002 had piston valves from the outset, operated by Walschaerts/Gresley valve gear. This arrangement did not operate sharply as in the case of poppet valves so that the draughting characteristics were not the same. At first the engine was given $5\frac{7}{8}$in. diameter blastpipe tops with No. 3 taper blocks. Observations were made on 12th December 1934 working the 12-2 p.m. Doncaster – King's Cross and back with the 5-45 p.m., with Doncaster driver A. Wooffindin. The up train had 9 vehicles (232) tons leaving Doncaster, attaching two coaches at Retford (load then 284 tons) and three more at Grantham (final load 341 tons). There were additional stops at Bawtry, Newark, Peterborough, Huntingdon, St. Neots, Hitchin and Finsbury Park, so that the working should by no means tax a P2 and in fact the engine maintained time throughout. However, although full boiler pressure was easily maintained at each stop, it quickly dropped when running, to 175 lb. for example at Bawtry or 165 lb. at Grantham. There was no lift on the fire and no sparks were emitted through the chimney at any time. It was considered that the blast was insufficient to maintain full boiler pressure.

On the return journey the load was 12 vehicles, 400 tons, and there were stops at Peterborough and Grantham only. Again full pressure was only obtained at the stops, and was quickly lost when running. On the climb up Stoke bank there was considerable difficulty maintaining 150 lb. pressure and the exhaust steam injector had to be shut off and the blower opened to assist. Nevertheless the engine regained on this section the three minutes which had been previously lost south of Peterborough due to signal checks.

New $5\frac{3}{4}$in. diameter blastpipe tops, with No. 3 taper blocks, were fitted to No. 2002 in January 1935. On the 24th of this month the engine again worked the 12-2 p.m. ex-Doncaster and back with the 5-45 p.m., with Doncaster driver A. E. Purdy. Observations were made on the return journey only, when the load was 12 vehicles, 400 tons. Steam pressure was well maintained throughout, at around 200-215 lb., except towards the top of Stoke bank when it dropped sharply to 165 lb. For most of the ascent the engine was worked at 15 per cent cut-off, with boiler and steam chest pressures coincident around 200-205 lb. The cut-off was only lengthened to 25 per cent when pressure started to fall near the summit. The engine lost 1 minute on the schedule between Peterborough and Grantham.

The combination of $5\frac{3}{4}$in. diameter blastpipe tops and No. 3 taper blocks was considered satisfactory for this engine and was afterwards made standard for Nos. 2003/4/6, and also for No. 2001 after it received piston valve cylinders in April 1938.

Details

Frames and Running Gear

The frames were 45ft. $5\frac{1}{4}$in. long overall, formed from three sections, consisting of main frames with front-end extension, overlapping each other in the vicinity of the leading coupled axle, together with the rear assembly which gave the usual double frame arrangement under the firebox and cab.

The main frames were 36ft. $9\frac{1}{2}$in. long and ran from just ahead of the leading coupled wheels to the rear end and were spaced 3ft. $11\frac{1}{4}$in. apart. At the rear end they were set in and the last 2ft. 0in. section was 3ft. 5in. apart. The front-end frames were 13ft. $1\frac{1}{4}$in. long and ran from just behind the leading coupled wheels forward to the front buffer plate. This section was 4ft. $1\frac{1}{2}$in. apart. Both the front-end and main frames were $1\frac{1}{8}$in. thick and the 4ft. $4\frac{1}{2}$in. overlap gave added strength around the leading driving horn gaps.

A 1in. thick stiffening plate was welded to the outer face of the main frames, giving extra strength where the set-in commenced. The 11ft. $3\frac{1}{4}$in.-long outside frames, 1in. thick, were bolted to the strengthened frames close to the firebox support stay and diverged outwards before becoming parallel over the last 8ft. $0\frac{1}{4}$in., which was set 6ft. $0\frac{1}{2}$in. apart. It should be noted that in the Gresley Pacifics the stiffening plate was welded to the inner face of the main frames. The change was brought about by the closer spacing of the main frames.

The width of the running plate at the cab end was 9ft. 0in. Ahead of the firebox it was reduced to 8ft. 9in. The width over the front buffer plate was 8ft. 6in. and the lower corners were scalloped with a radius of 7in. to clear platform edges.

On Nos. 2003-6 the distance between the frames at the rear end, where they were set in, was 3ft. $2\frac{1}{2}$in. instead of 3ft. 5in. as in Nos. 2001/2. The final parallel portion extended sufficiently forward beyond the trailing radial wheels to eliminate the need to dish the frames at this point to clear the wheel boss as had been necessary on the first two P2's. On Nos. 2003-6 also, the width over the front buffer plate was only 7ft. 6in. and Nos. 2001/2 were brought into line in this respect when they were fully streamlined.

The height above rail level to the underside of the running plate over the coupled wheels was 6ft. 8in. On No. 2001 when new the running plate remained horizontal to the front end where there was then a sharp drop to the lower platform (fig. 126). On No. 2002 there was a reverse curve in the running plate and the section over the cylinders was $7\frac{27}{32}$in. lower (fig. 127). There was only a shallow drop at the extreme front to the lower platform, which was $2\frac{5}{32}$in. higher than in No. 2001. On Nos. 2003-6, and the first two P2's after they were fully streamlined, the running plate curved gently downwards ahead of the leading coupled wheels.

The leading pony truck employed double swing links for centring though by this time Pacific bogies were being converted to helical spring side control. Gresley's assistant, B. Spencer, unsuccessfully tried to persuade his chief to adopt a Bissell truck arrangement for the P2's after being favourably impressed by the smooth riding of the Southern Railway River class 2-6-4 tank engines which were tested on 16th October 1927 between Huntingdon and St. Neots at speeds up to 83 m.p.h. Gresley saw no reason to depart from usual practice especially as his pony trucks were cheaper to construct.

The pony truck was therefore modelled on that of the K3 class, with ⅞in.-thick frames spaced 2ft. 11½in. apart and helical bearing springs on the outside of them. These springs had a combined vertical deflection of 0.17in. per ton. The wheels, which were 3ft. 2in. diameter, had a maximum translation of 4½in. to each side, in an arc. The radius arm was 6ft. 9½in. long and the journals were 6½in. diameter and 9in. long.

The swing links were 7in. between pin centres and arranged so that the effect of side translation was to raise the front of the engine. Its weight then tended to return the truck to its central position. The maximum lift, with full translation, was 1⅝in. Alternatively the bearing springs could be depressed instead or, what was more likely, there would be a combination of both factors. Whilst this method of centring may have been acceptable on straight track, it had a dubious effect on curves. It was thought that as the wheels followed the curve, the front of the engine first of all lifted, with a corresponding fall at the cab end. The engine as a whole would then lift throughout its entire length until the spring deflections gave the correct total weight and the same centre of gravity. Static tests in August 1934 with a K3 confirmed this supposition but also drew attention to the unexpected discovery that the altered weight distribution was not equally shared between the left and right sides of the engine.

Methods of lubricating the swing link pins were unsatisfactory and experience with the K3's had already shown that the pin holes tended to wear oval, thus nullifying the lifting concept. Later experience with the P2's in Scotland showed abnormally high wear of the outside crank pins on the leading coupled wheels which suggested that these wheels were leading the engine into curves as if the pony truck did not exist.

The minimum radius curvature that the engines could negotiate was originally given as 6 chains. Because of the long rigid wheelbase extra care was taken in shed yards to avoid derailment, with the engines restricted to certain roads. When the engines were built and again after each overhaul at Doncaster, they were taken to the old iron foundry in the Plant yard by the river where there was a particularly sharp curve. The P2's, and in fact Pacifics also, had to pass this strict test before being sent into traffic. On 29th December 1934 No. 2002's pony truck wheels were derailed in the locomotive yard at King's Cross station. The tyres were to size and appeared to be the correct distance apart, whilst the Civil Engineer could find nothing wrong with the track. The engine returned to Doncaster on 2nd January, working the 8-15 a.m. No. 2 braked goods from King's Cross, and the following day was sent into the works for examination. Everything appeared to be in order, at first, and so the engine was taken round to the iron foundry in an effort to derail it, but the only result was derailment of the shunting engine pushing it! It has been said that someone then noticed a movement in the wheels as they turned, and on careful checking it was realised that the axle was slightly bent. Whilst in works, static tests were made both in the Weigh house and in the Crimpsall Repair Shop to measure the actual sideway translation of the pony truck wheels, on a greased plate. This was found to be only 3½in. against the theoretical figure of 4½in. Longer swing links were fitted, 8in. between pin centres instead of 7in., which gave an additional 1in. sideway translation. No. 2002 returned to traffic on 19th January after this modification had been carried out. No. 2001 was afterwards brought into line, in March 1935, and the remaining P2's came out new in 1936 with this altered arrangement. Calculations were made of the effect of this new pony truck with the engine on a 5 chain radius curve, to see if there was sufficient lateral side play in the leading and trailing coupled wheels or whether it would be necessary to thin the flanges on the driving and intermediate coupled wheels to allow the engine to pass freely. The only action taken seems to have been to amend the minimum radius curvature that the engines could negotiate from 6 to 7 chains, which placed further restrictions on their availability in shed yards and stations.

Rapid wear in the swing link pin holes eventually resulted in the pony truck not functioning properly. Consequently the front coupled wheels took on the task of leading the engine into curves and the outside crank pins on the coupling rods of these particular wheels needed frequent renewal. The P2's also had a particularly bad record of over-heated middle big-ends which was in part due to the stresses and strains at the front end arising from faults in the pony truck and to the enormous piston load of 34 tons. However, the bearing surface of the middle big-end was 9¼in. diameter by 6in. wide and theoretical calculations showed that the piston thrust produced in the crank pin a bending or twisting stress of 9.69 tons per sq. in. which was appreciably less than the 11.22 tons in the smaller crank pin of the A3's. An over-heated middle big-end frequently resulted in the driving axle crank pin being badly scored and the middle connecting rod, piston rod, piston head and cylinder back being damaged. Sometimes the crank axle actually broke as a result of a big-end failure. On one occasion the axle broke just as the P2 was running into Edinburgh so that there was little delay. Not so on 18th July 1939 when No. 2005 was working the 7-35 p.m. Aberdeen – King's Cross with a load of 508 tons. Leaving Stonehaven the crank axle broke close to the right-hand driving wheel. The train suffered 2 hrs. 19 mins. delay. Then on 10th April 1942 No. 2004 was working the 2-0 p.m. Edinburgh – Aberdeen, with Haymarket driver L. Daniel, when the crank axle broke leaving Kirkcaldy. This seems to have been the last straw. At that time No. 2006 was already in Doncaster Works for new cylinders. It is perhaps significant that it was in April 1942 that the first outline drawing appeared showing the P2's as they would appear after rebuilding as Pacifics. The Thompson bogie had coil springs for centring, which overcame the problem associated with the swing links. This was a drastic course to take when it would have been simpler and cheaper to have substituted a pony truck with side spring control. E. Windle, the Chief Draughtsman at Doncaster, failed to persuade Thompson to adopt the simpler solution and the engines were rebuilt as Pacifics in 1942-44, after which there were no recorded instances of crank axle failures. The last such case with a P2 was on 29th July 1944, when No. 2003's axle broke two miles south of Aberdeen. The engine entered Doncaster Works on 2nd September and emerged rebuilt as a Pacific.

The three cylinders were cast together in one monobloc casting following Gresley's adoption of this N.E.R. practice in new designs where the front end arrangement permitted this. The outside cylinders were inclined at 1 in 30 and the inside one at 1 in 7.713 to clear the leading coupled axle. All three cylinders drove on the second pair of coupled wheels; the distance from the centre of the cylinders to the centre of the driving axle was a common 11ft. 8in. The poppet valves and gear for No. 2001 when new are described on page 171 *et seq.* On the remaining P2's, and No. 2001 subsequently, the piston valves were 9in. diameter and the maximum valve travel 5$\frac{5}{8}$in., at 65 per cent cut-off. Walschaerts valve gear was used for the outside piston valves and Gresley's 2 to 1 arrangement to actuate the centre valve. Screw reverse gear was fitted, with the screw arranged vertically in the cab. An inspection hole for the 2 to 1 levers was provided in the vertical running plate below the smokebox front. This had a hinged door to exclude dirt and ashes.

A large steam receiver was incorporated in the top of No. 2001's cylinder casting to maintain the steam chest pressure as near as possible to that of the boiler. Two 5$\frac{1}{2}$in. diameter bore pipes led from the superheater header to the top of this receiver, thus eliminating the need for outside steam pipes. The remaining P2's with their conventional cylinders, and No. 2001 subsequently, had three 5in. diameter bore steam pipes leading down from the header to the steam chests. The outside pipes had separate elbow joints following current practice, hence the need for sloping covers which were a protruberance from the streamline casing on Nos. 2003-6 for example. This feature had been avoided in the A4 class by redesigning the steam passages.

Two Wakefield No. 7 mechanical lubricators were provided on the left-hand running plate. The front one was for the cylinders and the rear one was for the coupled wheel axleboxes. Whilst No. 2001 was fitted with poppet valves, the drive for the lubricators was taken from a crank on the intermediate trailing coupled axle. On the remaining engines, and on *Cock o' the North* from April 1938, the lubricators were located further forward on the running plate and operated from the radius link in the standard manner (cf. figs. 126 and 127).

Boilers

The design of *Cock o' the North*'s boiler (Diagram 106) was based on the A3-type (Diagram 94HP). The distance between the tubeplates and the arrangement of the tubes were the same and consequently such particulars as the heating surface figure for the tubes were identical. However the firebox was enlarged to provide a grate area of 50 sq. ft. The barrel was constructed in two sections. The front ring was parallel, 5ft. 9$\frac{3}{16}$in. outside diameter, whilst the taper section was 6ft. 5in. outside diameter at the firebox end. An innovation was the perforated steam collector extension to the dome casing on the taper section. The straight top to the clothing plate gave the appearance that the barrel was parallel throughout.

The length of the firebox outer casing was 10ft. 8$\frac{7}{8}$in. and this was the dimension that appeared on the original engine diagram for No. 2001. However, the overall length of the complete firebox was 10ft. 9in., as measured from the rear of the casing to the front of the tubeplate, and this was the dimension that appeared on later engine diagrams. The outer casing had twenty-two rows of roof stays, two rows of expansion sling link stays at the front end and twelve transverse stays. These dictated the position and number of the wash-out plugs (which were situated over the boiler handrail). There were five on the left side (though the rear one was out of sight behind the vee-portion of the cab front) and four on the right (figs. 126 and 130).

With a wide firebox it was usual practice in Britain to run with a thin fire with the firehole flap left open for supplementary air to enter and aid combustion. French practice was to have a thicker fire with increased air space between the firebars, thus reducing the risk of a sharp blast tearing holes in it and obviating the need for supplementary air through the firehole door. Following the trials in France the firebars were redesigned on the lines of those fitted to the Est engine which had been at Vitry at the same time as No. 2001. The new grate was fitted to *Cock o' the North* in March 1935. The air space through the grate was increased from 30 to 56 per cent of the grate area which was a substantial improvement. Bulleid also recommended increasing the firebox volume as a further aid to complete combustion, by enlarging the combustion chamber. An extra P2 boiler incorporating this feature was ordered in August 1935 (Diagram 108) and fitted to No. 2006 *Wolf of Badenoch* when new. The distance between the tubeplates was reduced by 1ft. 0in. and the combustion chamber lengthened by a corresponding amount. The enlarged firebox had three extra rows of roof stays and two additional transverse stays. Instead of wash-out plugs above the boiler handrails, there were five inspection doors on each side (fig. 134), with the rear one on the right-hand side actually inside the cab.

The introduction of the Diagram 108 boiler rendered spare one of the Diagram 106 boilers which had been ordered originally for Nos. 2003-6. This remained unused until April 1940 when it was fitted at Doncaster to No. 2002. *Earl Marischal's* original boiler was repaired and sent to Cowlairs where it was fitted in October 1942 to No. 2003. These were the only boiler changes affecting the P2's prior to their rebuilding as Pacifics.

No. 2001 had the A.C.F.I. system of feed water heater until April 1938 (fig. 130). The horizontal tandem feed pump was mounted on the right-hand running plate with a common piston rod serving (respectively) the steam, cold water and hot water cylinders. Cold water was pumped from the tender to the mixing tank on the top of the boiler, hidden from view under the clothing plates. The water entered this tank as a fine spray which was heated by mingling with exhaust steam, both from the steam pump and diverted from the blastpipe. The heated water was forced under pressure into the adjacent settling tank from which waste gases, mainly oxygen and carbon dioxide which have a detrimental effect on the inside of the boiler if allowed to remain in the feed, were allowed to escape through two air vents. The water, now almost at exhaust steam temperature, was drawn into the hot water pump, which forced it through a clack valve on the side of the boiler.

The equipment was a constant source of trouble. To function properly it required the regulator to be open continuously which was not possible on the Edinburgh to Aberdeen line, with its numerous speed restrictions. One of the engine's regular firemen at Haymarket, J. Cunningham, could afterwards recall only one successful trip when the A.C.F.I. worked perfectly, and that was on a Newcastle to Edinburgh working, when *Cock o' the North* was returning home after a repair at Doncaster.

No. 2001 had "sine wave" superheater elements at first, (No. 2002 may also have had this type when new but this has not been confirmed). Such elements undulate throughout their length, in the shape of a sine wave, to create a turbulent steam flow within the element. This breaks down the potentially insulating layer of steam next to the flue walls and so increases the heat transfer from gases to steam. During the test run on 27th June 1934 a steam temperature as high as 750 degrees Fahr. was recorded, which was considerably higher than temperatures attainable in the A3's. However, it is understood that these elements were subject to rapid erosion.

Towards the end of July 1934 the sine wave elements were taken out of No. 2001 to permit trials with a new Robinson superheater, the return loops of which were 10ft. 6in. long with their ends only 9in. from the firebox tubeplate, as compared with 9ft. 0in. and 1ft. 7in. respectively at that time standard for the A3's. These new elements offered a substantial increase in heating surface over both the sine wave type and the normal A3 type (see accompanying table). During the road tests in France a figure of 765 degrees Fahr. was

Introduced	Type	Outside Diam. of Elements	Gauge (S.W.G.)	Heating Surface (sq. ft.)	Fitted to
12/1932	Short loop (9′ 0″)	$1\frac{1}{2}$″	10	706	Class A3
5/1934	Sine wave	$1\frac{1}{4}$″	11	695*	2001, class A3 2500-8
7/1934	Short loop (10′ 6″)	$1\frac{1}{2}$″	10	776.5	2001-5, class A3
9/1935	,, ,, ,,	$1\frac{1}{2}$″	10	748.9	2006, class A4

* Quoted in error as 635.5 sq. ft. on the engine diagrams.

registered during the last two runs. It was even suggested at that time that the superheat could be further increased as temperatures up to 800 degrees should cause no problem with poppet valves. No further improvement was attempted and in any case after these French trials, when the cam boxes were opened out for inspection back at Doncaster, Bulleid noticed discolouration of the valve gear due to the high temperature. The later P2's also received the new Robinson type, though in the case of No. 2006 (which had a shorter boiler barrel) the elements were 1ft. 0in. shorter. Similar elements afterwards became standard for the Gresley Pacifics. The different types are summarised in the accompanying table.

The double blastpipe arrangement was efficient in maintaining a high smokebox vacuum with low back pressure. The results from the Vitry trials showed that there was a considerable reduction in horsepower output when the blastpipe opening was restricted. The diameter was perhaps a little too large for the high power outputs and the figures suggested the need to fit a variable top so that the blast could be controlled. As a result No. 2004 had an experimental exhaust steam by-pass to reduce the effect of the blast, which tended to lift the fire when starting or working heavily at long cut-offs (see accompanying drawing). The 5in.

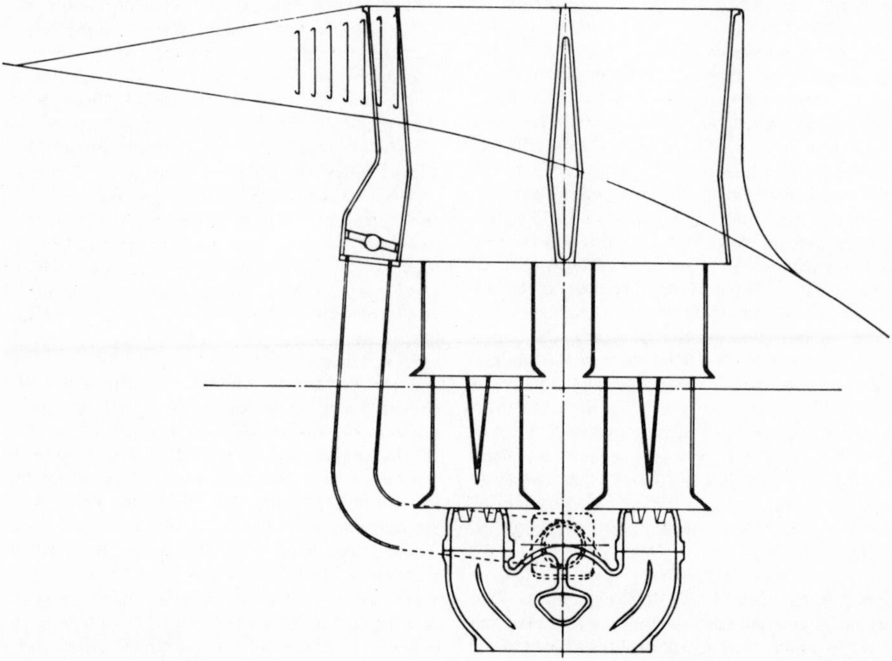

diameter by-pass ran from the blastpipe and ended in a crescent-shaped orifice behind the double chimney. A butterfly valve was located in this pipe, opened and closed at the discretion of the driver by means of rodding which passed along the left-hand side of the boiler, partly hidden from view behind the vacuum ejector exhaust pipe. The rod was pulled to open the valve and pushed to close it. When working in 40 per cent cut-off a slight reduction of about ½in. in the smokebox vacuum was obtained when the valve was open.

In service the butterfly valve frequently became clogged with carbonised oil. On one occasion the valve stuck and the engine had to be taken off its train at Thornton. L. Parker, the draughtsman at Doncaster who had been responsible for the drawings, was hurriedly sent to Thornton shed to unstick the valve. The outcome was that the arrangement was altered in July 1937. The by-pass valve was now 5½in. diameter, opening out into a 7⅜in. diameter circular orifice behind the double chimney. A plug valve was provided in place of the butterfly valve, operated as before by means of the horizontal rodding except that it was now pushed to open and pulled to close. The new arrangement effected a reduction of 1in. in the smokebox vacuum when working in 40 per cent cut-off.

It was then found that drivers were reluctant to use the by-pass valve as it made the engine steam badly when working uphill. Draughtsman Parker was again sent for and on 17th November 1938 he rode on the engine between Edinburgh and Dundee. It was clear that the apparatus had not been used for some time and as a result the operating mechanism was modified in June 1939. The manual control (which drivers shunned) was replaced by automatic operation working off the reversing shaft. This opened the plug valve when the cut-off was 38 per cent or longer, in fore gear only.

Carbonisation troubles persisted and it was necessary to remove and clean the plug valve monthly. In September 1940 an alternative arrangement was considered in which the plug valve was to be replaced by a flap valve, which fully opened when the cut-off was 40 per cent or longer, in fore gear, and fully closed at 25 per cent or shorter. The modification was not introduced, neither was a later scheme to operate the valve by steam.

No. 2005 was the only P2 with a single chimney. The blastpipe had a 6in. diameter orifice. Following the successful application of jumper tops of the A4's which had single chimneys, it was decided in December 1938 that it would be advantageous to equip No. 2005 similarly, and the appliance was fitted in April 1939. When working hard the heavy blast lifted the outer casing, effectively increasing the diameter of the orifice to 6¾in.

General

On Nos. 2001/2 the cab profile was basically that of the A3 class, with the same principal dimensions, but the front end was vee-shaped to present a streamline appearance which also hid the safety valves from view. There was the usual beading around the edge of the side sheets and the rear of the cab curved inwards to match the tender. The length of the vertical handrails was 3ft. 7in., but this was later increased to 4ft. 3in. when seat backs were fitted and the depth of the rear cut-out in the side sheets was reduced (cf. figs. 126 and 130). On Nos. 2003-6 the cab profile was very similar to that of the A4 class, but the bottom edge was horizontal. There was no beading around the rear edge of the side sheets which were straight to match the streamlined tender. The length of the vertical handrails was 4ft. 6in. (fig. 134), which was afterwards adopted as standard on the A4's from No. 4482 onwards.

Conditions in the cab were found to be unbearably hot and it was often necessary to keep open the front plate windows on the first catch. Firemen also complained about the heat from the firehole door when they were seated. The driver was protected in the usual manner by the hinged heat shield to the left of this door (fig. 124). However, this heat shield interfered with the fireman's movements when he was firing. An improvement was implemented on No. 2002 which became the standard arrangement for the P2's: the heat shield on the driver's side was shortened so as not to be in the fireman's way when it was pulled out and a separate shield was provided for the first time on the fireman's side.

On the fully streamlined engines, which had rubber sheeting across the gap between engine and tender, there were further complaints of hot conditions in the cab and two extra roof ventilators were provided on No. 2006 when new, one above each seat (fig. 134). The other P2's were afterwards brought into line.

No. 2001's boiler clothing plates hid the dome from view, and presented a smooth profile from the smokebox back to the cab. The casing also surrounded the smokebox, extending well forward beyond it, and below the centre line it dropped vertically to the running plate. "Alfol" corrugated aluminium foil (instead of asbestos mattresses) was used for clothing the boiler (fig. 121), and this material also filled the gap between the smokebox and smoke deflectors, thus enabling the casing to be painted green in its entire length without risk of heat blistering. The smokebox front plate and door sloped at an angle of 12 degrees from the vertical and the top sloped at 15 degrees from the horizontal. A curved plate was fitted on the top behind the double chimney to help deflect the flow of air upwards to carry with it the smoke and exhaust steam. The front end arrangement was similar to that employed for class W1 No. 10000 and appears to have been successful in the case of *Cock o' the North*.

No. 2002 had a similar arrangement though in its case the lower edge of the front casing followed the contour of the reverse curve in the running plate. In addition the outside steam pipe covers protruded through this casing (fig. 127). The arrangement failed to lift the smoke and exhaust steam clear of the cab, particularly when working in short cut-off positions, and this was considered to be due to the slower acting piston valves.

Following experiments with a scale model in the wind tunnel at the City & Guilds (Engineering) College, additional smoke lifting plates were fitted to No. 2002 in April 1935 which solved the problem (fig. 128). These were placed outside the original casing alongside the smokebox, 1ft. 5⅛in. away at running plate level, curving inwards to 6in. distance at their tops. The casing was shortened by 1ft. 0in. at the front end and the beading was removed from its edge. The nameplates were transferred from the casing to the smoke lifting plates, located 7¼in. lower down than before to clear their curved portion. Extra curved plates were finally fitted in the space between the original casing and the smoke lifting plates which deflected the air upwards.

The four P2's which appeared in 1936 had their smokeboxes and front ends streamlined in the manner of the A4's which had been introduced the previous September, this arrangement having proved most effective in lifting smoke and exhaust steam clear of the boiler top. An obvious point of difference was the extrusion of the steam pipe covers as the steam passages in the P2 cylinders had not been rearranged to avoid this necessity. Similar streamlined casings were fitted to No. 2002 in October 1936 and No. 2001 in April 1938 (figs. 132 and 133).

The front casing had the same mechanism as in the A4 class by which it could be opened to give access to the smokebox door itself. The top lampiron was located as close as possible to the upper casing door hinge, with its lamp support 9ft. 11in. above rail level, i.e. ¼in. lower than in the A4 class. Commencing with No. 2004 in May 1941, the lampirons were relocated 9in. lower down on the curve of the door, reducing the height above rail level to 9ft. 5⅜in. This was done at the request of the Running Department who, when changing tubes and elements at the shed, found that the upper door would not open sufficiently when cranked. Their remedy was to disconnect the operating mechanism and prop the door wide open, but when doing so it was found that the lampiron fouled the chime whistle on the P2's with double chimneys. (No. 2005 with its single chimney, had its chime whistle located 9¾in. further away from the upper hinge, fig. 137). When the alteration was made to the top lampiron, the operating gear on the lower door was dispensed with, enabling it to be opened more fully. This door was then supported by a chain when open.

As with the A4 class, the skirting ahead of the cylinders could be removed to give access to the 2 to 1 motion levers and piston valves. Wartime conditions brought about an inevitable deterioration in the standard of maintenance and valuable time was wasted removing this skirting. The skirting was permanently removed from late 1941, usually whilst in works, but No. 2004 was dealt with at Haymarket shed in June 1942.

The handrails which ran the full length of the boiler were positioned 1ft. 2¼in. above the boiler centre line. In the case of *Earl Marischal* they were cut back when the additional smoke lifting plates were added in April 1935 (fig. 128). On the sides of the firebox additional handrails were provided, pitched 4in. higher than those on the cab sides, except that in the case of *Cock o' the North* they were even higher on the left-hand side only, to clear the shafting for the reversing gear. This arrangement was not altered afterwards when the engine was changed to piston valve operation (cf. figs. 126, 127 and 132).

The vacuum ejector exhaust pipe ran along the left-hand side of the boiler below the handrail. On Nos. 2001/2 the pipe was pitched 6in. above the boiler centre line except alongside the firebox where it sloped down gradually towards the cab front to clear the window. On the later P2's the pipe was pitched $1\frac{1}{2}$in. lower and remained horizontal throughout (cf. figs. 126 and 134).

In April 1934 Captain Howey, of the Romney Hythe & Dymchurch Railway, presented Gresley with a Crosby tri-note whistle, which he decided to fit on No. 2001. It could not be fitted in front of the cab without the possibility of steam blistering the paint work and it was installed instead on top of the sloping smokebox immediately in front of the chimney (fig. 123). It was an immediate success and five more were ordered from Crosby's for Nos. 2002-6, though in the event four of these were fitted to class A4 Nos. 2509-12 instead. A replacement order for a further four for Nos. 2003-6 was placed in October 1935. These last four P2's were fully streamlined and the chime whistle was located immediately in front of the chimney. During the 1939-45 War it was considered that these chime whistles could possibly be confused with air raid sirens and about August 1942 they were replaced by the standard single-note L.N.E.R. whistle with a modified stand.

At an early date No. 2001 was provided with a "Teloc" speed recorder, manufactured by Hasler Telegraph Works. The mechanical drive was taken from the right-hand trailing coupled wheel crank pin whilst the recorder itself was in the cab, mounted on the boiler back plate on the fireman's side but set at an angle so as to be discernible by the driver. The remaining P2's were similarly equipped when new (fig. 128).

By the time Nos. 2001/2 went into regular service in Scotland they had been provided with tablet exchange apparatus for use over the single line section between Usan and Montrose South. The remaining P2's were fitted when new. An elliptical hole was cut in the left-hand side sheet of the tender at the cab end, through which the exchanger was operated (fig. 129). By comparison the A1's and A3's which were also fitted had theirs on the cab sides.

Nos. 2001/2 had footsteps at the front end when new. These steps were omitted from the remaining P2's and were also removed from the first two engines when they were fully streamlined (cf. figs. 125 and 132).

Brakes

Vacuum brake was fitted for engine and train, with four 18in. diameter cylinders located vertically between the frames. One pair was located in front of the first coupled axle and the other pair was in front of the third coupled axle.

Tenders

Tender Order 59 was placed at Doncaster on 3rd March 1933 for two New Type Non-Corridor eight-wheel tenders, as provided for the batch of A3's which appeared in 1930. The order was reduced on 12th April 1933 to one only. On 30th March Metropolitan-Vickers Electrical Co. Ltd., Trafford Park, was invited to prepare a drawing and quote for one or two 5,000-gallon tanks of all-welded construction. The drawing was completed two weeks later and on 27th April the firm quoted £352 for one tank or £644 for two. An order was placed early in June for one tank.

The base plate was 24ft. $4\frac{1}{4}$in. long after welding and 8ft. 9in. wide. This formed the bottom of the tank and the footplate surround. The back, side and front plates were welded into position to form the tank, 21ft. 9in. long and 8ft. 0in. wide inside. The side sheets were extended upwards and curved inwards at the top. The overall height to the top of the beading from footplate level was 7ft. $0\frac{1}{8}$in. The side sheets were also extended forward and at the front curved inwards, the distance between their ends being 6ft. 11in., the same as between the cab side arms. The self-trimming coal bunker was welded separately, complete with tank top plate. The whole unit was then lifted into the tank and welded into position. The tops of the front plate, division plate on the tank top and back plate followed the same contour and all had the same height on centre line of 7ft. $10\frac{3}{8}$in. above footplate. The well tank was also fabricated separately and welded into position as a complete unit. The minimum of angle irons went into the construction, and no rivets, so that there was a total saving in weight of 1 ton 5 cwt.

The firm experienced some difficulty in preventing distortion of the tender sides, which showed signs of slight caving in between the straps. However, when the completed tank was inspected on 5th September it was pronounced satisfactory and said to compare favourably with riveted tanks. The tank was sent to Doncaster for the fitting of coal gates, toolboxes, water gauges, lampirons, handrails, steps and lifting eyes.

The tank was assembled on the usual frame arrangement – 1in. thick plates, 24ft. $1\frac{1}{2}$in. long and set up 5ft. $6\frac{1}{2}$in. apart. The carrying wheels were 4ft. 2in. diameter and, surprisingly, had spokes, Since 1929 all new eight-wheel tenders had been built with steel disc centre wheels. However, on 19th April 1933 Gresley had instructed Doncaster to order suitable cast steel spoked wheel centres instead. No reason was given for this departure from standard practice. The axle bearings were outside the frames, with the springs 5in. wide and at 3ft. 6in. centres. One plate in each set was $\frac{5}{8}$in. thick whilst the remaining ten plates were $\frac{1}{2}$in. thick. Two 18in. diameter vacuum brake cylinders were mounted vertically side by side between the frames just in front of the first axle. The vacuum reservoir cylinder was located between the frames at the rear end of the tender. The Spencer double case buffers at the back were 1ft. 8in. long, with 1ft. 1in. diameter heads. The water scoop was placed between the two inner axles and was operated by screw gear. This tender remained attached to No. 2001 throughout its life, including after it was rebuilt to class A2 in 1944.

Tender Order 61 was placed on 7th November 1933 for the second P2. In the event No. 2002's intended tender went to class A3 No. 2505 which appeared at about the same time. No. 2002 then acquired the tender which should have gone to No. 2508. (As they were all New Type Non-Corridor tenders, these exchanges were not significant). Its construction differed from that of No. 2001's tender in that normal riveting methods were used, though as the rivets were countersunk flush the external appearance was the same. There was one obvious point of difference: the wheels had steel disc centres (cf. figs. 126 and 127). This tender remained attached to No. 2002 throughout its life, including after it was rebuilt to class A2 in 1944.

Tender Order 62 was also placed on 7th November 1933 for the last four P2 tenders, but it was not executed straight away. When the tenders were eventually completed in 1936 they were to the new Streamlined Non-Corridor design. Similar tenders were afterwards attached to a number of Pacifics of both classes A3 and A4. These tenders had the same coal and water capacities as the previously mentioned New Type but a visual external difference was the absence of beading around the edges. At the front end the side sheets remained straight to match the cabs on Nos. 2003-6 whose rear edges were also straight. The height to the top of the side sheets was raised to 7ft. 5$\frac{1}{2}$in. above footplate and the height to the top of the front plate became 8ft. 6$\frac{1}{4}$in. The division plate just behind the bunker was also made higher at 8ft. 3$\frac{1}{2}$in., but the back plate remained unaltered at 7ft. 10$\frac{3}{8}$in. The side sheets were curved over at the front end to form a canopy which extended back 2ft. 0in. behind the front plate and then tapered off, to allow rubber sheeting to be fitted across the gap between engine and tender (fig. 134). Between November 1937 and April 1938 the canopy on all four tenders was cut back to just a few inches behind the front plate and the coal capacity was shown as increased from 8 to 9 tons. At the same time the extra plating at the rear end around the manhole was removed and the manhole itself lowered by 6in. These four tenders remained with Nos. 2003-6 throughout their lives, including after they were rebuilt as Pacifics, though Nos. 2005/6 exchanged tenders at an unrecorded date prior to 1945.

Maintenance

The engines usually visited Doncaster for repair though there were visits to Cowlairs. The official minimum mileage to be attained between general repairs was 70,000, though figures well in excess of this were recorded before the War, in particular 118,930 miles achieved by No. 2006 before it entered Doncaster Works in May 1939 for its first heavy repair. Wartime mileages between overhauls generally decreased, possible partly due to the engines no longer being new as well as to the obvious reason of a reduced standard of maintenance.

The mileages run by these six engines prior to being rebuilt as Pacifics are shown below, with the figures in brackets relating to No. 2001 prior to its first rebuilding in April 1938 with conventional cylinders and valve gear.

No.	*Mileages*
2001	362,136 (125,670)
2002	360,907
2003	246,283
2004	294,243
2005	225,739
2006	287,187

Liveries

Nos. 2001/2 were painted in apple green livery with black and white lining, including the casing around the smokebox (and also the additional smoke lifting plates in the case of No. 2002) made possible by the "Alfol" insulation between the smokebox and aerofoil which prevented heat blistering. On Nos. 2003-6 the wedge-shaped front was painted black and there was a parabolic shaped division between the black and the green paint on the sides of the aerofoil. A similar style was adopted for class A4 No. 4482 which appeared shortly after the last P2. However, whilst blue livery was standardised for the A4's from October 1937 the P2's continued to run in green livery.

In November 1941 No. 2006 appeared in black overall with no lining, and the remaining P2's followed suit at their next repaint. From July 1942 the letters "N E" were applied to the tender instead of the full "L N E R", though in the case of No. 2005 (and probably No. 2006) this change only came on rebuilding as a Pacific.

Names

The six engines of class P2 were given names of historical significance appropriate to the route over which they were intended to work.

No. 2001 *Cock o' the North.* The nickname given to George, the proud fifth Duke of Gordon (1770-1836). When chosen for the first P2, this name was still carried by an N.B. Atlantic, No. 9903, but the latter was renamed *Aberdonian* (previously carried by sister engine No. 9868, withdrawn in September 1933) before No. 2001 entered traffic.

No. 2002 *Earl Marischal.* The hereditary title of the Keith family, whose seat was Dunnottar Castle, visible from the Aberdeen line near Stonehaven. The title was forfeited after the family took the Jacobite side in 1715 and has never been used since.

No. 2003 *Lord President.* Presumably the Lord President of the Court of Session sitting in Edinburgh, the Scottish equivalent of the Lord Chief Justice.

No. 2004 *Mons Meg.* Popular name given to a celebrated fifteenth-century cannon standing on the ramparts of Edinburgh Castle, overlooking the main line as it leaves Waverley station.

No. 2005 *Thane of Fife.* Ancient name given to the Earl of Fife (through which county the Aberdeen line passes). This name had been borne by an N.B. Atlantic, No. 9871, withdrawn in January 1935.

No. 2006 *Wolf of Badenoch.* Nickname of the notorious fourteenth-century Earl of Buchan, guilty of great depredation in north-east Scotland, whose response to episcopal criticism was to burn down Elgin Cathedral in 1390.

Exhibitions

As a prestige engine, No. 2001 was naturally called upon to appear at a number of exhibitions. It is therefore of interest to list all such occasions it has been possible to trace.

26th-27th May 1934	Doncaster Works
1st June 1934	King's Cross (a)
2nd June 1934	Ilford
5th June 1934	Aberdeen (b)
6th June 1934	Edinburgh Waverley (b)
17th February 1935	Paris Gare du Nord
4th-5th May 1935	Stratford
8th September 1935	Gateshead (c)
16th-17th May 1936	Kirkcaldy
14th-15th November 1936	Aberdeen

(a) Press demonstration.
(b) Also inspected by that city's Lord Provost.
(c) Former works.

Two other P2's are known to have been exhibited to the public. No. 2002 *Earl Marischal,* when new, was on view at York 14th October 1934 and No. 2004 *Mons Meg* was exhibited at Edinburgh Waverley 26th March 1939.

Allocation and Work

No. 2001 came off Plant late in May 1934 and its Press Exhibition was held at King's Cross station on 1st June, on its way to a rolling stock exhibition at Ilford next day. On the morning of 3rd June it was observed at Bounds Green passing through the siding connection between the G.E. Section Palace Gates branch and the G.N. Section carriage sidings. It regained the main line at Wood Green station and headed north light engine for Scotland. On Monday 4th June it left Edinburgh (Waverley) at 2-20 p.m. on a special test train of twelve coaches to Aberdeen. The Locomotive Running Superintendent for the Scottish Area (G. A. Musgrave) and his assistant (G. W. Phillips) both rode on the footplate on this trial run. Gresley was presumably in the train as next morning he showed the Lord Provost over the engine before it went on public view. It arrived back in Waverley just before the Aberdeen train booked to arrive at 4-14 p.m. On the Wednesday (6th June) No. 2001 was on exhibition at Waverley station, where it was inspected by Edinburgh's Lord Provost, but was back in London in time for a radio broadcast on 9th June. Between the 11th June and 30th July it was on trial in the Southern Area, working first from King's Cross shed and then, following a visit to Doncaster Works on 21st June, from Doncaster shed; see page 174 for details.

No. 2001 was handed over to the Scottish Area Running Department at Haymarket shed on 30th July 1934 and was put in the charge of driver D. Macguire, the senior man in No. 2 Link ("The

Dundees") at that time. Test runs were made with a 586-ton train from Edinburgh to Aberdeen and back on two successive days, 1st and 2nd August. Afterwards, it was regularly employed on the 2-0 p.m. ex-Waverley and 5-40 p.m. ex-Dundee (3-45 p.m. Aberdeen – King's Cross). On 23rd August No. 2001 was sent back to Doncaster and the opportunity was taken of using it to work the 11-30 p.m. parcels train from Edinburgh. By the end of August, No. 2001 was back at Haymarket and again used regularly on the 2-0 p.m. from Waverley as far as Dundee. Later, the engine was prepared at Doncaster Works for trial on the French Railway's Testing Plant at Vitry, to which it was despatched on 5th December. No. 2001 returned to England on 21st February 1935 but it was not until mid-June that it resumed normal duties at Haymarket shed, joining No. 2002 which had arrived there on 8th June. No. 2001 was officially allocated to Haymarket on 31st July 1934 (and never subsequently transferred whilst a P2) but, as described earlier, it was almost a year before that shed was able to have regular use of it.

No. 2002 had come off Plant in October 1934 and was exhibited at York on the 14th of that month, subsequently working from Doncaster shed until despatched to Scotland. It was employed on either of two regular diagrams, arriving at King's Cross at 1-55 p.m. and 3-55 p.m., and returning at 4-0 p.m. and 5-45 p.m. from the terminus. On 10th November 1934, No. 2002's leading pony truck wheels were derailed when leaving the locomotive yard at King's Cross station, preparatory to working the 4-0 p.m. down, blocking the down main lines, and having to be replaced on this duty. On 29th December the same wheels were derailed on entering the locomotive yard at King's Cross station, after working up from Doncaster. This time the engine was run back to Doncaster, slowly, where eventually a bent axle was diagnosed (see p. 181).

For about a month in April and May 1935, it was usual to see both P2's in London on the same day. One invariably appeared on the 11-4 a.m. ex-Doncaster and went back with the 4-0 p.m. from King's Cross. The other P2, when available, appeared on the 12-2 p.m. ex-Doncaster, returning with the 5-45 p.m. These regular workings ceased on 22nd May, with the departures of No. 2002 on the 4-0 p.m. and No. 2001 on the 5-45 p.m. The next day both engines entered Doncaster Works for a final check before being despatched to Scotland.

No. 2002 remained at Haymarket for only thirteen days before moving on to Dundee. Its principal duties were on the 5-32 a.m. to Aberdeen, returning on the 10-20 a.m., then on the 3-35 p.m. to Aberdeen and the 7-23 p.m. return, the two regular drivers being G. Arbuthnott and T. Campbell. Several runs about this time were reported in detail by O. S. Nock, from which it was clear that the engine could work competently and economically trains of 500 tons tare weight over this difficult route. With such loads, No. 2002 easily kept time with cut-off about 25 per cent and full regulator on the rising gradients, and 18 per cent cut-off and $\frac{1}{3}$ regulator on the level stretches. On 28th September 1935 No. 2002 failed with a hot axlebox at Montrose whilst working the 10-20 a.m. from Aberdeen, with a load of 510 tons. The P2 was replaced by class J36 No. 9776, assisted from Arbroath by a class G9 0-4-4 tank engine to Dundee, and between them this pair only lost 22 minutes in running between Montrose and Dundee. No. 2002 also appeared on the Dundee to Edinburgh train which arrived in Waverley at 11-6 a.m., returning on the 1-9 p.m. from Edinburgh.

In the winter of 1935-36, No. 2001 settled down to a regular daily diagram, double-shifted with two regular drivers, A. Douglas and A. Shedden. Driver Shedden's fireman at that time was J. Cunningham, who ultimately became Chief Locomotive Inspector in the Scottish Region of British Railways. He was a thoroughly experienced and highly skilled fireman, and he recalls that this was the hardest time of his whole career. No. 2001 had very quickly earned for itself the unenviable nickname of "The Miner's Friend", and even as late as the end of 1935, officials were still travelling with the engine whilst in normal service. These included E. Windle and O. V. S. Bulleid, but there was little they could say or do to improve the engine's performance in its form at that time. Although No. 2001 could not be trusted on the Edinburgh – Aberdeen through working which had been intended for the class, because of its extravagant coal consumption, there was a certain amount of such working by the P2/2's when they were all in service.

No. 2003 was delivered to Haymarket on 27th June 1936, having been noted on the 5-50 p.m. down at King's Cross two days previously, and was subsequently noted on the 2-0 p.m. and 6-0 p.m. Aberdeen expresses from Waverley. It was transferred to Dundee on 4th September 1936, where it joined No. 2005 which had arrived there on 20th August. No. 2005 had been seen at King's Cross four days before this, on 16th August. Nos. 2003/5 worked the following diagrams: 1) 8-40 a.m. Dundee to Edinburgh, 2-0 p.m. Edinburgh to Aberdeen (remanned at Dundee), 7-35 p.m. Aberdeen to Dundee; 2) 5-42 a.m. Dundee to Aberdeen, 10-20 a.m. Aberdeen to Dundee, 3-34 p.m. (fish) Dundee to Edinburgh, 8-25 p.m. Edinburgh to Dundee. No. 2002 moved on 10th September 1936 to Aberdeen, which also became the home of No. 2006 (delivered to Haymarket on 23rd September 1936 and then on to Aberdeen 16th November 1936). Incidentally, No. 2006 does not appear to have worked into King's Cross as a Mikado.

No. 2004 was turned out of Doncaster Works towards the end of July 1936, and initially it worked from Doncaster shed. It was seen at King's Cross on 31st July, when it failed with an overheated journal, and was on shed for several days before proceeding light to Doncaster on 8th August. Its next recorded visit to London was on 21st August when it was noted on the 4-0 p.m. down express (fig. 144). It was delivered to Haymarket shed on 25th August, joining No. 2001 in regular service on the Aberdeen main line, and it remained a Haymarket engine.

The Aberdeen engines (Nos. 2002/6) were not allocated to regular men, but along with the Pacifics (and later the V2's) they worked passenger trains manned by No. 1 Link, and fish and meat trains with No. 2 Link crews. Three typical passenger duties were: 1) 6-10 a.m. to Dundee and 11-30 a.m. return; 2) 3-45 p.m. to Dundee and 6-28 p.m. return; 3) 5-15 p.m. south with the 9-2 p.m. back from Dundee. The meat train for King's Cross left Aberdeen at 10-45 a.m. and was often worked by Aberdeen P2's to Dundee, as were the afternoon fish trains which ran when required. These latter duties were not always balanced by booked return workings.

During the period when through running between Edinburgh and Aberdeen was in force, it was possible for all six engines of the class to be seen in Waverley station in one day. For example, on 20th November 1936 a contemporary observer noted No. 2005 on the 9-55 a.m. to Aberdeen, No. 2002 on the 1-9 p.m. to Dundee, No. 2001 on the 2-0 p.m. for Aberdeen, No. 2004 on the 4-14 p.m. arrival ex-Aberdeen, No. 2003 on the fish train arriving at 5-10 p.m. from Aberdeen and No. 2006 on the 5-35 p.m. departure for Aberdeen. These were not necessarily all through engine workings.

The through running fell into abeyance (to be resumed during the War) and the Aberdeen engines then only worked southwards to Dundee, the Dundee engines working either to Aberdeen or to Edinburgh, whilst the Haymarket engines normally ran to Dundee. However, early in 1939 Nos. 2001/4 began to appear on passenger trains to Glasgow, previous P2 visits having been confined to light engine trips to Eastfield for Cowlairs Works. The trains on which the P2's were used (the 7-35 a.m. and 7-55 p.m. ex-Waverley) consisted of parts of the same Pacific diagram, and this duty was in the nature of a running-in turn for the P2's. The return working of the 7-35 a.m. was the 11-0 a.m. ex-Queen Street, which continued from Waverley to terminate at Leith Central, thence empty to Craigentinny. The engine of the 7-55 p.m. came back on the 10-40 p.m. from Glasgow.

By the winter of 1938-39, the two Haymarket P2's (Nos. 2001/4) worked double-shifted diagrams as follows:-

Haymarket No. 9 Engine. 7-35 a.m. Edinburgh to Dundee, 10-38 a.m. Dundee to Edinburgh (empty coaches to Craigentinny), 5-40 p.m. Edinburgh to Dundee, 9-30 p.m. Dundee to Edinburgh.

Haymarket No. 10 Engine. 4-15 a.m. Edinburgh to Dundee, 8-20 a.m. Dundee to Edinburgh, 1-9 p.m. Edinburgh to Dundee, 5-40 p.m. Dundee to Edinburgh. This engine was also booked to carry out a shunting movement at Dundee, attaching a van to the 1-45 p.m. (fish) ex-Aberdeen.

There were no Haymarket Sunday diagrams which specified class P2, but nevertheless these engines were used for instance on the 7-35 a.m. to Dundee (a Pacific diagram). The men took the engine to Dundee shed and booked off, returning on the 6-20 p.m. Dundee to Edinburgh with the engine off the 11-25 a.m. ex-Edinburgh. The Haymarket men who had worked the latter then prepared the engine off the 7-35 a.m. from Edinburgh and worked back on the 5-38 p.m. from Dundee, theirs being a straight shift.

From about 1939 onwards the Haymarket P2's ceased to be regularly manned, not only due to wartime conditions and the re-introduction of through running to Aberdeen, but also due to the inclusion in the same link of Perth trains (formerly worked by St. Margaret's) on which the P2's were not used. By this time, the P2 class had been authorised to work to Perth and, although they were not usually employed on this route, on two successive days during the War, No. 2004 worked military specials through from Perth to Newcastle with Haymarket men (one set from Perth to Edinburgh, relieved by another crew for the journey to Newcastle). No official authorisation for the running of the P2's from Edinburgh to Newcastle has been traced, but apart from the specials just mentioned, and the early trip of No. 2001 en route to Doncaster on a parcels train, one other instance has been recorded. This again involved the pioneer engine, No. 2001, which on its way back from Doncaster on one occasion took the place of the normal Haymarket Pacific on one of the East Coast expresses between Newcastle and Edinburgh. The driver was J. Binnie, and the fireman (J. Cunningham who had fired regularly on this engine on the Dundee road) averred that this was the best trip he had on this engine, and the only one on which he realised to the full the benefits of the A.C.F.I. feed water heater. Usually the P2's proceeded light to and from Doncaster Works.

In addition to the trains already mentioned in connection with the Dundee engines, there was another diagram for a time in which a P2 worked the 2-38 p.m. from Dundee to Edinburgh and the 7-25 p.m. Edinburgh to Dundee. A certain amount of Sunday work was undertaken by the Dundee engines, notably on the 7-37 p.m. ex-Aberdeen, usually a heavy train loading to about sixteen heavy vehicles, always of course taken without assistance.

Normally, only Haymarket, Dundee and Aberdeen men handled the P2's, but once on a summer Saturday No. 2001 was seen passing through Kinghorn with a southbound relief in the charge of a St. Margaret's Top Link crew. The driver was a rather lugubrious individual, and on this occasion he looked even more miserable than usual!

The maximum loads given for the P2 class (with corresponding figures for the A3's in brackets) were as follows:-

	Tons (tare)
Edinburgh – Aberdeen	530 (480)
Aberdeen – Edinburgh	530 (420)
Dundee – Edinburgh*	550 (450)
Edinburgh – Perth	500 (450)
Perth – Edinburgh	475 (425)
Edinburgh – Glasgow	550 (500)
Glasgow – Edinburgh	550 (500)

* Assisted to Forth Bridge North if stopped at Inverkeithing.

When No. 2001 made its appearance in 1934, it was stated that the L.N.E.R. intended to use this class also on the Waverley Route between Edinburgh and Carlisle. However, it would appear that these engines were never passed for running over the Carlisle road, and there is no record of their having done so.

During the War the P2's (like the Pacifics, Green Arrows and Shires) were given permission to run over certain L.M.S. routes as alternatives in the event of L.N.E.R. main lines being blocked. As far as is known, this facility was never used.

Thompson visited Edinburgh in May 1942, when he made known to local officials his avowed intention "to get the P2's off the Aberdeen road". This gave rise to speculation as to the possibility of the P2's being moved to the Southern Area for use on the very heavy trains then being worked over the G.N. main line from King's Cross. Then on 29th May 1942, rebuilt W1 No. 10000 arrived at Haymarket and was tried between Edinburgh and Aberdeen. This seemed to indicate the possibility of a new development of the 4-6-4 type for use on this particular stretch of line. In fact, what took place was the drastic rebuilding, in January 1943, of No. 2005 as a 4-6-2. Although this rebuild could hardly be described as an unqualified success, the other five P2's were similarly treated during 1944, and so passed from the scene one of the most outstanding developments in British locomotive history. This was the only class of eight-coupled express engines in Britain and represented a bold attempt to deal with the operating difficulties peculiar to the Edinburgh – Aberdeen main line. It is realised that all steam locomotive design was a compromise to a greater or lesser extent, and it was not surprising that certain criticisms have been levelled against the P2 class. For example, it was alleged that they were prone to "brass-cutting" in the axleboxes, but similar troubles beset the Pacifics working over this line. Then the P2's were said to be liable to derailment. Certainly No. 2002 was derailed at King's Cross early in its career, but in relation to the miles run by the class as a whole, these were hardly significant. The annual mileage figures, and mileages between shoppings of the P2's were on a par with those of the Scottish Pacifics. Admittedly, No. 2001 in its original form could be said to be something of a disappointment, but on the other hand it was a remarkable engine in some respects. Its capacity for free-running was noteworthy, and it was reputed to be able to get a heavy train from rest at Dundee up the 1 in 88 gradient through Esplanade on to the Tay Bridge more quickly than any other engine. The class P2/2 engines did their work very satisfactorily, and were highly esteemed by the men. Except possibly for No. 2005 (which had a single chimney), the P2's steamed freely; they rode well and their coal consumption was little different from that of a Pacific on a heavy train. As the Pacifics were not allowed to be double-headed on the Aberdeen road, the use of the P2's permitted the working of heavier trains which would otherwise have had to be divided and run in two portions. Their epitaph is perhaps appropriately expressed in the words of a Dundee running foreman: "If I haven't got a P2, I have to look for two engines and another set of men".

The full allocations of these engines prior to rebuilding are set out in the accompanying table.

No.	*Allocation*
2001	DON 5/34, HAY 7/34 (Rebuilt 9/44).
2002	DON 10/34, HAY 6/35, DEE 6/35, ABD 9/36 (Rebuilt 6/44).
2003	HAY 6/36, DEE 9/36, HAY 10/42 (Rebuilt 12/44).
2004	HAY 7/36 (Rebuilt 11/44).
2005	DEE 8/36 (Rebuilt 1/43).
2006	HAY 9/36, ABD 11/36, HAY 10/42 (Rebuilt 5/44).

The abbreviations used above for these sheds are as follows: ABD Aberdeen (Ferryhill), DEE Dundee, DON Doncaster, HAY Haymarket.

Engine Diagrams

P2/1 Section L.N.E., 1934. No. 2001, with rotary cam poppet valve gear. Engine rebuilt to P2/2 and diagram deleted 12/1938.

P2/2 Section L.N.E., 1934. No. 2002, with Walschaerts/Gresley valve gear. Engine streamlined and diagram deleted 12/1936.

P2/2 Section L.N.E., 1936. Nos. 2002-5, streamlined. Diagram replaced 12/1937.

P2/3 Section L.N.E., 1936. No. 2006 with long combustion chamber. Diagram replaced 12/1937.

P2/2 Section L.N.E., 1937. Revised diagram for Nos. 2002-5, with tender coal capacity 9 tons instead of 8 tons. Note added: No. 2001 has New Type Non-Corridor tender, 12/1940. Note added: No. 2002 has same tender type as No. 2001, 12/1941.

P2/3 Section L.N.E., 1937. Revised diagram for No. 2006, with tender coal capacity 9 tons instead of 8 tons.

Classification: Route availability 9.

Summary of P2 Class

No.	*Maker*	*Works No.*	*Built*	*Name*	*Orig. Cl. Pt.*	*Subs. Altn.*	*Streamlined casing*	*Rebuilt to A2*
2001	Doncaster	1789	5/1934	*Cock o' the North*	1	2 (4/38)	4/38	9/44
2002	,,	1796	10/1934	*Earl Marischal*	2	—	10/36	6/44
2003	,,	1836	6/1936	*Lord President*	2	—	As built	12/44
2004	,,	1839	7/1936	*Mons Meg*	2	—	,,	11/44
2005	,,	1840	8/1936	*Thane of Fife*	2	—	,,	1/43
2006	,,	1842	9/1936	*Wolf of Badenoch*	3	—	,,	5/44

Appendix

1946 No.	1924 No.	*R.O.D.* No.	*In store*	*Previous use*	
3898	6253	2157	Beachley	GWR	3045
3897	6254	2153	,,	,,	3041
3756	6255	1841	,,	,,	6002
3846	6256	2044	Queensferry	LNWR	2836
3842	6257	1998	Beachley	GWR	3052
3748	6258	1827	,,	LYR, GWR	3095
3822	6259	1948	,,	,,	3048
(3834)	6260	1975	,,	,,	3056
3838	6261	1981	,,	,,	3046
3819	6262	1937	,,	,,	3059
3817	6263	1933	,,	,,	3058
3818	6264	1936	,,	,,	6003
3812	6265	1923	,,	,,	3092
(3815)	6266	1928	,,	,,	3047
3776	6267	1870	,,	,,	3037
3774	6268	1868	,,	,,	3084
3781	6269	1878	,,	,,	3086
3771	6270	1864	,,	,,	3090
3765	6271	1858	,,	LYR, GWR	3093
3763	6272	1856	,,	,,	3080
(3762)	6273	1855	,,	,,	3036
3767	6274	1860	,,	,,	3060
3798	6275	1904	,,	,,	3061
3758	6276	1847	,,	,,	3034
3794	6277	1898	,,	,,	3077
3750	6278	1831	,,	,,	3088
(3757)	6279	1845	,,	,,	3039
3793	6280	1896	,,	,,	3083
3802	6281	1910	,,	LYR, GWR	3094
3759	6282	1848	,,	,,	3035
3792	6283	1895	,,	,,	3069
3744	6284	1819	,,	LYR, GWR	3097
3739	6285	1811	,,	,,	3087
3880	6286	2112	Queensferry	GCR	
3882	6287	2121	,,	LSWR, LNWR	2978
3879	6288	2110	,,	GCR	
3852	6289	2054	,,	LNWR	2855
3847	6290	2046	,,	,,	2837
3848	6291	2047	,,	,,	2838
3853	6292	2055	,,	,,	2851
3893	6293	2148	,,	,,	2852
3850	6294	2052	,,	,,	2849
3891	6295	2145	,,	,,	2847
3895	6296	2150	,,	,,	2840
(3892)	6297	2147	,,	,,	2842
3883	6298	1800	Queensferry	GCR	
3851	6299	2053	,,	LNWR	2854
3894	6300	2149	,,	,,	2843
(3831)	6301	1963	,,	,,	2865
3841	6302	1995	,,	,,	2949
3832	6303	1969	,,	,,	2875
3829	6304	1959	,,	,,	2947
3839	6305	1991	,,	,,	2861
3827	6306	1956	,,	,,	2945
3731	6307	1746	Beachley	GWR	3089
3728	6308	1739	,,	LSWR, GWR	3099
3729	6309	1741	,,	LSWR, GWR	6000
3716	6310	1696	,,	,,	3020
3720	6311	1643	,,	,,	3027
(3722)	6312	1636	,,	,,	3026
3718	6313	1699	,,	,,	3023
3717	6314	1697	,,	,,	3021
(3719)	6315	1700	,,	,,	3024
3714	6316	1694	,,	,,	3067
(3711)	6317	1691	,,	,,	3073
3708	6318	1688	,,	,,	3031
3706	6319	1650	,,	,,	3049
3705	6320	1649	,,	,,	3070
3702	6321	1685	,,	,,	3075
(3698)	6322	1680	,,	,,	3053
3696	6323	1678	,,	,,	3072
3687	6324	1669	,,	,,	3030
3679	6325	1661	,,	LYR, GWR	3096
3730	6326	1743	Queensferry	LYR, LNWR	2961
(3727)	6327	1738	,,	LSWR, LNWR	2977
3725	6328	1641	,,	,,	2832
3724	6329	1640	,,	,,	2831
(3723)	6330	1638	,,	,,	2830
3721	6331	1645	,,	,,	2858
(3678)	6332	1659	,,	,,	2909
3715	6333	1695	,,	,,	2898
3712	6334	1692	,,	,,	2917
(3710)	6335	1690	,,	,,	2916
3703	6336	1686	,,	GER	
3699	6337	1682	,,	SECR, LNWR	2973
3697	6338	1679	,,	SECR, LNWR	2972
(3692)	6339	1674	,,	,,	2914
(3693)	6340	1676	,,	GER	

1946 No.	1924 No.	*R.O.D.* No.	*In store*	*Previous use*	
3689	6341	1671	Queensferry	SECR, LNWR	2971
3691	6342	1673	,,	LYR, LNWR	2959
3688	6343	1670	,,	,,	2913
3685	6344	1667	,,	,,	2912
(3684)	6345	1666	,,	,,	2911
(3680)	6346	1662	,,	,,	2910
3681	6347	1663	,,	GER	
(3677)	6348	1658	,,	LNWR	2908
3694	6349	1675	,,	,,	2915
3676	6350	1657	,,	,,	2907
3674	6351	1655	,,	LYR, LNWR	2958
3673	6352	1654	,,	LYR, LNWR	2957
3675	6353	1656	,,	,,	2906
3672	6354	1653	,,	,,	2905
(3671)	6355	1652	,,	,,	2904
3670	6356	1651	,,	,,	2903
3665	6357	1627	Beachley	GWR	3064
3662	6358	1624	,,	,,	3057
3663	6359	1625	,,	,,	3074
3659	6360	1620	,,	,,	3062
3668	6361	1631	,,	,,	3066
(3669)	6362	1632	,,	,,	3065
3656	6363	1617	,,	,,	3068
3655	6364	1616	,,	,,	3076
3649	6365	1608	,,	,,	3082
3645	6366	1604	,,	,,	3081
3667	6367	1629	Queensferry	LYR, LNWR	2956
(3658)	6368	1619	,,	GER	
(3654)	6369	1614	,,	,,	
3653	6370	1612	,,	LNWR	2902
3652	6371	1611	,,	,,	2901
3648	6372	1607	,,	,,	2883
(3643)	6373	1601	,,	,,	2900
3646	6374	1605	,,	,,	2870
3638	6375	1723	Beachley	GWR	3054
3636	6376	1721	,,	,,	3055
(3634)	6377	1718	,,	,,	3050
3686	6495	1668	Aintree	GCR	
3695	6496	1677	,,	GER	
(3700)	6497	1683	,,	,,	
3701	6498	1684	,,	,,	
(3707)	6499	1687	,,	GCR	
3726	6500	1737	,,	NER	
3732	6501	1747	,,	,,	
3733	6502	1748	,,	,,	

1946 No.	1924 No.	*R.O.D.* No.	*In store*	*Previous use*	
3734	6503	1749	Aintree	NER	
(3777)	6504	1873	,,	GER	
3780	6505	1876	,,	,,	
3782	6506	1879	,,	,,	
3784	6507	1881	,,	,,	
(3825)	6508	1953	,,	,,	
(3826)	6509	1954	,,	,,	
3791	6510	1894	,,	,,	
3800	6511	1907	,,	,,	
3804	6512	1913	,,	,,	
3768	6513	1861	Queensferry	,,	
(3773)	6514	1867	,,	LNWR	2935
3786	6515	1884	,,	,,	2894
3824	6516	1952	,,	,,	2889
(3799)	6517	1905	,,	,,	2869
3807	6518	1916	,,	,,	2871
3808	6519	1917	,,	,,	2892
(3811)	6520	1922	,,	LYR, LNWR	2954
3821	6521	1943	,,	,,	2888
3836	6522	1978	,,	,,	2885
3837	6523	1979	,,	,,	2893
3840	6524	1993	,,	GER	
3872	6525	2094	,,	LNWR	2845
3854	6526	2056	,,	,,	2850
(3875)	6527	2098	,,	,,	2856
3876	6528	2099	,,	,,	2857
3877	6529	2101	,,	,,	2853
(3896)	6530	2152	,,	,,	2841
3833	6531	1971	Aintree	GCR	
3862	6532	2073	,,	NER	
3863	6533	2074	,,	,,	
3864	6534	2075	,,	,,	
3865	6535	2076	,,	,,	
3633	6536	1717	Queensferry	SECR, LNWR	2975
(3635)	6537	1719	Aintree	GCR	
3642	6538	1729	,,	NER	
3651	6539	1610	,,	GER	
3661	6540	1622	,,	,,	
(3664)	6541	1626	,,	,,	
3666	6542	1628	,,	GCR	
3644	6543	1603	Queensferry	GER	
3647	6544	1606	Morecambe	GCR	
3650	6545	1609	,,	,,	
3657	6546	1618	,,	,,	
(3660)	6547	1621	,,	,,	
3682	6548	1664	,,	,,	
(3683)	6549	1665	,,	,,	
3704	6550	1647	,,	,,	

Appendix (continued)

1946 No.	1924 No.	R.O.D. No.	In store	Previous use	
(3690)	6551	1672	Morecambe	GCR	
3709	6552	1689	,,	,,	
3713	6553	1693	,,	,,	
3629	6554	1701	Gretna	CR	
3630	6555	1712	,,	,,	
3631	6556	1713	Queensferry	GER	
(3632)	6557	1716	Morecambe	GCR	
3637	6558	1722	,,	,,	
3639	6559	1724	,,	,,	
(3640)	6560	1727	,,	,,	
3641	6561	1728	,,	,,	
3735	6562	1805	,,	,,	
(3736)	6563	1806	Queensferry	LNWR	2921
3737	6564	1807	,,	,,	2922
(3738)	6565	1809	,,	,,	2923
3740	6566	1812	Gretna	CR	
3741	6567	1815	Queensferry	LYR, LNWR	2962
3742	6568	1816	Gretna	CR	
(3743)	6569	1817	,,	,,	
(3745)	6570	1820	Queensferry	LNWR	2879
3746	6571	1821	,,	LYR, LNWR	2963
3747	6572	1824	Gretna	CR	
3749	6573	1829	Queensferry	LYR, LNWR	2965
3751	6574	1833	,,	GER	
3752	6575	1834	Gretna	CR	
3753	6576	1836	Queensferry	LNWR	2931
3754	6577	1839	,,	GER	
3755	6578	1840	,,	LYR, LNWR	2966
3760	6579	1849	,,	,,	2933
(3761)	6580	1854	,,	,,	2868
3764	6581	1857	,,	LYR, LNWR	2952
3766	6582	1859	,,	,,	2979
3769	6583	1862	Morecambe	GCR	
3770	6584	1863	,,	,,	
(3772)	6585	1866	,,	GER	
3775	6586	1869	Queensferry	,,	
(3778)	6587	1874	Morecambe	GCR	
3779	6588	1875	,,	,,	
3783	6589	1880	Queensferry	LNWR	2896
3785	6590	1882	,,	,,	2897
3787	6591	1885	Morecambe	GCR	
3788	6592	1886	,,	,,	
(3789)	6593	1887	Queensferry	LNWR	2980
3790	6594	1892	,,	,,	2940
3795	6595	1899	,,	,,	2941

1946 No.	1924 No.	R.O.D. No.	In store	Previous use	
3796	6596	1902	Morecambe	GCR	
(3797)	6597	1903	Queensferry	LNWR	2877
3801	6598	1908	Morecambe	GCR	
(3803)	6599	1911	Queensferry	GER	
(3805)	6600	1914	,,	,,	
3806	6601	1915	,,	LNWR	2884
(3809)	6602	1920	,,	GER	
(3810)	6603	1921	,,	,,	
3813	6604	1925	,,	,,	
(3814)	6605	1927	Morecambe	GCR	
3816	6606	1929	Queensferry	GER	
(3820)	6607	1939	,,	,,	
3823	6608	1949	,,	LNWR	2944
3828	6609	1957	,,	,,	2946
(3830)	6610	1962	,,	GER	
3835	6611	1976	Morecambe	GCR	
3843	6612	2000	,,	GCR	
(3844)	6613	2001	,,	,,	
3845	6614	2043	,,	,,	
3849	6615	2048	,,	,,	
3855	6616	2059	,,	,,	
3856	6617	2062	Queensferry	LNWR	2835
3857	6618	2063	Morecambe	GCR	
3858	6619	2064	,,	,,	
3859	6620	2065	,,	,,	
3860	6621	2066	,,	,,	
3861	6622	2068	,,	,,	
(3866)	6623	2078	Gretna	CR	
3867	6624	2079	,,	,,	
3868	6625	2081	,,	,,	
3869	6626	2082	,,	,,	
3870	6627	2084	,,	,,	
(3871)	6628	2087	,,	,,	
3873	6629	2095	Morecambe	GCR	
3874	6630	2096	,,	,,	
3878	6631	2104	Queensferry	LNWR	2833
3881	6632	2116	Morecambe	GCR	
3884	6633	2126	Gretna	CR	
3885	6634	2132	,,	,,	
3886	6635	2133	,,	,,	
3887	6636	2134	,,	,,	
3888	6637	2135	,,	,,	
3889	6638	2136	,,	,,	
3890	6639	2144	Queensferry	LNWR	2846
3899	6640	2160	Gretna	CR	
3900	6641	2162	,,	,,	
3901	6642	2165	,,	,,	